In the *Professional's Job Finder*, author Daniel Lauber applies to the private sector the same effective job–quest tools and techniques he introduced in the *Government Job Finder*, *Non–Profits' Job Finder*, and his breakthrough 1989 volume *The Compleat Guide to Finding Jobs in Government*.

Here are reviews of the author's other books on finding jobs in government which used the same techniques as those presented in the *Professional's Job Finder:*

"**Dynamite job hunting tool**...the most complete compendium of resources for... jobs I've ever seen."
—Joyce Lain Kennedy, *national careers columnist*

"We were **enthralled with the first edition of this book,** which used the title *The Compleat Guide to Finding Jobs in Government*, and **this is even better**. Like the rear section of **What Color is Your Parachute?**...it is packed with citations (1,400 in all) of resource books, newsletters, job services, etc....Good summary of government jobs at all levels plus much more."
—Career Opportunities News

"**Everything you ever wanted to know about locating... vacancies** (and possibly a few things you never even thought about)...**unlocks** seemingly limitless (and sometimes obscure) data about finding positions.... **Easy–to–use**, compact guide to a broad subject."
—Journal of Career Planning and Development

Career books by Daniel Lauber:

✎ **Government Job Finder**

✎ **Non–Profits' Job Finder**

✎ **Professional's Job Finder**

✎ **The Compleat Guide to Finding Jobs in Government**

✎ **The Compleat Guide to Jobs in Planning and Public Administration**

✎ **The Compleat Guide to Jobs in Planning**

PROFESSIONAL'S JOB FINDER

DANIEL LAUBER

Published by

PLANNING/COMMUNICATIONS

7215 Oak Avenue
River Forest, Illinois 60305-1935
708/366-5200

Cover design by Salvatore Concialdi

For information on distribution or quantity discount rates, contact
Planning/Communications. Distribution to the trade is by
National Book Network
4720 Boston Way, Lanham, MD 20706 301/459–8696.

Disclaimer of All Warranties and Liabilities

The author and publisher make no warranties, either expressed or
implied, with respect to the information contained herein. The
information about periodicals and job services reported in this book
is based on facts conveyed by their publishers and operators either
in writing or by telephone interview. The author and publisher shall
not be liable for any incidental or consequential damages in
connection with, or arising out of, the use of materials in this book.

ISBN: 0-9622019-2-8
Library of Congress Catalog Card Number: 90–92306

Table of Contents

Preface

While so many people are having a difficult time finding job vacancies in these recessionary times, there's a whole bundle of folks who have no trouble locating job vacancies. Somehow they know exactly where to look to find the 75 to 93 percent of all job vacancies that never make it into the classified ads of your local newspapers. They've got a secret that they don't want to share.

In a sense this book ''boldly goes where no one has gone before'' to reveal this secret key to the successful job quest. Instead of advertising in the local classifieds, companies that seek the best people to fill job vacancies rely on advertising in specialty or trade periodicals and use job-matching services, job hotlines, and computerized job databases to reach the top candidates for professional, trades, technical, labor, and office support positions.

There have been a few books that list periodicals that *may* contain job ads. And there have been a few books that identify job services that may, or may not, exist. But the *Professional's Job Finder* is the first to give you **full details on over 2,001 of the best of these job sources** so you can find job vacancies in any of the hundreds of career specialties reported on in this book.

In the 14 months it took to research this book and its companion volumes, the *Government Job Finder* and *NonProfits' Job Finder*, my researchers and I examined close to 8,000 potential job sources.

As you may have guessed, an awful lot of *alleged* job sources either do not carry announcements or ads for job vacancies. My researchers and I found that many job services had gone out of business years earlier, and a good many new ones had come along. We have culled out the duds and describe for you only those job services that carry the job vacancies you won't find in the classified section of your local newspaper.

This book and its companion volumes evolved from my first job-quest monograph, the 16-page *Compleat Guide to Jobs in Planning* (1976, 1978) which described the dozens of job sources for city planners I discovered when I looked for my second job in city planning. Since then, I've been expanding the scope of my job-quest books to fill the information void. Six years later I looked around and saw that nobody had gathered job sources for public administration. The result was the 44-page *Compleat Guide to Jobs in Planning and Public Administration* (1982, 1984).

And in 1989 when I was running out of copies of that booklet, I looked around and realized that all the rest of government lacked a similar one-stop shopping center for government job vacancies. The result was the 183-page *Compleat Guide to Finding Jobs in Government* which was a critical and commercial success.

When I started updating that book in November 1990, I realized that nobody had put together this sort information for the private sector. As a result, I expanded my research to cover the private sector as well. The 14 months of research culminated in the publication of the *Professional's Job Finder* (February, 1992) and the *Government Job Finder* (January, 1992).

In the course of the research, I found there was enough material for a book on the non-profit sector as well. A month after this book is published, the *Non-Profits' Job Finder* will leave the press to guide workers to over 1,001 job sources that carry vacancies in the non-profit sector.

Since job hunting can be a drag, I've included illustrations and comic strips to lighten things up a bit. Although the sample resumes illustrate proper resume form, I've tried to spice up one of them with references and puns on some of the musical and cultural ''icons'' of our day and age.

We have continued another tradition in the career books I've written: **we verified our job sources** as thoroughly as was practical. For periodicals, we actually obtained copies of nearly all of those listed herein. When we couldn't get a copy, we interviewed someone at the periodical. For job services, we obtained brochures that describe them, interviewed the head of the service, and, in some instances, tested them out ourselves.

This book could not have been prepared without the very kind cooperation of the people who publish and operate the job sources enumerated in these pages. I offer my deepest gratitude to them for providing the information needed to determine if the job-quest aides they produce and operate would really help people seeking work in the private sector.

Ronald Krannich of Impact Publications warrants my unending thanks for his very practical advice concerning the preparation and printing of my books and for his encouragement. He has been sort of a "fairy god-father" with his wise counsel.

I would particularly like to thank my research assistants—Christopher M. Wienke, Matthew B. Wienke, Quito Zuba, Christopher Lasch, and Gerrold Macoy—for a job well done. Little did they know that they would spend most of their summer vacation from college in libraries and on the phone eight hours a day tracking down leads and gathering information for inclusion in this book and its companion volumes.

Thanks also go to Edith Reposh and Nancy Raimondi who put in many hours of office support and without whose help this book could not have been written. And much appreciation is offered to cover designer Sam Concialdi for his patience and talent.

Most of all, I thank my wife, Diana, for not only putting up with my eccentricities while researching and writing this book (during which I did a dead-on impression of an obsessed workaholic), but for also offering valuable advice on the manuscript as well as moral support when the going got tough. I doubt if I could have written this book, much less three books at once, without her love and understanding.

I would be seriously remiss if I did not thank my parents for all they have done for me over the years. I love them, and appreciate them, far more than I can express in mere words.

While I have tried to make this book as inclusive as possible, I realize that some useful aides for the private sector job search may have escaped my attention (and that I have, no doubt, let a few typographical errors creep through). In some instances we were unable to obtain information about alleged job sources because the staff at a publication or association simply refused to answer our questions. So if you know any details about the job sources we did not include, please drop me a line so we can add them to the 1994 edition of this book. If you find any mistakes or know of any other sources of private sector vacancies, please drop me a note so I can include them in the next edition. Let me know if you've encountered a job source that has moved, changed its phone number, or altered how it operates. There's a "Reader Feedback Form" on page 487 to help you submit such information.

Thanks for purchasing the *Professional's Job Finder*. If you follow the suggestions in Chapter 1 on how to get the most out of this book, it will help you find the private sector job you want, where you wish to live.

Daniel Lauber

Daniel Lauber

February, 1992

Production notes for folks who really care about these things

The text of this book was prepared in WordStar 2000, Version 3.5. It was then imported into Ventura Publisher 3.0 and merged with the cartoons which had been scanned and clip art. The text is set in 11-point Palatine type to make reading easier, especially for the huge baby-boomer generation that is now discovering the joys of bifocals. Camera-ready copy was printed on a HP LaserJet III using HP Type Director.

Chapter 1

How to get the most out of the *Professional's Job Finder*

War is hell—and finding a job, particularly during an economic downturn, can be a real battle, especially if you rely solely on the local classifieds to find job vacancies. Some experts estimate that only seven to 25 percent of all job vacancies are advertised in the local classifieds. But if you know where to look for the hundreds of thousands of job vacancies available each month that aren't advertised in the local classifieds, your job quest can turn into a successful journey with the proverbial happy ending: the job you want, in the place you wish to live.

The *Professional's Job Finder* provides everything you need to know to locate professional, technical, labor, trades, and office support job vacancies, and business opportunities, in the vast private sector—it's literally a **one-stop shopping center for job vacancies in the private sector.** Sources of private sector internships are also identified. In addition, the *Professional's Job Finder* offers solid, no–nonsense advice on writing effective cover letters and resumes as well as preparing for job interviews.

Even if you're not one of those lucky people who knows exactly the type of work you want, the *Professional's Job Finder* is one of the places to start your career search. Used in conjunction with such books as *What Color is Your Parachute?* or *Careering and Re–Careering for the 1990's,* books that effectively help you decide what career to pursue, the entries in the *Professional's Job Finder* will give you a good idea of the current job outlook in each specialty. Each description of a job source tells you how many job openings are advertised or listed in that job source. You can get a real good idea if the professions that interest you are also likely to have jobs vacancies.

Whether you know the kind of job you want, or you are using this book to help determine what field you wish to enter, *it is essential that you read this chapter before you go any further in this book. If you don't read this chapter first, you will not be able to find all the job sources that will help you.* If you follow the suggestions this chapter presents for using the *Professional's Job Finder*, job openings in all segments of the private sector will soon be at your fingertips in the so–called "non–professional" technical, labor, trades, and office support (clerical, secretarial, etc.) fields, as well as in the hundreds of professional specialties identified in this book.

One of the most difficult parts of job hunting involves finding out what jobs are available in the geographic area in which you wish to ply your skills. Naturally, most job seekers turn to the local classifieds—where only 20 percent of job vacancies are advertised—to find a new position or use their contacts to network to identify vacancies even before they are advertised and find vacancies that don't get advertised. Few people realize that the best jobs aren't advertised in the local classifieds. You'll find them advertised in specialty periodicals, often published by professional or trade associations; on job hotlines, often accessible at no cost to the job seeker; and in job–matching services, frequently free to the job seeker, or available at very low cost. I'mnot talking about just a few jobs here. I'm talking about hundreds of thousands of jobs advertised every month almost exclusively through these three vehicles.

The *Professional's Job Finder* will lead you to the periodicals, job–matching services, and job hotlines that announce private sector job openings in your specialty. And because it is often necessary to contact an agency directly to learn about job openings, this book identifies hundreds of directories of businesses, corporations, and agencies to enable you to write to the correct person to inquire about job vacancies and/or to request job announcements to be sent to you.

In addition, this volume offers concise advice to help you prepare more effective cover letters and resumes. It also suggests techniques for preparing for a job interview so you can present the best possible portrait of yourself to the interviewer. The following chapters of this book also describe salary surveys that will enable you to be more effective when negotiating salary. Not only does this information clear up common misconceptions held by many entry–level job seekers, but it also serves as a refresher course for long–employed practitioners who have been out of the job market for years.

The *Professional's Job Finder* provides all the information you need to find and be hired for the private sector job you want, in the location you desire.

Types of job sources

There are at least two basic ways to find job openings in the vast private sector. One is the direct approach, in which you find actual job openings. The second is more circumspect, where you use networking contacts to locate job opportunities or you write, almost blindly, to possible employers to learn if there are any job openings, or if there are any expected in the near future. The *Professional's Job Finder* furnishes vital information to successfully use both techniques.

Using the direct approach

Periodicals

Newspapers. Always start with your local newspaper's classified and display advertising. In some locales, the Sunday edition of the local newspaper may be the only accessible source for local job openings. In some states, a major newspaper is the best source for job ads for locations throughout the state, and in areas like New England, throughout the region. The *Professional's Job Finder* identifies these newspapers in the chapter that presents job sources for individual states.

But not only do the local classifieds rarely carry ads for jobs outside your local area, the best jobs are rarely even advertised in the local classifieds. That's why you need the other job sources described in the *Professional's Job Finder*.

For some jobs, the local classifieds remain the best source of job vacancies. Most of these jobs are very locally-oriented professions, such as taxi drivers, which rarely have any reason to seek employees outside the local geographic area. The local classifieds are also the best job sources for so-called minimally skilled labor positions such as janitors and dish washers that do not require advanced skills. This book will not help you locate job vacancies in those specialties.

Even though most secretarial positions are advertised in the local classifieds, the *Professional's Job Finder* does include several nationwide job sources for secretaries. These are noted in the Index.

Specialty periodicals. The specialty periodical that a professional association or private publisher produces is one of the best sources for private sector job vacancies and business opportunities that aren't advertised in the local classifieds as well as for job openings located outside your local area. These are described in the chapters that follow. Chapter 2 introduces you to the job sources that cover the whole spectrum of the private sector. Beginning with Chapter 3, each chapter presents job sources for one or several related specialties. As explained later in this chapter, you should also consult the Index to locate job sources that are listed in places you would not intuitively expect them to be placed.

The vast majority of the specialty magazines are available to the general public, usually at higher subscription rates than for members. Some of these are available only to organization members. The *Professional's Job Finder* presents full information on these periodicals so you can focus on the ones most likely to carry ads for jobs for which you are qualified and in which you are interested.

Job listing periodicals. The best source of jobs in a particular specialty is usually a periodical devoted primarily or entirely to job ads or announcements. The number of job ads in a typical issue ranges from about a dozen to several hundred.

As with specialty periodicals, a job listing periodical may be available only to members of the organization that publishes it. Most, however, are available to nonmembers as well, although members often receive the job magazine for free as part of their membership package or for a reduced fee.

Since so many professional organizations publish job ads in their periodicals, the *Professional's Job Finder* also tells you about several directories of associations so you can track down any that might have escaped our attention. As your read this book, you'll find that some job listing periodicals are also published by private businesses rather than non–profit professional or trade associations.

State chapters of professional or trade associations. Many of the associations that publish periodicals with ads for private sector positions have state or regional chapters that also announce job openings in their chapter newsletters. Unfortunately, few of these national federations can provide information on which chapters publish job ads. You will have to contact an organization's national office to obtain the proper addresses and phone numbers to reach the chapter president or newsletter editor who can tell you if their newsletter features job openings. Throughout this book, the address and phone number given for a publication or job service issued by an association is almost always that for the association's headquarters.

Positions wanted. In addition to listing jobs which are available, many of these periodicals let job seekers advertise themselves under a category like "Positions Wanted." Many of these are identified in the *Professional's Job Finder*. Before seeking to place a "Positions Sought" ad, you'd be prudent to first examine the periodical. Try to get a sample copy or examine one in a library. After you've identified the periodicals in which you want to advertise yourself, contact them directly to learn if they publish "Position Wanted" ads, any restrictions that limit such self–advertising to members only, the rates charged, and whether you can publish a "blind" ad without your name in it. In a blind ad, a box number at the publication is given for responses. The periodical regularly mails the responses to you. This way you can remain anonymous and avoid tipping off your current employer that you are in the job market.

Inspect periodicals first. The *Professional's Job Finder's* descriptions of each periodical will give you a good idea whether it's worth subscribing to it. But in some cases you can't really decide without seeing a sample copy. Many publishers will be happy to send you a complimentary sample copy to help you decide if you want to subscribe. Others charge a few dollars for a single issue.

In addition, you can inspect many of the periodicals listed in the *Professional's Job Finder* at your local public library or a university library. The libraries of professional associations are also likely to carry relevant periodicals. However, it is usually worth the cost to subscribe to a periodical rather than rely on library copies since subscribers invariably receive their periodicals at least a few days before they are available at any library.

Internships. Throughout the chapters that follow, you'll come upon some directories of internships and a few periodicals that carry internship announcements. The directories are more like the periodicals described here since they provide what amounts to job descriptions for the internships they list. Also be sure to consult the Index to find job sources that include internships.

Listings for periodicals

For each periodical, the *Professional's Job Finder* provides the following information so you can make an informed decision whether or not to seek out the periodical:

- *Periodical's name.*

- *Address for subscriptions.*

- *Publisher's phone number.* Toll-free "800" numbers are given when available.

- *Frequency of publication.* To clear up the confusion, "biweekly" means every two weeks; "bimonthly" means every two months. Semimonthly is twice a month.

Publishers are like people. They move all the time. If you write to a periodical and it has moved without leaving a forwarding address (or its forwarding order has expired) try the following steps:

☐ Call the publisher at the phone number given in the *Professional's Job Finder.*

☐ If this phone number has been disconnected, call directory assistance in the same city or go to the public library to see a telephone directory for that city.

☐ If you still can't find the publisher, the publisher has probably moved to another city. Go to the public library and use one of the directories of periodicals or associations described in Chapter 2 and in the chapter on the media to find the periodical or the association which publishes it. Most of these directories are updated annually and they often have the new address and phone number.

☐ If you still can't find the new address or phone number, use the "Reader Feedback Form" near the end of this book to let us know and we will send you the new address or phone number if we have it.

☐ If you do find a new address or phone number, please use the "Reader Feedback Form" to let us know so we can correct it in the next edition of the *Professional's Job Finder.*

• *Subscription rates.* Both rates are given when a professional or trade association charges different rates for nonmembers and members. Contact the association for membership dues. Sometimes annual dues don't cost much more than the price of an annual subscription. In addition, some periodicals are free to qualified "professional." To receive one of these free subscriptions, you almost always must complete an application form which you can obtain in an issue of the periodical or from the publisher.

Prices given are for surface mail delivery to addresses in the United States and its possessions. Listings note when different rates are charged for Canada, Mexico, and/or other foreign countries. Most subscription rates are annual rates. Rates for shorter periods of time are noted. Contact the magazines if you wish to subscribe for more than 12 months since many offer discounts for two- or three-year subscriptions. Although prices were accurate when we found them during the year of researching this book, they are certainly subject to change without notice at any time. If you find that any information contained in this book has changed, please use the *Reader Feedback Form* near the end of the book to tell us what changes we should make in the next edition.

- *Special information about the periodical.* If a periodical is regional in scope, the states within its region are noted. Also provided is any other pertinent information that will help you decide if the periodical is worth your time and money.
- *Heading under which job openings appear.* For the periodicals that contain articles as well as job listings, the heading under which job ads appear is given.
- *Number of job openings in a typical issue.* "Few job ads" means no more than two or three appear in the average issue.

Job—matching services

Many trade and professional organizations, as well as state governments, operate a service in which the resumes of job candidates are matched with positions for which they qualify. These services can be quite effective for professionals and individuals seeking support, technical, trades, or labor positions in the private sector.

Some services supply a form for the job candidate to complete, while others allow you to submit your regular resume. Most place the information you submit in a computer database while others operate manually. Some charge job candidates for their services, while others do not (they will usually charge employers a fee to

access the candidates' database). The job–matching services operated by state Job Service Offices are free. These are described
in the chapter on "State–by–state job sources."

Listings of job banks or job–matching services provide the
following information:

- *Name of service.*
- *Operator of service.*
- *Operator's address and phone number.*
- *Type of resume used.* Does the service require you to fill out
  the service's own resume data form or do you submit your
  own regular resume? If you submit your own resume, how
  many copies should you send in? Many job–matching services, especially the free services, send you original resume
  to the potential employer. So they will require you to submit
  multiple copies of your resume.
- *How the service operates.* Is the service computer–based or
  manually operated?
- *Who contacts whom?* Does the job service tell the job candidate that an employer would like to contact her for an
  interview, or does the potential employer contact selected
  candidates directly?
- *Length of time resume is kept on file.*
- *Fees for applicants, if any.* Fees were accurate as of the
  beginning of 1992. These fees, though, are no exception to
  the adage "things change."
- *Other pertinent information.* Some job services may be available only to members of the organization that operates the
  service. A few privately–operated job services attempt to
  compensate for past (and, to be candid, current) discrimina-
  tion against minorities or women and, therefore, serve only
  members of the discriminated–against group.

Job hotlines

Many professional and trade associations operate job hotlines
which often offer tape recordings that describe available jobs.
These hotlines have become much more sophisticated than just
two years ago thanks to the wonders of the "automated attendant"
device. You will almost certainly need a touch-tone phone to call

these hotlines because the recorded voice at the other end will give you instructions that can be implemented only with a touch-tone phone. The most sophisticated job hotlines allow you to specify the geographic area(s) in which you are interested and the types of jobs about which you want to hear.

Some of the less high-tech hotlines simply give you a recording that lists jobs. You have no control over what you hear. Often you will first hear a list of all the job titles available. If you want to hear a detailed description and how to apply for a particular position that was just listed, keep listening because that information is often conveyed next.

When you call a few of these hotlines, a live person will answer and read job openings to you. Other job hotlines can be accessed by computer (via a modem) to generate printed listings. Those that are accessible by computer modem are noted. Some of these job hotlines offer thousands of job openings.

Pay attention to the area code of the job hotline you are about to call. If the area code is "900," the call not only isn't free, but you will be charged an additional fee directly on your phone bill. When a "900" number is listed here, the charges are generally identified.

The *Professional's Job Finder* offers the following information on each of job hotlines it describes:

- *Name of job hotline.*
- *Name of the association or private business that operates the hotline.*
- *Operator's address and regular telephone number.*
- *Hotline's phone number.* A small, but growing number of hotline operators offer a "Telecommunications for the Deaf" number as well. These are identified as **TDD** phone numbers.
- *Hours the hotline operates.* Most of these recordings can be called 24-hours a day, eight days a week. But hours are listed if they are limited.
- *When job listings are changed.* So you don't waste time calling too often, most of the listings note when recordings are updated.
- *Types of jobs included.* Some job hotlines are for specific types of jobs that may not be readily apparent from the name of the hotline.

- *Membership requirements, if any.* The description of a hotline notes when a hotline is available only to subscribers or to the sponsoring association's members.

Using the indirect approach

Unfortunately, many employers are less than aggressive when announcing job openings. Some companies will, upon request, place job candidates on a mailing list to receive announcements of certain types of job openings. Others will tell you about jobs available at the time you contact them. And in some instances, you just get lucky by contacting the right person at the right time.

Using directories

National directories. The *Professional's Job Finder* includes descriptions of hundreds of directories of professionals and businesses to steer job seekers to the right person concerning possible job openings in a wide variety of private sector fields. Speaking directly to the right person can give you a genuine competitive edge. It tells the hiring person that you've done your homework. Also, you can learn a lot more about the nature of vacant jobs and the character of the hiring agency by talking to someone in the know than just by reading job ads. As noted in the chapter on interviewing, you would be most prudent to know something about the company for which you are applying for a job when you step into that interview.

Many of the directories enumerated in this book include the name of a company's director of personnel or human resources. Most do not. You can, however, use these to contact a company and ask to whom to send a job inquiry or application.

Directories are also useful for networking purposes. They give you an opportunity to identify people who already work for the company to which you want to apply. By knowing who they are when you meet them at professional gatherings, you can ''network'' with them and place yourself in a position to hear about vacancies even before they officially occur. For details on the networking game, see books like *Great Connections: Small Talk and Networking*

SYLVIA by Nicole Hollander

for Businesspeople by Anne Baber and Lynne Wayman and *Network Your Way to Job and Career Success* by Ron and Caryl Krannich (for your convenience, both are available from Planning/Communications; see the catalog at the end of this book).

State Directories. We did not include individual state directories of businesses in this book. It would take a whole other book to do that. However, the *Professional's Job Finder* does tell you about several publishers who produce state directories of businesses. Contact them directly for information on the states that interest you.

Libraries. Some of the directories listed in the *Professional's Job Finder* are rather lengthy tomes that cost the proverbial arm and a leg. No rational individual would spend the hundreds, or even thousands, of dollars a few of these cost. Fortunately, most of them are available at well–stocked public libraries and can also be found through inter–library loan systems. Reference libraries and libraries at colleges and universities are even more likely to carry the directories described in this book. The libraries of professional associations are also likely to carry relevant directories.

The following details are furnished for each of the directories described in the *Professional's Job Finder:*

- *Title.*
- *Publisher.*
- *Publisher's address and phone number.*

- *Price.* Members of an association that publishes a directory can often purchase it at a lower price than nonmembers or receive it free as part of their membership package. The price of the most recent edition is given. Subsequent editions may cost more. When a directory is available only to association members, this restriction is noted. Some directories are available free to qualified "professionals." To obtain a free copy, you almost always must complete an application form which you can obtain from the publisher.

- *Frequency of publication.* Most of these directories are published annually or less frequently. The handful that are updated and republished several times a year are sold by subscription. The date of the most recent edition is usually given as well as how often the directory is published.

- *Description of contents.* Information on the subjects a directory covers is provided when the directory's title doesn't adequately describe its contents. When it's helpful, indexing information is presented. The number of entries and pages is often provided, especially for the really large and expensive directories.

Salary surveys

As the last chapter of the *Professional's Job Finder* explains, the more a job applicant knows about the wage scales in the locale or region for a particular position, the better he can negotiate salary and meet the employer's expectations in the job interview. In addition, knowing differences in salary between states and regions can help you decide where to look for a job.

Consequently, the following chapters include books, monographs, and articles that report the results of salary surveys. Many trade and professional associations collect salary data but do not widely publicize their findings. To obtain salary information on the professions for which salary survey information is not listed, contact the appropriate professional or trade association directly. To find associations not mentioned in this book, see the directories of associations cited herein.

The descriptions of these salary survey books include:

- *Title.*

- *Publisher.*
- *Publisher's address and phone number.*
- *Price.*
- *Most recent publication date and frequency of publication.*
- *Survey coverage.* Descriptions often include details of how data is presented (by size of city, type of city, region, etc.).
- *Types of positions included.*

How to use this book effectively

Nationwide job–hunting helpers. The periodicals, job hotlines, job–matching services, and directories described in the *Professional's Job Finder* can be divided into two classes based on the subject area they cover. The periodicals and other job–hunting aides that

A caution about area codes

Ma Bell has been rapidly adding new area codes to metropolitan areas during the past few years. Just while this book was at the printer, several new area codes went into effect. Part of the Los Angeles area, including Santa Monica, was assigned the area code "310." A number of other area codes were also changed, generally for suburban areas. For example, in 1989, the Chicago suburbs were given the area code "708," while the city kept its "312" code.

So when you call a phone number for a job source listed in the *Professional's Job Finder*, it is possible that you will hear a recording that your call cannot be completed. It is very possible that only the area code has changed and the phone number you called is still correct. To learn the new area code, try calling your local Bell System telephone operator for assistance. If he can't help you, call the operator for your long distance company or see a phone book at your public library.

feature job openings for a broad spectrum of private sector specialties, are listed in Chapter 2. The chapters that follow Chapter 2 focus on an individual specialty, or on related fields. When one or more specialties are closely related, a cross reference is provided to alert you to examine the job sources for the related specialties as well. When just one or two job sources listed under a different specialty is relevant, a cross reference to it is given.

Local sources of private sector vacancies. The other set of job-search aides presents information on jobs available within a state. Nearly all these job sources include the broad range of private sector job specialties. The chapter on "State-by-state job sources" identifies these periodicals, job hotlines, job-matching services, directories, and salary surveys.

Executive search and recruiting. The *Professional's Job Finder* does not offer information on individual executive search or recruiting firms. Describing them would fill a whole book. However, it does describe several directories of such firms in the chapter on "Personnel." Also see the Index entry "Executive search firms."

Cover letters, resumes, and interviews. The second to last chapter presents succinct guidelines for writing cover letters and for preparing and designing resumes. Two sample cover letters and resumes are presented. The last chapter explains how to prepare for job interviews, what to wear, and how to perform at the interview. It addresses some of the many myths regarding job interviews.

How to find technical, labor, trades, and support vacancies

Although they tend to concentrate on "professional" positions, most of the job sources enumerated throughout this book carry job vacancy advertisements for what are commonly called technical, trades, labor, and office support positions. Many of the entries specify when trade, labor, technical, and/or office support positions are included. With others, the title of the publication and its subject matter reveal that jobs in this classification are included.

Be sure to also look in the **Index** *where you will find references to job sources for specialties that are not listed where you would intuitively expect them to be.* When you find your specialty in the Index, be sure to read the whole section in which that specialty is listed because there are often several entries for that specialty in addition to the one on the page of the index entry.

Many chapters of this book start with a set of job sources that cover a broad subject area. Following the initial section on "general" job sources that cover all facets of that field are sections that focus on more specialized areas. For example, the "Media" chapter starts with "Media in general" and then continues with narrower disciplines labeled "Broadcasting and film," "Print media," "Photography," "Graphic arts and print production," "Models," "Advertising and public relations," and "Translators." Don't look just in the section on your specialty. Also see the initial section on general sources at the beginning of the chapter because many of those job sources will include your specialty. And be sure to also see the other chapters that are cross-referenced in the "Media" chapter.

Local newspapers. A fairly good source of advertisements for these types of private sector positions is the classified advertising section in a local newspaper. However, these rarely contain ads from outside the local geographic area. Many libraries and newspaper vendors, though, carry newspapers from around the country.

Job Service Offices. One of your best bets is to examine the job sources described in the chapter on "State-by-state job sources." These include state-operated Job Service or Employment Security offices which generally operate a computer-based system that matches applicants with the local and/or state government jobs for which they qualify. Many companies hire for these sorts of positions almost exclusively from state Job Service offices. See the discussion at the beginning of that chapter for details. This chapter also explains how to identify the local and state chapters of professional association that may publish a newsletter with job ads or operate a job service.

How to find
professional positions

Start with the nationwide job–quest aides identified in Chapter 2. These job helpers are quite broad in coverage. Each issue of these periodicals is almost certain to include ads for professional positions in most, if not all, of the classifications into which job specialties are divided in the following chapters.

Next, turn to chapters whose titles tell you they are likely to include your specialty. These chapters are cross–referenced so periodicals, job–matching services, job hotlines, directories, and salary surveys that serve more than one discipline can be easily found. Virtually all of the job–search aides identified here are nationwide in scope. Any regional and state job sources for a particular field are generally listed here with the nationwide job sources, rather than in the state–by–state listings of Chapter 3.

You'll find that the number of items presented in each chapter varies significantly. There are simply more job sources available for some specialties than for others. For those specialties with few job sources, you will have to rely more heavily on the job sources in Chapter 2 and in the state–by–state chapter.

Be sure to also look in the Index where you will find references to job sources for specialties that are not listed where you would intuitively expect them to be. When you find your specialty in the Index, be sure to read the whole section in which that specialty is listed because there are often several entries for that specialty in addition to the one on the page of the index entry.

Many chapters of this book start with a set of job sources that cover a broad subject area. Following the initial section on "general" job sources that cover all facets of that field are sections that focus on more specialized areas. For example, the "Media" chapter starts with "Media in general" and then continues with narrower disciplines labeled "Broadcasting and film," "Print media," "Photography," "Graphic arts and print production," "Models," "Advertising and public relations," and "Translators." Don't look just in the section on your specialty. Also see the initial section on general sources at the beginning of the chapter because many of those job sources will include your specialty. And be sure to also see the other chapters that are cross-referenced in the "Media" chapter.

Finally, turn to the chapter on "State-by-state job sources" for job-search aides that cover multi-state regions and individual states. Be sure to read the material at the beginning of the chapter. Job sources for a state include local newspapers that cover the whole state or a multi-state region; state-operated job-matching services; books on finding a job in a major city; and how to locate state Job Service offices. This chapter also explains how to identify the local and state chapters of professional association that may publish a newsletter with job ads or operate a job service.

How to find business opportunities

A great many of the periodicals described in this book include advertisements for business opportunities. The entry for a periodical states if business opportunities are advertised in that periodical.

Start with the nationwide job-quest aides identified in Chapter 2. These job helpers are quite broad in coverage. A small number of these include ads for business opportunities.

Next, turn to chapters whose titles tell you they are likely to include the specialty that interests you. Many of the periodicals listed in each specialty include business opportunities.

Be sure to also look in the Index where you will find references to job sources for specialties that are not listed where you would intuitively expect them to be. When you find your specialty in the Index, be sure to read the whole section in which that specialty is listed because there are often several entries for that specialty in addition to the one on the page of the index entry.

Some periodicals listed in the *Professional's Job Finder* contain ads for business opportunities that, to the prudent person, may sound too good to be true. They usually are! Those ads for you to make abundle by working at home often fall into this cateory. Be very careful with those sorts of ads. If you are tempted to reply to those types of ads, you might be prudent to check it out first with the local or national Better Business Bureau. When the periodical prints a warning that it is not responsible for the claims made in the ads it prints, you ought to be very cautious of many of the business opportunities advertised therein.

If you follow these directions, you will find all the job sources cited in the *Professional's Job Finder* for the private sector specialty or specialties in which you want a new job or internship, or in which you wish to start or acquire a business. Armed with this information, you will be able to find the most desirable jobs, internships, or business opportunities where you want to live.

Chapter 2

General job sources

Unlike the chapters that follow, this chapter features the job–hunting aides that cover more than a single specialty. For job sources that focus on individual private sector specialties such as accounting, engineering, entertainment, health care, telecommunications, and dozens of other disciplines—and their related technical, trades, labor, and office support positions—see the chapters that follow this one. Because so many of these specialities overlap, cross references are made to related fields and to specific periodicals, directories, job banks, and hotlines listed elsewhere in the *Professional's Job Finder*. For the disciplines which do not have helpful job aides that focus on them alone, job openings can be found in the periodicals and other job aides listed in this chapter. Also, be sure to consult the Index for references to the specialties that interest you.

For some fields, the best job sources that include private sector positions are those that actually focus more on government jobs or non–profit positions. In those instances, you will be referred to one or both of the companion books to this volume, the *Government Job Finder* or the *Non–Profits' Job Finder*. For your convenience, the catalog at the end of this book describes these books in detail and tells you how to order them. The job sources in those two books include a fair number of private sector positions in addition to government or non–profit positions.

General job sources

How to proceed. The periodicals, job services (primarily job-matching services and job hotlines), directories, and salary surveys described in this chapter are broad in scope: each covers a wide variety of private sector disciplines. As noted in Chapter 1, you should examine these first to see which of them would be helpful to your job search. Many of these sources include openings for office support jobs, labor, trades, and technical positions.

After examining the job sources in this chapter, you should examine the sources in the chapters that follow. Also be sure to look in the Index at the end of this book to find job sources in a specialty that are not listed where you would intuitively expect to find them.

Job sources are presented under these labels: Job openings, Job services, Directories, and Salary surveys. Within each classification, job sources are listed in this order: those with the broadest coverage and the most job openings come first, followed by those with a more narrow focus and/or fewer job openings. Job sources that cover the same specialties are generally listed together.

Job openings

The National Ad Search (P.O. Box 2983, Milwaukee, WI 53201; phone: 414/351–1398) 50 issues/year, $40/six–week subscription, $75/three–month subscription, $235/annual subscription. Each issue overflows with 2,000 classified ads reprinted from 75 newspapers around the country. Job ads are divided into 54 disciplines. The advertised jobs require at least some post–high school training. Most are at the managerial level or higher.

National Employment Review (Recourse Publications, 334 Knight St., Warwick, RI 02887–1040; phone: 401/732–9850) monthly, $14.95/three-issue subscription, $26.95/six–issue subscription, $39.95/annual subscription, $2.50/single issue. Hundreds of jobs are advertised under the categories: professional, health care, general, business, franchises, and engineering. The most ads are in engineering, health care, and franchising.

The Job HUNTER (University of Missouri at Columbia, 100 Noyes Building, Columbia, MO 65211; phone: 314/882-2097) biweekly, $40/six-month subscription, $50/annual subscription. Around 400 job openings for holders of liberal arts degrees fill every issue. This tabloid covers the full range of private sector job opportunities.

National Business Employment Weekly (Dow Jones & Company, P.O. Box 9100, Springfield, MA 01101; phone: 800/535-4868) weekly, $35/eight-week subscription, $199/annual subscription, $3.95/single issue. Ads that appear in the regional issues of the *Wall Street Journal* are for hundreds of jobs in every major employment category fill each issue. Also includes ads for employment services including recruiting firms and a "Talent for Hire" section where you advertise yourself.

Rocky Mountain Employment Newsletter (Intermountain Publishing, 703 S. Broadway, Suite 100-B0, Denver, CO 80209; phone: 303/988-6707) 18 issues/year, $19/three-month subscription to one edition, $30/any two editions, $39/three editions. Two and one month subscriptions also available. Published in three editions: Colorado-Wyoming, Arizona-New Mexico, and Idaho-Montana. Combined, the three editions include over 400 positions, about 75 to 80 percent of them in the private sector. The positions tend to orient toward the outdoors, with quite a few in natural resources, environmental, wildlife, construction, farming, ranches, livestock, and resorts as well as automotive, industrial, medical, professional, and technical.

Affirmative Action Register (Warren H. Green, Inc., 8356 Olive Blvd., St. Louis, MO 63132; phones: 800/537-0655, 314/991-1335) monthly, individuals: $15/annual subscription, $8/six-month subscription; free to institutional and organizational minority, female, or disabled candidate sources. Hundreds of positions in all segments of the private sector appear throughout this magazine.

The Black Collegian (Black Collegiate Services, 1240 S. Broad Ave., New Orleans, LA 70125; phone: 504/821-5694) quarterly, $10/annual subscription (U.S.), $15/foreign. The annual jobs issue published in March or April includes advertisements for 50 to 150 professional positions under "JASS" and in display ads throughout the magazine.

Journal of Minority Employment (National Consortium for Black Professional Development, 2210 Goldsmith Office Center, Suite 228-A, Louisville, KY 40218; phone: 5502/451-8199) monthly, $24/annual subscription. About 20 job openings for professionals in the private sector are in "Job Mart."

If you didn't read Chapter 1 first, you will be unable to find all the job sources applicable to your job search. Chapter 1 explains how to get the most out of this book—exactly the sort of chapter nobody ever wants to read. But you will be lost without it—guaranteed!

Careers and the disABLED (Equal Opportunity Publications, 44 Broadway, Greenlawn, NY 11740; phone: 516/261-9080) three issues/year, $10/annual subscription. Over 60 display ads throughout this magazine feature positions in all areas of government (and the private sector) for college graduates from employers who certify they are equal opportunity employers who will hire people who have disabilities. Readers can submit their resume to the magazine which then forwards them to advertising employers the job seeker names—for free.

Mainstream Magazine (2973 Beech St., San Diego, CA 92102; phone: 619/234-3138) 10 issues/year, $20/annual subscription (U.S.), $32/Canada. More than five ads appear under "Classifieds—Employment" from employers who certify they are equal opportunity employers who will hire people who have disabilities.

CareerWOMAN (Equal Opportunity Publications, 44 Broadway, Greenlawn, NY 11740; phone: 516/261-8899) three issues/year, $13/annual subscription, free to female college graduates and female students within two years of graduation (request application form). Around a dozen or so job ads appear throughout the magazine. Readers can submit their resume to the magazine which then forwards them to advertising employers the job seeker names—for free.

Executive Female Magazine (National Association for Female Executives, 127 W. 24th, New York, NY 10011; phone: 212/645-0770) bimonthly, free/members only. A few ads for a broad range of executive and management positions appear in "Classified."

The Retired Officers Magazine (The Retired Officers Association, 201 N. Washington St., Alexandria, VA 22314; phones: 800/245-8762, 703/549-2311) monthly, $20/annual subscription (U.S.), $36/foreign, free/members, $20/annual dues. Membership is limited to active or retired officers and warrant officers who serve or have served in the U.S. military. Under "TOPS Job Mart" you'll find about 15 job ads for physicians, engineers, instructors, salespeople, and others.

Managing Your Career (Dow Jones & Company, P.O. Box 435, Chicopee, MA 01021; phone: 609/520-4305) $5/issue, five issues/year. Regular issues are published in March and October. Three additional special issues are published at other times during the year. Subscriptions are available only in bulk quantities. Each issue carries at least 20 to 30 job ads in all employment categories.

Roll Call (Levitt Communications, 900 Second St., NE, Washington, DC 20002; phone: 202/289-4900) twice weekly, $175/annual subscription. Among the 15 or so job ads under "Roll Call Classifieds—Employment," are positions in the private sector that require a knowledge of politics and Capitol Hill: lobbyists, government affairs/relations directors, legislative assistants, press directors, etc.

AMBA Network News (Association of MBA Executives, 227 Commerce St., East Haven, CT 06512; phone: 203/467-8870) quarterly, free/members only. About five ads in business are under "Marketplace." Twice as many "Positions Wanted" ads are nearby.

Contract (Gralla Publications, 1515 Broadway, New York, NY 10022; phones: 800/688–7318, 212/869–1300) monthly, $35/annual subscription. Ten to 12 job ads for sales representatives, contract designs, and research firms are in "Help Wanted."

Quality (Hitchcock Publications, 191 Gary Ave., Carol Stream, IL 60188;; phone: 708/665–1000) monthly, $70/annual subscription, free to qualified professionals. Five to ten ads for quality management, technicians, and engineers are under "Positions Available."

Journal of Quality Assurance (National Association of Quality Assurance Professionals, 5700 Old Orchard Rd., Skokie, IL 60077; phone: 708/940–8800) bimonthly, $90/annual nonmember subscription, free/members. Five to 20 job openings for quality assurance professionals appear in the back under "Classified."

BLONDIE reprinted with special permission of King Features
Syndicate, Inc. Copyright © 1991. All rights reserved.

Career Guide (Dun's Market Service, 3 Sylvan Way, Parsipanny, NJ 07054; phones: 800/526–0651, 201/455–0900) $450 plus $10/postage, published each December, 4,000 pages. This tome provides intimate details on over 5,000 U.S. companies that have indicated that they expect to hire during the coming year. Included in each company description are the name and phone number of a contact person to whom to send a job inquiry, a list of the disciplines the company expects to hire, a description of career opportunities and benefits with the company, and a list of the company's locations.

Job Opportunities for Business and Liberal Arts Graduates (Petersons Guides, P.O. Box 2123, Princeton, NJ 08543-2123; phone: 800/338-3282) $20.95 plus shipping, issued each August. This book features descriptions on over 500 companies that are actively seeking employees.

The Part-Time Professional (Association of Part-Time Professionals, 7700 Leesburg Pike, Suite 216, Falls Church, VA 22043; phone: 703/734-7975) available only to members, included in dues. The typical issue includes about 15 positions under "Part-Time Job Leads Private Sector."

The National Directory of Internships (National Society for Internships and Experiential Education, Suite 207, 3509 Haworth Dr., Raliegh, NC 27609; phone: 919/787-3263) biannual, $24/nonmember U.S., $20/member. Lists 28,000 internship opportunities in 72 different fields with chapters on the arts, business, clearinghouses, communications, consumer affairs, education, environment, government, health, human services, international affairs, museums and history, public interest, sciences, women's issues, and resources for international internships.

1992 Internships (Petersons Guides, P.O. Box 2123, Princeton, NJ 08543-2123; phone: 800/338-3282) $27.95. Updated annually, this 300+ page book provides detailed descriptions and application instructions for 38,000 short-term job opportunities for 23 fields including arts and entertainment, human services, public affairs, and science and industry. It includes 6,400 overseas internship opportunities, geographic and alphabetical indexes, and details on regional and national internship clearinghouses.

Job Opportunities Bulletin (TransCentury Corporation, 1724 Kalorama Rd., NW, Washington, DC 20009; phone: 202/328-4400) bimonthly, $25/annual subscription (U.S., Canada, Mexico), $40/elsewhere (air mail). Lists job vacancy announcements and "Jobseekers" ads in international development, primarily for work in Third World countries. About 25 to 35 job ads, including a moderate number of government positions, appear in the typical issue. Typical positions include accountants, agriculturalists, administrators, medical personnel, teachers, refugee affairs, engineers, project managers, forestry, and environment.

International Jobs Bulletin (Southern Illinois University Placement Center, Woody Hall, Carbondale, IL 62901; phone: 618/453–1047) biweekly, monthly, $25/20 issues, $15/ten issues, $1.50/single issue. Write for free sample issue. The typical issue contains over 75 ads for jobs overseas for accountants, physicians, computer, economists, engineers, translators, teachers, physical therapists, horticulturists, etc.

USA Today (1000 Wilson Blvd., Arlington, VA 22229; phones: 800/872–0001, 703/276–3400) daily, Monday through Friday, $32.50/13–week subscription, $61.75/six-month subscription, $97.50/annual subscription. "USA Today Classified" runs dozens of job ads, business and franchising opportunities ads, and career service ads.

Catholic Standard (P.O. Box 4464, Washington, DC 20017; phone: 301/853–4599) weekly, $20/annual subscription. Among the 15 to 20 job ads in the "Classifieds" are vacancies for secretaries and salespeople.

Harper's (P.O. Box 7511, Red Oak, IA 51591–0511; phone: 800/444–4653) monthly, $18/annual subscription U.S., $20/Canada and U.S. possessions, $38/elsewhere. Half a dozen employment and business opportunities are in the "Classified" section.

The Atlantic (P.O. Box 51044, Boulder, CO 80321–1044; phone: 800/234–2411) monthly, $15.94/annual subscription, $21.94/Canada, $23.94/elsewhere. "Atlantic Classified" lists about 10 job and business opportunities.

Popular Mechanics (Hearst Corporation, 224 W. 57th St., New York, NY 10019; phone: 212/649–2000) monthly, $15.94/annual subscription (U.S.), $31.94/foreign. "Classified Advertisements" carry eight to ten ads for all sorts of jobs under "Help Wanted" and "Employment Opportunities" as well as dozens of "Business Opportunities." As always, be cautious with some of those business opportunities.

The National Review (150 E. 35th St., New York, NY 10016; phones: 800/222–6806, 212/679–7330) semimonthly, $57/annual subscription (U.S.), $71.50/foreign. Five to ten job ads, often for positions with conservative political leanings, are in the "Classified Advertisements—Situations Available."

New Age Journal (Rising Star Associates, 342 Western Ave., Brighton, MA 02135; phone: 617/787–2005) bimonthly, $24/annual subscription. Five to 15 job vacancies and business opportunities are advertised in the "Classifieds."

The Progressive (P.O. Box 421, Mount Morris, IL 61054–0421; phone: 800/435–0715) monthly, $30/annual subscription, $22/students, $50/libraries and institutions, $36/foreign individuals, $56/foreign libraries and institutions. Just one or two job ads appear under "Classified Advertising."

Internships Leading to Careers (Graduate Group, 86 Norwood Rd., West Hartford, CT 06117; phones: 203/232–3100, 203/236–5570) $27.50, published annually.

1992 Summer Employment Directory of the United States (Petersons Guides, P.O. Box 2123, Princeton, NJ 08543–2123; phone: 800/338–3282) $14.95. Published annually in the autumn. Its 200+ pages list over 75,000 summer job openings at resorts, camps, amusement parks, national parks, and government.

Job services

Career Placement Registry (Career Placement Registry, Inc., 302 Swann Ave., Alexandria, VA 22301; phones: 800/368–3093, 703/683–1085) registration fees: $15/students, others by salary sought: $25/through $20,000 salary, $35/$20,001–$40,000 salary, $45/$40,001+. Complete detailed data entry form. Resume information kept in database for six months. Database updated weekly. Maintains resume database that employers access through DIALOG Information Services computer network. Employers contact registrant directly. Over 110,000 potential employers have access to CPR's database.

kiNexus (Information Kinetics, Inc., Suite 560, 640 N. LaSalle St., Chicago, IL 60610; phones: 800/828–0422, 312/642–7560) $24.95/annual fee, free if you are a student at one of the 1,500+ universities that subscribe to this service—check with your school's placement office. This is an online resume database service for college students and graduates with up to five years work experience. You complete their resume form and kiNexus puts your information into the computer. Businesses that subscribe to kiNexus can ask kiNexus staff to conduct searches to identify candidates for specific positions or can conduct their own searches since the database is online. The potential employer is responsible for contacting job candidates for an interview. As of this writing, over 250,000 college students and recent graduates have their resumes in this system.

University Placement Service (Southern Illinois University Placement Center, Woody Hall, Carbondale, IL 62901; phone: 618/453-1047) $30/year, $25/year SIU students. Submit 15 resumes. Resumes are given to appropriate employers who submit vacancy notices. The employer is responsible for contacting the job seeker. These are for international jobs including accountants, physicians, computer, economists, engineers, translators, teachers, physical therapists, horticulturists, etc.

JOBSource (Computerized Employment Systems, Inc., 1720 W. Mulberry, Suite B9, Fort Collins, CO 80521; phones: 800/727-5627, 303/493-1779) There are three services available using an extensive database of over 700 positions, mostly in the environmental arena, but also including: administration, agricultural sciences, biological sciences, botany, business administration, camp personnel, chemistry, communication and the arts, computer science and mathematics, education, engineering, finance, fisheries, forestry, geology, health care, horticulture, hotel/resort/restaurant management, hydrology/water quality, law, marketing and sales, microbiology, natural resources, natural sciences, therapeutics, wildlife biology, and zoology.

For individuals, the most useful is JOBSource's in-house search program. Obtain a resume application form from JOBSource. Within two weeks of receiving your completed form, JOBSource will conduct a job search of its database for you. JOBSource guarantees from six to 25 matches per search. The cost is $30. If fewer than six matches are found, JOBSource will run a second search the next month for free. If the second run turns up fewer than six matches, there is a $5 charge for that second run.

However, if you have a computer and modem, you can download the entire database onto your computer for $20 plus your phone call. It takes 20 to 40 minutes to download the three files. To update, you need download just one file which takes about 20 minutes and costs $15. The database is updated every Thursday. A growing number of universities and colleges are subscribing to JOBSource. They receive the database and user programs around the 24th of each month and can conduct their own job searches. Subscriptions are available for a year ($495), the nine months of September through May ($375), or for the three months of January, April, and November ($189).

SYLVIA

ADNET ONLINE (ADNET Employment Advertising Network, 5987 E. 71st St., Suite 206, Indianapolis, IN 46220; phones: 800/543-9974, 317/579-6922) requires computer modem: free/via Prodigy®, $4/month plus $4 per hour via America OnLine®, free trial via computer modem by dialing 317/579-4857 (2,400 baud, 7 bits, even parity, 1 stop bit; at prompt type: guest. Also available through BIX®, PORTAL Online®, The Well®, ExecPC Bulletin®, and GEnie®. This job vacancy database covers the whole gamut of the employment world. The job candidate gets a menu listing 14 job categories (the number of job ads in a recent week are in parentheses): executive, CEO, plant management, and division management (111); engineering, construction, maintenance, and facilities (324); data processing, computer operations, and tele-communications (189); sales, marketing, advertising, and communications media (234); accounting, finance, and general administration (145); human resources, labor relations, training, and safety (89); purchasing, transportation, and traffic (76); manufacturing, production, quality, and materials (167); management—hotel, restaurant, food, retail, and property (92); natural and physical sciences (134); social sciences (52); education (113); legal occupations (32); and health professions (64).

Once you select a one of these 14 categories, you get a more specific menu of classifications with the number of job ads in each. Then you get another menu with narrower classifications, and the number of job ads in each, from which you select your specialty. Then you can browse the ads for each job and take down the information needed to apply.

Connexion (Petersons Guides, P.O. Box 2123, Princeton, NJ 08543–2123; phone: 800/338–3282) $40/non–college students, free/college students, Peace Corps, U.S. military. Obtain a registration form from Petersons or on the Prodigy computer service. When a match is made, the employer contacts you.

Human Resource Information Network (Executive Telecom System, Inc., 9585 Valparaiso Ct., Indianapolis, IN 46268; phone: 800/421–8884, 317/872–2045) contact for costs. Among the databases on this service is the *Job Ads USA* database which lists 20,000 to 25,000 private sector job openings gleaned from over 100 newspapers. Users can search for jobs by job title, job abstract, geographic location, date advertised, and more. Ads are kept online for six weeks. Updated weekly. Contact Executive Telecom System for details on how to use this service.

Also on this network is a database called *Resumes–On–Computer* which, in June 1991, contained 5,000 resumes from active job seekers that have been gathered from outplacement firms, quick–print shops, and resume writing services. Resumes are kept on file for 24 weeks. Updated weekly. Contact Curtis Development Company (1000 Waterway Blvd., Indianapolis, IN 46202; phone: 317/636–1000) for details on how to get your resume into this database.

The *College Recruitment Database* is an up–to–date resume retrieval service that provides essential data about 13,000 graduating undergraduate and graduate students. All colleges and universities can participate in this service. Have your college placement office contact Executive Telecom Systems for details on how to participate.

Similarly, the *Minority Graduate Database* is a current listing of 6,000 minority graduates from 300 schools as well as older job candidates with extensive experience in specific fields. Updated annually. Contact McClure Lundberg Associates, 1515 U St., NW, Washington, DC 20009; phone: 202/482–4107) to learn how to get listed in this database.

The *Military in Transition Database (MILITRAN)* features current resumes of over 21,000 officers and noncommissioned officers from the Armed Forces who are entering the civilian work force. Updated monthly. Contact Employment Transition Service/ETS, Inc. (1255 Drummers Ln. Suite 306, Wayne, PA 19087; phone: 215/687–3900) to learn how to be included in this database.

ECHO Opportunities Database (ECHO, Suite 860, 100 Wilshire Blvd., Santa Monica, CA 90401; phone: 310/576–4884) free. Hundreds of job vacancies are described on this database which can be accessed only by computer modem by calling 310/319–0164. In the past the emphasis has been on computer and financial jobs, but ECHO has recently expanded the scope of this service to include the whole private sector. ECHO will move in mid–1992 to a new address which is unknown as of this writing.

Employment Assistance Resource Network (Direct Link for the Disabled, Inc., P.O Box 1036, Solvang, CA 93463; phone: 805/688–1603 [voice/**TDD**]). As of this writing, Direct Link is seeking funding to establish a national network of employment–related resources to assist people who have disabilities locate job vacancies and help meet these needs: transportation, adaptive equipment, job training, financial assistance, attendant care, independent living, vocational rehabilitation, and job accommodations. During the first year of funding, Direct Link will develop this network of resource during the first year of funding. During the second year it will be able to offer personalized one–stop information and assistance through this EARN program.

Job Placement Exchange (4–Sights Network, 16625 Grand River, Detroit, MI 48227; phone: 313/272–3900) free. This is part of a national computer system for people who are blind or visually–impaired. It requires the use of a computer modem. Set your communications program with the following parameters: full duplex, VT–100 or TTY emulation, 300, 1,200, or 2,400 baud; choose either 8–bit word, 1 stop bit, no parity; or 7–bit word, 1 stop bit, even parity. Then dial 313/272–7111. When you have reached 4–Sights, type the single word *newuser* in lower case letter at the login: prompt. Answer the questions about yourself and type in a personal code name of three to seven characters in lower case letters. Then select a password of three to seven lower case characters. This information will be recorded by the 4–Sights system administrator on the next business day so that the next time you call 4–Sights you can simply use your login and password to enter the system. You would be prudent to contact 4–Sights for written instructions on how to dial 4–Sights and get around the program.

4–Sights maintains a *Job Placement Exchange* on this computer database. Contact 4–Sights for instructions on how to add your resume to the database. The database contains both a roster of jobs and resumes of persons looking for employment. The idea is to connect people who are blind or visually-impaired with job opportunities and specialized training.

Also on this database is 4–Sights' *Occupational Information Library for the Blind*. This database directory describes over 500 jobs successfully performed by people who are blind or visually-impaired. It itemizes the educational requirements, technical devices needed to accomplish each job listed, and the sort of organizations or businesses most likely to hire people for each job. Jobs listed range from simple tasks in agriculture or manufacturing to positions that require advanced degrees. If you are blind or have a visual impairment, this directory is a great resource for career ideas.

To access the OILB, follow the instructions given above for entering the 4–Sights Network. Once on 4–Sights, type *oilb* at the first Ok: prompt. Then choose to run the OILB program and follow the instructions to search through the ten ''job families'' or create a personal profile that identifies job titles that match your interests. You may download onto your computer those job descriptions that interest you.

Senior Community Service Employment Program (National Council on Aging, 600 Maryland Ave., SW, Washington, DC 20024; phone: 202/479-1200) free. This service has already helped put over 6,400 older Americans back to work or in job training. You meet with a local project staff person to identify the sort of work that interests you and what else you might need to work such as transportation assistance, better eyeglasses, or other supportive services. Job training that pays at least the minimum wage is offered for about 20 hours a week. The local project office then helps you find a job using your new skills. Eligibility requirements: 55 or older, household income no more than 25 percent over the federal poverty level, and out of work or having trouble finding a suitable job. To identify a local project near you, contact the program at its Washington address.

Resume File (American Society of Corporate Secretaries, 1270 Avenue of the Americas, New York, NY 10020; phone: 212/765-2620) $100/annual nonmember fee, free/members. Obtain a registration form from ASCS and submit and your resume to the service. When a match is made, the employer is given your complete resume and is responsible for contacting you for a corporate secretarial position.

TOPS: TROA's Officer Placement Service (The Retired Officers Association, 201 N. Washington St., Alexandria, VA 22314; phones: 800/245-8762, 703/549-2311) free/members only, $20/annual dues. Membership is limited to active or retired officers and warrant officers who serve or have served in the U.S. military. You submit five copies or your resume and complete the service's detailed form which is coded into the TOPS database and kept on file for 18 months at a time. When a match is made, you are sent a copy of the job announcement and are responsible for contacting the employer yourself. Jobs are for a wide variety of professionals.

MBA Employment Guide (Association of MBA Executives, 227 Commerce St., East Haven, CT 06512; phone: 203/467-8870) $10/report plus $1.75/shipping. This service produces a customized report for the industry and region you specify. It lists the names and addresses of companies in that region and industry that employ MBAs. Also included is the name and phone number of a contact person at most of the companies.

Database (National Women's Economic Alliance Foundation, 1440 New York Ave., NW, Washington, DC 20005; phone: 202/393-5257) free. Your resume is kept on file indefinitely. This service connects board of director level women with job opportunities.

Computer Assisted Matching Program (Air Force Association/Militran, 1501 Lee Highway, Arlington, VA 22209-1198; phones: 800/727-3337, 703/247-5800) available only to AFA members, free. Submit the completed "Mini-Résumé" form and this very sophisticated service will match you to available jobs in virtually any profession.

Talent Bank (TransCentury Corporation (1724 Kalorama Rd., NW, Washington, DC 20009; phone: 202/328-4400) free. Obtain their "Professional Skills Registration Form." Submit a completed form with your resume. This service refers your resume to international employers seeking people with your background. Resumes are kept on file for two years. Typical positions include accountants, agriculturalists, administrators, medical personnel, teachers, refugee affairs, engineers, project managers, forestry, and environment.

Directories

Job Hunter's Sourcebook: Where to Find Employment Leads and Other Job Search Resources (Gale Research, Inc., 835 Penobscot Bldg., Detroit, MI 48226-4094; phone: 800/877-4253) $49.95, published in December of even-numbered years, 1,106 pages. This tome lists sources of help wanted ads, placement and job referral services, employer directories and networking lists, handbooks and manuals about each profession, employment agencies and search firms, and other leads, primarily associations that don't offer any job services but can provide general information about a profession.

This is a great source for identifying job recruiters and executive search firms for the 100+ specialties into which the book is divided. It also identifies extremely useful books and manuals that will help you learn about a specific field.

Unfortunately, many of the job sources (periodicals and job placement services) listed in the first edition (1990) either do not include ads for job openings or no longer exist. One association listed as providing job services had disbanded in 1985. These comments, however, apply *only* to the 1990 first edition. We're sure that the next edition will make corrections.

Corporate Technology Directory (CorpTech, 12 Alfred St., Suite 200, Woburn, MA 01801; phone: 617/932-3939) $425, published each March, 5,500 pages, four volumes. Profiles over 35,000 businesses with 110,000 key executive identified and products and services described. These are technology companies in automation, biotechnology, chemicals, computers and software, defense, energy, environment, manufacturing equipment, advanced materials, medical, pharmaceuticals, photonics, subassemblies and components, testing and measurements, telecommunications, transportation, and holding companies.

CorpTech Fast 5,000 Company Locator (CorpTech, 12 Alfred St., Suite 200, Woburn, MA 01801; phone: 617/932-3939) $95, issued each March. This is a state-by-state listing of the 5,000 fastest growing companies listed in the *Corporate Technology Directory* described immediately above. Each entry includes phone number and address, number of employees, sales, and industries in which the company is active.

Sales Guide to High-Tech Companies (CorpTech, 12 Alfred St., Suite 200, Woburn, MA 01801; phone: 617/932-3939) $145/regional edition, quarterly, 400 pages, available in ten regional editions. Each edition averages 3,300 company profiles with 12,000 executive contacts and details on each firms products and services.

Corporate Jobs Outlook! (P.O. Drawer 100, Boerne, TX 78006; phones: 800/325-8808, 512/755-8810) $159.99/annual subscription, bimonthly. Although technically a newsletter, for our purposes this is more of a directory since it does not include actual job vacancies. Instead, each issue offers a pretty in-depth look at 16 or 17 major firms usually with at least 5,000 employees with offices in every part of the country. Each report rates the firm and its salaries and benefits, analyzes its current and projected development, and tells what parts of the company to apply for various types of jobs and what parts to avoid due to financial or operating problems, or potential layoffs. The name of the personnel director is also given. It also examines the firm's "corporate culture," benefit plans, record for promoting women or minorities to top posts, and its practices concerning tuition reimbursement.

Each issue also includes a "Hot Idea!" section that identifies companies experiencing or expected to undergo growth and expansion—and therefore likely to offer career opportunities—as well as a report on the fastest growing occupations. In addition, this section tells you which of the firms profiled in that issue are offer the most promising opportunities for different specialties.

This newsletter is also available via computer modem on NewsNet (phones: 800/345-1301, 215/527-8030) and is available to personnel professionals on HRIN, the *Human Resources Information Network* (Executive Telecom System, 9585 Valparaiso Ct., Indianapolis, IN 46268; phones: 800/421-8884, 317/872-2045). Contact the appropriate computer service for details.

The Almanac of American Employers (Corporate Jobs Outlook!, P.O. Drawer 100, Boerne, TX 78006; phones: 800/325-8808, 512/755-8810) contact for price. This book profiles and ranks 500 of the nation's most successful large corporations by salaries and benefits, financial stability, and advancement opportunities.

Directory of Corporate Affiliations (National Register Publishing Company, 3004 Glenview Rd., Wilmette, IL 60091; phones: 800/323-6772, 708/441-2210) $687 plus $13.75 shipping, annual, includes five cumulative supplements during the year. Identifies key personnel in America's 40,000 most influential multi-companies: 4,700 parent companies; 40,000 divisions, subsidiaries, and affiliates; 500 privately-owned companies; plus hard-to-find facts about each company including phone numbers and addresses of key executive decision makers.

International Directory of Corporate Affiliations (National Register Publishing Company, 3004 Glenview Rd., Wilmette, IL 60091; phones: 800/323-6772, 708/441-2210) $497 plus $14.25 shipping, annual, 1,900 pages. Details over 1,400 major foreign companies and their 30,000 U.S. and foreign holdings: 44,000 listings.

Directory of Leading Private Companies (National Register Publishing Company, 3004 Glenview Rd., Wilmette, IL 60091; phones: 800/323-6772, 708/441-2210) $497 plus $8.75 shipping, annual, 1,900 pages. Gives details on over 7,000 U.S. private companies in the service, manufacturing, distribution, retail, and construction industries as well as health, high technology, entertainment, fast–food franchises, leasing, publishing, communications, and much more.

National Trade and Professional Associations of the United States (Columbia Books, 1212 New York Ave., NW, Suite 300, Washington, DC 20005; phone: 202/898–0662) $55. With information on over 6,450 trade and professional associations, this annual volume enables you to identify any of these associations beyond those included in this volume.

Encyclopedia of Associations 1992 (Gale Research, Inc., 835 Penobscot Bldg., Detroit, MI 48226; phone: 800/877–4253) Volume 1: *National Organizations of the U.S.* $320/set of three parts, published July 1991, includes entries on over 22,000 associations including hundreds for government professionals. Usually available at public libraries. Volume 2: *Geographic and Executive Indexes*, $265, published July 1991, enable you to locate organizations in a particular city and state to identify association executives. Volume 3, $275, published in November 1991, provides full entries on associations not listed in Volume 1.

The *Encyclopedia of Associations* is available on the DIALOG online computer service (File number 114) on which records can be accessed by name, key word, description, publications, and other fields. For information on online subscriptions, contact DIALOG Information Services (3460 Hillview Ave., Palo Alto, CA 94304; phone: 800/334–2564)

The *Encyclopedia of Associations* is also available on CD–ROM as part of *Gale GlobalAccess: Associations* ($995/annual single–user subscription. Issued every June and December. Includes one updated replacement disc after six months.

Directories in Print (Gale Research, Inc., 835 Penobscot Bldg., Detroit, MI 48226–4094; phone: 800/877–4253) $250, 1991, 2,059 pages in two volumes. Details on 14,000 directories in the U.S. and worldwide.

Life Sciences Organizations and Agencies Directory (Gale Research, Inc., 835 Penobscot Bldg., Detroit, MI 48226–4094; phone: 800/877–4253) $175, 1988, 864 pages. Over 7,500 organizations active in the life sciences, from agriculture to wildlife and zoology are profiled.

"Well, sir, now that you have a minute, let me tell you
about my company's product."

The Salesman's Guide: National Directory of Association Meeting Planners & Conference/Convention Directors (National Register Publishing Company, 3004 Glenview Rd., Wilmette, IL 60091; phones: 800/323-6772, 708/441-2210) $193 plus $11 shipping, annual. Includes 8,000 national associations that hold off-site conventions and meetings with 12,400 meeting planners by city and state.

The Salesman's Guide: The Nationwide Directory of Corporate Meeting Planners (National Register Publishing Company, 3004 Glenview Rd., Wilmette, IL 60091; phones: 800/323-6772, 708/441-2210) $235 plus $13.50 shipping, annual. Includes the names and number for 16,600 elusive corporate meeting planners at over 11,000 corporations.

The Salesman's Guide: The Nationwide Directory of Premium Incentive & Travel Buyers (National Register Publishing Company, 3004 Glenview Rd., Wilmette, IL 60091; phones: 800/323-6772, 708/441-2210) $187 plus $11 shipping, annual. Lists 20,000 buyers who purchase premiums, incentives, and incentive travel programs for over 11,000 corporations.

National Displaced Homeworkers Directory (Displaced Home-workers Network, 1411 K St., NW, Suite 930, Washington, DC 20005; phone: 202/628-6767) $22, issued each fall.

Consultants and Consulting Organizations Directory (Gale Research, Inc., 835 Penobscot Bldg., Detroit, MI 48226-4094; phone: 800/877-4253) $410, last published in 1991, 2,571 pages. Lists over 16,500 consulting firms and individual consultants in 14 general fields. This directory is also available as a database on the *Human Resource Information Network* (Executive Telecom System, Inc., 9585 Valparaiso Ct., Indianapolis, IN 46268; phone: 800/421-8884, 317/872-2045) contact for costs. Updated semiannually.

The Futures Research Directory: Individuals (World Future Society, 4916 Saint Elmo Ave., Bethesda, MD 20814; 301/656-8274) $29.95/nonmembers, $25.95/members, $30/annual dues, published in January of odd-numbered years. Lists individuals who are professionally involved in the study of the future.

Salary surveys

American Salaries and Wages Survey(Gale Research, Inc., 835 Penobscot Bldg., Detroit, MI 48226; phone: 800/877-4253) $89.50, 1991, 1,125 pages. Covers more than 4,500 occupational classifications with salary ranges, entry level, highest paid. Figures are derived from more than 300 publications issued by trade and professional organizations.

Inter-City Wage & Salary Differentials (Abbott, Langer & Associates, 548 First St., Crete, IL 60417; phone: 708/672-4200) $225, annual. Gives average hourly rates for each of 90 different jobs in 200 locations in the U.S.: office, professional and technical; maintenance, toolroom, and powerplant; and material movement and custodial/guard functions.

The American Almanac of Jobs and Salaries (Avon Books, 105 Madison Ave., New York, NY 10016) $15.95. 665 pages. This is a good general source on salaries. It covers a broad spectrum of careers. However, it is not nearly as thorough as the salary studies conducted by trade and professional organizations. Most recent 1990-1991 edition; expect a new edition by 1993.

"The boss thought you might like to read this while
you're waiting to ask him for a raise."

College Recruiting Report (Abbott, Langer & Associates, 548 First St., Crete, IL 60417; phone: 708/672–4200) $195, annual. Reports on the actual starting salaries of 10,000 inexperienced college graduates. Salaries are reported for all degree levels by curriculum types and type of employer. Covers 34 different college curricula and 10 junior or community college curricula and 15 types of employers.

Available Pay Survey Reports: An Annotated Bibliography (Abbott, Langer & Associates, 548 First St., Crete, IL 60417; phone: 708/672–4200) Part 1: U.S. surveys, $350; Part 2: Non–U.S. surveys, $125. Covers over 1,100 individual pay survey reports. Heavily indexed to help you find the specialities that interest you.

National Fringe Benefit Survey (Abbott, Langer & Associates, 548 First St., Crete, IL 60417; phone: 708/672–4200) $79.95, annual. Findings are reported by employer size and geographic location.

National Executive Compensation Database included on the *Human Resource Information Network* (Executive Telecom System, Inc., 9585 Valparaiso Ct., Indianapolis, IN 46268; phone: 800/421–

8884, 317/872–2045) contact for costs. This database furnishes annual survey results on salaries, bonuses, and other benefits for 28 executive positions.

AMBA's MBA Career and Salary Census (Association of MBA Executives, 227 Commerce St., East Haven, CT 06512; phone: 203/467–8870) $6/nonmembers, $3/members, annual. Lists average salaries earned by MBAs in 17 different industries and by 12 job functions.

Management Salaries Report (Abbott, Langer & Associates, 548 First St., Crete, IL 60417; phone: 708/672–4200) $150, annual. Covers 22 management positions based on a survey of 20,000 management employees at 2,100 companies in 60 metropolitan areas.

Office, Professional, and Data Processing Salaries Report (Abbott, Langer & Associates, 548 First St., Crete, IL 60417; phone: 708/672–4200) $250, annual. This survey of 160,000 employees at 2,100 companies reports on salaries for 40 different positions by metropolitan area and nationally. Includes programmers, word processing operators, systems analyst, personal computer specialists, data entry operators, and clerk typists; accountants; human resources; shipping and receiving clerk; credit and collection clerk; customer service representative; purchasing agents; secretary; executive secretaries; and much more.

Surveys of Nonexempt Compensation (Abbott, Langer & Associates, 548 First St., Crete, IL 60417; phone: 708/672–4200) $49/state, annual. Shows salaries for nonexempt office employees in 26 jobs categories. Reports for 26 states are available.

Chapter 3

Animals

Also see the chapter on ''Farming and ranching'' for job sources in the bee, horse, and livestock industries.

Job openings

Animal Keepers Forum (American Association of Zoo Keepers, 635 Cage Blvd., Topeka, KS 60606; phone: 913/272–5821) available only to members, annual dues: $30/full–time zoo keeper, $25/affiliates and associates, $20/libraries. Six to eight vacancies for animal keepers, veterinary technicians, and education specialists appear under ''Opportunity Knocks.''

The Animals' Agenda (Animal Rights Network, PO Box 6809, Syracuse, NY 13217; phone: 800/825–0061) 10 issues/year, $22/annual subscription, $28/Canada and Mexico, $35/elsewhere. Fewer than five employment and business opportunities appear under ''Classified.''

Directories

The Official Museum Directory and Products and Services Guide (National Register Publishing Company, 3004 Glenview Rd., Wilmette, IL 60091; phones: 800/323–6772, 708/441–2210) $194,

$112/members of the American Association of Museums; plus $8.25 shipping, annual. Provides details on 6,700 U.S. museums including zoos and aquariums.

Pets

Job openings

Pet Supplies Marketing (Edgell Communications, 1 E. First St., Duluth, MN 55802; phones: 800/346–0085, 218/723–9870) monthly; $25/annual subscription (U.S.); $50/Canada; $100/elsewhere. "PSM Classified" features about three ads, usually for pet store managers or manufacturers' sales reps and managers. The December directory issue by itself costs $55.

Pet Product News (Fancy Publications, P.O. Box 6050, Mission Viejo, CA 92690; phone: 714/855–8822) monthly, $32/annual subscription, free to qualified pet industry professionals. "Classified Advertising " carries about eight ads for sales and manufacturers' representatives, and business opportunities.

Pet Age (207 S. Wabash, Suite 504, Chicago, IL 60604; phone: 312/663–4040) monthly, controlled free circulation to qualified professionals in the pet store industry. Two or three ads for salespersons, sales managers, manufacturers' representatives, and pet store managers are in the "Classified" section.

Dog World (Maclean Hunter, 29 N. Wacker Dr., Chicago, IL 60606; phone: 312/726–2802) monthly, $28/annual subscription (U.S.), $38/Canada, $43/elsewhere. About three job ads are in "Help Wanted" with another 40 ads in "Kennel Property (for Sale)" and eight ads under "Business Opportunities."

Dog Fancy (P.O. Box 53264, Boulder, CO 80322–3264; phone: 303/447–9330) $23.97/annual subscription, $31.97/Canada, $35.97/elsewhere. The "Classified Dog" section features over a dozen business opportunities. Also includes a directory of breeders.

Cat Fancy (P.O. Box 52864 Boulder, CO 80322–2864; phone: 303/447–9330) $23.97/annual subscription, $31.97/Canada, $35.97/elsewhere. The "Classified Cat" section features over a dozen business and employment opportunities. Also includes a directory of breeders.

Groom & Board (207 S. Wabash, Suite 504, Chicago, IL 60604; phone: 312/663–4040) controlled free circulation to qualified professionals in the kennel and grooming industry. Four to eight job vacancies and business opportunities for groomers and kennel operators are in the "Classified" section.

Borderline (American Breeding Kennels Association, 4575 Galley Rd., Suite 400A, Colorado Springs, CO 80915; phone: 719/591–1113) bimonthly, $50/annual subscription. An occasional job vacancy in the kennel industry makes it into "Employment Market."

Freshwater and Marine Aquarium (144 West Sierra Madre Blvd., Sierra Madre, CA 91024; phones: 800/523–736, 818/355–1476) monthly, $22/annual subscription, $27.50/Canada and Mexico. Five to ten job and business opportunities are listed under "Business."

Bird Talk (P.O. Box 57347, Boulder, CO 80322; phone: 303/447–9330) monthly, $25.97/annual subscription, $33.17/Canada, $37.17/elsewhere. About ten job vacancies and business opportunities appear in the "Classifieds" section.

Directories

Pet Age Directory (Pet Age, 207 S. Wabash, Suite 504, Chicago, IL 60604; phone: 312/663–4040) $45, published each September. Includes details on manufacturers and distributors of pet products as well as livestock wholesalers.

American Breeding Kennels Association Membership Directory (ABKA, 4575 Galley Rd., Suite 400A, Colorado Springs, CO 80915; phone: 719/591–1113) $3.50/nonmembers, free/members, issued each June. Lists member animal kennels.

Birds USA (PO Box 6050 Mission Viejo, CA 92690; phone: 714/855-8822) annual, $5.95. Includes national directories of breeders and pet shops.

Veterinary care

Job openings

Journal of the American Veterinary Medical Association (American Veterinary Medical Association, 1931 N. Meacham Rd., Suite 100, Schaumburg, IL 60173; phone: 708/925-8070) biweekly, $70/annual nonmember subscription, included in dues. Among the 300 to 450 "Classifieds" are many positions for veterinarians and veterinary technicians.

DVM: The Newsmagazine of Veterinary Medicine (Edgell Communications, 1 E. First St., Duluth, MN 55802; phone: 800/346-0085) monthly, $28/annual subscription. "DVM Classified Advertising" runs 40 to 50 ads for job vacancies for veterinarians.

Veterinary Technician (Veterinary Learning Systems, 475 Phillips Blvd., Suite 100, Trenton, NJ 08616; phone: 609/882-5600) ten issues/year, $31/annual subscription (U.S.), $38/Mexico and Canada, $46/elsewhere. Around 40 job vacancies for veterinary technicians fill the "Classified" section.

Veterinary and Human Toxicology (c/o Comparative Toxicology Laboratories, Kansas State University, Manhattan, KS 66506-5606; phone: 913/532-4334) bimonthly, $40/annual subscription (U.S.), $46/Canada, $50/elsewhere. Forty to 50 openings, including positions for veterinarians, toxicologists, biologists, and health professionals appear under "Job Opportunities." A membership directory of several related organizations is published once a year in this journal.

Journal of Veterinary Internal Medicine (J. B. Lippincott Company, Downville Pike, Route 3, Box 20-B, Hagerstown, MD 21740; phones: 800/638-3030, 215/238-4206) bimonthly, $40/annual subscription (U.S.), $20/students, $55/foreign. You'll find about five job openings featured under "Classified."

Veterinary Surgery (J. B. Lippincott, P.O. Box 350, Hagerstown, MD 21741-9901; phones: 800/638-3030, 509/335-0711) bimonthly, $65/annual nonmember subscription, free to members of the American College of Veterinary Anesthesiologists. Ads for veterinary surgeons and anesthesiologists appear in the ''Classified Ad Section.''

Job services

AVMA Job Placement Service (American Veterinary Medical Association, 1931 N. Meacham Rd., Suite 100, Schaumburg, IL 60173; phone: 708/925-8070) available only to AVMA members, free. Complete a resume form and this service will match you with vacancies in clinical practice or private industry.

Directories

ACVS Directory of Diplomates (American College of Veterinary Surgeons, 4330 East West Highway, Suite 1117, Bethesda, MD 20814; phone: 301/718-6504) free, published in late autumn of odd-numbered years.

Chapter 4

Apparel and accessories

Clothing industry

Job openings

American Textiles (Billian Publishing Company, 2100 Powers Ferry Rd., Atlanta, GA 30339; phone: 404/955-5656) monthly, $43/annual subscription (U.S.), $115/foreign (airmail). The "Classified" section lists ten to 20 ads for a wide range of positions from labor to technical, to chemists and executives.

DNR (7 W. 34th St., NY, NY 10001; phone 609/461-6248) daily, Monday through Friday, $62/annual subscription (U.S.), $140/Canada & Mexico (airmail), $250/elsewhere (airmail). Twenty vacancies for salespeople, graphic artists, store and plant managers, and clothing designers are advertised under "The DNR Marketplace" and "Sales Help Wanted."

Earnshaw's Infants, Girls, Boys Wear Review (Earnshaw's, 225 W. 34th St., NY, NY 10001; phone: 212/563-2742) monthly, $24/annual subscription (U.S.), $36/Canada, $114/elsewhere. There are from five to ten ads for infants and children clothes and accessories sales and marketing representatives and district managers.

Apparel Industry Magazine (Shore Publishing, 180 Allen Rd., NE, Atlanta, GA 30328; phone 404/252-8831) free/professionals in the apparel industry. "Classified" lists two or three positions for management positions in plant operations.

AAMA News (American Apparel Manufacturers Association, 2500 Wilson, Blvd., Suite 301, Arlington, VA 22201; phone: 703/524–1864) every other month, free/members. Around three ads appear under "Classified" for positions in the apparel industry.

Knitting Times (National Knitwear and Sportswear Association, 386 Park Ave., NY, NY 10022; phone: 212/683-7520) monthly, $35/annual (U.S.), $56/foreign. "Market Place – Help Wanted" lists about eight ads for production and supervisors in the mill industry.

Sew News (PJS Publications, P.O. Box 3134 Harlan, IA 51537-3134; phone 800/289-6397) $19.94/annual subscription (U.S.), $32.04/Canada, $40/elsewhere. Around eight job ads appear under "Classified—Business Opportunities."

Bobbin Magazine (Bobbin Blenheim Media, P.O. Box 1986, Columbia, SC 29202; phone: 800/845-8820) monthly, $48/annual subscription. From ten to 20 ads appear under "Classifieds–Career Opportunities" for apparel and sewing positions from engineers to sales to sewing operators.

American Drycleaner (Crain Associated Enterprises, 500 N. Dearborn, Chicago, IL 60610; phone: 312/337-7700) monthly, $30/annual subscription (U.S.), $65/foreign. Nine ads for plant managers, salespeople, and spotters are in "Classified."

Modern Salon (Vance Publishing, 400 Knightsbridge Pkwy., Lincolnshire, IL 60069; phone: 708/634-2600) monthly, $20/annual subscription (U.S.), $29.50/Canada. A few ads for stylists and other beauty salon employees are under "Help Wanted."

Directories

Women's & Children's Wear Specialty Stores (Chain Store Guide Information Services, 425 Park Ave., New York, NY 10022; phone: 212/371-9400, ext. 306) $179, published each September. Describes 5,400 women's and children's wear specialty stores, mail order companies, and sport shops/activewear retailers who operate 55,000 stores. Also free–standing shoe companies with 25,000 stores. Includes 23,600 key executive, buying, and administrative personnel.

American Apparel Manufacturers Association Membership Directory (AAMA, 2500 Wilson, Blvd., Suite 301, Arlington, VA 22201; phone: 703/524-1864) $100/nonmembers, $15/members, annual. In addition to listing all AAMA members and associate members, this directory includes product, brand name, and government contracting indexes and listings of key personnel, plant locations, and products or services. Also included is sourcing/private label contracting information.

The Fashion Resource Directory (Fairchild Books, 7 E. 12th St., New York, NY 10003; phones: 800/247-6622, 212/630-3880) $35, 262 pages. While much of this directory covers New York City where so much of the fashion industry is situated, it is national in scope. Included are all specialties within the industry including fabric sources, make-up artists, apparel marts, buying offices, public relations agencies, and much more.

The Fashion Guide: International Designer Directory 1991 (Fairchild Books, 7 E. 12th St., New York, NY 10003; phones: 800/247-6622, 212/630-3880) $245, annual, 688 pages. Includes names, addresses, phone, and fax numbers for 250 major fashion houses, 1,800 designers, 5,000 fashion-related companies, 1,200 buyers, 10,000 directors and managers, 900 public relations leaders, and 850 fashion publishers and writers. Also includes country-by-country guides and special indexes on public relations and designers.

Who's Who in Fashion (Fairchild Books, 7 E. 12th St., New York, NY 10003; phones: 800/247-6622, 212/630-3880) $27.50, 260 pages. Includes profiles of more than 200 of the world's top designers. A 75-page supplement ($15) adds profiles of another 40 influential designers.

Men's and Boys' Wear Specialty Stores (Chain Store Guide Information Services, 425 Park Ave., New York, NY 10022; phone: 212/371-9400, ext. 306) $179, published each September. Profiles 3,800 men's and boys' wear specialty stores, mail order companies, and sport shops/activewear retailers who operate 35,000 stores. Includes 18,100 key executive, buying, and administrative personnel.

IACD Yearbook (International Association of Clothing Designers, 240 Madison Ave., NY, NY 10016; phone: 212/685-6602), free/members only, annual. Includes clothing designers and companies.

American Salon's Green Book (Edgell Communications, 1 E. First St., Duluth, MN 55802; phone: 800/346-0085) $70, annual. Includes manufacturers and their sales representatives, salon products and brand names, salon chains, national distributors, professional and trade organizations, accredited barber schools in the U.S. and Puerto Rico, and cosmetology schools in the U.S. Canada, and the Caribbean.

Salary surveys

Management Compensation Survey (American Apparel Manufacturers Association, 2500 Wilson Blvd., Suite 301, Arlington, VA 22201; phone: 703/524-1864) $600, $450/participants in the survey. This report includes information on average salary, average bonuses, company sales, and number of employees for 42 management positions in the apparel manufacturing industry.

Apparel Plant Wages Survey (American Apparel Manufacturers Association, 2500 Wilson Blvd., Suite 301, Arlington, VA 22201; phone: 703/524-1864) $60/nonmembers, $25/members. Survey includes information on workers and supervisors from 1981 to the present.

Apparel Sales/Marketing Compensation Survey (American Apparel Manufacturers Association, 2500 Wilson Blvd., Suite 301, Arlington, VA 22201; phone: 703/524-1864) $60/nonmembers, $25/members. Survey includes information on trainee and sales positions.

Footwear

Job openings

Footwear News (Footwear Industries of America, P.O. Box 1402 Riverton, NJ 08077; phone: 609/461-6248) weekly, $62/annual subscription (U.S.), $140/Canada, $175/elsewhere. Around five ads are listed under "Market Place" for sales managers, production, and secretaries.

Shoe Service (Shoe Service Institute of American Service Corporation, 5024 Campbell Blvd., Baltimore, MD 21236; phone: 301/931-8100) monthly, $18/annual subscription (U.S.), $25/Canada, $33/elsewhere. When job ads appear, there can be as many as six jobs for shoe repair personnel. Job ads, however, do not appear in every issue.

Directories

1991 US Footwear Industry Directory (Footwear Industries of America, 1420 K St., Suite 600, Washington, DC 20005; phone 202/789-1420) $70/nonmembers, $40/members, annual.

Footwear Distributors and Retailers of America Member List (FDRA, 1319 F St. NW, Washington, DC 20004; phone: 202/737-5660) free, annual, three pages.

Salary survey

Annual Compensation and Benefits Survey (Footwear Distributors and Retailers of America, 1319 F St. NW, Washington, DC 20004; phone: 202/737-5660) free/members only, annual. Covers footwear retail store salaries for store level employees, operations managers, and buying and merchandising staffs.

Jewelry and timepieces

Job openings

National Jeweler (Gralla Publications, P.O. Box 7614, Riverton, NJ 08077; phone: 609/461–3838) semimonthly, $100/annual subscription (U.S.), $122/Canada, $190/elsewhere, $39/qualified professionals in the jewelry industry (U.S.), $72/foreign. "Positions Available" and "Reps Wanted" run ads for 40 to 60 vacancies for everything in the jewelry industry, but mostly for salespeople and manufacturers' representatives.

Jewelers' Circular–Keystone (Chilton Company, 1 Chilton Way, Radnor, PA 19089; phones: 800/247–8080, 215/964–4000) monthly, $29/annual subscription (U.S.), $65/Canada, $86/elsewhere. Around 50 job vacancies for manufacturing and sales representatives as well as jewelers, bench jewelers, goldsmiths, silversmiths, and watchmakers are under "Help Wanted" and "Sales Reps Wanted." Also publishes "Situations Wanted" ads.

American Jewelry Manufacturer (Chilton Company, 1 Chilton Way, Radnor, PA 19089; phones: 800/247–8080, 215/964–4145) monthly, $36/annual nonmember subscription (U.S.), $46/Canada, $74/elsewhere, free/members of Manufacturing Jewelers and Silversmiths of America (100 India St., Providence, RI 02903; phone: 401/274–3840). Around 20 job vacancies for jewelers and silversmiths are in the "Marketplace."

Modern Jeweler (Vance Publishing, 400 Knightbridge Pkwy., Lincolnshire, IL 60069; phone: 708/634–2600, ext. 306) monthly, $35/annual subscription (U.S.), $100/foreign, free/members of the trade. The "Classifieds" run ads for five to 15 goldsmiths, silversmiths, jewelers, salespeople, managers, and clock makers.

Horological Times (American Watchmakers Institute, 3700 Harrison Ave., Cincinnati, OH 45211; phone: 513/661–3838) monthly, free/members only. Four to eight "Classifieds" advertise job openings for watchmakers, clock makers, and jewelers.

Watch & Clock Review (2403 Champa St., Denver, CO 80205; phone: 303/296–1600) monthly, $19.50/annual subscription. Two or three ads for watch and clock makers, repair people, retail sales, service technicians, and manufacturers' or importers' representatives are in "Help Wanted" and "Sales Reps Wanted."

Repairing Metalware (Institute of Metal Repair, 1558 S. Redwood, Escondito, CA 92025; phone: 619/747–5978) monthly, $12/annual subscription. One or two ads for platers, silversmiths, and metal repairers are under "Jobs Wanted/Offered."

The Jewelry Appraiser (National Association of Jewelry Appraisers, 4210 N. Brown Ave., Suite A, Scottsdale, AZ 85251; phone: 602/941–8088) quarterly, $39/annual nonmember subscription, free/members. One or two ads for jewelry appraisers are in "Employment."

Job services

Job Placement (Gemological Institute of America, 1660 Stewart St., Santa Monica, CA 90404; phone: 800/421–7250) free. This service is for folks who seek a job in retail jewelry. It usually is for students and operates through schools. Contact GIA for details on how to participate.

Informal Job–Matching Service (National Association of Jewelry Appraisers, 4210 N. Brown Ave., Suite A, Scottsdale, AZ 85251; phone: 602/941–8088) free/members only. Members contact NAJA to let the association know they are looking for work. Employers contact NAJA when they are looking for jewelry appraisers. NAJA gives the phone numbers of these job seekers to each employer who is then responsible for contacting desirable candidates for the next step in the hiring process. This is a very informal service.

Directories

Manufacturing Jewelers and Silversmiths of America Buyers Guide (MJSA, 100 India St., Providence, RI 02903; phone: 401/274–3840) $35, published in March of odd–numbered years. Lists all member companies and their products and services.

Watch Industry Directory (Watch & Clock Review, 2403 Champa St., Denver, CO 80205; phone: 303/296–1600) $3, issued each May. Describes watch manufacturers and importers.

Clock Industry Directory (Watch & Clock Review, 2403 Champa St., Denver, CO 80205; phone: 303/296–1600) $3, released every June. Describes clock manufacturers and importers.

Who's Who in Jewelry Appraisal (National Association of Jewelry Appraisers, 4210 N. Brown Ave., Suite A, Scottsdale, AZ 85251; phone: 602/941–8088) $10/nonmembers, free/members, annual.

RM Mailing List (Institute of Metal Repair, 1558 S. Redwood, Escondito, CA 92025; phone: 619/747–5978) $50/nonmembers, $35/members, published when ordered. Includes members of IMR.

Salary survey

Manufacturing Jewelers and Silversmiths of America Annual Wage and Benefit Survey (MJSA, 100 India St., Providence, RI 02903; phone: 401/274–3840) $100/nonmembers, $50/members, issued each April. Includes salaries and benefits by region and position.

Chapter 5

Architecture

Job openings

Also see entries under "Engineering" in the "Science and engineering" chapter, and under "Construction" in the "Real estate" chapter.

Progressive Architecture (P.O. Box 95759, Cleveland, OH 44101; phone: 216/696-7000) monthly; annual subscription: $36/professional architects, designers, engineers, and draftspersons, $45/others (U.S.), $75/Canada, $140/elsewhere. Jobs listed under "Job Mart." Very extensive list of job openings in good times. During recessions there are only about ten job openings listed plus "Situations wanted." Largely architecture and engineering positions. Some federal positions.

Architectural Record (1221 Avenue of the Americas, New York, NY 10020; phone: 619/416-7070) monthly, annual subscription: $42.50/architects, engineers, interior designers, design and other directly related firms or students (U.S. and Canada), write for other subscription prices. Ten to 20 jobs are listed under "Classified Advertising," largely architecture and engineering positions.

AIA Referral Network Job Bulletin (American Institute of Architects, 1735 New York Ave., NW, Washington, DC 20006; phone: 202/626-7300) weekly, available only to members and student members for $20 for 12 weeks. Lists jobs by category and geographic location. You can call the *AIA Referral Network*, 800/242-6381 (see below under "Job Services"), for a computer printout of each job ($2/each job printout).

AIA Memo (American Institute of Architects, 1735 New York Ave., NW, Washington, DC 20006; phone: 202/626–7300) monthly, $75/non-member annual subscription, free/members. Typical issue has about five job announcements, although some issues have none.

Messages (Society of Environmental Graphic Designers, 47 Third St., Cambridge, MA 02141; phone: 617/577–8225) quarterly, available only to members. About seven positions in graphic design and architecture appear under "Job Openings."

Job services

AIA Referral Network (American Institute of Architects, 1735 New York Ave., NW, Washington, DC 20006; phones: 800/242–6381, 202/626–7364) available only to AIA members and student members; call or write for fee structure and resume form to submit. Resume forms are kept on file for six months. A job seeker can call the network for a position search to get a printout of positions that match her qualifications.

Directories

Profile (American Institute of Architects, 1735 New York Ave., NW, Washington, DC 20006; phone: 800/242-4140) $175/nonmembers, $142/members, issued annually. Lists architects and firms.

Profile (Association of Women in Architecture, 911 Washington, Ave., Suite 225, St. Louis, MO 63101; phone: 314/621–3484) $15 to $20, contact for precise price, published each January beginning in 1992.

Chapter 6

The arts

Also see the job sources described in the "Entertainment" and "Media" chapters.

Job openings

American Artist (BPI Communications, 1515 Broadway, New York, NY 10036; phones: 800/347-6969, 212/764-7300), monthly, $24.95/annual subscription (U.S.), $34.95/foreign. About six ads for artists appear under "Classified—Artists Wanted."

WESTAF's National Arts Jobbank (236 Montezuma Ave., Santa Fe, NM 87501; phone: 505/988-1166) biweekly, U.S.: $36/annual subscription, $24/six-month subscription, $15/three-month subscription; foreign: $45/annual subscription, $27/six-month subscription, $17/three-month subscription. Over 100 job vacancies in arts administration, performance, production/technical, and academia are described in a typical issue.

Sculpture (International Sculpture Center, 1050 Potomac St., NW, Washington, DC 20007; phone: 202/965-6066) bimonthly, $40/annual subscription (U.S. and Canada), $55/elsewhere. "Opportunities" lists five to 15 jobs for sculptors and artists as well as dozens of competitions, grants and fellowships, residencies, calls for artists, and studio exchanges. Also lists "Wanted/Apprenticeships."

Afterimage (Visual Studies Workshop, 31 Prince St., Rochester, NY 14602; phone: 716/442-8676) ten issues/year, $30/annual subscription (U.S.), $35/foreign. Under "Notices—Etc." there are listed about ten jobs in media arts and photography, curators, administrative, and visual arts museums. In addition, there are about ten grants, five internships and residencies plus 30 notices to submit to exhibitions.

Bulletin (National Association of Artists' Organizations, 918 F St., NW, Washington, DC 20005; phone: 202/347-6350) bimonthly, available only to members. About four or five positions in art administration appear under "Help Wanted."

Antique Monthly (Trans World Publishing, 2100 Powers Ferry Rd., Atlanta, GA 30339; phone: 404/955-5656) monthly, $19.95/annual subscription (U.S.), $25.95/foreign. You'll find one or two job openings in sales or antique restoration advertised under "Collectors' Exchange—Job Opportunities." The companies that advertise in "Professional Services" are also potential employers.

American Craft (American Craft Council, 72 Spring St., New York, NY 10012; phone: 212/274-0630) bimonthly, $50/annual membership includes subscription, $60/foreign; available at newsstands. The "Marketplace"has about five "positions available" ads for arts and crafts including camp jobs and several residency positions listed under "Opportunities."

Woodshop News (Woodshop News, Subscriptions Department, Pratt St., Essex, CT 06426; phone: 800/341-1522) monthly, $12.97/annual subscription (U.S.), $22.97/foreign. "Classified Advertising" features about a dozen job vacancies and business opportunities in all aspects of the woodshop and related industries.

Job service

Sculpture Source (International Sculpture Center, 1050 Potomac St., NW, Washington, DC 20007; phone: 202/965-6066) $40/annual nonmember registration fee, free/members. Registrants complete this service's forms and also submit slides of their work. The computerized database is used to match sculptors with potential art sponsors. Over 1,200 referrals were made in 1990.

Directories

National Association of Artists' Organizations Directory (National Association of Artists' Organizations, 918 F St., NW, Washington, DC 20005; phone: 202/347-6350) write for price, published in autumn of odd-numbered years.

American Art Directory (R. R. Bowker, P.O. Box 31, New Providence, NJ 07974-9903; phone: 800/521-8110) $159.95 plus 5 percent shipping and handling, published in February of odd-numbered years, 782 pages. Offers details on more than 7,000 art organizations, museums, libraries, schools, and galleries throughout the U.S. and Canada.

Who's Who in American Art (R. R. Bowker, P.O. Box 31, New Providence, NJ 07974-9903; phone: 800/521-8110) $159.95 plus 5 percent shipping and handling, published in February of odd-numbered years, 1,404 pages. Lists over 11,500 artists, critics, curators, administrators, librarians, historians, collectors, and art dealers in the U.S., Mexico, and Canada.

International Directory of Art (Gale Research, Inc., 835 Penobscot Bldg., Detroit, MI 48226-4094; phone: 800/877-4253) $175, biennial, 1,800 pages. Contains over 130,000 names and addresses of working artists, individual collectors, art dealers and galleries, art museums, and much more.

Who's Who in Art (Gale Research, Inc., 835 Penobscot Bldg., Detroit, MI 48226-4094; phone: 800/877-4253) $95, most recent edition 1990, 566 pages. Contains biographical sketches on over 3,000 artists, designers, craftspersons, critics, writers, teachers, collectors, curators, and other exponents of art.

Stained Glass Association of America Membership Directory appears in *Stained Glass* (Stained Glass Association of America, 6 SW Second St., Suite 7, Lee's Summit, MO 64063; phone: 800/888-7422) quarterly, $24/annual subscription (U.S), $40/foreign.

Art & Auction International Directory (P.O. Box 11344, Des Moines, IA 50340; phones: 800/777-8718, 212/582-5633) 11 issues/year, $42/annual subscription (U.S.), $54/Canada, $90/Europe; single issue available for $12 in book stores. Essentially a directory of over 7,000 antique dealers and shows, auction houses, art galleries, art services, and art fairs.

Sunshine Artists U.S.A. (Sun Country Enterprises, 1700 Sunset Dr., Longwood, FL 32750; phone: 407/323-5927) monthly, $22.50/annual subscription (U.S.), $36.50/Canada and Mexico. Features a calendar directory of art fairs and craft shows.

Where It's At: A Guide to Arts and Crafts Shows (7204 Buckmell Dr., Austin, TX 78723; phone: 512/926-7954) ten issues/year, $23.95/annual subscription, $11.25/three-month subscription, $5/single issue. This is essentially a monthly directory of arts and crafts shows in these "southwestern" states: Alabama, Arizona, Arkansas, Colorado, Georgia, Kansas, Louisiana, Mississippi, Missouri, New Mexico, Oklahoma, Tennessee, and Texas. Each issue covers five months at a time.

Art in America (Brant Art Publications, 575 Broadway, New York, NY 10012; phones: 800/247-2160, 212/941-2800) $39.95/U.S., $59.95/Canada, $69.95/elsewhere, published each month. Contains an alphabetical list by city and state of museums, galleries, non-profit exhibition spaces, corporate consultants, private dealers, and print dealers. Provides basic information plus a short description of the type of art shown and artists presented.

Jobs in Arts and Media Management (American Arts Council, 1285 Avenue of the Americas, New York, NY 10019; phone: 212/245-4510) $21.95/nonmembers plus $4 shipping, $19.75/members plus $4 shipping, last published autumn 1991. In addition to career planning tips, detailed explanations of different types of management positions, and an industry forecast for the 1990s, this valuable paperback also lists some of the periodicals, job-matching services, and job hotlines described in the *Professional's Job Finder* and the *Non-Profits' Job Finder*. However, many of the listings in the 1990 edition were out-of-date as of mid-1991. We presume the next edition will update them. This book also describes university programs in arts and media management and lists relevant professional organizations.

Chapter 7

Business

Also see many of the entries in Chapter 2 and for different specialities throughout this book. Many of the job source periodicals described throughout this book include business opportunities.

Job openings

The Search Bulletin (The Beacon Group, 8300 Boone Blvd., Suite 500, Vienna, VA 22182; phones: 800/486–9220, 703/848–9220) bi-weekly, $97/six–issue subscription, $177/12–issue subscription, $300/21–issue subscription, $7.50/single sample issue. Intended for executives earning $50,000 to $250,000 per annum, each issue of *The Search Bulletin* carries announcements of 110 to 130 job openings in general management, finance, accounting, banking, marketing, sales, and consulting and corporate planning. Over 80 percent of these have not been advertised elsewhere.

Business and Industry Bulletin (Career Development and Placement Services, Campus Box 14, Emporia State University, Emporia, KS 66801; phone: 316/343–5407) weekly, $56.57/annual subscription, $31.43/six–month subscription. This three–page newsletter includes jobs in all aspects of business and industry.

Women in Business (American Business Women's Association, 9100 Ward Pkwy., Kansas City, MO 64114; phone: 816/361–6621) bimonthly, $12/annual nonmember subscription, free/members. Five to ten ads for engineers, paralegals, salespeople, and other professionals appear in the "Classifieds." In addition, there are three to five listings under "Business Opportunities" and "Franchise Opportunities."

Income Opportunities (P.O. Box 7063; Red Oak, IA 51591) ten issues/year, $17.89/annual subscription, $22.50/foreign. Hundreds of business opportunities and maybe a dozen actual jobs are advertised in each issue. Caution is urged: *some* of these business opportunities sound so suspect that it is no surprise that the publisher includes a disclaimer about the advertisements.

SYLVIA   by Nicole Hollander

Reprinted by permission of Nicole Hollander. Copyright ©1991. All rights reserved.

Contracting Business (Penton Publishing, 1100 Superior Ave., Cleveland, OH 44114; phone: 216/696–7000) monthly; free to qualified professionals, call or write for application form; otherwise: $45/annual subscription (U.S.), $65/Canada, $80/elsewhere. "Classified—Employment Opportunities" will have only one or two job ads for technicians or managers.

Entrepreneur (2392 Morse Ave., Irvine, CA 92714; phone: 714/261–2325) monthly, $19.97/annual subscription, $29.97/Canada, $39.97 elsewhere. Hundreds of business opportunities are advertised under "Opportunity Mart" and "Classified."

Entrepreneurial Woman (2392 Morse Ave.; Irvine, CA 92714; phone: 714/261-2325) ten issues/year, $16.95/annual subscription, $24.95/Canada, $32.95/elsewhere. The sections labeled "Opportunity Mart" and "Classified" include advertisements for around 100 business opportunities. These advertisements appear to be largely a subset of the ads that run in its brother publication *Entrepreneur.*"New Business Mart" features ads for dozens of books on operating different types of businesses.

Inc. (P.O. Box 54129, Boulder, CO 80322; phone: 617/248-8426) monthly, $25/annual subscription. Sixty or more advertisements appear under "Business Opportunities" each issue.

Fortune (P.O. Box 60001, Tampa, FL 36660; phone: 800/621-8000) biweekly, $49.95/annual subscription, $54/Canada. While few job ads appear in the "Fortune Exchange," there are 10 to 20 business opportunities advertised.

Nation's Business (1615 H St., NW, Washington, DC 20062; phone: 800/638-6582) monthly, $22/annual subscription, $42/foreign. "Classified Ads" feature ten to 20 business opportunities.

Black Enterprise (P.O. Box 3009, Harlan, IA 51537; phone: 800/727-7777) monthly, $19.95/annual subscription, $29.95/foreign. About 15 business opportunities are advertised under "Black Enterprise Classifieds."

Success (P.O. Box 3038, Harlan, IA 51537-3038; phone: 800/234-7324) bimonthly, $14.97/annual subscription, $21.97/Canada, $24.97/elsewhere. Dozens of jobs, franchises, and business opportunities listed under "Business Marketplace" and "Classified."

New Business Opportunities (P.O. Box 58932, Boulder, CO 80306; phone: 714/261-2083) monthly, $14.97/annual subscription, $24.97/Canada, $24.97/elsewhere. Over 100 business opportunities are listed in "Opportunity Mart" and in "Classifieds" as well as about a dozen employment opportunities.

Business Opportunities Handbook (Enterprise Magazines, 1020 N. Broadway Ave., Suite 111, Milwaukee, WI 53202; phone: 414/272-9977, quarterly, $15.95/annual subscription, $4.95/single issue plus $2 shipping. Each issue describes around 2,200 business and franchising opportunties.

Income Plu$ (73 Spring St., Suite 303, New York, NY 10012; phone: 212/925–3180) monthly, $15.89/annual subscription (U.S.), $21.89/foreign. Over 100 business opportunities appear in display ads and under "Classifieds."

Successful Home Business (P.O. Box 7063, Red Oak, IA 51591; phone: 212/557–9100) monthly, $17.89/annual subscription. Over 50 business opportunities and about a dozen jobs listed under "Classified Marketplace."

In Business (419 State Ave., Emmaus, PA 18049; phone: 215/967–4135) bimonthly, $23/annual subscription (U.S.), $29/foreign. Over two dozen business and job opportunities grace the "Classified" section.

Forbes (60 Fifth Ave., New York, NY 10011) biweekly, $52/annual subscription. Five to ten business opportunities are listed under "Forbes Market Classified."

SOCAP Update (Society of Consumer Affairs Professionals in Business, 801 Fairfax, Alexandria, VA 22312; phone: 703/519–3700) monthly, free/members only. Two or three jobs for consumer affairs and customer service managers are listed under "Positions Available."

Directories

Executive Employment Guide (American Management Association, 135 W. 50th St., New York, NY 10020; phone: 212/903–7912) $20/nonmembers, free/members, published each month. This directory describes hundreds of executive search firms in over 100 specialties. It identifies the kinds of positions handled, the minimum salary, whether a firm is willing to review resumes and is willing to interview job candidates. A contact person is also named.

Try Us (National Minority Business Campaign, 2105 Central Ave., SE, Minneapolis, MN 55418; phone: 612/781–6819) $42, published each January. Describes minority–owned companies divided into 84 classifications and by state.

Ward's Business Directory of U.S. Private and Public Companies (Gale Research, Inc., 835 Penobscot Bldg., Detroit, MI 48226–4094; phone: 800/877–4253) $1,050/four volumes, $950/volumes 1–3, $655/volume 4, annual. The first two volumes offer an alphabetical list of 107,000 U.S. businesses that includes key personnel, number of employees, SIC code classification, financial information, and other details. Volume 3 is a geographical section that lists companies in zip code order by state. Volume 4 is a rankings section where companies are ranked by sales volume within the four-digit SIC classifications.

American Wholesalers & Distributors Directory (Gale Research, Inc., 835 Penobscot Bldg., Detroit, MI 48226–4094; phone: 800/877–4253) $135, published Dec. 1991. Includes descriptions of over 20,000 wholesalers and distributors on the national, regional, state, and major local levels. Gives the number of employees, principal product lines, generic brands and private labels, number of employees, annual sales volume, and principal officers.

Business Organizations, Agencies, and Publications Directory (Gale Research, Inc., 835 Penobscot Bldg., Detroit, MI 48226–4094; phone: 800/877–4253) $315, last published in 1990, 1,900 pages. Gives you 23,000 names of exactly who to contact for information on 39 types of businesses. Also available on computer disk on via modem.

National Directory of Minority-Owned Business Firms (Gale Research, Inc., 835 Penobscot Bldg., Detroit, MI 48226-4094; phone: 800/877-4253) $195, annual, 1,500 pages. Gives details to contact more than 40,000 minority-owned businesses in the U.S.

National Directory of Women-Owned Business Firms (Gale Research, Inc., 835 Penobscot Bldg., Detroit, MI 48226-4094; phone: 800/877-4253) $195, annual, 900 pages. Gives details on over 25,000 businesses owned by women in the U.S.

Regional Directories of Minority and Women-Owned Business Firms (Gale Research, Inc., 835 Penobscot Bldg., Detroit, MI 48226-4094; phone: 800/877-4253) $145/edition, published in 1990, available in eastern, central, and western editions. These provide the same information as the national directories described immediately above, but on a regional basis.

Directory of Public Companies (American Business Directories, 5711 S. 86th Cr., Omaha, NE 68127; phone: 402/593-4600) $145, $95/one-year lease, annual. Provides information on 9,000 publicly-traded companies including the number of employees, sales figures, key personnel, phone, and address.

Directory of Blue Chip Companies (American Business Directories, 5711 S. 86th Cr., Omaha, NE 68127; phone: 402/593-4600) $450, $295/one-year lease, annual. Provides details on 120,000 companies with 100 or more employees. Includes number of employees, sales volume, chief executive, phone, and address.

U.S. Business Directories (American Business Directories, 5711 S. 86th Cr., Omaha, NE 68127; phone: 402/593-4600) contact for prices. ABD offers nationwide directories for hundreds of types of businesses. These specify the name, address, city, phone, name of owner or manager, and number of employees. Contact for a catalog of these directories.

State Business Directories (American Business Directories, 5711 S. 86th Cr., Omaha, NE 68127; phone: 402/593-4600) available for almost every state, prices range from $120 to $325, contact for prices and number of businesses listed; $6,100/complete set. Lists basic information on businesses in each state alphabetically and by business classification.

Directory of Business to Business Catalogs (Grey House Publishing, Pocketknife Square, Lakefill, CT 06039; phones: 800/562-2139, 203/435-0868) $110, annual, 400 pages. Thirty-five chapters describe catalogs that supply goods and services for businesses, everything from computers to laboratory supplies, office products and office design, marketing resources and safety equipment, landscaping and maintenance supplies, building construction, and much more. Includes key executives by job function, phone and fax numbers, top product lines, number of employees, and how long they've been in business.

Be Your Own Boss "How–To" Business Guides Catalog (Entrepreneur Magazine, 2392 Morse Ave., Irvine, CA 92713; phones: 800/421-2300, [in California: 800/352-7449]) free, annual, 50 pages. Over 150 guides to starting a wide variety of businesses are described in this catalog.

Directory of Mail Order Catalogs (Grey House Publishing, Pocketknife Square, Lakefill, CT 06039; phones: 800/562-2139, 203/435-0868) $135, annual. Includes details on over 6,000 catalogs arranged in 35 broad chapters with 140 subchapters. Key personnel, job titles, company size, and number of employees are reported.

Salary surveys

Officer Compensation Report (Abbott, Langer & Associates, 548 First St., Crete, IL 60417; phone: 708/672-4200) $365, annual. Details compensation practices of over 1,400 small to medium-sized companies for 16 positions.

SOCAP Salary and Job Description Study (Society of Consumer Affairs Professionals in Business, 801 Fairfax, Alexandria, VA 22312; phone: 703/519-3700) $70/nonmembers, $35/members, published in odd-numbered years, 25 pages. Reports on salaries by gender, geography, age, experience, company revenues, job title, and type of business.

Franchising

Job openings

Franchise Opportunities Guide (International Franchise Association, Suite 900, 1350 New York Ave., NW, Washington, DC 20005; phone: 202/628–8000) semiannual in April and October, $15 plus $4/shipping per issue. Describes hundreds of franchise possibilities from 2,600 companies including over 250 ads for current franchise opportunities. It also includes articles that explain start–up and operating costs, checklists of steps to take, and other advice to help you determine if franchising is for you.

The Franchise Handbook (Enterprise Magazines, 1020 N. Broadway Ave., Suite 111, Milwaukee, WI 53202; phone: 414/272–9977, quarterly, $15.95/annual subscription, $4.95/single issue plus $2 shipping. Each issue contains detailed descriptions of over 1,700 franchising opportunities.

Franchising World (International Franchise Association, Suite 900, 1350 New York Ave., NW, Washington, DC 20005; phone: 202/628-8000) bimonthly, $12/annual nonmember subscription (U.S.), $20/Canada, $39/elsewhere, free/members. About six job ads for franchise executives, franchise sales personnel, and even chief executive officers are in the "Classifieds."

Directories

Worldwide Franchise Directory (Gale Research, Inc., 835 Penobscot Bldg., Detroit, MI 48226-4094; phone: 800/877-4253) $129.50, published 1991. Full details are given on over 1,500 franchises

Chapter 8

Cemeteries and mortuaries

Cemeteries and mortuaries

Job openings

Cemetery Management (American Cemetery Association, 5201 Lees-burg Pike, Suite 1111, Falls Church, VA 22041; phone: 703/379-5838) monthly, $45/annual nonmember subscription, free/members. The "Classifieds" typically carry ten to 15 job ads largely for sales positions with cemeteries, and mortuaries as well as monument repairs.

Stone in America (American Monument Association, 933 High St., Suite 220, Worthington, OH 43085; phone: 614/885-2713) monthly, $18/annual nonmember subscription, free/members. Up to five job ads for salespeople, sandblasters, carvers, letterers, layout designers, shop fore-persons, office managers, and sculptors are under "Job Opportunities."

Chapter 9

Computers and electronics

Computers

Also see the entries in the chapter "Telecommunications" as well as the listings in this chapter under "Electronics."

Job openings

High Technology Careers (Westch Publishing, 4701 Patrick Henry Dr., Suite 1901, Santa Clara, CA 95054; phone: 408/970-8800) bimonthly, $29/annual subscription, free to residents of northern California. From 500 to 700 positions in engineering, technology, and computers fill each issue.

Computer (Computer Society of the Institute of Electrical and Electronics Engineers, 10662 Los Vaqueros Cr., Los Alamitos, CA 90720-1264; phone: 714/821-8380) available only to members. Two to 15 pages of "Career Opportunities" listing ten to 100 job openings for computer engineers and scientists are in the typical issue.

PD News (P.O. Box 399, Cedar Park, TX 78613; phones: 800/678-9724, 512/250-8127) weekly, $51/annual subscription (U.S.), $88/Canada, $152/elsewhere. Positions in data processing, design, drafting, technical writers, programmers, and engineering are among the roughly 800 positions listed in a typical issue. These are positions with technical service firms that provide employees to companies that need temporary help.

Career Opportunity Update (CRS Publications, 3621 S. Harbor Blvd., Santa Ana, CA 92704; phone: 714/556–1200) bimonthly, $72/annual subscription. About 50 job vacancies in computer science and engineering fill this newsletter.

AIIM Job Bank Bulletin (Association for Information and Image Management, 1100 Wayne Ave., Suite 1100, Silver Spring, MD 20910; phone: 301/997–2200) semimonthly, $100/nonmember four-month subscription, $25/members. About 20 vacancies in information and image management for programmers, systems analysts, quality assurance engineers, management, and sales people pack the first half of this jobs bulletin. The second half is filled with "Positions Wanted" announcements. Obtain the *AIIM Job Bank* brochure for the advertising form and rates.

Market Place (International Society for Hybrid Micro–Electronics, 1861 Wiehle Ave., Suite 340, Reston, VA 22090; phone: 800/232–4746) bimonthly, free/members only. Fifteen to 20 openings for technological engineers for computer components are listed in "Positions Available."

Computerworld (375 Cochituate Rd., Framingham, MA 01701-9171; phones: 800/669-1002, 508/879-0700) weekly; $48/annual subscription (U.S.), $110/Canada. About 75 to 100 ads for all types of computer industry positions appear under "Computer Careers."

ASIS Jobline (American Society for Information Science, Suite 501, 8720 Georgia Ave., Silver Springs, MD 20910–3602; phone: 301/495–0900) monthly, free. About 15 jobs appear in the typical issue.

PC Week (Ziff–Davis Publishing, P.O. Box 1770, Riverton, NJ 08077-7370; phone: 609/461–2100) weekly, $160/annual subscription (U.S.), $250/Mexico and Canada, $300/elsewhere. Ten to 20 ads for programming, technical, management, and sales positions with companies that use MS–DOS computers are listed under "Career Opportunities." There are also some jobs for companies that use Macintosh computers.

MacWeek (Ziff–Davis Publishing, P.O. Box 1764, Riverton, NJ 08077–7370; phone: 609/461–2100) 42 issues/year, $99/annual subscription (U.S.), $150/Mexico and Canada, $300/elsewhere, free to qualified professionals. Fifteen to 30 jobs for everything in the Macintosh computer world (software development, hardware design, programming, sales, management) are under "Career Opportunities."

UNIX Today! (CMP Publications, 600 Community Dr., Manhasset, NY 11030; phone: 516/562–5000) biweekly, $59/annual subscription, free to qualified professionals in UNIX users organizations. Ten openings for software engineers and programmers for the UNIX operating environment are advertised in "Career Opportunities."

Datamation (Cahners Publishing Company, 275 Washington St., Newton, MA 02158; phone: 617/964–3030) 23 issues/year, $69/annual subscription (U.S.), $108.86/Canada. "Career Opportunities" sports about a dozen jobs in computer and system programming, software development, and system architecture.

Government Computer News (Cahners Publishing, 8601 Georgia Ave., Suite 300, Silver Spring, MD 20910; phone: 301/650–2000) biweekly, $52.95/annual subscription (available only to U.S. addresses). Although every issue does not carry job ads, when they do appear, there are as many as ten openings for private sector computer programmers, analysts, and software engineers advertised under "Career Opportunities."

EDN (Cahners Publishing, P.O. Box 5262, Denver, CO 80217; phone: 303/388–4511) 48 issues/year, $119.95/annual subscription (U.S.), $169.95/Mexico, $181.85/Canada, $209/95/elsewhere, free to qualified engineers. A dozen job openings for computer design engineers are in the "Careers Opportunities" section.

Electronic Engineering Times (CMP Publications, 600 Community Dr., Manhasset, NY 11030; phone: 516/562–5000) weekly, $115/annual subscription, free to qualified managers and engineers in electronics. "Classified" carries ads for about nine software engineers, digital hardware/software engineers, and systems engineers.

Mother Goose and Grim reprinted by permission of MGM L&M
and Grimmy, Inc. Copyright 1991. All rights reserved.

Information Executive (Data Processing Management Association,
505 Bussie Highway, Park Ridge, IL 60068-3091; phone: 708/825-
8124) quarterly, $16/annual nonmember subscription, included in
dues. About seven ads placed by executive search firms seeking
programmers, software developers, and system analysts appear
under "Classifieds–Careers."

Journal of Systems Management (Association of Systems Management, P.O. Box 38370, Cleveland, OH 44138; phone: 216/243-6900)
monthly, $48/annual nonmember subscription, free/members.
About five positions are listed under "Joblink."

Computers in Nursing (J. B. Lippincott Company, Downville Pike,
Route 3, Box 20-B, Hagerstown, MD 21740; phones: 800/638-3030,
215/238-4206) bimonthly, $35/annual subscription, $30/students,
$45/foreign. About five jobs for nurses who use computers appear
under "Classifieds."

Electronic Design (Penton Publishing, 1100 Superior Ave., Cleveland, OH 44114; phone: 216/696-7000) semimonthly, $85/annual
subscription (U.S.), $160/Canada, $230/elsewhere, free to qualified
professionals. About six job ads for design engineers and circuit
designers for computer components appear under "Classifieds—
Employment Opportunities."

AI Magazine (American Association of Artificial Intelligence,445 Burgess Dr., Menlo Park, CA 94025; phone: 415/328–3123) quarterly, $40/annual subscription (U.S., Canada), $65/elsewhere. About five job openings in computer science and artificial intelligence are listed under "Career Opportunities."

Journal of Object–Oriented Programming (SIGS Publications, P.O. Box 3000, Denville, NJ 07834; phone: 212/274–0640) nine issues/year, $59/annual subscription. "Career Opportunities and Training" has two or three ads for software design engineers and development managers.

INTERCOM (Society for Technical Communications, 901 N. Stuart St., Suite 304, Arlington, VA 22203; phone: 703/522–4114) ten issues/year, available to members only. One to three display ads for technical writers and editors in the computer field are in the usual issue.

Electronic Buyers News (CMP Publications, 600 Community Dr., Manhasset, NY 11030; phone: 516/562–5000) weekly, $89/annual subscription, free to qualified electronics purchasers. Twenty to 25 openings for sales, buyers, and management positions in computer parts and components are advertised under "Employment."

Computer Reseller News (CMP Publications, 600 Community Dr., Manhasset, NY 11030; phone: 516/562–5000) weekly, $150/annual subscription, free to qualified management personnel in companies that sell computers. Just one or two jobs for manufacturers' representatives are listed in "Classified—Career Opportunities."

Job services

CU Career Connection (University of Colorado, Campus Box 133, Boulder, CO 80309–0133; phone: 303/492–4127) $20/two–month fee entitles you to a "passcode" which unlocks this job hotline. You need a touch-tone phone to call and request computer or electronics jobs and the geographic area in which you want to hear job openings. The hotline is turned off Monday through Friday, 2 to 4 p.m. for daily updating.

Resume Service (P.O. Box 399, Cedar Park, TX 78613; phones: 800/678-9724, 512/250-8127). _Weekly Mailing Service_ mails your prepared resume to all advertisers in that week's _PD News_, described above under "Job openings." Cost: $40/first page, $5/each addition page. _Monthly Mailing Service_ sends your prepared resume to all advertisers in the _Directory of Technical Service Firms_ described below under "Directories." Resumes must be received by the 25th of the month. Cost: $195/first page, $20/each additional page.

PD News Hot List (P.O. Box 399, Cedar Park, TX 78613; phones: 800/678-9724, 512/250-8127) weekly. Job seekers submit their name, address, phone, and job description (of no more than 70 letters) for publication in this weekly mailing to contract service firms in the computer industry that are advertising vacancies in _PD News_, described above under "Job opernings." Jobs include data processing, design, drafting, technical writers, programmers, and engineering. Free to PD Passport holders ($89/annual fee gets you _PD News_, this service, the _Directory of Technical Service Firms_, and discounts on car rentals, etc.); $3/week for others, $10/four consecutive listings. You do not have to subscribe to _PD News_ to use this service.

Bulletin Board Service (P.O. Box 399, Cedar Park, TX 78613; phones: 800/678-9724, 512/250-8127) available only to subscribers to _PD News_ described above under "Job openings," free access, you still pay for the phone call. Hook up your computer via modem to the latest listings in _PD News_,described above under "Job Openings."

Computers in Healthcare (Cardiff Publishing Company, 6300 S. Syracuse Way, Suite 650, Englewood, CO 80111; phone: 303/220-0600) 18 issues/year, $28/annual subscription (U.S.), $38/Canada, $40/elsewhere. About two openings for MIS directors, sales, marketing, and administration appear under "Positions."

Association for Computing Machinery Resume Databank (ACM, 11 W. 42nd St., New York, NY 10036; phone: 212/869-7440) free, available to members only. Members are matched with job vacancies in computer-related positions.

Directories

Job Opportunities for Engineering, Science, and Computer Graduates (Peterson's P.O. Box 2123, Princeton, NJ 08543-2123; phones: 800/338-3282, 609/243-9111) $20.95 plus $4.75 shipping, issued each August for the following year. This is essentially a directory of over 1,000 firms that recruit in these fields. Actual vacancies cannot be guaranteed, but this serves as a good directory of firm descriptions.

Northwest High Tech (Resolution Business Press, 11101 NE 8th St, Suite 208, Bellevue, WA 98004; phones: 800/866-0327, 206/455-4611) $24.95/U.S., $29.95/Canada, annual. Available as a computer database in dBase and ASCII formats, $69.95/U.S., $79.95/Canada. Its 464 pages profile more than 1,700 companies in the computer software, hardware, sales, and support services industries in Oregon, Washington, Idaho, Alberta, and British Columbia. Provides contact names, sales figures, staff size, specialization, services, and products.

Northwest Computer Jobs (Resolution Business Press, 11101 NE 8th St, Suite 208, Bellevue, WA 98004; phones: 800/866-0327, 206/455-4611) $39.95/U.S., $47.95/Canada, issued every winter. Also available as a computer database. Its 464 pages profile 1,700 companies in the computer software, hardware, sales, and support services industries in Oregon, Washington, Idaho, Alberta, and British Columbia—both countries' fastest growing computer regions. About 600 of them are expected to recruit new staff each year.

Directory of Top Computer Executives (Applied Computer Research, 11242 N. 19th Ave., Phoenix, AZ 85029; phones: 800/234-2227, 602/995-5929). This directory comes in three separate editions: East (U.S.), West (U.S.), and Canada. All three are published every April and October. Prices: $180/single edition, $325/both East and West editions, $470/all three editions. Also available as mailing labels, prospect sheets, customized directories, and on magnetic tape. Each edition lists details on the executive at each company who oversees all computer functions for both mainframe and personal computers. Provides information on types of computers used and the company's industry classification.

Directory of Technical Service Firms (P.O. Box 399, Cedar Park, TX 78613; phones: 800/678–9724, 512/250–8127) $10, or free with subscription to *PD News* listed above under "Job openings." Published each June.

International Society for Hybrid Micro–Electronics Industry Guide (ISHME, 1861 Wiehle Ave., Suite 340, Reston, VA 22090; phone: 800/232–4746) $60/nonmembers, free/members, issued each April. Lists members and companies in this aspect of the computer components industry.

ACIL Directory: A Guide to the Leading Independent Testing, Research, and Inspection Laboratories of America (American Council of Independent Laboratories, 1725 K St., NW, Washington, DC 20006; phone: 202/887–5872) contact for details.

ASIS Handbook and Directory (American Society for Information Science, Suite 501, 8720 Georgia Ave., Silver Spring, MD 20910–3602; phone: 301/495–0900) $100/nonmembers, free/members, published each March.

Handbook and Directory of Members (Videotext Industry Association, 8403 Colesville Rd., Suite 865, Silver Spring, MD 20910) phone: 301/495–4955) $55/nonmembers, free/members, annual. Describes in some detail the member information service provider companies that develop (software and hardware), sell, and maintain interactive electronic services like PRODIGY™.

Computer Dealers and Lessors Association Membership Directory (CDLA, 1212 Potomac St., NW, Washington, DC 20007; phone: 202/333-0102) $100, annual.

Members Phone Directory (Computer Aided Manufacturing, International, 1250 E. Copeland, Arlington, TX 76011; phone: 817/860-0070) available only to members, annual.

Electronic Mail Association Membership Directory (EMA, 1555 Wilson Blvd., Suite 300, Arlington, VA 22209; phone: 703/875-8620) $50/nonmembers, $10/members, annual.

The AI Directories (American Association of Artificial Intelligence, 445 Burgess Dr., Menlo Park, CA 94025; phone: 415/328-3123) contact for current price, issued each January. Lists companies involved in the artificial intelligence field.

Computer + Software Storefront Dealers (Chain Store Guide Information Services, 425 Park Ave., New York, NY 10022; phone: 212/371-9400, ext. 306) $289, published each February. Also available on computer disk. Describes 2,700 computer and software storefront dealers operating 5,900 stores. Includes 11,600 key executive, buying, and administrative personnel.

Information Sources (Information Industry Association, 555 New Jersey Ave., NW, Suite 800, Washington, DC 20001; phone: 202/639-8262) $106, annual. This is a list of information sources that use "800" and "900" telephone numbers.

Salary surveys

Compensation in the MIS/dp Field (Abbott, Langer & Associates, 548 First St., Crete, IL 60417; phone: 708/672-4200) $495, annual. Sponsored by the Data Processing Management Association, this 600-page study reports on salaries and benefits for 76 job functions from junior data entry operator to MIS/dp director.

Computer Salary Survey and Career Planning Guide (Source edp, P.O. Box 152109, Irving, TX 75015-9831; phones: 214/387-1600, 214/387-0795) free. Published annually by this computer recruiting firm.

Office, Professional, and Data Processing Salaries Report (Abbott, Langer & Associates, 548 First St., Crete, IL 60417; phone: 708/672–4200) $250, annual. This survey of 160,000 employees at 2,100 companies reports on salaries for 40 different positions by metropolitan area and nationally. Includes programmers, word processing operators, systems analyst, pc specialists, data entry operators, and clerk typists.

Profile of Systems Professional (Association of Systems Management, P.O. Box 38370, Cleveland, OH 44138; phone: 216/243–6900) write for price, included in dues, most recent edition, 1991.

Northwest Computer Jobs (Resolution Business Press, 11101 NE 8th St, Suite 208, Bellevue, WA 98004; phones: 800/866–0327, 206/455–4611) $39.95, issued every winter. Its 500 pages profile 1,700 companies in the computer software, hardware, sales, and support services industries in Oregon, Washington, Idaho, Alberta, and British Columbia; also includes a salary survey and job outlook chapter.

Technical Communicator Salary Survey (Society for Technical Communications, 901 N. Stuart St., Suite 304, Arlington, VA 22203; phone: 703/522–4114) free/members only, released in even-numbered years. Reports on salaries and benefits for technical writers and editors, visual communicators (illustrators, artists, photographers), and consultants in the U.S.

Electronics

Also see the listings in the chapters "Telecommunications" and "Science and engineering" as well as the entries under "Computers" in this chapter.

Job openings

IEEE Spectrum (Institute of Electrical and Electronics Engineers, P.O. Box 1331, Piscataway, NJ 08885–1331; phones: 800/678–4333, 212/705–7555) monthly, $29.95/annual nonmember subscription, free/members. Around 30 openings for electrical engineers are advertised under "Classified."

Career Opportunities in Electronics (International Society of Certified Electronics Technicians, 2708 W. Berry St., Fort Worth, TX 76109; phone: 817/921–9101) free, quarterly. Lists around 25 to 30 job openings for electronics technicians and service engineers and technicians with repair services and within private companies and research facilities. Includes television and VCR repair.

Semiconductor International (P.O. Box 5700, Denver, CO 80217–9889; phone: 708/390–2219) monthly, $60/annual subscription, free to qualified semiconductor professionals. Ten or more openings are advertised under "Classified Advertising—Positions Available" and in display ads under "Career Opportunities."

Association News (Electronics Technicians Association, 602 N. Jackson, Greencastle, IN 46135; phone: 317/653–8262) monthly, $30/annual subscription (U.S.), $40/Canada, $50/foreign. Six ads for electronics technicians in communications, computers, industrial, video distribution, medical, and consumer fields run under "Career Opportunities."

Electronic Servicing & Technology (CQ Communications, 76 N. Broadway, Hicksville, NY 11801; phone: 516/681–2922) $29/annual subscription (U.S.), $35/foreign. A handful of jobs for electronics servicing technicians and businesses are under "Classified."

Job services

Professional Engineering Employment Registry (Career Technologies Corp., Suite 6, 44 Nashua Rd., Londonderry, NH 03053; phone: 603/437–7337) free to members of Institute of Electrical and Electronics Engineers. IEEE members submit their resume (in their own format) to PEER which places it in its computer database which potential employers access via modem to identify job candidates to interview. Resumes are viewed without the job candidate's name, address, or phone, and are coded to prevent a current employer from ever seeing any portion of a current employee's resume. PEER never discloses a job candidate's identity. PEER contacts the job candidates employers wish to interview. Job candidates then can contact the employer directly.

Electronics Technicians Association Jobs Program (ETA, 602 N. Jackson, Greencastle, IN 46135; phone: 317/653-8262) free/members only. Complete the resume form which is kept on file for six months. When a match for an electronics technician position (in all aspects of the industry including broadcasting) is made, your resume is sent to the company which is responsible for contacting you.

Directories

North American Directory of Contract Manufacturers in Electronics (Miller Freeman, P.O. Box T, Gilroy, CA 95021-9968; phone: 408/848-5296) $177 plus $5/shipping (U.S.), $8.50/Canada, annual. Also available on computer disk in dBaseIII, ASCII or Lotus formats for $250 plus $5/shipping (U.S.), $8.50/Canada. Included in this directory is data on 1,350 contract manufacturing facilities in the U.S., Canada, and Mexico, 400 that provide SMT assembly, 830 with test services, 650 design locations, 390 final assembly sites, 190 consultants, and 700 suppliers to the industry.

IEEE Membership Directory (Institute of Electrical and Electronics Engineers, P.O. Box 1331, Piscataway, NJ 08885-1331; phones: 800/678-4333, 212/705-7555) $189.95/nonmembers, $64.95/members, issued each April.

Electronics Industries Association Directory and Membership List (EIA, 2001 Pennsylvania Ave., NW, Washington, DC 20006; phone: 202/457-4900) $200/nonmembers, $85/members, published every April.

Consumer Electronics (Chain Store Guide Information Services, 425 Park Ave., New York, NY 10022; phone: 212/371-9400, ext. 306) $199, published biennially in June. Features descriptions of

4,500 consumer electronics, photography, and major appliance retailers with over 18,700 stores. Includes over 11,000 key executive, buying, and administrative personnel.

Semiconductor Industry Association Yearbook and Directory (SIA, 4300 Stevens Creek Blvd., Suite 271, San Jose, CA 95129; phone: 408/246-2711) $76/nonmembers, free/members, published in August of odd-numbered years. Describes 300 semiconductor companies in the U.S.

Semiconductor Equipment and Material Institute Membership Directory (SEMI, 805 E. Middlefield, Rd., Mountain View, CA 94043; phone: 415/764-5111) $100/nonmembers, $70/members, issued in January of odd-numbered years.

Salary survey

IEEE U.S. Membership Salary and Fringe Benefit Survey (Institute of Electrical and Electronics Engineers, P.O. Box 1331, Piscataway, NJ 08885-1331; phones: 800/678-4333, 212/705-7555) $99.95/nonmembers, $79.95/members, released in May of odd-numbered years. Reports on income and benefits by technical expertise, geography, education, experience, and age.

Chapter 10

Defense industry

Job openings

Defense Transportation Journal (National Defense Transportation Association, 50 S. Pickett St., Suite 220, Alexandria, VA 22304; phone: 703/751–5011) bimonthly, $35/annual subscription (U.S., Canada), $45/elsewhere. "Job Bank" carries 15 to 20 job openings in the defense transportation industry.

Directories

Defense Organization Service Industry (Carroll Publishing, 1058 Thomas Jefferson St., NW, Washington, DC 20007; phone: 202/333–8620) $625/one–year subscription, updated every 90 days. Identifies more than 11,000 key defense business managers with 140 of the top U.S. defense contractors.

NSIA Annual Report and Directory (National Security Industrial Association, 1025 Connecticut Ave., NW, Suite 300, Washington, DC 20036; phone: 202/775–1440) contact for price, annual, 112 pages. Describes hundreds of member companies; identifies products, services, and key personnel. However, this directory does not provide addresses or phone numbers.

Chapter 11

Education

See the "Education" chapter in the Non–Profits' Job Finder for a very extensive listing of job sources for all levels of education. The job sources listed in this chapter feature jobs in the private sector arm of education.

Job openings

Chronicle of Higher Education (Suite 700, 1255 23rd St., NW, Washington, DC 20037; phone 202/466–1050) weekly; $62.50/annual subscription. Hundreds of jobs are listed under "Bulletin Board." Includes teaching and administrative positions as well as jobs as university planners. Extensive "Positions wanted" section.

Jobs in Education (Career/Consultants in Education, Suite 455, 615 Main St., Stroudsburg, PA 18360) monthly, $20/four–month subscription, $14/two–month subscription. Lists teaching and administrative positions at colleges and schools.

The Insider (PRONET, Inc., P.O. Box 6095, Rockville, MD 20850; phones: 800/444–7650, 301/251–5356) 24 issues/year, $30/annual subscription, $16/eight–week subscription, $12/six–week subscription. Announces job openings for non–faculty professional and technical positions at public and private institutions of higher education.

The Women's Review of Books (828 Washington St., Wellesley, MA 02181; phone: 617/431–1453) 11 issues/year, $16/annual subscription for individuals and $30 for institutions, add $3 for Canada, elsewhere add $20 for airmail, $5 for surface mail. ''Classified'' features two or three ads for jobs, generally in education or library work.

Chapter 12

Entertainment

Also see the chapters on "The media" and "Arts."

Job openings

The Hollywood Reporter (6715 Sunset Blvd., Hollywood, CA 90028; phone: 213/464-7411) weekdays, $110/six-month subscription (U.S.), $425/elsewhere (airmail). "The Reporter Classifieds" feature about 60 positions in all aspects of broadcasting, writing, film, video, acting, music, public relations, and models as well as positions for secretaries, receptionists, bookkeepers, and management in the entertainment industry.

Back Stage (330 W. 42nd St., New York, NY 10036; phone: 800/648-1436) weekly, $55/annual subscription. "Casting" section features announcements of 50 to 100 available positions in stage, music, television, film, student film, staff, and technical. The "Job Market" section contains ads for over 20 jobs as well.

Spotlight Casting Magazine (P.O. Box 3720, Hollywood, CA 90078; phone: 213/462-6775) weekly, $40/annual subscription. The "Casting Board" section features about 100 ads for actors, singers, dancers, technicians, cinmatographers, and most everything else in show business.

Daily Variety (5700 Wilshire Blvd., Los Angeles, CA 90036; phone: 213/857-6600) daily, $129/annual subscription. As many as 50 openings in all aspects of entertainment appear under "Job Opportunities."

Variety (475 Park Ave., South, New York, NY 10016; phone: 212/779-1100) weekly edition, $100/annual subscription, $124/Canada, $250/Europe. Five to 10 jobs plus business opportunities are listed under "Classifieds."

Village Voice (P.O. Box 1905, Marion, OH 43302; phone: 800/336-0686) weekly, $47.95/annual subscription (U.S.), $79.20/foreign. The classifieds section has about 50 job openings under "Music Notes—Public Notice-Musicians," and 15 under "Stage & Screen Notes—Jobs & Auditions." Includes both performing and behind the scenes positions.

Casting Call (Mel Pogue Enterprises, 3365 Cahuenga Blvd., Hollywood, CA 90068; phone: 213/874-4012) biweekly, $36/annual subscription, $1/single issue. About 40 positions for just about any aspect of show biz appear under "Auditions."

Boxoffice (1020 S. Wabash, Chicago, IL 60605; phone: 312/922-9326) monthly, $35/annual subscription (U.S.), $45/Canada, $65/elsewhere. The "Clearinghouse" section lists a few job openings in the entertainment industry.

WESTAF's National Arts Jobbank (Western Arts Federation, 236 Montezume Ave., Santa Fe, NM 87501; phone: 505/988-1166) biweekly, $36/annual subscription, $24/six-month subscription, $15/three-month subscription. Each issue contains over 100 vacancies in theater, dance, and music: arts administration, performance, production, technical, and academic as well as information on grants, residencies, internships, and competitions.

Audition News (Chicago Entertainment Company, 6272 W. North Ave., Chicago, IL 60639; phone: 312/637-4695) monthly, $24.95/annual subscription, $14.95/six-month subscription. Dozens of job openings appear throughout. Positions are mostly in acting, singing, dancing, and modeling as well as in production. Covers the midwest.

Amusements industry

Job openings

Amusement Business (BPI Communications, 1515 Broadway, New York, NY 10036; phone: 800/648–1436) weekly, $75/annual subscription. About 15 ads for concessions, ride foremen, ride men, agents, and other jobs in amusement parks appear under "Showmen's Marketplace."

Funworld (International Association of Amusement Parks and Attractions, 1448 Duke St., Alexandria, VA 22314; phone: 703/836–4800) 11 issues/year, $30/annual nonmember subscription, free/members. An occasional ad appears in "Trading Post" for amusement park jobs including general managers.

Souvenirs (Kane Communications, 7000 Terminal St., Upper Darby, PA 19082; phone: 215/734–2420) seven issues/year, $17/annual subscription (U.S.), $23/Canada. Over 100 ads for distributors and sellers of souvenirs are in the "Classifieds."

Tourists Attractions and Parks (Kane Communications, 7000 Terminal St., Upper Darby, PA 19082; phone: 215/734–2420) seven issues/year, $25/annual subscription (U.S.), $31/foreign. Five or six job openings are in the "Classifieds."

Gaming & Wagering Business Magazine (7 Penn Plaza, New York, NY 10001; phones: 800/223–9638, ext. 234) monthly, $48/annual subscription (U.S.), $64/Canada, $88/elsewhere. Two or three ads for "Help Wanted" and the same number under "Business Opportunities" appear for lottery and gaming executives, casino management, sales, and government lobbyists.

Directories

Talent and Carnival Guide in an issue of *Tourists Attractions and Parks*, described above under "Job openings," annual.

IAAPA Directory and Buyers Guide (International Association of Amusement Parks and Attractions, 1448 Duke St., Alexandria, VA 22314; phone: 703/836–4800) $50, published each October. This directory provides details on amusement parks throughout the country as well as their suppliers (food, rides, costumes, acts).

Dance

Job openings

Dance Magazine (33 W. 60th St., New York, NY 10023; phones: 800/227–7585, 212/245–9050) monthly, $29.95/annual subscription (U.S.), $41.95/foreign. About 20 positions are listed under "Classifieds." Certain issues also include the "Dance Directory of Schools, Teachers, Dancers, Regional Companies" which includes several hundred listed by state.

Job Express Registry (American Dance Guild, 31 W. 21st St., New York, NY 10010; phone: 212/627–3790) monthly, $33/three–month nonmember subscription, $18/members. Fifteen to 20 job ads for positions in dance administration and education fill this newsletter.

Update (American Alliance for Health, Physical Education, Recreation and Dance, 1900 Association Dr., Reston, VA 22091; phone: 703/476–3400) eight issues/year, $45/annual nonmember subscription, included in $85/annual membership. "Job Exchange" features 30 or more jobs largely with camps and universities as well as numerous graduate assistantships and grants.

Journal PERD (American Alliance for Health, Physical Education, Recreation and Dance, 1900 Association Dr., Reston, VA 22091; phone: 703/476–3400) monthly, $65/annual nonmember subscription. The "Classifieds" feature about five positions usually with camps and universities.

Directory

American Dance Guild Membership Directory (ADG, 31 W. 21st St., New York, NY 10010; phone: 212/627–3790) $15/nonmembers, $12/members, published every January.

Film industry

Also see the entries under "Broadcasting and film" in the chapter "The media" for the more serious side of the film and video industries. Many of those listings also include jobs in the film industry. The "Broadcasting and film" section in that chapter also includes the entertainment side of television and radio.

Job openings

On Location Magazine (On Location Publishing, P.O. Box 2810, Hollywood, CA 90028; phone: 213/541–4363) quarterly, $102/annual subscription. You'll find over 100 positions in all aspects of film and video, mostly technical, described under "Professional Job Opportunities."

In Motion Magazine (1203 West St., Suite D, Annapolis, MD 21401; phone: 301/269–0605) monthly, $24.95/annual subscription. The "Classifieds" carry about ten openings for film and video professionals, videographers, writers, directors, performers, and more.

In Motion Film and Video Production Magazine (1203 West St., Suite D, Annapolis, MD 21401; phone: 301/269–0605) monthly, $24.95/annual subscription. The "Classifieds" carry about 20 openings for film and video professionals, videographers, writers, directors, performers, and more.

Millimeter (Penton Publishing, 1100 Superior Ave., Cleveland, OH 44114; phone: 216/696–7000) monthly; free to qualified professionals, call or write for application form; otherwise: $60/annual subscription (U.S.), $90/elsewhere. Under "Marketplace—Employment Opportunities" you'll find about five ads for film engineers, editors, colorists, and artist/designers.

American Cinematographer (American Society of Cinematographers Holding Company, 1782 N. Orange Dr., Hollywood, CA 90028; phones: 800/448-0145, 213/876-5080) monthly, $24/annual subscription (U.S.), $39/Canada and Mexico, $49/elsewhere. Three or four ads for cinematographers, lighting crew, repair and optical technicians appear under "Classified Ads—Situations Available."

Directories

Back Stage Shoot (BPI Communications, 330 W. 42nd St., New York, NY 10036; phone: 212/947-0020) $37.90, annual. This 400 plus page national directory includes advertising agencies, aerial services/helicopters, animal rentals, catering, edge coding, equipment rental and sales, film commissions, makeup and stylists, location management and scouting, music and sound, post-production, studios and stages, talent casting, unions and guilds, visual effects, writing and consulting.

Who's Who in the Motion Picture Industry (Packard Publishing, P.O. Box 2187, Beverly Hills, CA 90213; phone: 213/854-0276) $19.95, published each May. Gives address, phone, and credits for directors, producers, writers, cinematographers, and executives. For the major studios, production companies, and distribution companies, this directory also names their officers.

Directory of Working Members American Society of Cinematographers (ASC, P.O. Box 2230, Los Angeles, CA 90078; phones: 800/448-0145, 213/876-5080) free, published each May. Gives names, agents, credits, and awards of cinematographers.

Locations (Association of Film Commissioners International, 159 W. Main St., Suite 344, Webster, NY 14580-2967; phone: 716/671-6727) semiannual, free. Includes names, addresses, and phone numbers for municipal and state filmcommissions as well as film commissions abroad.

On Location Annual Directory (On Location Publishing, P.O. Box 2810, Hollywood, CA 90028; phone: 213/541-4363) $99, issued each October. In over 1,000 pages, this directory provides details on the companies that provide the goods and services needed to conduct filming and videotaping in the U.S. and other English-speaking countries.

AIVF Guide to International Film and Video Festivals (Association for Independent Video and Film, 625 Broadway, New York, NY 10012; phone: 212/473-3400) $25 plus $2.50 postage, available only as part of a package with two audio tapes of a seminar called the "Festival Circuit Confidential." This directory is a fully-indexed compendium of over 370 international film and video festivals that includes dates, deadlines, contact person, fees, locations, regulations, awards, and more.

Music

Job openings

Music Trades (80 West St., Englewood, NJ 97670; phone: 201/871-4965) monthly, $12/annual subscription. Under "Classified," you'll find 40 to 60 ads for just about every type of job in the music industry.

The Music Paper (PO Box 304; Manhasset, NY 11030; phone: 516/883-8898) monthly, $12/annual subscription, $30/first class mail in U.S., $40/foreign. About 15 ads appear under "Musicians Wanted" while "Musicians Available" sports around 50 ads. Are they trying to tell us something about the job market? These positions are almost exclusively for rock/pop musicians.

Administrative Service Announcements (American Symphony Orchestra League, 777 14th St., NW, Suite 500, Washington, DC 20005; phone: 202/628-0099) biweekly, available only to members, included in $75/annual dues. About ten to 15 job openings in arts administration, marketing, community relations, and development fill the typical issue.

Billboard (P.O. Box 2011, Marion, OH 43306-2111; phone: 800/669-1002) weekly, $199/annual subscription (U.S.), $205/Canada. About five ads for musicians, jobbers, and other aspects of the music business appear under "Classified Action Mart" and "Help Wanted."

Conducting Service Announcements (American Symphony Orchestra League, 777 14th St., NW, Suite 500, Washington, DC 20005; phone: 202/628-0099) monthly, available only to members, included in $75/annual dues. About five to ten job openings for conductors are in the typical issue.

Musician Service Announcements (American Symphony Orchestra League, 777 14th St., NW, Suite 500, Washington, DC 20005; phone: 202/628-0099) monthly, available only to members, included in $75/annual dues. About five to ten work opportunities for classical musicians are in the typical issue.

New York Opera Newsletter (P.O. Box 278, Maplewood, NJ 07040; phone: 201/378-9549) 11 issues/year, $40/annual subscription. From 30 to 50 positions (primarily for singers, some musicians) with opera companies and choruses with symphony orchestras appear under "Auditions." Despite the periodical's title, these jobs come from across the country.

Intercompany Announcement (Opera America, 777 14th St., NW, Suite 520, Washington, DC 20005; phone: 202/347-9262) monthly, available only to members, salary-based dues system starts with $25/students. Three to ten potions in opera management are listed under "Positions Available."

Music City News (50 Music Square West, Suite 601, Nashville, TN 37203) monthly, $23.50/annual subscription, $15/six-month subscription. The "Classifieds" feature around 25 ads for writers and singers of country music.

Hot Line News (Musicians National Hot Line Association, 277 East 6100 South, Salt Lake City, UT 84107; phone: 801/268-2000) bimonthly, available only to members, included in dues: $20/annual dues, $10/students. Lists job openings for technicians, agents, management, instructors, musicians seeking bands, and bands seeking musicians.

Spin (P.O. Box 420193, Palm Coast, FL 32142-0193; phone: 800/829-9093) monthly, $18/annual subscription, $30/Canada, $50/elsewhere. Just a few jobs under "Spin Classifieds."

Electronic Musician (6400 Hollis St., Suite 12, Emeryville, CA 94608; phone: 415/653–3307) monthly, $24/annual subscription (U.S.), $44/foreign. About five job openings in the music industry appear under "Classifieds."

Musician (BPI Communications, 33 Commercial St., Gloucester, MA 01950; phones: 800/347–6969, 508/281–5110) monthly, $17/annual subscription (U.S.), $29/elsewhere. The "Classified" section sports about three or four job ads under "Employment" and "Musicians."

The Diapason (Scranton Gillette, 380 Northwest Highway, Des Plaines, IL 60016; phone: 708/298–6622) monthly, $15/annual subscription (U.S.), $25/foreign. Under "Classified Advertising—Positions Available," you'll find about ten job ads for organists, organ builders and designers, and sales.

Street Sound (174 Spadina Ave., Suite 506, Toronto, Ontario, Canada M5T 2C2; phone: 416/369–0070) monthly, $42/annual subscription (U.S. air mail, Canada ground mail), $30/U.S. (surface mail), $75/elsewhere. About five ads will appear under "Classifieds—Talent Wanted" for performers of popular music and radio disk jockeys.

Mix (6400 Hollis St., Suite 12; Emeryville, CA 94608; phone: 415/653–3307) monthly, $46/year, $61/foreign. About three ads for audio engineers and sales opportunities appear under "Classifieds."

Job services

Hot Line (Musicians National Hot Line Association, 277 East 6100 South, Salt Lake City, UT 84107; phone: 801/268–2000) available only to members, included in dues: $20/annual dues, $10/students. The job seeker completes the MNHLA's membership application which includes detailed information about your music type, specialities, and experience as well as whether you are seeking full–time or part–time work and how far you are willing to travel. When the Hot Line receives a request for, say, a musician, it provides a list of those who meet the employer's criteria. The employer is responsible for contacting the potential employees.

Resume Clearinghouse (American Symphony Orchestra League, 777 14th St., NW, Suite 500, Washington, DC 20005; phone: 202/628-0099) free, available only to members. You complete their registration form and submit it with your resume. When matched to a job opening, your resume is sent to the employer who is responsible for contacting you directly. Fields covered include: classical musicians, conductors, and arts administration and management (primarily orchestras, but also some theater): development, marketing, operations, education, and public relations.

Directories

Musical American: International Directory of Performing Arts (Musical American Publishing, 825 Seventh Ave., New York, NY 10019; phone: 212/265-8360) $75 includes shipping, published each December. Lists performers, managers, festivals, concert sites, and schools—only for classical music.

The Christian Music Marketing Manual (James Lloyd Group, P.O. Box 3, Ashland, OR 87520; phone: 503/488-5627) $20. This is a detailed guide to Christian-oriented recording labels, publishing companies, and managers and booking agents. If you wish to work within this segment of the music industry, this book is pretty essential for understanding it.

Theater

Job openings

ArtSEARCH (355 Lexington Ave., New York, NY 10017; phone: 212/697-5230) 23 issues/year, $48/annual subscription. Features from 100 to 200 positions in theater for administrators, actors, technicians, production, marketing, interns, and faculty.

THEatre JOBLIST: The National Employment Service Billboard for Theatre Arts (THEater Service, P.O. Box 15282, Evansville, IN 47716-0282) phone: 812/474-0549) 11 issues/year, $45/annual non-

member subscription, $30/members; $36/members of Alliance for Theater and Education or United States Institute for Theatre Technology. From 20 to 90 positions appear throughout for technicians, designers, and mostly for college teaching positions.

Drama Logue (P. O. Box 38771, Los Angeles, CA 90038; phone: 213/464–5079) weekly, $55/annual subscription (U.S.), $110/Canada. Several hundred job opportunities for performers (actors, singers, dancers, etc.) and technical and production crew (in film, video, and stage) appear under "Casting Notices." In addition, there are dozens of ads for performers, technicians, production staff, and sales positions scattered throughout.

Job Contact Bulletin (Southeastern Theatre Conference, 506 Stirling, University of North Carolina, Greensboro, NC 27412; phone: 919/272–3645) monthly, available only to members: $35/annual member subscription, $15/member students. From 20 to 50 ads for everything in theater except actors appear in the typical issue.

Performing Arts Forum (International Society of Performing Arts Administrators, 6065 Pickerel Dr., Rockford, MI 49341; phone: 616/874–6200) ten issues/year, $25/nonmember annual subscription, free/members. One or two ads for CEOs, directors of marketing, and other senior arts positions for performing arts centers appear under "Position Openings."

Call Board (Theatre Bay Area, 657 Mission, Suite 402, San Francisco, CA 94105; phone: 415/957–1557) monthly, $32/annual subscription (includes membership in TBA), single copy available at Bay Area bookstores. Over 20 technical, production, acting, and administrative positions appear under "Job Bank." "Auditions" features about 35 opportunities. These openings are located almost entirely in the San Francisco Bay Area.

Dramatics Magazine (International Thespian Society, 3368 Central Parkway, Cincinnati, OH 45225; phone: 513/559–1996) monthly, $18/annual nonmember subscription. Five to seven ads for drama teachers and directors appear under "Classified."

Newsletter (Box Office Management International, 333 E. 46th St., New York, NY 10017; phone: 212/949–7350) eight issues/year, free, available only to members. About four positions in box office management appear under "BOMI/Search."

Teaching Theatre (International Thespian Society, 3368 Central Parkway, Cincinnati, OH 45225; phone: 513/559–1996) quarterly, available only to members. Features three or four positions for directors and drama teachers under "Positions Available."

Short Subjects (Greater Philadelphia Cultural Alliance, 320 Walnut St., Philadelphia, PA 19106; phone: 215/440–8100) annual, $15. Under "Job Bank" you'll find around 20 ads for administrative and other support staff.

Job service

Skills Registry (Greater Philadelphia Cultural Alliance, 320 Walnut St., Philadelphia, PA 19106; phone: 215/440–8100) free. Fill out their resume form which is kept on file for up to one year. When you are matched with an administrative or other support position in the cultural arts or theater, the service gives a copy of your resume to the potential employer who is then responsible for contacting you.

Directories

Regional Theatre Directory (American Theatre Works, Inc., P.O. Box 519, Dorset, VT 05251; phone: 802/867–2223) $12.95, published each spring. Lists regional theaters and programs for the U.S., Canada, and Great Britain.

Summer Theatre Directory (American Theatre Works, Inc., P.O. Box 519, Dorset, VT 05251; phone: 802/867–2223) $12.95, published each winter. Covers the May to September theater season in the U.S., Canada, and Great Britain.

Membership Directory (International Society of Performing Arts Administrators, 6065 Pickerel Dr., Rockford, MI 49341; phone: 616/874–6200) free/members only, published each February.

Theatre Directory of the Bay Area (Theatre Bay Area, 657 Mission, Suite 402, San Francisco, CA 94105; phone: 415/957–1557) $22/nonmembers, $18/members. Published in March of odd–numbered years. Provides details on the theater companies in the nine-county San Francisco area.

Directory (Southeastern Theatre Conference, 506 Stirling, University of North Carolina, Greensboro, NC 27412; phone: 919/272–3645) available only to members. The major value of this directory is its list of theater companies that belong to the STC in the southeastern U.S.

Chapter 13

Environment

Also see the job sources in the chapters on "Science and engineering,"
"Forestry and horticulture," and "Parks, recreation, and sports."

Job openings

Environmental Careers Bulletin (11693 San Vicente Blvd., Suite
327, Los Angeles, CA 90047; phone: 213/399-3533, no phone
orders) monthly, free, but when you write for a subscription you
must provide your job title, college major, college degree, and
year awarded. From 150 to 200 display ads for environmental
positions, largely private sector, appear in the typical issue. Details
on this company's environmental job fairs held around the
country are included.

The Job Seeker (Route 2, Box 16, Warrens, WI 54666; phone:
608/378-4290) biweekly, $60/annual subscription, $36/six-month
subscription, $19.50/three-month subscription. Over 200 environ-
mental and natural resource positions in every aspect of these
fields, including environmental education, fill these pages. Special
supplement in one December issue features dozens of summer
internships.

Environmental Opportunities (P.O. Box 4957, Arcata, CA 95521; phone: 707/839-4640) monthly, $47/annual subscription, $26/six-month subscription (U.S.), $52/Canada, $60/elsewhere. Over 125 jobs, internships, seasonal work, educational offerings, and conferences. Includes administrative positions, fisheries, wildlife, forestry, research, parks, outdoor recreation, and ecology. Write for free sample copy.

Employment Opportunity Service (National Association of Interpretation P.O. Box 1892, Ft. Collins, CO 80522; 303/491-6434) $3.00/week. This is a printout of the *Dial-a-Job* and *Dial-an-Internship* jobs listed by phone as described below under ''Job services.'' Be sure to indicate the week or weeks for which you want a printout.

EarthWorks includes **Job Scan** (Student Conservation Association, P.O. Box 550, Charlestown, NH 03603; phone: 603/826-5206) monthly, $29.95/nonmember annual subscription, $25.95/members. About 70 jobs in a typical issue plus 20 to 30 internships.

Environmental Action (Environmental Action, Inc., 6930 Carroll Ave., Takoma Park, MD 20912; phone: 202/745-4870) bimonthly; annual subscription: $30/profit-making institutions, $20/annual membership for individuals includes subscription. Jobs listed under ''Eco-Exchange.''

1992 Summer Employment Directory of the United States (Petersons Guides, P.O. Box 2123, Princeton, NJ 08543-2123; phone: 800/338-3282) $14.95, published each autumn. Its 200+ pages list over 75,000 summer job openings at resorts, camps, amusement parks, national parks, ranches, restaurants, businesses, and conference and training centers.

HAZMAT WORLD (Tower-Borner Publishing, Building C, Suite 206, 800 Roosevelt Rd., Glen Ellyn, IL 60137-5851; phone: 708/858-1888) monthly; $30/annual subscription, $50/elsewhere (surface), $80/air. The ''Classifieds'' section features about five to ten job openings for engineers and other environmental specialists.

Fisheries (American Fisheries Society, 5410 Grosvenor Ln., Suite 110, Bethesda, MD 20814-2199; phone: 301/897-8616) bimonthly, $43.50/annual nonmember subscription, $47/Canada, $54/elsewhere, included in dues which, coincidentally, are $43.50/U.S. and $47/foreign, $21.75/students. "Current events and Announcements" sports four or five job ads.

The Caretaker Gazette (P.O. Box 342, Carpentersville, IL 60110; phone: 708/658-6554, no phone orders) quarterly, $8/three issues, $14/six issues. Among its 60 job announcements are jobs and internships in forestry, fisheries, environment, and caretaking.

Job's Clearinghouse (Association for Experiential Education, University of Colorado, Box 249, Boulder, CO 80309; phone: 303/492-1547, **TDD:** 303/492-0526) monthly, $25/nonmember annual subscription, $15/members. Many environmental-related positions are among the 30-plus pages of opportunities in a typical issue.

Environmental Science & Technology (American Chemical Society, P.O. Box 3337, Columbus, OH 43210; phone: 614/447-3776) monthly, $73/nonmember annual subscription (individuals), $39/members. The "Classified Section" carries around 25 job vacancies.

The Wildlifer (The Wildlife Society, 5410 Grosvenor Ln., Bethesda, MD 20814; phone: 301/897-9770) bimonthly, available only to members: $33/annual dues, $17/student dues. About 20 positions in conservation, wildlife, and natural resources appear under "Positions Available."

Employment Announcements (American Meteorological Society, 45 Beacon St., Boston, MA 02108-3693) monthly, $25/annual nonmember subscription, $12/members. About 25 jobs for weather forecasters and meteorologists grace these pages.

E Magazine (Earth Action Network, 28 Knight St., Norwalk, CT 06851; phone: 203/854-5559) bimonthly, $20/annual subscription (U.S.), $25/Mexico and Canada, $30/elsewhere. Five to ten job openings are in "Classified—Job Opportunities."

Journal of Soil and Water Conservation (Soil and Water Conservation Society, 7515 NE Ankeny Rd., Ankeny, IA 50021–9764; phone: 515/289–2331) bimonthly, $35/annual subscription (U.S. and Canada), $40/elsewhere. Jobs listed under "Classified Advertising." About five job ads per issue.

Journal of Air and Waste Management (Air Pollution Control Association, P.O. Box 2861, Pittsburgh, PA 15230; phone: 412/232–3444) monthly, $200/annual nonmember subscription, $90/nonprofit libraries and institutions, free/members. About three or four vacancies in environmental engineering are listed under "Manpower."

Environmental Science and Technology (American Chemical Society, 1155 16th St., NW, Washington, DC 20036; phones: 800/227–5558, 202/872–4363) monthly, $329/annual nonmember subscription, $39/members. Includes job ads.

Job services

JOBSource (College of Natural Resources, Colorado State University, Fort Collins, CO 80523; phone: 800/727–5627). *JOBSource* consists of three services that use an extensive database of 700+ vacancies, mostly in the environmental arena (fisheries, natural resources, wildlife, forestry, biology, recreation, parks). For individuals, the most useful is *JOBSource's* in–house search program. Obtain a resume application form from *JOBSource*. Within two weeks of receiving your completed form, *JOBSource* will conduct a job search of its database for you. *JOBSource* guarantees from six to 25 matches per search. The cost is $30. If fewer than six matches are found, *JOBSource* will run a second search the next month for free. If the second run turns up fewer than six matches, there is a $5 charge for that second run.

However, if you have a computer and modem, you can download the entire database onto your computer for $20 plus your phone call. It takes 20 to 40 minutes to download the three files. To update, you need to download just one file which takes about 20 minutes and costs $15. The database is updated every Thursday. A growing number of universities and colleges are subscribing to *JOBSource*. They receive the database and user programs around the 24th of each month and can conduct their own job searches. Subscriptions are available for a year ($495), the nine months of September through May ($375), or for the three months of January, April, and November ($189).

Environmental Career Hotline (1224 Washington Ave., Suite 104, Golden, CO 80401; phone: 303/231-6144) $5/minute charged directly to your phone bill. Call this interactive hotline at 900/933-3393 from a touch-tone phone, 24-hours a day, seven days a week, to hear job descriptions in air quality, water quality, waste management, industrial hygiene, and regulatory compliance. You are able to specify the specific field(s) that interest you. Updated weekly.

Dial-a-Job and *Dial-an-Internship* (National Association of Interpretation P.O. Box 1892, Ft. Collins, CO 80522; 303/491-6434) Call 301/491-7410 24-hours a day for a recording of full-time, seasonal, and temporary jobs in environmental education, interpretation, and related fields: naturalists, park rangers, outdoor education, biologists, historians, archaeologists, museum personnel, and publication designers. The tape runs from 10 to 30 minutes. Updated weekly. For internships, call 301/491-6784 24-hours a day. The tape runs from 5 to 20 minutes. Updated weekly.

Environmental Action Job Book (Environmental Action, Inc., 1525 New Hampshire Ave., NW, Washington, DC 20036; phone: 202/745-4870) free. This up-to-date book of environmental jobs and internships can be seen only at the Environmental Action office.

Directories

Environmental Services Directory (Environmental Information, 4801 W. 81st St., Suite 119, Minneapolis, MN 55437; phone: 612/831-2473) $275/national edition (two volumes), also available in five editions ($70/each) that coincide with the regions of the U.S. Environmental Protection Agency: regions I, II, and III; region IV; region V; regions VI, VII, and VIII; and regions IX and X. The national edition profiles over 4,500 environmental services and firms by state, including hazardous waste treatment, storage, and disposal facilities; spill response firms; transportation services; laboratories; soil boring and well drilling firms; and consultants.

Careers in Hazardous Waste Management: A Job Hunters Guide to the Hazardous Waste Management Field (Environmental Employment Clearinghouse, 3304 Marcus Ave., Newport Beach, CA 92663; phone: 714/675–8278) $12.95, most recent edition published January, 1992. We've generally excluded these sorts of books, but this one is different. It includes a good list of job hunting resources (periodicals and directories) and a thorough directory of private sector businesses.

Environmental Information Directory Gale Research, Inc., 835 Penobscot Bldg., Detroit, MI 48226; phone: 800/877–4253) $75, 1991. Divided into 20 chapters, this directory includes information on federal government and state agencies that deal with the environment in addition to private and non–profit players in the environmental field.

NAI Membership Directory (National Association of Interpretation P.O. Box 1892, Ft. Collins, CO 80522; 303/491–6434) available only to members, included in dues, published each spring. Lists members and institutional members.

The Wildlife Society Membership Directory and Certification Registry (The Wildlife Society, 5410 Grosvenor Ln. Bethesda, MD 20814; phone: 301/897–9770) $3/nonmembers, included in dues, published each September.

Journal of Air and Waste Management Consultants Guide (Air Pollution Control Association, P.O. Box 2861, Pittsburgh, PA 15230; phone: 412/232–3444) monthly, $200/annual nonmember subscription, $90/non–profit libraries and institutions, free/members. Published in the December issue of the *Journal of Air and Waste Management*, this is an extensive 28–page guide to individual consultants and firms in air pollution control and waste management.

Sanitation/solid waste management

Job openings

Employment Hotline Newsletter (HCI Publications, 410 Archibald St, Kansas City, MO 64111; phone: 816/931–1311) weekly, $98/annual subscription, $59/six–months, $35/12 weeks. Twenty to 30 jobs in all facets of solid waste management appear in each issue. Many of these ads are the same ads as those in *Solid Waste & Power* described immediately below.

Solid Waste & Power (HCI Publications, 410 Archibald St, Kansas City, MO 64111; phone: 816/931–1311) bimonthly, $49/annual subscription (U.S.), $60/foreign. About ten job vacancies in all aspects of solid waste management are listed under "Job Mart." Many of these ads are the same ads as those in *Employment Hotline Newsletter* described immediately above.

Biocycle (P.O. Box 351, 18 S. Seventh St., Emmaus, PA 18049; phone: 215/967–4135) monthly, $55/annual subscription (U.S.), $75/foreign. About ten job ads in typical issue, generally focusing on recycling.

Recycling Today Municipal Market Edition (4012 Bridge Ave., Cleveland, OH 44113; phone: 216/961–4130) monthly, $32/annual subscription. About three vacancies for recycling coordinators, operations handlers, and directors of solid waste operations appear under "Classifieds."

Resource Recycling (P.O. Box 10540, Portland, OR 97210; phones: 800/227–1424, 503/227–1319) monthly, $42/annual subscription. About two recycling and solid waste management positions are listed under "Positions Available."

Management of World Wastes (Communication Channels, 6255 Barfield Rd., Atlanta, GA 30328; phones: 800/241–9834, 404/256–9800) monthly; $40/annual subscription (U.S.), $60/Canada. Five to ten jobs are listed under "The Job Mart."

Waste Age (Suite 1000, 1730 Rhode Island Ave., NW, Washington, DC 20036; phone: 202/861-0708) monthly; $45/annual subscription (U.S. and Canada), but free to professionals in the industry (U.S. and Canada only); $125/elsewhere. Jobs listed under "Classifieds."

Solid Wastes News (Solid Waste Association of North America, P.O. Box 7219, Silver Spring, MD 20910; phone: 301/585-2898) monthly, available only as part of membership package ($50/year membership fee for individual government employee, $10/students). Jobs listed under "Jobs." About four job ads per issue.

Environmental Management (Environmental Management Association, 9255 Detroit St., Suite 200, Denver, CO 80206; phone: 303/320-7853) quarterly, $80/annual nonmember subscription, free/members. About six jobs for sanitation operators, building sanitarians, and housekeeping managers appear in "Career Opportunities."

Pollution Engineering (Cahners Publishing, 44 Cook, St., Denver, CO 80206; phone: 303/388-4511) 13 issues/year, $24/annual subscription (U.S.), $32/Canada and Mexico, elsewhere: $72/surface mail, $92/air mail; free to qualified professionals. Thirty to 40 positions fill the "Classified" section.

Environment Today (Enterprise Communications, P.O. Box 7389, Marietta, GA 30065; phone: 404/989-9558) nine issues/year, $42/annual subscription, $76/foreign. "ET Classified" usually includes around five job ads for environmental engineers, industrial hygienists, and hazardous waste experts.

Hazardous Materials Control (Hazardous Materials Control Research Institute, 7237A Hanover Pkwy., Greenbelt, MD 20070-3602; phone: 301/982-9500) bimonthly, $18/annual subscription (U.S.), $25/Canada, $25 elsewhere via surface mail, $50/elsewhere via air mail. Jobs listed under "Focus." Few job ads.

Directories

Solid Waste & Power's Industry Directory (HCI Publications, 410 Archibald St, Kansas City, MO 64111; phone: 816/931-1311) $12, issued each December. Lists companies related to the solid waste management industry.

Solid Wastes Association of North American Membership Directory (Solid Waste Association of North America, P.O. Box 7219, Silver Spring, MD 20910; phone: 301/585-2898) $500.

Hazardous Materials Control Directory (Hazardous Materials Control Research Institute, 7237A Hanover Pkwy., Greenbelt, MD 20070-3602; phone: 301/982-9500) $65/nonmembers, included in dues, published each November.

Water/wastewater operations

Job openings

The Jobank (Water Pollution Control Federation, 601 Wythe St., Alexandria, VA 22314; phone: 703/684-2400) bimonthly, $36/nonmember six-month subscription, $18/members. About 16 positions in pollution control and wastewater operations are in the typical issue.

Water Environment Technology (Water Pollution Control Federation, 601 Wythe St., Alexandria, VA 22314; phone: 703/684-2400) monthly, $144/nonmember annual subscription (U.S.), $187/nonmember elsewhere; included in membership package. Jobs listed under "Classifieds." About ten to 15 ads in typical issue.

Water Well Journal (National Water Well Association, 6375 Riverside Dr., Dublin, OH 43017; phone: 614/761-3222) monthly, $12/annual subscription (U.S.), $24/foreign, free/members. About 12 vacancies for drillers, hydrogeologists, and hydrologists are listed under "Opportunities."

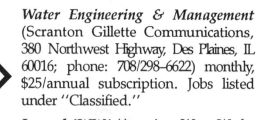

Water Engineering & Management (Scranton Gillette Communications, 380 Northwest Highway, Des Plaines, IL 60016; phone: 708/298-6622) monthly, $25/annual subscription. Jobs listed under "Classified."

Journal AWWA (American Water Works Association, 6666 W. Quincy, Denver, CO 80235; phone: 303/794-7711) monthly, $85/nonmember annual subscription

(North America), $110/elsewhere; included in annual dues ($65/U.S., $93/foreign). Jobs listed under "Classified." Fifteen to 18 job ads grace these pages each issue.

Ground Water (Association of Groundwater Scientists and Engineers, 6375 Riverside Dr., Dublin, OH 43017; phones: 800/423–7748 (outside Ohio), 614/761–1711) bimonthly, $63/annual nonmember subscription, $20/members. Forty to 50 ads for geologists, hydrogeologists, environmental engineers, and hazardous waste engineers are printed under "Ground-Water Employment Opportunities."

Mainstream (American Water Works Association, 6666 W. Quincy, Denver, CO 80235; phone: 303/794–7711) monthly, $13/nonmember annual subscription (U.S.), $18.50/foreign, included in dues (annual dues: $65/U.S., $93/foreign). Jobs listed under "Employment." About 20 job ads appear in the typical issue.

Waterworld News (American Water Works Association, 6666 W. Quincy, Denver, CO 80235; phone: 303/794–7711) bimonthly, free to qualified people in the profession, write for application form, free/members. About 12 jobs for engineers, utility directors, and related positions are listed under "Classified."

Water Conditioning & Purification (4651 N. First Ave., Suite 101, Tucson, AZ 85718; phone: 602/293–5446) monthly, $34/annual subscription (U.S., Canada), $85/elsewhere. "Classified" normally carries about four job ads for water treatment salespeople, servicepeople, installers, and management.

Job service

Job Mart (National Water Well Association, 6375 Riverside Dr., Dublin, OH 43017; phone: 614/761–3222) $20/12 months. Job seeker completes resume forms and a "blind ad." The blind ads are sent to employers who pay a fee to see the full resume of promising candidates. It's up to the employer to contact the job seeker. Resumes are kept on file until you find a job, or one year. Positions include geologists, hydrogeologists, contractors, scientists, and engineers.

Directories

Monitoring Contractors Directory (National Water Well Association, 6375 Riverside Dr., Dublin, OH 43017; phone: 614/761–3222) available only to members, published each May.

Directory of Consultants and Contractors (National Water Well Association, 6375 Riverside Dr., Dublin, OH 43017; phone: 614/761–3222) $5.50/nonmembers, free/members, published annually.

AWWA Membership Roster (American Water Works Association, 6666 W. Quincy, Denver, CO 80235; phone: 303/794–7711) free/members only, published in 1989 and every three years thereafter.

National Water Supply Improvement Association Membership Directory (NWSIA, P.O. Box 102, St. Leonard, MD 20685; phone: 301/855–1173) free/members only, issued each May.

Water Conditioning & Purification Buyer's Guide (4651 N. First Ave., Suite 101, Tucson, AZ 85718; phone: 602/293–5446) $18, published each April. Lists manufacturers, distributors, and products in the water treatment industry.

Salary survey

Survey: The Ground Water Profession (Association of Groundwater Scientists and Engineers, 6375 Riverside Dr., Dublin, OH 43017; phones: 800/423–7748 [outside Ohio], 614/761–1711) $31.25/nonmembers, $25/members, issued in odd–numbered years. This booklet reports on the results of a random sample survey of 1,000 AGSE members.

Chapter 14

Farming and ranching

Beekeeping

Job openings

American Bee Journal (51 S. Second St., Hamilton, IL 62341; phone: 217/847-3324) monthly, $14.40/annual subscription (U.S.), $22.15/foreign. "The Market Place—Help Wanted" includes five to ten ads for beekeepers.

American Beekeeping Foundation Newsletter (ABF, P.O. Box 1038, Jesup, GA 31545; phone: 912/427-8447) bimonthly, available only to members. One or two beekeeping jobs are under "Employment."

Farming

Also see entries in the "Environment" chapter.

Job openings

Agronomy News (American Society of Agronomy, 677 S. Segoe Rd., Madison, WI 53711; phone: 608/273–8080) monthly, $7/annual nonmember subscription, free/members. About 30 openings for agronomists and crop and soil scientists are described under "Personnel."

Hog Farm (Miller Publishing, 12400 Whitewater Dr., Suite 160, Minnetonka, MN 55343; phones: 800/333–8261, 612/931–0211) monthly, $25/annual subscription (U.S.), $35//Canada, free to qualified professionals. The number of job ads under "Positions Available" varies widely by the time of year. Jobs advertised include herdspersons, nutritionists, and other positions in swine farming.

Feedstuffs (Miller Publishing, 191 S. Gary Ave., Carol Stream, IL 60188; phones: 800/333–8261, 708/690–5600) weekly, $75/annual subscription (U.S.), $120/Canada. The number of job ads under "Positions Available" varies considerably with the time of year. A July issue had ten ads for technical sales managers, veterinarians, nutritionists, dairy specialists, manufacturers representatives plus a few ads from agribusiness recruiting firms.

Women in Agribusiness Bulletin (WIA, P.O. Box 10241, Kansas City, MO 64111; phone: 816/361–5846) quarterly, annual subscriptions: $15/U.S., $20/elsewhere. Four or five jobs appear under "Classifieds."

Successful Farming (1716 Locust St., Des Moines, IA 50336; phone: 800/678–2711) monthly, $12/annual subscription (U.S.), $24/foreign. Two or three job openings for farming positions (farm managers, herdspeople, farm hands) are under "Classified Shopper—Help Wanted" and "Business Opportunities." Also includes "Help Available" ads.

Alternative Agriculture News (Institute for Alternative Agriculture, Suite 117, 9200 Edmonton Rd., Greenbelt, MD 20770; phone: 301/441–8777) monthly, $15/annual membership includes subscription. Few ads in typical issue.

Seed World (Scranton Gillette Communications, 380 E. Northwest Highway, Des Plaines, IL 60016; phone: 708/298-6622) monthly, $18/annual subscription (U.S.), $28/foreign. "Marketplace" tends to carry two or three job ads, largely from recruiters for all aspects of the seed business.

Solutions (339 Consort Dr., Manchester, MO 63011; phone: 314/256-4900) seven issues/year, free. About three job ads for plant managers, sales, and applicators in the fertilizer industry appear in "Classified."

Farm Chemicals (37841 Euclid Ave., Willoughby, OH 44094; phone: 216/942-2000) monthly, free to qualified professionals. One to five display ads include jobs in agricultural chemicals, fertilizers, seed, and related regulatory and research positions.

FMRA News (American Society of Farm Managers and Rural Appraisers, Inc., Suite 500, 950 Cherry, Denver, CO 80222; phone: 303/758-3513) bimonthly, available only as part of membership package. Jobs listed under "Job Mart." Usually two to four job ads per issue, but some issues have no ads.

Shortliner (Farm Equipment Manufacturers Association, 243 N. Lindberg Blvd., St. Louis, MO 63141; phone: 314/991-0702) semimonthly, available only to members. About three ads for positions in management and sales are advertised in a typical issue.

Job services

Career Development and Placement Service (American Society of Agronomy, 677 S. Segoe Rd., Madison, WI 53711; phone: 608/273-8080) $15/nonmember annual fee, free/members. Job seeker submits resume which is matched with jobs. The potential employer contacts the job seeker. Resume kept on file for 12 months; $7.50 fee to update resume during that time.

APS Placement Service (American Phytopathological Society, 3340 Pilot Knob Rd., St. Paul, MN 55121; phone: 612/454-7250) $35/nonmembers, free/members. This service sends all resumes to participating employers who then select whom they will interview. At the APS annual meeting, current resumes are placed in a bound volume for employers to examine. Positions are generally in plant pathology, genetics, or pesticides.

Directories

Names to Know (National Association of Farmer Cooperatives, 50 F St., NW, Washington, DC 20001; phone: 202/626-8700) contact for price, annual, 40 pages. Includes member farmer cooperatives and state councils of farmer cooperatives.

National Corn Growers Association Membership Directory (NCGA, 201 Massachusetts Ave., NE, Suite C-4, Washington, DC 20002; phone: 202/546-7611) free, issued each September.

Cattle Ranch/Feedlot Directory (Intermountain Referral, 703 S. Broadway, Suite 100, Denver, CO 80209; phone: 303/988-6707) $7/each directory, available as mailing labels: $19/each directory. Directory lists are available for Arizona, northern California, southern California, northern Colorado, southern Colorado, Idaho, Kansas, Montana (counts as two directories, pay $14), Nebraska, Nevada, New Mexico, North Dakota, Oklahoma, South Dakota,

Texas (counts as two directories, pay $14), Utah, Washington, and Wyoming. A total of over 5,000 ranches are listed between the 17 directory lists. These are updated daily.

American Feed Industry Association Annual Membership Directory (AFIA, 1501 Wilson Blvd., Suite 1100, Arlington, VA 22209; phone: 703/524-1921) $100/nonmembers, free/members, annual. Over 400 pages of key feed industry contacts in over 600 companies.

National Grain and Feed Association Membership Directory (1201 New York Ave., NW, Suite 830, Washington, DC 20005; phone: 202/289-0873) $150/nonmembers, free/members, annual.

Accredited and General Membership Directory (American Society of Farm Managers and Rural Appraisers, Inc., Suite 500, 950 Cherry, Denver, CO 80222; phone: 303/758-3513) free, published each February.

National Association of Tobacco Distributors Directory of Membership and Services (NATD, 1199 N. Fairfax, Suite 701, Alexandria, VA 22314; phone: 800/642-6283) $50/nonmembers, $20/members, annual, 180 pages. Includes state associations as well as members and nonmembers in the tobacco distribution industry.

Farm Equipment Manufacturers Association Directory (FEMA, 243 N. Lindberg Blvd., St. Louis, MO 63141; phone: 314/991-0702) free/members only, annual.

Farm Equipment Wholesalers Association Membership Directory (FEWA, 1927 Keokuk St., Iowa City, IA 52240; phone: 319/334-5156) $40/nonmembers, free/members, annual.

Horses and livestock

Job openings

The Chronicle of the Horse (301 W. Washington St., Middleburg, VA 22117; phone: 703/687-6341) weekly, $42/annual subscription (U.S.), $57/foreign. "Help Wanted" carries 15 to 20 job ads in the equine industry.

Western Horseman (3850 N. Nevada Ave., Colorado Springs, CO 80907-5339; phone: 800/545-9364) monthly, $18/annual subscription (U.S.), $25/foreign. About 15 jobs for riders, cowboys, grooms, wranglers, horse appraisers, and cooks are advertised under "Classified."

The Blood-Horse (Thoroughbred Owners and Breeders Association, 1736 Alexandria Dr., Lexington, KY 40504; phones: 800/866-2361, 606/278-2361) weekly, $75.50/annual subscription (U.S.), $125.25/foreign. About four ads for farm trainers and riders are in the "Classifieds—Help Wanted." One issue each year includes an industry directory.

The Morgan Horse (American Morgan Horse Association, P.O. Box 960, Shelburne, VT 05482; phone: 802/985-4944) monthly, $25/annual subscription. Two or three ads for horse trainers, breeding farm managers, and grooms are under "Help Wanted."

Horse Illustrated (Fancy Publications, P.O. Box 52898, Boulder, CO 80323-2898; phone: 303/447-9330) monthly, $21.97/annual subscription (U.S.), $29.97/Canada, $33.97/elsewhere. A few ads for exercise riders, stable help, and other horse industry positions appear under "Business Opportunities."

Saddle Horse Report (730 Madison St., Shelbyville, TN 37160; phone: 615/684-8123) weekly, $50/annual subscription. "Bulletin Board" runs two or three job ads for trainers and others.

Job service

Equimax (1625 Cardwell Rd., Crozier, VA 23039; phones: 800/759-9494, 804/784-3020). Job seekers have two options with this service. You can become an Equimax Candidate where a summary of your resume is placed in Equimax's *List of Candidates* which potential employers receive. They are responsible for contacting you for the next step in the hiring process. It costs $40 to place a listing for up to six months. It costs $70 for a confidential listing where a code number is substituted for your name.

In addition, Equimax publishes a *List of Jobs* which you receive for free if you are a Job Candidate. You can receive an updated list as frequently as every two weeks. From 40 to 80 jobs are on the list. This list is also available to anybody for a $40 (add $8/foreign) fee which entitles you to one initial list and up to 12 updates. You can contact employers directly. Positions include horse trainers, assistant trainers, working farm help, instructors, grooms, barn help, and summer camp instructors.

Directory

Horse Industry Directory (American Horse Council, 1700 K St., NW, Washington, DC 20006; phone: 206/296–4031) contact for price; it's not expensive. Lists breed registries, show, health, and research, humane, educational, racing, trail, sports, and general interest horse organizations, horse libraries and museums, state horse councils, transportation companies, equine periodicals, trade directories and annuals, and more.

Chapter 15

Financial industry

Financial industry in general

Job openings

Position Alert (Professional Communications, Inc., 714 Peninsula, Suite 200, Ann Arbor, MI 48105; phone: 313/662–0250) semi-monthly, $45/three–month subscription, $81/six–month subscription, $12.50/single issue. Over 150 jobs in accounting, auditing, banking, investing, and finances fill these pages. These include some, but far from all of the jobs listed in Professional Communications' job hotline, *PRESORT*, described below under "Job services."

Position Report (David J. White & Associates, Suite 200, 809 Ridge Rd., Wilmette, IL 60091; phone: 708/256–8826) weekly, $42.50/four week subscription, $115/12 weeks, $220/24 weeks, $440/48 weeks. This is a collection of 500 + job ads in finance and accounting taken from over 100 newspapers and periodicals nationwide.

Journal of Taxation (Warren, Gorham & Lamont, 210 South St., Boston, MA 02111; phone: 800/950–1205) monthly, $145/annual subscription. Ads, largely for accountant and attorney tax professionals, appear under "Classified."

Corporate Cash Flow (Communication Channels, Inc., P.O. Box 41369, Nashville, TN 37204; phone: 615/377–3322) monthly, $66/annual subscription. The "Classifieds" have a handful of job ads for administrators and financial officers with corporations.

Internal Auditor (Institute of Internal Auditors, 249 Maitland Ave., Altamonte Springs, FL 32701–4201; phone: 407/830–7600) bimonthly, $36/nonmember annual subscription (U.S.), $56/foreign (air mail), $42/foreign (surface mail), included in membership package. Typical issue features four to eight job ads plus ads from recruitment agencies. Includes ads for positions overseas.

Job services

1–900–PRE–SORT (Professional Communications, Inc., 714 Peninsula, Suite 200, Ann Arbor, MI 48105; phone: 313/662–0250) $1.95/first minute, 95¢ each additional minute. Call 900/773–7678 on a touch-tone phone to hear descriptions of available jobs in accounting, finance, and banking. You can specify the geographic area, salary level, and specialty you seek. As of late 1991, over 700 positions are available at any one time. They expect to have up to 2,000 positions listed at a time within a year or two. The hotline is updated weekly.

Counseling and Referral Service (Financial Executives Institute, 10 Madison Ave., Morristown, NJ 07960; phone: 201/898–4600) free, available only to members, $300/annual dues. FEI matches your resume to jobs. The potential employer contacts the job seeker directly. Positions covered include chief executive officers, chief financial officers, comptrollers, and treasurers.

Jobline Placement Service (Financial Analysts Federation, 5 Boar's Head Lane, Charlottesville, VA 22903; phone: 804/980–3688) free, available only to members, $100/annual dues. Members can call a 24-hour recording of positions for financial analysts which is updated every two weeks. They can then send their resume to the service with the code number for the job in which they are interested. The employer contacts the job candidate for an interview.

Directories

The Corporate Finance Sourcebook (National Register Publishing Company, 3004 Glenview Rd., Wilmette, IL 60091; phones: 800/323–6772, 708/441–2210) $377 plus $10.25 shipping, annual. In over 1,000 pages, this directory lists 15,700 corporate financial officers with direct-line phone numbers and high-risk venture capital firms, major private lenders, commercial banking services, investment bankers, pension managers, master trusts, cash managers, business insurance brokers, corporate real estate services, securities analysts, CPA firms, accounting firms, and auditors.

The Corporate Finance Bluebook (National Register Publishing Company, 3004 Glenview Rd., Wilmette, IL 60091; phones: 800/323-6772, 708/441-2210) $427 plus $11.75 shipping, annual. Among the 2,000 pages are the names, title, direct phone line, and area of responsibility for executives in 11 financial specialties for thousands of U.S. companies.

National Association of Surety Bond Producers Membership Directory (NASBP, 55301 Wisconsin Ave., NW, Suite 450, Washington, DC 20015; phone: 202/686-3700) free, available only to members, issued each September.

American Bankruptcy Institute Membership Directory (American Bankruptcy Institute, 51 C St., NE, Washington, DC 20002; phone: 202/543-1234) available only to members, published annually. Includes bankruptcy judges and clerks.

Salary surveys

Accounting and Finance Salary Survey and Career Planning Guide (Source Finance, P.O. Box 152112, Irving, TX 75015-2112; phone: 214/754-0600) free, annual. Identifies average national compensation for 45 position titles and responsibility levels in both public and private accounting and finance. Reviews local data on salaries in 32 metropolitan areas in the U.S. and Canada. Based on survey of 35,000 accounting and financial professionals.

Compensation in the Accounting/Financial Field (Abbott, Langer & Associates, 548 First St., Crete, IL 60417; phone: 708/672-4200) $375, annual. In-depth analysis of salary and benefits for 18 different positions from junior accountants to chief corporate financial officers in business, industry, education, government, and non-profit organizations.

Accounting

Job openings

Journal of Accountancy (American Institute of CPAs, 1211 Avenue of the Americas, New York, NY 10036–8775; phone: 212/575–5505) monthly, $50/annual nonmember subscription, included in dues. About 30 to 40 openings for accountants appear under "Classified" and in occasional display ads. Ads also list executive search firms, job services, and business opportunities.

CA Magazine (150 Bloor St., West, Toronto, Quebec M5S 2Y2 Canada; phone: 416/962–1242) monthly, $46/annual subscription. About 36 jobs for chartered accountants appear under "Classifieds."

SHOE copyright © 1990. All rights reserved. Reprinted by permission. Tribune Media Services.

National Public Accountant (National Society of Public Accountants, 1010 N. Fairfax St., Alexandria, VA 22314; phone: 703/549–6400) monthly, $18/annual subscription. "Ad Classifieds" has five to ten ads for accounting practices.

Management Accounting (10 Paragon Dr., Montvale, NJ 07645–1760; phone: 201/573–6280) monthly, $115/annual subscription. About five ads for corporate accountants and financial executives appear under "Classified."

Bottomline (International Association of Hospitality Accountants, P.O. Box 27649, Austin, TX 78755; phone: 512/346–5680) bimonthly, $50/annual nonmember subscription, free/members.

Published in alternating months with *The President's Log* described immediately below. "Job Opportunities" lists about ten jobs for accountants and comptrollers for hotels, resorts, and cruise lines.

The President's Log (International Association of Hospitality Accountants, P.O. Box 27649, Austin, TX 78755; phone: 512/346–5680) bimonthly, available only to members, included in dues. Published in alternating months with *Bottomline* described immediately above. "Job Opportunities" features about eight positions for accountants and comptrollers with hotels, resorts, and cruise lines.

The Attorney–CPA (American Association of Attorney–Certified Public Accountants, 24196 Alicia Pkwy., Suite K, Mission Viejo, CA 92691; phone: 714/768–0336) five issues/year, $30/annual nonmember subscription, free/members. "Position Clearinghouse" will have as many as two or three jobs openings for attorney–CPAs.

Job services

Job Referral Service (Alliance of Practicing CPAs, 3909 California Ave., Long Beach, Ca 90807; phone: 213/988–5052) free, available only to members. Twenty to 25 certified public accountant positions are listed in this job database at any one time. The job seeker submits a copy of his resume from which the service extracts information for the database. When a match is made, the employer contacts the job seeker. Employers may also browse the database and receive a copy of job seekers' resumes. Resumes are kept on file indefinitely.

Resume Service (International Association of Hospitality Accountants, P.O. Box 27649, Austin, TX 78755; phone: 512/346-5680) free, available only to members. The job seeker submits her resume along with a short advertisement for the IAHA's two newsletters. An employer interested in the candidate receives a copy of the resume from this service and then is responsible for initiating contact with the job seeker. Positions are for accountants and comptrollers with hotels, resorts, and cruise lines.

Directories

National Society of Public Accountants Membership Directory (NSPA, 1010 N. Fairfax St., Alexandria, VA 22314; phone: 703/549–6400) free, available only to members, released each October.

National CPA Group Roster (NCPAG, 233 Broadway, New York, NY 10279; phone: 212/766–4260) free, available only to members, issued twice a year.

AWSCPA Roster (American Women's Society of Certified Public Accountants, 111 E. Wacker Dr., Chicago, IL 60601; phone: 312/644–6610) available only to members, included in dues, published annually.

International Association of Hospitality Accountants Membership Directory (IAHA, P.O. Box 27649, Austin, TX 78755; phone: 512/346–5680) free, available only to members, published each year. Includes accountants and comptrollers with hotels, resorts, and cruise lines.

American Association of Attorney–Certified Public Accountants Membership Directory (AAA–CPA, 24196 Alicia Pkwy., Suite K, Mission Viejo, CA 92691; phone: 714/768–0336) $160/nonmembers, free/members, annual. Includes biographies of member CPA–attorneys.

Economists

Job openings

Job Openings for Economists (American Economic Association, 2014 Broadway, Suite 305, Nashville, TN 37203; phone: 615/322–2595) bimonthly, $25/annual nonmember subscription (U.S.), $32.50/foreign, $15/AEA regular members, $7.50/AEA junior members. About 150 job vacancies are announced in a typical issue.

Employment Opportunities for Business Economists (National Association of Business Economists, 28790 Chagrin Blvd., Suite 300, Cleveland, OH 44122; phone: 216/464–7986) quarterly, available only to members. Around 35 vacancies for economists, financial analysts, strategic planners, marketing executives, and

"Say what you want, but she's been right more
times than a lot of prominent economists."

related positions fill this newsletter. The jobs listed here appear on the NABE's Electronic Bulletin Board, described below under "Job services," which is accessible only to members.

NABE News (National Association of Business Economists, 28790 Chagrin Blvd., Suite 300, Cleveland, OH 44122; phone: 216/464–7986) bimonthly, $55/annual subscription. Just three or four positions are advertised here.

Job services

National Registry for Economists (c/o Illinois Department of Employment Security, 401 S. State St., Chicago, IL 60605; phone: 312/793–4904; operated in conjunction with the Allied Social Science Association) free. Request application form. Completed forms kept on file for one year. The Registry submits forms of qualified registrants to employers seeking economists. Employers then contact registrants directly.

National Home Economists in Business Dial-a-Job (National Home Economists in Business, 5008 Pine Creek Dr., Suite B, Westerville, OH 43081) free. Call 614/890-0090 for a recording of available job vacancies, each of which is assigned a code number. To apply for a position, send your resume and cover letter to NHEB—be sure to put the job's code number in your cover letter and on the outside of your envelope. Then put this envelope containing your letter into another envelope which you address to NHEB.

Electronic Bulletin Board (National Association of Business Economists, 28790 Chagrin Blvd., Suite 300, Cleveland, OH 44122; phone: 216/464-7986) available only to members. Members can complete a resume form which is then added to the "positions wanted" database which even nonmembers can access. Members, however, can also access the continuously updated "Employment Opportunities" listing of job descriptions, which are also published in the NABE's newsletter *Employment Opportunities for Business Economists*, described earlier under "Job openings."

Directories

Directory of Black Economists (National Economic Association, School of Business, University of Michigan, Ann Arbor, MI 48109-1234; phone: 313/763-0121) $25/nonmembers, included in dues. New edition scheduled for 1992 and even-numbered years thereafter.

Business Economics Membership Directory (National Association of Business Economists, 28790 Chagrin Blvd., Suite 300, Cleveland, OH 44122; phone: 216/464-7986) free to members and to subscribers to *Business Economics*, $35/annual subscription. This March issue of *Business Economics* offers short biographies on NABE members.

Roster for Committee on the Status of Women in the Economics Profession (CSWEP, American Economic Association, c/o Joan Haworth, 4901 Tower Ct., Tallahasse, FL 32303; phone: 904/562-1211) $35/nonmembers, free/members, issued in April of even-numbered years. Includes job, fields of specialization, and education.

Salary survey

Salary Characteristics (National Association of Business Economists, 28790 Chagrin Blvd., Suite 300, Cleveland, OH 44122; phone: 216/464–7986) $15, released in even–numbered years.

Financial institutions

Also see listings under "Real estate finance" in this chapter.

Job openings

American Banker (Thomson Financial Information, 1 State Street Plaza, New York, NY 10004; phone: 212/943–6700) daily, $675/annual subscription (U.S.), $815/foreign. The number of ads for banking positions, mostly vice president level, ranges from one to 20 in the "Help Wanted" section.

Job/OPS (National Association of Federal Credit Unions, 3138 N. 10th St., Suite 300, Arlington, VA 22201; phone: 703/522–4770) monthly, free/members, available only to members. Around 30 positions in upper–level management are carried.

Credit Union Magazine (Credit Union National Association, 431 Madison, WI 53704; phone: 800/356–9655, 608/231–4000) monthly, $30/annual subscription. "Classified—Career Opportunities" features announcements for almost ten positions of all types with credit unions.

Credit Union Management (Credit Union Executives Society, P.O. Box 14167, Madison, WI 53714; phones: 800/252–2664, 608/271–2664) monthly, $48/annual nonmember subscription, $36/members. The "Classifieds" feature about five ads for financial CEOs, marketers, operations, data processing, and accountants.

Job services

Job (National Bankers Association, 122 C St., NW, Suite 580, Washington, DC 20001; phone: 202/783–3200) free, available only to members. Covering bank positions from tellers to CEOs, this job–matching service has the job seeker submit a resume which is kept on file for six to 12 months. When a match is made, the resume is forwarded to the employer who is responsible for contacting job candidates for an interview.

Placement Service (American League of Financial Institutions, 1709 New York Ave., NW, Suite 801, Washington, DC 20006; phone: 202/628–5624) free, available only to members. ALFI sends employers' job announcements to members.

Directories

American Financial Directory (McFadden Business Publications, 6195 Crooked Creek Rd., Norcross, GA 30092–9986; phones: 800/247–7376, 404/448–1011) $385, published every June and December. Covers the entire U.S. and Canadian financial services industry: 75,000 banks, non–banks, savings and loans, brokers with CMAs, credit unions, financial holding companies, and more. Lists all major managers by function and formal title, includes their addresses and phone numbers. Also available on computer disk. Contact for information.

Thomson Bank Directory (Thomson Financial Information, P.O. Box 668, Skokie, IL 60076) $265, published every May and December. Provides details on U.S. and foreign banks.

Association of Reserve City Bankers Membership Directory (ARCB, 1710 Rhode Island Ave., NW, Suite 500, Washington, DC 20036; phone: 202/296–5709) free, available only to members, issued each August.

MR. BOFFO reprinted by permission. Tribune Media Services. Copyright ©1991.

Polk's Bank Directory: North American Edition (R. L. Polk & Co., P.O. Box 305100, Nashville, TN 37230-5100; phones: 800/827-2265, 615/889-3350) $256.50 plus $8.63 shipping for current edition, prepaid, published each spring and fall. Provides details and officers of banks in the U.S., Mexico, Canada, Central America, and the Caribbean.

Polk's Bank Directory: International Edition (R. L. Polk & Co., P.O. Box 305100, Nashville, TN 37230-5100; phones: 800/827-2265, 615/889-3350) $222.75 plus $6.08 shipping for current edition, prepaid, published at mid-year. Provides details and officers of banks outside North America as well as U.S. banks engaged in international banking.

American Savings Directory (McFadden Business Publications, 6195 Crooked Creek Rd., Norcross, GA 30092-9986; phones: 800/247-7376, 404/448-1011) $145, published each January. Covers savings and loan associations, major credit unions, mutual savings banks, and non-bank financial companies. Also available on computer disk. Contact for information.

State and Regional Directories (McFadden Business Publications, 6195 Crooked Creek Rd., Norcross, GA 30092-9986; phones: 800/247-7376, 404/448-1011) $35/each for all financial institutions in a single state, $12/each additional state; $25/each for all banks in a single state, $11/each additional state. These are customized financial references for only the state or states you want.

National Automated Clearinghouse Association Participant Directory (607 Herndon Pkwy., Suite 200, Herndon, VA 22070; phone: 703/742-9190) $100/nonmembers, $60/members, published twice a year.

Credit Union Executive Society Annual Membership Directory (Credit Union Executives Society, P.O. Box 14167, Madison, WI 53714; phones: 800/252-2664, 608/271-2664) free, available only to members, published annually.

National Association of Federal Credit Unions Membership Handbook (NAFCU, 3138 N. 10th St., Suite 300, Arlington, VA 22201; phone: 703/522-4770) free, available only to members, issued every October.

Financial Operation Association Directory (Credit Union Executives Society, P.O. Box 14167, Madison, WI 53714; phones: 800/252–2664, 608/271–2664) free, available only to members, published annually. Details on operations managers of credit unions.

Financial Marketing Association Directory (Credit Union Executives Society, P.O. Box 14167, Madison, WI 53714; phones: 800/252–2664, 608/271–2664) free, available only to members, issued annually. Details on marketing directors of credit unions.

Commercial Finance Association Roster of Members (CFA, 225 W. 34th St., Suite 1815, New York, NY 10122; phone: 212/594–3490) free, 46 pages. Lists firms involved in the commercial credit market. The addendum gives details on each firm.

Financial Executives Institute Membership Directory (FEI, 10 Madison Ave., Morristown, NJ 07960; phone: 201/898–4600) free, available only to members, $300/annual dues, published annually.

Insurance

Job openings

National Underwriter: Property & Casualty/Risk & Benefits Management (505 Gest St., Cincinnati, OH 45203; phone: 513/721–2140) weekly, $74/annual subscription (U.S.), $108/foreign. About 25 ads for property and casualty agents and brokers, risk managers, and insurance company executives appear under "Classified."

National Underwriter: Life & Health/Financial Services (505 Gest St., Cincinnati, OH 45203; phone: 513/721–2140) weekly, $69/annual subscription (U.S.), $90/foreign. "Classified" has about 25 ads for life and health agents and brokers, financial planners, and insurance company executives.

Business Insurance (Crain Communications, 740 N. Rush St., Chicago, IL 60611; phone: 800/992–9970) weekly, $80/annual subscription (U.S.), $118/Canada (surface mail), $185/Canada (air mail, $118/elsewhere (surface mail). About 20 job ads appear in the typical issue.

National Health Lawyers' Association Members Corner (NHLA, 1620 I St, NW, Suite 900, Washington, DC 20006; phone: 202/833–1100) monthly, $150/annual nonmember subscription, free/members. "Job Opportunities" lists six to ten vacancies for attorneys, risk managers, health care executives, and academicians.

Directories

Insurance Phone Book and Directory (U.S. Directory Service, 655 NW 128th St., Miami, FL 33168; phone: 305/769–1700) $59.95 plus $4/shipping, most recent edition 1991–92. Provides addresses and phone numbers (lots of toll-free numbers) for over 3,000 insurance companies throughout the U.S.

Insurance Field Directories (Insurance Field Company, P.O. Box 24244, Louisville, KY 40224; phone: 502/491–5857) $55/each state, issued annually. Directories are available for each of these states (publication date in parentheses): Kentucky (May), Louisiana (October), Mississippi (October), New Jersey (February), New York (December), North Carolina (August), South Carolina (August), Tennessee (June), north Texas (April), south Texas (April), and Virginia (September). Details the facilities and services of licensed property, liability, and life insurance companies in the state. The New York edition, for example, runs 512 pages.

Best's Insurance Reports, Property/Casualty Edition (A. M. Best Company, Ambest Road, Oldwick, NJ 08858–9988; phone: 201/439–2200) $480, annual. Vital information on 2,100 major U.S. property/casualty insurance companies.

Best's Insurance Reports, Life/Health Edition (A. M. Best Company, Ambest Road, Oldwick, NJ 08858–9988; phone: 201/439–2200) $480, annual. Vital information on 1,425 major U.S. life/health insurance companies.

Best's Insurance Reports, International Edition (A. M. Best Company, Ambest Road, Oldwick, NJ 08858–9988; phone: 201/439–2200) $365, includes spring and fall editions. Vital information on 800 major insurance companies in over 50 countries.

Advance Company Reports (A. M. Best Company, Ambest Road, Oldwick, NJ 08858-9988; phone: 201/439-2200) $15/single sheet report, two to 25 reports: $10/each. Each report contains most of the major data and significant narrative on individual insurance companies as it will appear later in *Best's Insurance Reports*.

Best's Agents Guide to Life Insurance Companies (A. M. Best Company, Ambest Road, Oldwick, NJ 08858-9988; phone: 201/439-2200) $60. Profiles 1,425 insurers.

Best's Directory of Recommended Insurance Adjusters (A. M. Best Company, Ambest Road, Oldwick, NJ 08858-9988; phone: 201/439-2200) $50, annual. Lists 1,200 U.S. and foreign adjusting offices that insurance companies recommend.

Best's Directory of Recommended Insurance Attorneys (A. M. Best Company, Ambest Road, Oldwick, NJ 08858-9988; phone: 201/439-2200) $60, annual. Lists 5,000 law firms that insurance companies recommend. Includes names of insurance company officials in legal and claims departments.

American Council of Life Insurance Directory (ACLI, 1001 Pennsylvania Ave., NW, Suite 500-S, Washington, DC 20004; phone: 202/624-2000) free, available only to members, issued every September. Lists member companies.

Casualty Actuarial Society Yearbook (CAS, 1100 N. Glebe, Suite 600, Arlington, VA 22201; phone: 703/276-3100) $20, annual.

The Society of Actuaries Yearbook (Society of Actuaries, P.O. Box 95668, Chicago, IL 60694; phone: 708/706-3500) $75/nonmembers, free/members, published each January.

American Academy of Actuaries Yearbook (American Academy of Actuaries, 1720 I St., NW, Washington, DC 20006; phone: 202/223-8196) $50/nonmembers, free/members, published each January.

Roster: National Association of Catastrophe Adjusters (NACA, P.O. Box 1128, Hilltop Lakes, TX 77871; phone: 409/855-2155) available only to members, $55/annual dues, released each March, 36 pages. Lists 260 members. Catastrophe adjusters work to adjust losses that arise from natural disasters and other catastrophes.

National Association of Independent Insurers Directory (NAII, 2600 River Rd., Des Plaines, IL 60018; phone: 708/297-7800) free, available only to members, published every spring and autumn.

Investments, pensions, securities

Job openings

Pensions and Investments (Crain Communications, 965 E. Jefferson Ave., Detroit, MI 48207; phone: 800/992-9970) biweekly, $135/annual subscription (U.S.), $156/Canada (surface mail), $190/Canada (air mail). "Professional Marketplace" carries ten to 15 ads for positions in the employment benefits field including management, marketing, sales, brokers, equity managers, and market analysts. Also includes business opportunities and "positions wanted."

Registered Representative (Plaza Communications, 18818 Teller Ave., Suite 280, Irvine, CA 92715; phone: 714/851-2220) monthly, $18/annual subscription (U.S.), $30/foreign. From 20 to 30 ads for securities salespeople appear in display ads and under "Classifieds."

Futures: The Magazine of Commodities and Options (219 Parkade, Cedar Falls, IA 50613; phone: 800/221-4353) monthly, $69/annual subscription. About six ads for commodity traders appear under "Classified."

Job service

AIMR Jobline (Association for Investment Management and Research, 5 Boar's Head Lane, Charlottesville, VA 22903; phone: 804/980-3682) free, available only to members. Members can call a 24-hour recording of investment positions in the U.S. and Canada which is updated every two weeks. They can then send their resume to the service with the code number for the job in which they are interested. The employer contacts the job candidate for an interview.

"Mr. Wayne's stock analyst is leaving now. He'll see you now, Mr. Fox."

Directories

AIMR Membership Directory (Association for Investment Management and Research, P.O. Box 3668, Charlottesville, VA 22901; phone: 804/977–5724) $150/nonmembers, free/members, published each October. Almost 1,000 pages, this directory lists certified financial advisors by state and local society along with an alphabetical index. Many of the 60+ societies which belong to AIMR publish newsletters with job vacancies as well as job opening bulletins. The job placement officer for each society is identified. Alternatively, you could contact AIMR for a free list of job placement chairpeople for these state and local societies.

Securities Industry Yearbook (Securities Industry Association, 120 Broadway, New York, NY 10271; phone: 212/608–1500) $100/nonmembers, $65/members, published each August. Provides details on each of the 600 member firms (investment banks, brokers, dealers, mutual fund companies, and firms active in all exchange markets, the over–the–counter market, and all phases of corporate and public finance) including department heads. Also included is a directory of major exchanges and selected entities and a guide to products and services.

Salary survey

Report on Office Salaries in the Securities Industry (Securities Industry Association, 120 Broadway, New York, NY 10271; phone: 212/608-1500) $1,400/nonmembers, $450-$675/members, $50/firms that participated, annual. Reports on weekly, monthly, and annual base salaries for 78 non-exempt administrative, secretarial, sales assistant, clerical and "back office" positions.

Real estate finance

Also see listings under "Financial institutions" in this chapter and see the "Real estate" chapter.

Job openings

Real Estate Finance Today (Mortgage Bankers Association of America, 1125 15th St., NW, Washington, DC 20005; phone: 202/861-6500) biweekly, $85/annual subscription. Ten positions in banking (financial officers, mortgages, sale consultants) appear under "Help Wanted."

Trusts & Estates (Communication Channels, Inc. 6255 Barfield Rd., Atlanta, GA 30328; phone: 404/256-9800) 13 issues/year, $66/annual subscription. Carries just one or two display ads in trust and estate management and marketing.

Directories

Directory of Trust Institutions (*Trusts & Estates*, Communication Channels, Inc. 6255 Barfield Rd., Atlanta, GA 30328; phone: 404/256-9800) $44.95/U.S., $64.95/foreign. This issue is included in the annual subscription to *Trusts & Estates*, $66/annual subscription.

Mortgage Insurance Companies of America Factbook and Membership Directory (MICA, 805 15th St., NW, Suite 1110, Washington, DC 20005; phone: 202/371-2899) contact for price, published in even-numbered years.

National Association of Real Estate Investment Trusts Membership Directory (NAREIT, 1129 20th St., NW, Washington, DC 20036; phone: 202/785-8717) $195/nonmembers, free to members, last issued May 1991, next edition in December 1992. Detailed information on over 500 NAREIT members including officers and advisors, trustees and directors, counsel, and auditor.

Salary survey

REIT Executive Compensation Survey (National Association of Real Estate Investment Trusts Membership Directory, 1129 20th St., NW, Washington, DC 20036; phone: 202/785-8717) $500/nonmembers, $300/members, free/participants in survey, issued biennually. Covers executive compensation within the real estate investment trust industry for the top five positions.

Chapter 16

Forestry and horticulture

Forestry

Also see the job sources in the chapters "Manufacturing," "Environment," and "Parks, recreation, and sports." The Government Job Finder contains an extensive set of job sources in forestry and horticulture, many of which include private sector in addition to government vacancies.

Job openings

American Forests (American Forestry Association, 1516 P St., NW, Washington, DC 20005; phone: 202/667-3300) bimonthly, $24/annual subscription. Less than five job openings appear in the typical issue under "The Green Page." "Situations Wanted" also listed.

The Northern Logger & Timber Processor (North East Loggers Association, P.O. Box 69, Old Forge, NY 13420; phone: 315/369-3078) monthly, $10/annual subscription. "Wood Industries Marketplace" features ten to 12 job ads for foresters, sawyers, woods workers, mechanics, kiln operators, timber buyers, academics, and sales representatives.

Southern Lumberman (P.O. Box 681629, Franklin, IN 37068; phone: 615/791–1961) monthly, $16/annual subscription. Three to five job ads for foresters, sawyers, engineers, lumber graders, and sales representatives are in the "Classifieds—Help Wanted."

Timber Harvesting (Hatton–Brown Publishers, 225 Hanrick St., Montgomery, AL 36104; phone: 205/834–1170) monthly, $24/annual subscription (U.S.), $40/Canada. One to ten job ads for loggers, crew leaders, buyers, and management are under "THExchange." Also includes "Position Wanted" advertising.

Journal of Arborculture (International Society of Arborculture, P.O. Box 908, Urbana, IL 61801; phone: 217/328–2032) monthly, free/members only. Two to four ads for arborists are listed under "Opportunities."

Forest Products Journal (Forest Product Research Society, 2801 Marshall Ct., Madison, WI 53705; 608/231–1361) ten issues/year, $115/annual nonmember subscription, included in dues. Three to six positions are listed under "Employment Referral Service."

Journal of the National Technical Association (Black Collegiate Services, Inc., 1240 S. Broad St., New Orleans, LA 70125; phone: 504/821–5694) quarterly, $30/annual subscription, $35/foreign. Ten or more vacancies appear in display ads and under "Job Opportunities Bulletin." Most positions are for health physicists, biologists, and environmental scientists.

Directories

The Northern Logger & Timber Processor (North East Loggers Association, P.O. Box 69, Old Forge, NY 13420; phone: 315/369-3078) $2 plus shipping. Each year, the December issue includes a directory of logging operations in the northeastern and Great Lakes states.

International Society of Arborculture Member Directory (ISA, P.O. Box 908, Urbana, IL 61801; phone: 217/328-2032) contact for details.

American Society of Consulting Arborists Membership Directory (ASCA, 3895 Upham St., Suite 12, Wheat Ridge, CO 80033; phone: 303/420-9554) free, annual, 40 pages. A state-by-state listing of arborist consultants.

The FPRS Membership Directory (Forest Product Research Society, 2801 Marshall Ct., Madison, WI 53705; 608/231-1361) available only to members, free/members, published annually.

Grounds and horticulture

Job openings

AABGA Newsletter (American Association of Botanical Gardens and Arboreta, 786 Church Rd., Wayne, PA 19087; phone: 215/688-1120) monthly, available only to members; annual dues: $50, $25/students. About 15 positions in public horticulture ranging from gardener to director appear under "Positions Available."

Internship Directory (American Association of Botanical Gardens and Arboreta, 786 Church Rd., Wayne, PA 19087; phone: 215/688-1120) $4/nonmember, $3/member, published each October. This is a very extensive state-by-state listing of summer internships available in public horticulture and private estates.

Landscape Management (Edgell Communications, 1 E. First St., Duluth, MN 55802; phone: 800/346-0085) monthly, $30/annual subscription. Includes a dozen job ads for labor, estimating, management, design, and sales positions with lawn care and landscaping firms.

SAF Business News of the Floral Industry (Society of American Florists, 1601 Duke St., Alexandria, VA 22314; phone: 800/433-5612, 800/336-4743) monthly, $24/annual nonmember subscription, free/members. Five to seven jobs for growers, designers, and sales are under "Classified."

Horticulture: The Magazine of American Gardening (P.O. Box 53879, Boulder, CO 80321; phone: 617/482-5600) ten issues/year, $24/annual subscription (U.S.), $30/foreign. Two job openings and about five business opportunities are in the "Classified" section.

The Horticulturist (American Horticultural Society, 7931 East Boulevard Dr., Alexandria, VA 22308; phone: 800/777-7931) bimonthly, free/members only. About three ads for horticulturists are in the "Classifieds."

Grounds Maintenance (Intertec Publishing, 9221 Quivira Rd., Overland Park, KS 66215; phone: 913/888-4664) monthly, $30/annual subscription, free to qualified professionals. Ten to 20 openings for positions ranging from landscapers to management are advertised under "Classified—Help Wanted."

Grounds Management Forum (Professional Grounds Management Society, 10402 Ridgeland Rd., Suite 4, Cockeysville, MD 21030; phone: 301/667-1833) monthly, $95/annual subscription, available only to members. Ads for job openings are rare. However, even nonmembers can submit a brief one or two paragraph "Positions Wanted" ad for grounds management and horticulture positions. These ads can be "blind" ads where your name is replaced by a box number to which an interested employer can write for more information.

Garden Supply Retailer (Chilton Publishing, Chilton Way, Radnor, PA 19089; phone: 215/964-4000) ten issues/year, $30/annual subscription. One or two ads for sales or manufacturers' representatives are under "Help Wanted."

Nursery Retailer (Brentwood Publications, 3023 Eastland Blvd., Clearwater, Fl 34621; phone: 813/796-3877) contact for price. Two or three job ads are in the "Classifieds," but we couldn't get any details about the magazine, or about any of the other magazines they publish in the horticultural field, because they said they did not wish to be troubled with giving us the information we requested. Maybe they'd change their minds if nobody wanted to be troubled with subscribing to their magazines. (Meow!)

Job services

Jobs Hotline (American Association of Botanical Gardens and Arboreta, 786 Church Rd., Wayne, PA 19087; phone: 215/688-1120) free. Call 215/688-9127 weekdays 5 p.m. to 8 a.m. (eastern time) and 24 hours on weekends for a tape recording that lists four to eight jobs in horticulture.

Florapersonnel (2180 W. State Rd. 434, Suite 6152, Longwood, FL 32779-5008; phone: 407/682-5151) free. The job seeker completes Florapersonnel's form and submits it along with her resume. Resumes are kept on file indefinitely. When a match is made, Florapersonnel contacts the job seeker and, if the job seeker gives the okay, Florapersonnel gives her name and resume to the potential employer who then contacts the employer. (Normally, we don't list recruiters in this book, but the horticulture field has so few job sources that it seems essential to include this listing.) Job range from greenhouse growers to directors. Includes nursery, landscape, and irrigation.

Informal Job–Matching Service (American Horticultural Society, 7931 East Boulevard Dr., Alexandria, VA 22308; phone: 800/777-7931) free/members only. A member submits his resume which is sent to employers that have job openings for which the member qualifies. The employer is responsible for contacting the job candidate. Resumes are kept on file indefinitely.

Directories

AABGA Membership Directory (American Association of Botanical Gardens and Arboreta, 786 Church Rd., Wayne, PA 19087; phone: 215/688-1120) available to members, free/members: annual dues: $50, $25/students. Lists institutional members of AABGA

The Official Museum Directory and Products and Services Guide (National Register Publishing Company, 3004 Glenview Rd., Wilmette, IL 60091; phones: 800/323-6772, 708/441-2210) $194,

$112/members of the American Association of Museums, plus $8.25 shipping, annual. Provides details on 6,700 U.S. institutions including arboreta.

Who's Who in Landscape Contracting (Associated Landscape Contractors of America (405 N. Washington St., Falls Church, VA 22046; phones: 800/395-2522, 703/241-4004) $25/nonmembers, $3/members, published each April.

Professional Plant Growers Association Membership Directory (PPGA, P.O. Box 27517, Lansing, MI 48909; phone: 517/694-7700) free/members only, issued each April.

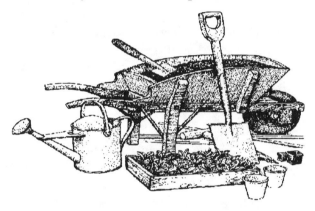

Professional Grounds Management Society Membership Directory (PGMS, 10402 Ridgeland, Suite 4, Cockeysville, MD 21030; phone: 301/667-1833) $30/nonmembers, free/members, annual. Also available on labels.

National Bark and Soil Producers Association Membership Directory (NBSPA, 13542 Union Village Cr., Clifton, VA 22024; phone: 703/830-5367) free/members only, annual. Lists member companies that manufacture mulch.

National Roadside Vegetation Management Association Membership Directory (NRVMA, 309 Center Hill Rd., Centerville, DE 19807; phone: 302/655-9993) free/members only, annual.

Grounds Maintenance Buyers' Guide (Intertec Publishing, 9221 Quivira Rd., Overland Park, KS 66215; phone: 913/888-4664) $5 plus shipping. This is the December issue of *Grounds Maintenance* described above under ''Job openings.'' It includes grounds equipment, landscape accessories and materials, seed and sod, horticultural chemicals and plant foods, maintenance supplies and services, and addresses of manufacturers, growers, and suppliers.

Who's Who in the Nursery Industry (American Association of Nurserymen, 1250 I St., NW, Suite 500, Washington, DC 20005; phone: 202/789–2900) $150/nonmembers, free/members, issued every September. Includes member companies by state.

National Lawn and Garden Distributors Association Membership Directory (1900 Arch St., Philadelphia, PA 19103; phone: 215/564–3484) $100/nonmembers, free/members, released each September. Includes product lines.

Members of the Southwest Turfgrass Association (STA, c/o Lynn Ellen Doxon, Extension Horticulture Specialist, 9301 Indian School Rd., NE, Albuquerque, NM 87112; phone: 505/293–1443) free/members only, issued each October.

Salary survey

Grounds Maintenance Salary Survey (Intertec Publishing, 9221 Quivira Rd., Overland Park, KS 66215; phone: 913/888–4664) $5 plus shipping. This is the October issue of *Grounds Maintenance* described above under "Job openings." It includes a salary survey of the landscaping industry.

Landscape architecture

Job openings

Landscape Architecture (American Society of Landscape Architects, 4401 Connecticut Ave., NW, Washington, DC 20008–2302; phone: 202/686–2752) bimonthly; $38/annual subscription, $28/students (U.S.), elsewhere: $65/surface mail, $117/air mail. Jobs listed under "Buyers Guide." Few job ads.

Also see the Employment Referral Service of the Golf Course Superintendents Association of America listed under "Parks and recreation" in the "Sports, parks, and recreation" chapter.

Directory

ASLA Membership Handbook (American Society of Landscape Architects, 4401 Connecticut Ave., NW, Washington, DC 20008–2302; phone: 202/686–2752) $29.95/nonmember individuals, $40/institutions, $12.50/libraries, free/members, published annually. Includes national listing of landscape architecture firms.

Chapter 17

Health care

Reminder: *To find the job sources that will benefit you the most, start with the listings under "Health care in general" which cover more than one specialty. Then read the listings in your specialty as well as those under any section which is cross-referenced. Remember to also consult the Index to find additional job sources which are not where you would intuitively expect them to be located in this book.*

*Some of the job sources described in this chapter include a few positions in academia and research. For more job sources in academia and research, see the **Non-Profits' Job Finder.***

Health care in general

Job openings

American Journal of Medicine (Cahners Publishing Company, P.O. Box 173377, Denver, CO 80217-3377; phones: 800/327-4511, 303/388-4511) 23 issues/year, $19.90/annual subscription first year, $57/second year, $9.95/students. There are about ten display ads for physicians and nurses at the beginning and end of the magazine.

Southern Medical Journal (35 Lakeshore Dr., Birmingham, AL 35219–0088; phones: 800/423–4992, 205/945–1840) monthly, $45/annual subscription. The "Classifieds" tend to carry about ten job ads for everything in medicine.

National Hospital Job Guide (Outcalt & Associates, P.O. Box 14153, Gainesville, FL 32604; phones: 800/874–7777, 904/373–2200) $15, annual, 144 pages. In addition to 40 pages of display ads for job openings, there are listings for over 400 hospitals actively recruiting health care professionals.

Hospitals (American Hospital Association, 737 N. Michigan Ave., Chicago, IL 60611; phones: 800/621–6902, 312/440–6836) bimonthly, $50/annual nonmember subscription. From five to 15 positions, mostly for hospital administrators, but also for a handful of maintenance and patient care positions (doctors, nurses, etc.) appear under "Classified."

Group Practice Journal (American Group Practice Association, 1422 Duke St., Alexandria, VA 22314) bimonthly, $65/annual nonmember subscription, free/members. "Professional Opportunity" generally runs ads for five to ten physician and administrative positions with medical centers and health maintenance organizations (HMOs).

American Review of Respiratory Disease (American Lung Association, 1740 Broadway, New York, NY 10019; phone: 212/315–8700) monthly, $130/annual nonmember subscription, free/members. "Professional Recruitment" is filled with around 30 job openings in all facets of medicine.

Anesthesiology (J. B. Lippincott Company, Downville Pike, Route 3, Box 20–B, Hagerstown, MD 21740; phones: 800/638–3030, 215/238–4206) monthly, $70/annual subscription, $120/foreign. About 200 positions for anesthesiologists and nurses appear under "Classifieds."

Journal of Nuclear Medicine (Society of Nuclear Medicine, 136 Madison Ave., New York, NY 10016; phone: 212/889–0717) monthly, $120/annual nonmember subscription, $130/Canada, $160/elsewhere; included in membership package. Twenty to 25 positions for physicians, technologists, and radiologists are listed.

The American Journal of Infection Control (Mosby Year Book, Journal Subscription Services, 11830 Westline Industrial Dr., St. Louis, MO 63146; phones: 800/325-4177, ext. 4351, 314/872-8370, ext. 4351) bimonthly, $34/annual subscription (U.S.), $20/student (U.S.), $117.88/Canada, $112/elsewhere. Two or three display ads are printed for epidemiologists and clinical instructors in infection control.

Journal of Allied Health (American Society of Allied Health Professions (1101 Connecticut Ave., NW, Suite 700, Washington, DC 20036; phone: 202/857-1150) quarterly, $65/annual nonmember subscription, free/members. Two or three job ads for nursing, pharmacy, dentistry, physical/occupational therapy, medical record administration, medical technicians, or home care appear under "Advertisements and Notices."

Healthcare Forum Journal (The Healthcare Forum, 830 Market St., San Francisco, CA 94102; phone: 415/421-8810) bimonthly, $35/annual subscription (U.S.), $38/Canada and Mexico, $55/elsewhere. Jobs listed under "Classified." Four or five job ads per issue.

Modern Healthcare (Crain Communications, 740 N. Rush St., Chicago, IL 60611; phone: 312/649-5350) weekly, $110/year. Jobs listed under "People/Career Opportunities." Five or six job ads per issue.

Cancer (J. B. Lippincott Company, Downville Pike, Route 3, Box 20-B, Hagerstown, MD 21740; phones: 800/638-3030, 215/238-4206) semimonthly, $95/annual subscription (U.S.), $165/foreign. "Classifieds" feature ten to 15 positions in all aspects of medicine.

FASA Update (Federated Ambulatory Surgery Association, 700 N. Fairfax St., Suite 520, Alexandria, VA 22314; phone: 703/836-8808) bimonthly, $50/annual nonmember subscription, free/members. Under "Classifieds Ads—Positions Available" you'll find around ten openings for physicians, administrators, and registered nurses.

Journal of Burn Care & Rehabilitation (Mosby Year Book, Journal Subscription Services, 11830 Westline Industrial Dr., St. Louis, MO 63146; phones: 800/325-4177, ext. 4351, 314/872-8370, ext. 4351) bimonthly, $41/annual subscription (U.S.), $23/student (U.S.), $54.87/Canada, $52/elsewhere. About 17 positions for physicians and nurses appear in display ads.

Fertility and Sterility (American Fertility Society, 2140 11th Ave., South, Suite 200, Birmingham, AL 35202-2800; phone: 205/933-8494) monthly, $100/annual nonmember subscription. About 12 to 15 positions for reproductive health doctors, nurses, and scientists appear under "Classified Announcements."

Heart & Lung: The Journal of Critical Care (Mosby Year Book, Journal Subscription Services, 11830 Westline Industrial Dr., St. Louis, MO 63146; phones: 800/325-4177, ext. 4351, 314/872-8370, ext. 4351) bimonthly, $36/annual subscription (U.S.), $19/student (U.S.), $50.52/Canada, $48/elsewhere. About ten vacancies are advertised in display ads and under "Professional Opportunities."

Veterinary and Human Toxicology (c/o Comparative Toxicology Laboratories, Kansas State University, Manhattan, KS 66506-5606; phone: 913/532-4334) bimonthly, $40/annual subscription (U.S.), $46/Canada, $50/elsewhere. Forty to 50 openings for physicians, nurses, pharmacists, toxicologists, biologists, and health professionals appear under "Job Opportunities." A membership directory of several related organizations is published once a year in this journal.

Laboratory Medicine (American Society of Pathologists, 2100 W. Harrison St., Chicago, IL 60612; phone: 312/738-1336) monthly, $40/annual nonmember subscription (U.S.), $55/foreign, free/members. About 45 openings for pathologists, technicians, and other laboratory-related positions are listed under "Professional Exchange."

American Journal of Pathology (J. B. Lippincott Company, Downville Pike, Route 3, Box 20-B, Hagerstown, MD 21740; phones: 800/638-3030, 215/238-4206) monthly, $145/annual subscription (U.S.), $205/foreign. Ten to 12 "Classifieds" appear for pathologists in government and private practice.

Archives of Pathology & Laboratory Medicine (American Medical Association, 515 N. State St., Chicago, IL 60610; phone: 312/464-0183) $72/annual nonmember subscription (U.S.), $87/foreign. About ten job ads for pathologists including business opportunities and residencies, appear under "Classified Advertising."

CAP Today (College of American Pathologists, 325 Waukegan Rd., Northfield, IL 60093; phone: 708/446-8800) monthly, $15/annual nonmember subscription, free/members. Two or three ads for pathologists and executive search firms appear under "Classifieds."

CLAS Newsletter (Clinical Ligand Assay Society, 3139 S. Wayne Rd., Wayne, MI 48184; phone: 313/722-6290) bimonthly, free, available only to members. Currently only a few job ads appear under "Positions Open," but the CLAS expects many more job ads in 1992. Many of these positions are in large corporations that make diagnostic reagents.

Arthritis & Rheumatism (J. B. Lippincott Company, Downville Pike, Route 3, Box 20-B, Hagerstown, MD 21740; phones: 800/638-3030, 215/238-4206) monthly, $90/annual subscription (U.S.), $100/foreign. The "Classifieds" feature 40 to 50 job openings.

Career Services Bulletin (American College of Sports Medicine, 401 W. Michigan St., Indianapolis, IN 46202-3233; phone: 317/637-9200) monthly, $20/annual nonmember subscription, $10/members. Around 50 positions, including doctors and nurses, in sports medicine and exercise science appear throughout.

HMO Practice (J. B. Lippincott Company, Downville Pike, Route 3, Box 20-B, Hagerstown, MD 21740; phones: 800/638-3030, 215/238-4206) monthly, $50/annual subscription (U.S.), $28/students, $65/foreign. Five job openings in all aspects of medicine and administration are advertised under "Classifieds."

The Neuroscience Newsletter (Society for Neuroscience, 11 Dupont Cr., NW, Suite 500, Washington, DC 20036; phone: 202/462-6688) bimonthly, $50/annual nonmember subscription, free/members. About 50 positions appear under "Positions Available."

Investigative Radiology (J. B. Lippincott Company, Downville Pike, Route 3, Box 20-B, Hagerstown, MD 21740; phones: 800/638-3030, 215/238-4206) monthly, $110/annual subscription (U.S.), $40/students, $140/foreign. You'll find around 40 job openings under "Classifieds."

Radiology Today (SLACK, Inc., 6900 Grove Rd., Thorofare, NJ 08086-9447; phones: 800/257-8290, 609/848-1000) monthly, $110/annual subscription (U.S.), $128/Canada, $146/elsewhere. Around 10 job openings and practices for sale appear under "Classified Marketplace." Includes both physician and technical positions.

Nationwide Jobs in Dietetics (P.O. Box 3537, Santa Monica, CA 90408-3537; phone: 213/453-5375) monthly, $72/annual subscription, $36/four-month subscription, $24/two-month subscription. About 300 dietitian and nutritionist jobs are announced in a typical issue. Your first issue will include a sheet that names additional sources of private sector and government positions.

Journal of the American Dietetic Association (ADA, 216 W. Jackson Blvd., Chicago, IL 60606; phone: 312/899-0040) monthly, $90/nonmember annual subscription, included in dues. About 40 ads for dietitians appear under "Classified Advertising" each issue.

American Journal of Clinical Nutrition (American Society for Clinical Nutrition, c/o Williams & Wilkins, 428 E. Preston St., Baltimore, MD 21202; phone: 301/528-4105) monthly, $80/annual nonmember subscription, $40/members. Four to six job ads appear on the front and back pages.

Journal of Perentology (25 Van Zant St., East Norwalk, CT 06855; phone: 203/838-4400) quarterly, $60/annual subscription (U.S.), $80/foreign. The "Classified" section has around ten positions for nutritionists, perentologists (prenatal), and nurses.

California Jobs in Dietetics (P.O. Box 3537, Santa Monica, CA 90408-3537; phone: 213/453-5375) biweekly, $48/six-issue subscription. Around 230 dietitian and nutritionist jobs are advertised in a typical issue. Your first issue will include a sheet that names additional sources of private sector and government positions in California and nationally.

American Industrial Hygiene Association Journal (AIHA, 345 White Pond Dr., Akron, OH 44320; phone: 216/873-2442) monthly, $75/annual nonmember subscription (U.S.), $90/foreign, free/members. "Classified/Employment Advertising" features 15 to 20 openings for industrial hygienists, occupational health scientists, ergonomists, safety engineers, and health and safety supervisors.

The Synergist (American Industrial Hygiene Association, 345 White Pond Dr., Akron, OH 44320; phone: 216/873-2442) monthly, free (U.S.), $10/foreign. Positions for industrial hygienists and environmental and health specialists appear under "Classified Ads."

Journal of Environmental Health (National Environmental Health Association, Suite 970, South Tower, 720 S. Colorado Blvd., Denver, CO 80222; phone: 303/756-9090) bimonthly, $40/nonmember annual subscription, included in dues ($50/year, $15/students). Jobs listed under "Opportunities." Five to ten job ads appear in the typical issue for sanitarians, toxicologists, health planners, and related positions.

AIUM Reporter (American Institute of Ultrasound in Medicine, 11200 Rockville Pike, Suite 205, Rockville, MD 20852-3139) monthly, $85/non-physicians annual subscription, $140/physicians. Positions advertised include physicians, sonographers, and technicians. Includes "Positions Wanted."

Pressure (Undersea and Hyperbaric Medical Society, 9650 Rockville Pike, Bethesda, MD 20814; phone: 301/571-1818) bimonthly, $25/annual nonmember subscription, free/members. Two or three openings for hyperbaric technicians, nurses, and doctors are listed under "Jobs/Help Wanted."

OAA News (Opticians Association of America, P.O. Box 10110, Fairfax, VA 22030-8010; phone: 703/691-8355) seven issues/year, free, available only to members. As of this writing, *OAA News* was just starting to include job announcements.

American Journal of Health Promotion (1812 S. Rochester Rd., Rochester Hills, MI 48307-3532; phone: 313/650-9600) bimonthly, $49.50/annual subscription. About two positions for wellness programs administrators and postdoctoral research fellowships appear under "Job Opportunities."

National Health Lawyers' Association Members Corner (NHLA, 1620 I St., NW, Suite 900, Washington, DC 20006; phone: 202/833-1100) monthly, $150/annual nonmember subscription, free/members. "Job Opportunities" lists six to ten vacancies for attorneys, risk managers, health care executives and academicians.

MLA News (Medical Library Association, 6 N. Michigan Ave., Suite 300, Chicago, IL 60602; phone: 312/419-9094) ten issues/year, $50/nonmember annual subscription, included in dues. From 15 to 20 ads appear in the "Classifieds" for librarian posts in the health sciences.

Job services

CU Career Connection (University of Colorado, Campus Box 133, Boulder, CO 80309-0133; phone: 303/492-4127) $20/two-month fee entitles you to a "passcode" which unlocks this job hotline. You need a touch-tone phone to call and request the health care field and the geographic area for which you want to hear job openings. The hotline is turned off Monday through Friday, 2 to 4 p.m. for daily updating. This service has a very extensive listing of health care vacancies.

Health Personnel Options Traveling Service (Health Personnel Options Corporation, 2221 University Ave., SE, Suite 140, Minneapolis, MN 55414; phones: 800/441-0357, 612/379-0408) no charge to job candidates. This "job-matching service" places nurses and allied health professionals (everything except physicians) in positions for four to 26 weeks. You must complete several forms and also submit a copy of your credentials, certification or registration, and any state licenses.

Health Personnel Options Supplemental Staffing Service (Health Personnel Options Corporation, 2221 University Ave., SE, Suite 140, Minneapolis, MN 55414; phones: 800/441-0357, 612/379-0408) no charge to job candidates. This "job-matching service" places nurses and allied health professionals (everything except physicians) in positions for short-term positions of as little as one day. You must complete several forms and also submit a copy of your credentials, certification or registration, and any state licenses.

Jobs for Dietitians Job Advice Hotline (P.O. Box 3537, Santa Monica, CA 90408–3537; phone: 213/453–5375) available only to subscribers to either the national or California edition of *Jobs for Dietitians* described above under "Job openings." Hotline number is given in the newsletter.

National Hospice Organization Job Bank (NHO, 1901 N. Moore St., Suite 901, Arlington, VA 22209; phone: 703/243–5900) free. Call 703/243–4348 24–hours a day to hear a recording that briefly describes about 30 positions in hospices: administrative, nursing, social workers, spiritual care, etc. You pay only regular long distance phone rates for this job hotline which is updated weekly.

AIHA Employment Service (American Industrial Hygiene Association, 345 White Pond Dr., Akron, OH 44320; phone: 216/873–2442) $100/nonmember six–month fee, $30/members. Job candidates are mailed a monthly listing of job openings. They contact the employer directly. Positions include industrial hygienists, occupational health scientists, ergonomists, safety engineers, and health and safety supervisors.

Safety and Industrial Hygiene Recruiting (Safety Recruiting Specialist, Southern Management Registry, P.O. Box 35036, Charlotte, NC 28235; phone: 704/372–7640) free. Submit resume to this nationwide executive search firm. The firm contacts a registrant when an employer is interested. Resumes are kept on file as long as applicant requests. Includes junior level through top–level professional positions.

Position Placement Service (American Fertility Society, 2140 11th Ave., South, Suite 200, Birmingham, AL 35202–2800; phone: 205/933–8494) $20/annual fee. You submit a resume which is kept on file for 12 months. Every three months, a list of about 80 job openings in reproductive endocrinology, gynecology, embryology, andrology, and for laboratory technicians and nurses is mailed to you. At the same time, resumes of job seekers registered with this service are sent to employers. Interviewing can be conducted at the AFS's annual meeting.

AIUM Placement Referral Service (American Institute of Ultrasound in Medicine, 11200 Rockville Pike, Suite 205, Rockville, MD 20852-3139) $60/nonmembers, $10/members. You fill out the ''Applicant Data Form'' and return it with ten copies of your resume. Every week for six months, AIUM will notify you how many of your resumes were sent to potential employers. Positions include physicians, sonographers, and technicians.

Directories

AHA Guide to the Health Care Field (American Hospital Association, ATTEN: AHA Services, P.O. Box 92683, Chicago, IL 60675-2683; phone: 800/242-2626) $195/nonmembers, $70/members, annual. Provides details on hospitals, health care systems, health care organizations, agencies, and providers. Also available on computer disk, $2000/nonmembers, $1800/members.

AHA Directory of Health Care Professionals (American Hospital Association, ATTEN: AHA Services, P.O. Box 92683, Chicago, IL 60675-2683; phone: 800/242-2626) $289/nonmembers, $119/members, annual.

Hospital Phone Book (U.S. Directory Service, 655 NW 128th St., Miami, FL 33168; phone: 305/769-1700) $47.95 plus $4 shipping. Information on over 7,940 government and private hospitals in the U.S. Most recent edition, 1991.

U.S. Medical Directory (U.S. Directory Service, 655 NW 128th St., Miami, FL 33168; phone: 305/769-1700) $150 plus $5 shipping. Over 1,000 pages of information on doctors, hospitals, nursing facilities, medical laboratories, and medical libraries. Most recent edition, 1990.

Billiam's Hospital Blue Book (Billiam Publishing Company, 2100 Powers Ferry Rd., Atlanta, GA 30339; phone: 404/955-5656) $99.50, released each May. Extensive listings of hospitals, services, and top employees.

Directory of Hospital Personnel (Medical Device Register, 655 Washington Blvd., Stamford, CT 06901) $295, published each December. Lists over 110,000 healthcare professionals.

Listing of Children's Hospitals (National Association of Children's Hospitals and Related Institutions, 401 Wythe St., Alexandria, VA 22314; 703/684-1355) $50/nonmembers, $10/members, released each November.

Blue Book Digest of HMOs (National Association of Employers on Health Care Action, P.O. Box 220, Key Biscayne, FL 33149; phone: 305/361-2810) $59.50/nonmembers, free/members, issued each August.

Federation of American Health Systems Directory (FAHS, 1405 N. Pierce St., Suite 311, Little Rock, AR 72207; phone: 501/661-9555) $60/nonmembers, free/members, published each December. Lists details, by state, on investor-owned hospitals, residential treatment facilities and centers, hospital management companies, and health systems. Includes key top personnel and specialties.

American Group Practice Association Directory (AGPA, 1422 Duke St., Alexandria, VA 22314) $125/nonmembers, free/members.

American Lung Association Membership Roster (ALA, 1740 Broadway, New York, NY 10019; phone: 212/315-8700) free/members, published in even-numbered years.

American Osteopathic Hospital Association Membership Directory (AOHA, 1454 Duke St., Alexandria, VA 22314; phone: 703/684-7700) $125/nonmembers, free/members, annual, 60 pages. Lists information on over 200 osteopathic hospitals including their CEOs, and state osteopathic hospital associations.

Clinical Ligand Assay Society Membership Directory (CLAS, 3139 S. Wayne Rd., Wayne, MI 48184; phone: 313/722-6290) $200/nonmembers, free/members, published in odd-numbered years. This is a specialty within pathology that deals with blood diseases.

American Society of Allied Health Professions Membership and Resource Directory (ASAHP, 1101 Connecticut Ave., NW, Suite 700, Washington, DC 20036; phone: 202/857-1150) available only to members, annual. Covers allied health professions—everything except physicians.

Federated Ambulatory Surgery Association Membership Directory (FASA, 700 N. Fairfax St., Suite 520, Alexandria, VA 22314; phone: 703/836–8808) free, available only to members, released annually.

American Industrial Health Council Membership Directory (AIHC, 1330 Connecticut Ave., NW, Suite 300, Washington, DC 20036; phone: 202/659–0060) free, available only to members, issued each spring.

Health Industry Manufacturers Association Membership Directory (HIMA, 1030 15th St., NW, Suite 1100, Washington, DC 20005; phone: 202/452–8240) free, available only to members, published annually. Includes contact names at manufacturers of health care items.

The Membership Directory (Health Industry Distributors Association, 225 Reinekers Ln., Suite 650, Alexandria, VA 22314; phone: 202/452–8240) $35, annual. Provides details on distributors of medical products.

New Careers: A Directory of Jobs and Internships in Technology and Society (Student Pugwash USA, 1638 R St., NW, Suite 32, Washington, DC 20009; phone: 202/328–6555) $18, $10/students (add $3 shipping). Offers full details on where and how to apply for internships and entry–level jobs in health care and related fields. Published in even–numbered years.

Encyclopedia of Medical Organizations and Agencies (Gale Research, Inc., 835 Penobscot Bldg., Detroit. MI 48226–4094; phone: 800/877–4253) $195, last published 1990, 1,079 pages. Provides information on 11,250 major public and private agencies in medicine and related fields.

Association of Academic Health Centers Directory (AAHC, 1400 16th St., NW, Washington, DC 20036; phone: 202/265–9600) $10/nonmembers, free/members, issued each January.

Directory of the Medical Library Association (MLA, 6 N. Michigan Ave., Suite 300, Chicago, IL 60602; phone: 312/419–9094) $42.75/nonmembers, free/members, published each October.

Salary surveys

Hospital Salary Survey Report (Hospital Compensation Service, 69 Minnehaha Blvd., Oakland, NJ 07436; phone: 201/405-0075) $190 prepaid, annual. Reports on salary and bonus payments, perquisites, and other data for over 120 job titles in management and administration, nursing, rehabilitation and mental health, radiology, laboratory, medical records and library, dietary, pharmacy, and technical. Data is reported both nationally and for nine regions.

Twenty-Eight Allied Health Careers (American Medical Association, P.O. Box 2964, Milwaukee, WI 53201-2964; phone: 800/621-8335) free/members, nonmembers can receive this item only if they purchase the *Allied Health Education Directory* for $36 (then this item is included free if you request it), published annually. Includes starting salaries and required education for many physician-support professions.

Dentistry

Job openings

Journal of the American Dental Association (ADA, 211 E. Chicago Ave., Chicago, IL 60611; phone: 312/440-2500) monthly, $50/annual nonmember subscription (U.S.), $70/foreign, free/members. Between 70 and 100 openings for dentists and practices for sale appear under "Opportunities Available" and other headings in the classifieds section.

Journal of Dentistry for Children (American Society of Dentistry for Children, 211 E. Chicago Ave., Chicago, IL 60611; phone: 312/943-1244) bimonthly, $65/annual nonmember subscription (U.S.), $75/foreign, free/members. About 11 positions and practices for sale appear under "Opportunities for Pedodontists." Also "positions wanted."

Trends and Techniques (National Association of Dental Laboratories, 3801 Mt. Vernon Ave., Alexandria, VA 22305; phone: 703/683-5263) ten issues/year, $40/annual nonmember subscrip-

tion (U.S. and Canada), $50/elsewhere, free/members. The "Classifieds" contain 15 to 20 openings for dental laboratory technicians, waxers, and ceramacists.

Proofs: The Magazine of Dental Sales (PennWell Publishing, P.O. Box 1260, Tulsa, OK 74101; phones: 800/331–4436, 918/835–3161) ten issues/year, $50/annual nonmember subscription, $15/members. Under "Want Ads" you'll find about 15 ads for manufacturers' reps and salespersons.

Journal of Dental Hygiene (American Dental Hygienists Association, 444 N. Michigan Ave., Suite 3400, Chicago, IL 60611; phone: 312/440–8900) nine issues/year, $40/annual nonmember subscription (U.S.), $55/foreign, free/members. About seven positions appear under "Classifieds."

Journal of Prosthetic Dentistry (Mosby Year Book, Journal Subscription Services, 11830 Westline Industrial Dr., St. Louis, MO 63146; phones: 800/325–4177, ext. 4351, 314/872–8370, ext. 4351) monthly, $71/annual subscription (U.S.), $48/student (U.S.), $100.97/Canada, $96/elsewhere. A handful of display ads for prosthetic dentists appear throughout.

Directories

International Association for Orthodontics Membership Directory and Referral Guide (IAO, 211 E. Chicago Ave., Suite 950, Chicago, IL 60611; phone: 312/642–2602) $15, annual.

Buyers' Guide and Manufacturers Directory (PennWell Publishing, P.O. Box 1260, Tulsa, OK 74101; phones: 800/331–4436, 918/835–3161) $15, published as the January issue of *Proofs: The Magazine of Dental Sales* described above under "Job openings."

Salary survey

Economic Conditions Survey (National Association of Dental Laboratories, 3801 Mt. Vernon Ave., Alexandria, VA 22305; phone: 703/683–5263) $25/nonmembers, free/members, last issued in June 1990. Reports on salaries for laboratory dental employees.

Doctors

Job openings

New England Journal of Medicine (Massachusetts Medical Society, 10 Shattuck St., Boston, MA 02115-6094; phone: 617/893–3800) weekly, $89/annual subscription. From 300 to 500 physician positions are advertised in the "Classifieds" section and in display ads throughout the magazine.

JAMA: The Journal of the American Medical Association (American Medical Association, Subscription Dept., 515 N. State St., Chicago, IL 60610; phone: 312/464–0183) weekly, $69/annual nonmember subscription, $86/foreign (surface mail), $126/foreign (air mail), free/members. "Classified Advertising" offers openings for 275 to 325 physicians of all types.

American Family Physician (American Academy of Family Physicians, 8880 Ward Pkwy., Kansas City, MO 64114; phone: 800/274–2237 ext. 3166) monthly, $60/annual subscription, free/student members. "AFP Classified Information" overflows with over 300 available positions.

Journal of Family Practice (25 Van Zant St., East Norwalk, CT 06855; phone: 203/838–4400) monthly, $66/annual nonmember subscription, free/American Medical Association members. Close to 80 ads for family practitioners and fellowships appear under "Classified."

Canadian Medical Association Journal (RBW Graphics, 1749 20th St., East Owen Sound, Ontario N4K 5R2 Canada) biweekly, $85/annual subscription (U.S.), $70/Canada, $100/elsewhere. From 80 to 120 positions for physicians appear in the "Classifieds."

Medical Tribune (257 Park Ave., South, New York, NY 10010; phone: 212/674-8500) biweekly, $75/annual subscription (U.S.), $125/Canada, $160/elsewhere. Over 50 ads for physicians fill the "Classified" section.

American Chiropractic Association Journal (ACA, 1701 Clarendon Blvd., Arlington, VA 22209; phone: 314/862-7800) monthly, $80/annual nonmember subscription (U.S.), $100/foreign, $24/members. From 50 to 60 job ads for chiropractors and practices for sale fill "Classified Advertising."

American Medical News (American Medical Association, Subscription Dept., 515 N. State St., Chicago, IL 60610; phone: 312/464-0183) 48 issues/year, $60/annual nonmember subscription (U.S.), $75/foreign (surface mail), free/members. About ten ads for physicians appear in "Classified Advertising."

Journal of the American Medical Women's Association (AMWA, 801 N. Fairfax St., Suite 400, Alexandria, VA 22314; phone: 703/838-0500) bimonthly, $35/annual nonmember subscription, free/members. The "Classifieds" carry 30 to 40 job openings for physicians of all types.

Journal of the National Medical Association (SLACK Inc., 6900 Grove Rd., Thorofare, NJ 08086; phone: 609/848-1000) monthly, $60/annual subscription (U.S.), $40/students and residents (U.S.), $78/Canada, $96/elsewhere, free/NMA members. About 20 openings for physicians, surgeons, staff, and faculty appear under "Positions Available."

Physicians' Professional Development Review (Prime National Publishing Company, 470 Boston Post Rd., Weston, MA 02193; phones: 800/869-2700, 617/899-2702) monthly, $50/annual subscription (U.S.), $75/foreign. Ten to 20 job openings for physicians are advertised throughout.

Annals of Internal Medicine (American College of Physicians, Independence Mall West, 6th St. at Race, Philadelphia, PA 19106; phone: 800/523-1546) $75/annual nonmember subscription (U.S.), $120/Canada, $138/elsewhere; $56.25/nonmember physicians, $37.50/nonmember medical students, included in membership package. From 250 to 400 vacancies for physicians in internal medicine appear under "Classified."

Archives of Internal Medicine (American Medical Association, Subscription Dept., 515 N. State St., Chicago, IL 60610; phone: 312/464-0183) monthly, $65/annual subscription (U.S.), $80/foreign (surface mail), $95/foreign (air mail), contact for reduced student and residents' rates. "Classified Advertising" offers about 40 residencies and practitioner positions.

The New Physician (American Medical Student Association, 1890 Preston White Dr., Reston, VA 22091; phone: 703/620-6600) nine issues/year, $22/annual nonmember subscription, free/members. Five to ten residency positions appear under "Classifieds/Opportunities."

Physician's Management (Edgell Communications, 1 E. First St., Duluth, MN 55802; phone: 800/346-0085) monthly, $35/annual subscription (U.S.), $60/Canada, $110/elsewhere. Three or four doctors are sought in the "Classified Ads."

"Just follow the advice God gave Moses—take two tablets and call me in the morning."

Resident and Staff Physician (80 Shore Rd., Port Washington, NY 11050; phone: 516/883-6530) monthly, $57/annual subscription (U.S.), $95/foreign. The typical issue will have one or two pages of "Classified" ads for physicians in private practice and hospitals.

APMA News (American Podiatric Medical Association, 9312 Old Georgetown Rd, Bethesda, MD 20814; phone: 301/571-9200) monthly, $25/annual subscription (U.S.), $35/foreign. Around 30 to 35 opportunities for podiatric medical doctors are printed under "Positions Available."

Medical Economics (5 Paragon Dr., Montvale, NJ 07645-1742; phones: 800/833-0197, 201/358-7200) semimonthly, $89/annual subscription. About six ads for physicians and administrators are printed under "Classified."

Critical Care Medicine (Williams & Wilkins, 428 E. Preston St., Baltimore, MD 21202; phone: 800/638-6423) monthly, $80/annual subscription (U.S.), $45/physicians in training (U.S.), add $35 for foreign delivery. About 25 physician positions in intensive and critical care appear under "Classified Advertising."

Emergency Medicine (Cahners Publishing Company, 249 W. 17th St., New York, NY 10011; 212/645-0067) monthly, $49/annual subscription. About five positions for emergency room and staff physicians are under "Classified."

Hospital Physician (Turner White Communications, 353 W. Lancaster Ave., Suite 200, Wayne, PA 19087) monthly, $55/annual subscription (U.S.), $65/Canada, $100/elsewhere. About four job ads appear under "Classified."

Rural Health Care (National Rural Health Care Association, 301 E. Armour Blvd., Kansas City, MO 64111; phone: 816/756-3140) monthly, available only to members, included in dues. About 15 physician and nursing positions appear under "Classified."

The DO (American Osteopathic Association, 142 Ontario St., Chicago, IL 60611-2864; phone: 312/280-5800) monthly, $20/annual subscription (U.S.), $50/foreign. About 120 openings for osteopaths appear under "Classifieds—Opportunities."

ACOS News (American College of Osteopathic Surgeons, 123 N. Henry St., Alexandria, VA 22314; phone: 703/684-0416) monthly, available only to members. Only one or two job ads appear in the "Classifieds."

ASA Placement Bulletin (American Society of Anesthesiologists, 515 Busse Highway, Park Ridge, IL 60068; phone: 708/825-5586) monthly, free, available only to members. From 100 to 125 positions for anesthesiologists fill this bulletin (no nursing positions; only doctors).

Anesthesiology (J.B. Lippincott Company, Downville Pike, Route 3, Box 20-B, Hagerstown, MD 21740; phones: 800/638-3030, 215/238-4206) monthly, $100/annual subscription (U.S.), $150/elsewhere. Two or three pages of job openings appear at the end of this magazine.

American Journal of Diseases of Children (American Medical Association, Subscription Dept., 515 N. State St., Chicago, IL 60610; phone: 312/464-0183) monthly, $58/annual subscription (U.S.), $73/foreign (surface mail). Around 40 openings for pediatricians and practices appear under "Classified Advertising—Professional Opportunities."

Journal of Allergy and Clinical Immunology (Mosby Year Book, Journal Subscription Services, 11830 Westline Industrial Dr., St. Louis, MO 63146; phones: 800/325-4177, ext. 4351, 314/872-8370, ext. 4351) monthly, $80/annual subscription (U.S.), $38/student (U.S.), $116.60/Canada, $111/elsewhere. About 25 job openings and practices for sale appear under "Opportunities Available" plus a few display ads.

Gerontology News (Gerontological Society of America, 1275 K St., NW, Washington, DC 20005; phone: 202/842-1275) monthly, $50/annual nonmember subscription, free/members. About five to eight positions for geriatric physicians appear under "Jobs."

Annals of Surgery (J.B. Lippincott Company, Downville Pike, Route 3, Box 20-B, Hagerstown, MD 21740; phones: 800/638-3030, 215/238-4206) monthly, $65/annual subscription (U.S.), $75/Canada, $95/elsewhere. About 30 job openings appear under "Positions Available."

Archives of Surgery (American Medical Association, Subscription Dept., 515 N. State St., Chicago, IL 60610; phone: 312/464-0183) monthly, $62/annual subscription (U.S.), $77/foreign (surface mail). Over 30 job opportunities and residencies for surgeons of all types appear under "Classified Advertising–Professional Opportunities."

American Journal of Surgery (Cahners Publishing Company, P.O Box 173306, Denver, CO 80217; phone: 800/637–6072) monthly, $57/annual subscription (U.S.), $85/Canada, $$135/elsewhere. Twelve openings for all types of surgeons appear in the "Classifieds."

American Journal of Surgical Pathology (Raven Press, 1185 Avenue of the Americas, New York, NY 10036; phone: 212/930–9500) monthly, $125/annual subscription (U.S.), $175/foreign. Over ten display ads for pathology surgeons are scattered throughout.

Transplantation Proceedings (25 Van Zant St., East Norwalk, CT 06855; phone: 203/838–4400) bimonthly, $156/annual subscription (U.S.), $205/foreign. Ten or fewer ads for transplant surgeons and immunologists appear in the "Classifieds."

Current Surgery (J. B. Lippincott Company, Downville Pike, Route 3, Box 20–B, Hagerstown, MD 21740; phones: 800/638–3030, 215/238–4206) monthly, $60/annual subscription (U.S.), $45/students, $85/foreign. About five ads appear under "Classifieds."

Surgery (Mosby Year Book, Journal Subscription Services, 11830 Westline Industrial Dr., St. Louis, MO 63146; phones: 800/325–4177, ext. 4351, 314/872–8370, ext. 4351) monthly, $81/annual subscription (U.S.), $38/student (U.S.), $106.67/Canada, $101/elsewhere. Three or four display ads for job openings are in the typical issue.

Surgical Rounds (80 Shore Rd., Port Washington, NY 11050; phone: 516/883–6530) monthly, $50/annual subscription. Three or four ads for general surgeons appear in the "Classified Ads."

Journal of Vascular Surgery (Mosby Year Book, Journal Subscription Services, 11830 Westline Industrial Dr., St. Louis, MO 63146; phones: 800/325–4177, ext. 4351, 314/872–8370, ext. 4351) monthly, $89/annual subscription (U.S.), $40/student (U.S.), $119.23/Canada, $113/elsewhere. An even dozen display ads for jobs appear.

The Journal of Thoracic and Cardiovascular Surgery (Mosby Year Book, Journal Subscription Services, 11830 Westline Industrial Dr., St. Louis, MO 63146; phones: 800/325–4177, ext. 4351, 314/872–8370, ext. 4351) monthly, $102/annual subscription (U.S.), $49/student (U.S.), $137.14/Canada, $130/elsewhere. Contains job ads for thoracic and cardiovascular surgeons.

AAO–HNS Bulletin (American Academy of Otolaryngology–Head and Neck Surgery, 1 Prince St., Alexandria, VA 22314; phone: 703/836–4444) free/residents, $75/annual subscription for other health personnel. "Employment Classifieds" publish 150 to 200 positions for otolaryngologists.

Otolaryngology–Head and Neck Surgery (Mosby Year Book, Journal Subscription Services, 11830 Westline Industrial Dr., St. Louis, MO 63146; phones: 800/325–4177, ext. 4351, 314/872–8370, ext. 4351) monthly, $93/annual subscription (U.S.), $48/student (U.S.), $123.51/Canada, $117/elsewhere. Around ten positions are advertised in display ads.

Journal of Hand Surgery (American Volume) (Mosby Year Book, Journal Subscription Services, 11830 Westline Industrial Dr., St. Louis, MO 63146; phones: 800/325–4177, ext. 4351, 314/872–8370, ext. 4351) bimonthly, $655/annual subscription (U.S.), $32/student (U.S.), $82.55/Canada, $78/elsewhere. Over 15 positions appear in display ads.

Orthopedics Today (SLACK, Inc., 6900 Grove Rd., Thorofare, NJ 08086–9447; phones: 800/257–8290, 609/848–1000) monthly, $110/annual subscription (U.S.), $128/Canada, $146/elsewhere. Around 10 job openings and practices for sale appear under "Classified Marketplace."

Orthopedics (SLACK, Inc., 6900 Grove Rd., Thorofare, NJ 08086–9447; phones: 800/257–8290, 609/848–1000) monthly, $95/annual subscription (U.S.), $113/Canada, $131/elsewhere. Around five job openings and practices for sale appear under "Classified Marketplace."

American Journal of Cardiologists (Cahners Publishing, P.O. Box 173377, Denver, CO 80217; phone: 800/637–6073) semimonthly, $66/annual subscription (U.S.), $105/Canada, $150/elsewhere. Around 12 job ads for cardiologists, electrophysiologists, and others appear in the "Classifieds" and display ads.

American Heart Journal (Mosby Year Book, Journal Subscription Services, 11830 Westline Industrial Dr., St. Louis, MO 63146; phones: 800/325–4177, ext. 4351, 314/872–8370, ext. 4351) monthly, $84/annual subscription (U.S.), $42/student (U.S.), $117.88/Canada, $112/elsewhere. Only a handful of positions for cardiologists and cardiovascular surgeons appear near the back of the magazine.

Journal of Immunology (P. O. Box 64471, Baltimore, MD 21264–0471; phone: 800/638–6423) semimonthly, $170/annual subscription (U.S.), $260/foreign. About four job openings appear near the front.

Aviation, Space and Environmental Medicine (Aerospace Medical Association, 320 S. Henry St., Alexandria, VA 22314; phone: 703/739–2240) monthly, $80/annual subscription. Just two or three ads for aviation medical examiners, flight surgeons, aerospace medicine specialists, and researchers appear under "Classified Ads" and "Medical News."

AGA News (American Gastroenterological Association, 6900 Grove Rd., Thorofare, NJ 08086; phone: 609/848–1000) bimonthly, free, available only to members. "Personnel" describes 200 to 300 positions for gastroenterological physicians, researchers, and assistants.

Opportunities in Dermatology (American Academy of Dermatology, P.O. Box 3116, Evanston, IL 60204–3116; phone: 708/869–3954) quarterly, $100/annual nonmember subscription, $50/members. Your subscription gets you four different quarterly editions: *Clinical Positions Available*, *Dermatologists Seeking Clinical Positions*, *Academic Positions Available*, and *Dermatologists Seeking Academic*

Positions. Hundreds of positions are listed state–by–state in each "positions available" edition. Only about 70 dermatologists are listed in the "seeking positions" editions.

Archives of Dermatology (American Medical Association, Subscription Dept., 515 N. State St., Chicago, IL 60610; phone: 312/464–0183) monthly, $73/annual subscription (U.S.), $88/foreign. From 50 to 75 job openings for practitioners, businesses, and faculty appear under "Classified Advertising."

Journal of the American Academy of Dermatology (Mosby Year Book, Journal Subscription Services, 11830 Westline Industrial Dr., St. Louis, MO 63146; phones: 800/325–4177, ext. 4351, 314/872–8370, ext. 4351) monthly, $93/annual subscription (U.S.), $47/student (U.S.), $131.51/Canada, $125/elsewhere. Around 20 openings appear in display ads.

Dermatology Times (Edgell Communications, 1 E. First St., Duluth, MN 55802; phone: 800/346–0085) monthly, $60/annual subscription (U.S.), $115/Canada, $175/elsewhere. Around ten ads for dermatologists appear under "Professional Notices."

Pediatrics (American Academy of Pediatrics, P.O. Box 927, Elk Grove Village, IL 60009; phone: 708/981–7904) monthly, $60/annual nonmember subscription, $45/members. About 30 pages of "Classified Ads" for pediatricians, neonatologists, and pediatric subspecialists are in the typical issue.

Journal of Pediatrics (Mosby Year Book, Journal Subscription Services, 11830 Westline Industrial Dr., St. Louis, MO 63146; phones: 800/325–4177, ext. 4351, 314/872–8370, ext. 4351) monthly, $80/annual subscription (U.S.), $38/student (U.S.), $110.60/Canada, $105/elsewhere. Around 100 to 125 positions are advertised under "Classified."

Obstetrics and Gynecology (Elsevers Science, 655 Avenue of the Americas, New York, NY 10010; phone: 212/989–5800) monthly, $98/annual subscription, $68/interns and residents. Sixty to 70 small display ads for job openings appear toward the end of each issue.

American Journal of Obstetrics and Gynecology (Mosby Year Book, Journal Subscription Services, 11830 Westline Industrial Dr., St. Louis, MO 63146; phones: 800/325–4177, ext. 4351, 314/872–8370, ext. 4351) monthly, $96/annual subscription (U.S.), $42/student (U.S.), $134.72/Canada, $128/elsewhere. Close to 60 practitioner and faculty positions appear in display ads.

The Dendrite (American Academy of Neurology, 2221 University Ave., SE, Minneapolis, MN 55414; phone: 612/623–8115) bimonthly, $60/annual nonmember physician subscription, $20/junior AAN members, $40/AAN members and nonmember residents, $150/hospitals and physician groups, $200/executive search firms. Over 100 positions plus 30 fellowships, 15 placement firms, and "positions wanted" fill each issue.

Archives of Neurology (American Medical Association, Subscription Dept., 515 N. State St., Chicago, IL 60610; phone: 312/464–0183) monthly, $74/annual subscription (U.S.), $89/foreign. Fifty to 100 positions for neurologists, residencies, administration, and faculty are published under "Classified Advertising."

Neurology— Official Journal of the American Academy of Neurology (Edgell Communications, 1 E. First St., Duluth, MN 55802; phone: 800/346–0085) monthly, $180/annual subscription (U.S. and Canada), $230/elsewhere. Fifty to 80 openings for neurologists are advertised under "Professional Notices."

Spine (J. B. Lippincott Company, Downville Pike, Route 3, Box 20–B, Hagerstown, MD 21740; phones: 800/638–3030, 215/238–4206) monthly, $150/annual subscription (U.S.), $95/students, $190/foreign. About 15 job openings are advertised in the typical issue.

American Journal of Clinical Pathologists (J.B. Lippincott, 100 Insurance Way, Hagerstown, MD 21740; phone: 215/238–4200) monthly, $105/annual subscription (U.S.), $150/foreign. About 20 to 30 positions in clinical pathology, research, and teaching are printed under "Classified."

Archives of Physical Medicine and Rehabilitation (American Academy of Physical Medicine and Rehabilitation, 78 E. Adams, Chicago, IL 60603; phone: 312/922-9371) monthly, $100/annual nonmember subscription (U.S. and Canada), $120/foreign, $36/members. Fifty to 60 openings for physicians, rehabilitation practitioners, administrators, and faculty appear under "Classified Advertising."

CAMS Newsletter (Chinese American Medical Society, 281 Edgewood Ave., Teaneck, NJ 07666; phone; 201/833–1506) quarterly, available only to members, $100/annual dues. Three or four practitioner and academic positions appear under ''Positions Available.''

Mother Goose and Grim reprinted by permission of MGM L&M and Grimmy, Inc. Copyright 1991. All rights reserved.

Ophthalmology Times (Edgell Communications, 1 E. First St., Duluth, MN 55802; phone: 800/346–0085) semimonthly, $100/annual subscription (U.S.), $145/Canada, $175/elsewhere. Thirty to 40 job ads fill the ''Professional Notices'' section.

Ophthalmology (J. B. Lippincott Company, Downville Pike, Route 3, Box 20–B, Hagerstown, MD 21740; phones: 800/638–3030, 215/238–4206) monthly, $81/annual subscription (U.S.), $40/students, $108/foreign. You'll come upon 30 to 40 job openings advertised under ''Classified.''

Archives of Ophthalmology (American Medical Association, Subscription Dept., 515 N. State St., Chicago, IL 60610; phone: 312/464–0183) monthly, $65/annual subscription (U.S.), $80/foreign. Around 30 openings for practitioners, residencies, faculty, and businesses appear under ''Classified Advertising.''

American Optometric Association News (AOA, 243 N. Lindberg Blvd., St. Louis, MO 63141; phone: 314/991–4100) semimonthly, $35/annual nonmember subscription, free/members. ''Professional Opportunities'' carries 15 to 20 job openings for optometrists.

American Journal of Ophthalmology (435 N. Michigan Ave., Chicago, IL 60611; phone: 312/787-3853) monthly, $52/annual subscription (U.S.), $80/foreign. Around 20 job ads grace the pages of "Positions Available."

Ocular Surgery News (SLACK, Inc., 6900 Grove Rd., Thorofare, NJ 08086-9447; phones: 800/257-8290, 609/848-1000) semimonthly, $150/annual subscription (U.S.), $186/Canada, $230/elsewhere. Around 60 job openings and practices for sale appear under "Classified Marketplace."

Journal of Visual Impairment and Blindness (American Foundation for the Blind, 15 W. 16th St., New York, NY 10011; phone: 212/620-2155) ten issues/year, $45/annual subscription (U.S.), $65/foreign. "Classified" contains about ten ads for practitioners, teachers (elementary school through university), researchers, and administrators.

Investigative Ophthalmology & Visual Science (J. B. Lippincott Company, Downville Pike, Route 3, Box 20-B, Hagerstown, MD 21740; phones: 800/638-3030, 215/238-4206) monthly, $118/annual subscription (U.S.), $80/students, $159/foreign. About ten positions are advertised under "Classifieds."

Journal of Pediatric Ophthalmology & Strabismus (SLACK, Inc., 6900 Grove Rd., Thorofare, NJ 08086-9447; phones: 800/257-8290, 609/848-1000) bimonthly, $85/annual subscription (U.S.), $101/Canada, $121/elsewhere. Around seven openings in pediatric eye care appear under "Classified Marketplace."

Urology (Cahners Publishing Company, P.O. Box 633, Holmes, PA 19043; phone: 800/345-8112) monthly, $75/annual subscription (U.S. and Canada), $120/elsewhere. Around 22 positions for urologists are described under "Career Opportunities."

Urology Times (Edgell Communications, 1 E. First St., Duluth, MN 55802; phone: 800/346-0085) monthly, $60/annual subscription (U.S.), $105/Canada, $140/elsewhere. About 20 positions are advertised under "Professional Notices."

The Journal of Urology (Williams & Wilkins, 428 E. Preston St., Baltimore, MD 21202; phones: 800/638-6423, in Maryland call: 800/638-4007) monthly, $150/annual subscription, $215/foreign. About 15 urologist openings appear in "Classified Advertising."

Job services

National Physicians Register (295 Cambridge St., Suite 422, Dept. JF, Boston, MA 02114; phone: 800/342-1007) free. A physician submits a copy of her resume and gives her geographic preference and type of position sought. NPR creates a synopsis of the resume and assigns a code number to it. These synopses are published with code numbers rather than the physician's name in a bulletin sent bimonthly to 7,500 hospitals, clinics, group practices, and health maintenance organizations. The potential employer tells NPR which doctors interest it and NPR sends the full resume to the employer. However, if the physician tells NPR that he doesn't want his name given out, NPR sends the job seeker a letter telling him a particular facility is interested in him and that he should contact the potential employer directly. About 300 physicians are registered at any one time, although that number is growing. This service serves both M.D.s and osteopathic physicians.

Physicians Career Resource (American Medical Association, P.O. Box 10012, Chicago, IL; phones: 800/955-3565, 312/464-5000). The AMA's Physicians Career Resource consists of several components. The major component is the *Physician Recruiting Service* which is a multidimensional operation that offers several techniques to match physicians with openings.

- *Physician Placement Service* $50/nonmembers, free/members, add $25 for a confidential listing. Complete the four-page registration questionnaire. The information you provide will be forwarded to employers who ask for information about you unless you select the confidential option in which case employers will get a code number rather than your name and address.

- *Physician Placement Register* (semimonthly, $350/members six-month registration fee for employers/recruiters, $450/nonmembers six-month registration fee for employers/recruiters) is where an abbreviated version of your registration form—curriculum vita or CV—is published. Potential employers and recruiters subscribe to this item. Their cost includes one job listing. Additional listings are available at $175 each.

↬ *Computer–Generated CVs* can be requested by interested prospective employers and recruiters. This includes all the information you provided on your registration form.

↬ *Opportunity Placement Register*, included as part of your registration in the *Physician Placement Service*, is a monthly newsletter that lists practice openings by state, specialty, type of practice, and community. The listings include compensation method, qualifications, whom to contact, starting date, description of the position, and demographic characteristics and distinguishing geographic or professional features. This newsletter also includes classified ads placed by recruiters and health care organizations seeking physicians.

↬ *Practice Profiles* are included in your registration to the *Physician Placement Register*. Based on the synopses of job openings in the *Opportunity Placement Register*, you can request computer–generated detailed descriptions of the opportunities that interest you the most. Contact the AMA for the nominal fee.

Locum Tenens Service (American Medical Association, P.O. Box 10012, Chicago, IL; phones: 800/955–3565, 312/464–5000) free/physicians, $350/member employers/recruiters, $450/nonmember employers/recruiters. All the services listed immediately above in the AMA's *Physicians Career Resource* are included in this recruiting/placement service for short–term (one year or less) physician placements. Physician registrants have a different registration questionnaire to complete. However, they are not charged any fee to participate even if they are not AMA members.

Practices for Sale (American Medical Association, P.O. Box 10012, Chicago, IL; phones: 800/955–3565, 312/464–5000) $65/members per month, $85/nonmembers per month. Complete the "Practices for Sale Registration Form" to list your practice each month in the AMA's *Opportunity Placement Register*. Confidential listings are available for free.

COMPASS (American Academy of Family Physicians, 8880 Ward Pkwy., Kansas City, MO 64114; phone: 800/274–2237, ext. 4122) $340/nonmember annual fee, $225/member annual fee. You complete their resume form and they match you to the appropriate family physician positions among the 800 to 900 openings in their database.

National Medical Network—Physicians' Network (Boyds Branch Rd., Rt. 1, Box 1230, Manchester, TN 37355; phone: 800/752–1906) free. Tell them the type of work you seek and the geographic area in which you wish to work, and they'll send you a list of hospitals that are looking for physicians like you. This is not a recruiting service.

National Resident Matching Program (1 Rotary Center, Suite 807, Evanston, IL 60201; phone: 708/328–3440) contact for rates. Matches graduating medical students with residencies.

AMA–FREIDA—AMA Fellowship and Residency Electronic Interactive Database (American Medical Association, P.O. Box 2964, Milwaukee, WI 53201–2964; phone: 800/621–8335) $500/members, $1,000/nonmembers, available on 3.5 inch and 5.25 inch MS-DOS disks. The only official listing of residency and fellowship programs accredited by the Accreditation Council for Graduate Medical Education, these disks provide detailed information on over 70 percent of the residency and fellowship programs available.

The Job Opportunity Program (National Medical Association, 1012 10th St., NW, Washington, DC 20001; phone: 202/347–1895) free, available only to member physicians. You complete this service's form which is kept on file until you find a position. You are sent a list of employers who meet your criteria and you are responsible for contacting them.

Placement Service (American College of Radiology, ATTEN: Professional Bureau, 1891 Preston White Dr., Reston, VA 22091; phone: 703/648–8900) $500/nonmembers six–month fee, free/members. You complete this service's resume form which is kept on file for six months. The service matches you to openings and sends your resume to potential employers who are responsible for contacting you. You can select their "stealth" option and have a code number assigned to you to keep your name confidential.

American College of Osteopathic Surgeons Placement Service (ACOS, 123 N. Henry St., Alexandria, VA 22314; phone: 703/684–0416) free, available only to members. ACOS maintains a list of practice opportunities and a list of physicians who seek a practice opportunity at its headquarters. It attempts to match the two. Contact for details.

Teratology Society Placement Service (Teratology Society, c/o Dr. Stanley Kaplan, Anatomy and Cellular Biology, Medical College of Wisconsin, 8701 Watertown Plank Rd., Milwaukee, WI 53226; phone: 414/257-8473) $10/annual fee. Complete the service's resume form. This service sends your form to all registered employers. It is kept on file for a year or until you find a new job, whichever comes first. Positions are for physicians and scientists who do clinical work or research on birth defects.

Directories

AMWA Membership Directory (American Medical Women's Association, 801 N. Fairfax St., Suite 400, Alexandria, VA 22314; phone: 703/838-0500) $35/nonmembers, free/members, published in January of odd-numbered years, over 350 pages. Lists physician members in all specialties.

Yearbook and Directory of Osteopathic Physicians (American Osteopathic Association, 142 Ontario St., Chicago, IL 60611-2864; phone: 312/280-5800) $50, annual. In nearly 700 pages, this directory offers both alphabetical and geographical listings of osteopathic physicians plus osteopathic hospitals, research centers, and postdoctoal training programs.

American College of Osteopathic Surgeons Membership Directory (ACOS, 123 N. Henry St., Alexandria, VA 22314; phone: 703/684-0416) free, available only to members, issued each January, 56 pages.

American Chiropractic Association Membership Directory (ACA, 1701 Clarendon Blvd., Arlington, VA 22209; phones: 800/368-3083314/862-7800) $100/nonmembers, free/members, annual. Lists information on over 2,300 practitioners.

CAMS Membership Directory (Chinese American Medical Society, 281 Edgewood Ave., Teaneck, NJ 07666; phone; 201/833-1506) free/members, available only to members, issued in odd-numbered years.

American Society of Anesthesiologists Directory of Members (ASA, 515 Busse Highway, Park Ridge, IL 60068; phone: 708/825-5586) $5/nonmembers, free/members, annual.

American College of Radiology Membership Directory (ACR, 1891 Preston White Dr., Reston, VA 22091; phone: 703/648-8900) free/members, released each December.

Directory (American Academy of Dermatology, P.O. Box 3116, Evanston, IL 60204-3116; phone: 708/869-3954) $100/nonmembers, free/members, published in April of odd–numbered years. This 150–page directory is jammed packed with dermatologists in the U.S. and worldwide.

Directory of Services for Blind and Visually Impaired Persons in the United States (American Foundation for the Blind, 15 W. 16th St., New York, NY 10011; phone: 212/620-2155) $50/print edition plus $4.50 shipping, 472 pages; $50/cassette edition (four track, 15/16 ips) plus $4.50 shipping; price includes quarterly update newsletters. Lists details on over 1,000 local, state, regional, and national services  including medical and research organizations, schools, and clinics.

Referral Directory (College of Optometrists in Vision Development, 353 H St., Suite C, Chula Vista, CA 92010; phone: 619/425-6191) contact for cost, annual.

Blue Book of Optometrists (Butterworth Publishers, 80 Montvale Ave., Stoneham, MA 02180: phone: 800/366-2665) $90, published in odd–numbered years. Includes optometrists in the U.S., Mexico, and Canada.

Red Book of Ophthalmology (Butterworth Publishers, 80 Montvale Ave., Stoneham, MA 02180: phone: 800/366-2665) $75, published in even–numbered years. Includes ophthalmologists in the U.S., Mexico, and Canada.

Membership Directory of the Gerontological Society of America (GSA, 1275 K St., NW, Washington, DC 20005; phone: 202/842-1275) $15/nonmembers, $9/members, most recently issued in 1991.

Directory of the American Academy of Orthopedic Surgeons (AAOS, 222 S. Prospect, Park Ridge, IL 60068; phone: 708/823-7186) available only to members, annual.

Membership Directory for the Society of Nuclear Medicine (Society of Nuclear Medicine, 136 Madison Ave., New York, NY 10016; phone: 212/889-0717) $50/nonmembers, free/members. Last published in September 1991. New edition expected in 1993.

American Society of Clinical Pathologists Directory (P.O. Box 122270, Chicago, IL 60612; phone: 312/738-1336) free/members only, annual.

U.S. Medical Licensure Statistics and Current Licensure Requirements (American Medical Association, P.O. Box 2964, Milwaukee, WI 53201-2964; phone: 800/621-8335) $60/nonmembers, $35/members plus your local sales tax. Although not a typical directory, this book will help any doctor who is thinking of relocating to a different state. It reports on every state's licensing policies, reciprocity/endorsement policies, fees, CME requirements, and much more.

Salary survey

Compensation Report on Hospital-Based and Group Practice Physicians (Hospital Compensation Service, 69 Minnehaha Blvd., Oakland, NJ 07436; phone: 201/405-0075) $245 prepaid, annual. Reports on salary and benefits nationally and in nine regions for 30 physician specialties. Also reports on hours worked, housing and meal allowances, incentive bonuses, and more.

Health care administration

Job openings

Healthcare Financial Management (Healthcare Financial Management Association, 2 Westbrook Corporate Center, Suite 700, Westchester, IL 60154; phones: 800/252-4362, 800/821-6459 [Illinois only]) monthly, $70/annual nonmember subscription, $120/foreign, free/members. You'll find 25 to 50 ads for hospital financial officers, business office managers, controllers, billing and collection managers, patient accounts managers, reimbursement specialists, and other administrators under "Classifieds—Positions Available."

Career Mart (American College of Healthcare Executives, 840 N. Lake Shore Dr., Chicago, IL 60611; phone: 312/943-0544) monthly, available only to members, $30/member six-month subscription. Typical issue includes more than 40 upper-level healthcare management positions listed under "Career Mart."

Health Week (CMP Publications, 600 Community Dr., Manhasset, MY 11030; phones: 800/645-6278, 516/562-5000) biweekly, $75/annual subscription. Around 35 openings for hospital administrators, business officers, marketing, sales, and claims adjusters are advertised under "Classifieds."

College Digest (American College of Physician Executives, 4890 W. Kennedy Blvd., Suite 200, Tampa, FL 33609; phones: 800/562-8088, 813/287-2000) bimonthly, free, available only to members. "Career Opportunities" features 15 to 20 openings for physician managers and administrators of all sorts.

Catholic Health World (The Catholic Health Association, 4455 Woodson Rd., St. Louis, MO 63134; phone: 314/427-2500) semimonthly, $24/annual subscription (U.S.), $28/foreign. Ten to 20 positions in hospital administration, including pastoral care, are printed under "Executive Referral."

HMO Managers Letter (Group Health Association of America, 1129 20th St., NW, Suite 600, Washington, DC 20036; phone: 202/778-3247) semimonthly, $125/annual nonmember subscription, free/members. You'll find ten to 15 job openings for medical and administrative positions with HMOs under "Managed Care Careers."

AMCRA's Manager Care Monitor (American Managed Care and Review Association, 1227 25th St., NW, Suite 610, Washington, DC 20037; phone: 202/728-0506) eight issues/year, contact for current subscription rates. About ten ads for managerial positions appear under "Career Advantage."

Update (Medical Group Management Association, 104 Inverness Terrace East, Englewood, CO 80112; phone: 303/799-1111) monthly, free, available only to members. Eight to ten medical management positions are in "Update Classified Advertising."

AAMA Executive (American Academy of Medical Administrators, 30555 Southfield Rd., Suite 150, Southfield, MI 48076-7747; phone: 313/540-4310) bimonthly, $60/annual nonmember subscription, free/members. Under "Career News" you'll find about ten openings for administrative positions as well as "Careers Wanted."

NAHC Report (National Association for Home Care, 519 C St., NE, Washington, DC 20002; phone: 202/547-5277) weekly, $325/annual nonmember subscription, free/members. About four ads for health care directors and supervisors appear under "Classifieds."

Journal of the American Medical Record Association (AMRA, 919 N. Michigan Ave., Chicago, IL 60611-1601; phone: 312/787-2672) monthly, $50/annual nonmember subscription, $7/members. Ten to 15 job openings in medical records administration appear under "Classified."

Trustee (American Hospital Publishing Company, 211 E. Chicago Ave., Suite 700, Chicago, IL 60611; phone: 312/440-6800) monthly, $22/annual subscription (U.S.), $30/foreign. Around three ads for hospital administrators and healthcare consultants appear in "Classified."

Provider (American Health Care Association, 1201 L St., NW, Washington, DC 20005; phone: 202/842-4444) monthly, $48/annual nonmember subscription, free/members. The "Classifieds" contain ads for administrators, controllers, and other long-term care professionals.

Computers in Healthcare (Cardiff Publishing Company, 6300 S. Syracuse Way, Suite 650, Englewood, CO 80111; phone: 303/220-0600) 18 issues/year, $28/annual subscription (U.S.), $38/Canada, $40/elsewhere. About two openings for MIS director, sales, marketing, and administration appear under "Positions."

Job services

GHAA Placement Referral Service (Group Health Association of America, 1129 20th St., NW, Suite 600, Washington, DC 20036; phone: 202/778-3247) $25/resume listing fee. Fill out this service's form and submit it with your resume which will be kept on file for six months. Resumes and job openings are published for review at the GHAA's semiannual national conferences. Each party is responsible for contacting the other.

Placement Service (Medical Group Management Association, 104 Inverness Terrace East, Englewood, CO 80112; phone: 303/799-1111). This service covers management positions from business managers to Chief Executive Officers. Forty-five to 50 positions are available at any one time. You can choose to receive bulletins of the positions listed with the service ($280/nonmember annual fee, $144/members) and have your resume circulated to employers ($335/nonmember annual fee, $195/members).

Exec-U-Trak (Healthcare Financial Management Association, 2 Westbrook Corporate Center, Suite 700, Westchester, IL 60154; phones: 800/252-4362 ext. 580, 800/821-6459 [Illinois only]) free, available only to HFMA members. This resume referral service is for healthcare financial and administration professionals.

Directories

American College of Healthcare Executives Directory (American Association of Healthcare Executives, 840 N. Lake Shore Dr., Chicago, IL 60611; phone: 312/943-0544) $75/nonmembers, $60/members, published in the winter of even-numbered years. Lists over 16,000 health care executives in public and private sectors.

Directory of Member Consultants & Affiliated Firms (American Association of Healthcare Consultants, 11208 Waples Mill Rd., Suite 109, Fairfax, VA 22030; phone: 703/691-2242) $100/nonmembers, free/members and their clients, annual, 31 pages. Offers great detail on each firm and consultant including areas of specialization.

GHAA National Directory of HMOs (Group Health Association of America, 1129 20th St., NW, Suite 600, Washington, DC 20036; phone: 202/778-3247) $100/nonmembers, free/members, published each June. Includes names of top management and owners of health maintenance organizations.

National Home Care and Hospice Directory (National Association for Home Care, 519 C St., NE, Washington, DC 20002; phone: 202/547-5277) $135/nonmembers, $50/members, plus $5 shipping, issued each winter. In 500 pages, this directory lists the nation's home care and hospice providers by city and state as well as 13,000 home care providers including visiting nurse associations, home-maker–home health aide agencies, large chain providers, and HMO-based and for-profit agencies. It also includes the names, addresses, and phones for home care agency directors and an updated list of state associations in home care.

MGMA Directory (Medical Group Management Association, 104 Inverness Terrace East, Englewood, CO 80112; phone: 303/799-1111) available only to members, issued each January.

American Association of Physicists in Medicine Membership Directory (AAPM, 335 E. 45th St., New York, NY 10017-3483) $10/nonmembers, free/members, released each June.

Salary survey

Compensation Report—Management Employees in Hospital and Nursing Home Management Companies (Hospital Compensation Service, 69 Minnehaha Blvd., Oakland, NJ 07436; phone: 201/405-0075) $245 prepaid, annual. Reports on salary and bonus payments for 25 hospital management positions, both nationally and by region.

Nursing

Also see listings under "Technical, medical assistants" later in this chapter.

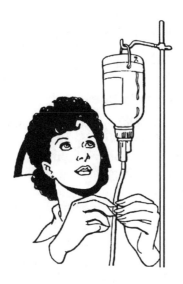

Job openings

The Nurse Practitioner (Vernon Publications, 3000 Northup Way, Suite 200, Bellevue, WA 98004; phone: 206/827-9900) monthly, $36/annual subscription (U.S.), $42/foreign. You'll find around 60 to 70 job openings in display ads and under "Positions and Opportunities" for nurse practitioners, pediatric, psychiatric, ob/gen, geriatric, family, public health, occupational medicine, and faculty positions.

Nursingworld Journal (Prime National Publishing Company, 470 Boston Post Rd., Weston, MA 02193; phones: 800/869-2700, 617/899-2702) monthly, $22/annual subscription (U.S.), $26/foreign. Between 30 and 50 job openings are advertised throughout.

American Journal of Nursing (555 W. 57th St., New York, NY 10019; phone: 212/582-8820) monthly, $30/annual subscription (U.S.), $40/Canada, $46/elsewhere. Ten to 20 nursing and nursing administrative and academic positions, plus privately operated placement services, appear in the "Classifieds Ads."

Journal of the American Academy of Nurse Practitioners (J. B. Lippincott Company, Downville Pike, Route 3, Box 20-B, Hagerstown, MD 21740; phones: 800/638-3030, 215/238-4206) quarterly,

$30/annual subscription (U.S.), $20/students, $40/foreign. This relatively new periodical features ten to 15 job openings under "Classifieds."

Nursing and Hospital Job Guide (Outcalt & Associates, P.O. Box 14153, Gainesville, FL 32604; phones: 800/874–7777, 904/373–2200) free/first state, $3/each additional state, order five states and you get their *National Hospital Job Guide* which includes everything in each of the 50 state job guides. Lists all hospitals in the individual state.

AORN Journal (Association of Operating Room Nurses, Inc., 10170 E. Mississippi Ave., Denver, CO 80231; phone: 303/369–9560) monthly, $50/annual nonmember subscription (U.S.), $60/foreign, $35/members. You'll come upon 80 to 100 ads for operating room nurses in this journal.

Today's OR Nurse (SLACK, Inc., 6900 Grove Rd., Thorofare, NJ 08086–9447; phones: 800/257–8290, 609/848–1000) monthly, $30/annual subscription (U.S.), $48/Canada, $66/elsewhere. About a dozen ads for operating room nurses and search firms that serve them appear under "Classified Marketplace."

Focus on Critical Care (Mosby Year Book, Journal Subscription Services, 11830 Westline Industrial Dr., St. Louis, MO 63146; phones: 800/325–4177, ext. 4351, 314/872–8370, ext. 4351) bimonthly, $31/annual subscription (U.S.), $15/student (U.S.), $40.67/Canada, $38.50/elsewhere. Ten to 20 display ads for nursing positions are in the typical issue.

Critical Care Nurse (Cahners Publishing Company, P.O. Box 633, Holmes, PA 19043–9894; phone: 800/345–8112) ten issues/year, $27/annual subscription (U.S.), $31/Canada and Mexico, $37/elsewhere. Around 25 openings for mostly intensive care nurses appear under "Regional Recruitment Highlights."

Registered Nurse (P.O. Box 182194, Columbus, OH 43272; phone: 800/669–1002) monthly, $35/annual subscription (U.S.), $40/foreign. From 20 to 30 ads for registered nurses, traveling nurses, and related health care positions appear under "Classified."

NANPRH Newsletter (National Association of Nurse Practitioners in Reproductive Health, 325 Pennsylvania Ave., SE, Washington, DC 20003; phone: 202/544–3208) three issues/year, $50/annual subscription. About 50 openings for nurse practitioners appear under "Job openings." Most openings are with affiliates of Planned Parenthood.

IOGNN: Journal of Obstetric, Gynecologic, and Neonatal Nursing (J. B. Lippincott Company, Downville Pike, Route 3, Box 20-B, Hagerstown, MD 21740; phones: 800/638-3030, 215/238-4206) bimonthly, $35/annual subscription (U.S.), $20/students, $45/foreign. You'll spot 30 to 50 job openings under "Classifieds."

NAACOG Newsletter (Nurses Association of the American College of OBGYNs, 409 12th St., SW, Washington, DC 20024; phone: 202/638-0026) monthly, $30/annual subscription (U.S. and Canada), $40/elsewhere. Twelve to 20 job ads for all aspects of obstetric nursing, women's health nursing, and baby birthing nurses appear under "Classified."

The Journal of Nursing Administration (J. B. Lippincott Company, Downville Pike, Route 3, Box 20-B, Hagerstown, MD 21740; phones: 800/638-3030, 215/238-4206) monthly, $45/annual subscription (U.S.), $30/students, $55/foreign. Twelve to 20 positions for nurse administrators appear under "Classified."

Nursing and Health Care (National League for Nursing, 350 Hudson St, New York, NY 10014; phone: 800/669-1656) ten issues/year, $30/annual subscription. The "Classified" section features ten to 20 ads for hospital nursing staff as well as academic positions.

Journal of Nursing Staff Development (J. B. Lippincott Company, Downville Pike, Route 3, Box 20-B, Hagerstown, MD 21740; phones: 800/638-3030, 215/238-4206) bimonthly, $40/annual subscription (U.S.), $50/foreign. About five positions are advertised under "Classified."

Nurse (Anesthesia) (25 Van Zant St., East Norwalk, CT 06855; phone: 203/838-4400) quarterly, $38/annual subscription. Four to eight nursing positions appear under "Classified."

Nursing Outlook (American Journal of Nursing Company, 555 W. 57th St., New York, NY 10019; phone: 212/582-8820) bimonthly, $25/annual subscription (U.S.), $35/Canada, $41/elsewhere. "Advertising—Classifieds" includes ten to 20 ads for nursing administrators, nurse educators, and deans of nursing schools.

Home Healthcare Nurse (National Fulfillment Services, 100 Pine Ave., Holmes, PA 19043; phone: 800/638–3030) bimonthly, $30/annual subscription (U.S.), $40/foreign. Ten job ads currently fill the "Classifieds," but the number of job ads is growing in this relatively new publication.

Journal of Pediatric Health Care (Mosby Year Book, Journal Subscription Services, 11830 Westline Industrial Dr., St. Louis, MO 63146; phones: 800/325–4177, ext. 4351, 314/872–8370, ext. 4351) bimonthly, $32/annual subscription (U.S.), $19/student (U.S.), $44.24/Canada, $42/elsewhere. About six to ten job vacancies appear under "Opportunities Available" and in display ads.

Journal of Emergency Nursing (Mosby Year Book, Journal Subscription Services, 11830 Westline Industrial Dr., St. Louis, MO 63146; phones: 800/325–4177, ext. 4351, 314/872–8370, ext. 4351) bimonthly, $35/annual subscription (U.S.), $20/student (U.S.), $46.45/Canada, $44/elsewhere. A dozen positions appear in display ads and under "Professional Opportunities."

Journal of ET Nursing (Mosby Year Book, Journal Subscription Services, 11830 Westline Industrial Dr., St. Louis, MO 63146; phones: 800/325–4177, ext. 4351, 314/872–8370, ext. 4351) bimonthly, $40/annual subscription (U.S.), $25/student (U.S.), $52.80/Canada, $50/elsewhere. Only one or two display ads appear for enterostomal therapists and nurses.

AAOHN News (American Association of Occupational Health Nurses, 50 Lenox Pointe, Atlanta, GA 30324; phones: 800/241–8014, 404/262–1162) monthly, $12/annual nonmember subscription, free/members. "Employment Information Service" includes ads for about eight nurse practitioners, wellness coordinators, and administrative positions.

AAOHN Journal (SLACK, Inc., 6900 Grove Rd., Thorofare, NJ 08086-9447; phones: 800/257–8290, 609/848–1000) monthly, $40/annual subscription (U.S.), $58/Canada, $76/elsewhere. Four or five display ads for occupational health nurses appear throughout.

Cancer Nursing (Raven Press, 1185 Avenue of the Americas, New York, NY 10036; phone: 212/930–9500) bimonthly, $38/annual subscription. Five to 15 jobs are advertised in display and classified ads.

Journal of Practical Nursing (National Association for Practical Nurse Education and Service, 1400 Spring St., Suite 310, Silver Spring, MD 20910; phone: 301/588-2491) quarterly, $15/annual subscription (U.S.), $22/foreign. Six to ten job openings for licensed practical and vocational nurses appear under "Employment."

Computers in Nursing (J. B. Lippincott Company, Downville Pike, Route 3, Box 20-B, Hagerstown, MD 21740; phones: 800/638-3030, 215/238-4206) bimonthly, $35/annual subscription, $30/students, $45/foreign. About five jobs for nurses who use computers appear under "Classifieds."

Also see the Journal of Gerontological Nursing and Journal of Psychosocial Nursing listed under "Therapy—mental" in this chapter.

Job services

Toll-Free Instant RSVP Nursing Career Directory (Springhouse Corp., 1111 Bethlehem Pike, Springhouse, PA 19477; phone: 215/646-8700) free. Published each January, this directory lists over 600 hospitals and health centers that are looking for nursing professionals. Job openings are listed under "Nurse Recruitment." You can be put directly in touch with a facility's nurse recruiter by calling 800/633-2648 (in Pennsylvania, call 800/633-2649) and giving your qualifications and specialty interests or sending in the reader service card from the directory. The RSVP line calls the nurse recruiter at the facilities of your choice. The nurse recruiter sends you an application form.

American Nurses Association Placement Service (ANA, 2420 Pershing Rd., Kansas City, MO 64108; phone: 816/474-5720). Call 800/969-7952 for details.

Pharmaceuticals

Job openings

Pharmacy Update (American Pharmaceutical Association, 2215 Constitution Ave., NW, Washington DC 20037; phones: 800/237-2642, 202/628-4410) weekly, free. Around 100 ads for pharmacists appear in the typical issue.

American Journal of Hospital Pharmacists (American Society of Hospital Pharmacists, 4630 Montgomery Ave., Bethesda, MD 20814; phone: 301/657-3000) monthly, $105/annual nonmember subscription, free/members. Thirty to 40 vacancies for pharmacists, generally at hospitals, appear under "Career Opportunities."

Hospital Pharmacy (J. B. Lippincott Company, Downville Pike, Route 3, Box 20-B, Hagerstown, MD 21740; phones: 800/638-3030, 215/238-4206) monthly, $60/annual subscription (U.S.), $80/foreign. Around ten job openings are advertised under "Classifieds."

Pharmaceutical Engineering (International Society of Pharmaceutical Engineers, 3816 W. Linbaugh Ave., Tampa, FL 33624; phone: 813/960-2105) bimonthly, $20/annual nonmember subscription

(U.S.), $35/foreign, free/members. Around 20 positions for process engineers and pharmaceutical validation specialists appear in display ads and under "Classifieds."

Pharmaceutical Executive (Aster Publishing Corp., 859 Willamette St., Eugene, OR 97440; phone: 503/343-1200) monthly, $54/annual subscription. Up to eight positions with pharmaceutical manufacturers and distributors appear in display ads throughout the magazine. Positions tend to be for executives, business mangers, market research, and research.

Journal of Pharmaceutical Sciences (American Pharmaceutical Association, 2215 Constitution Ave., NW, Washington, DC 20037; phone: 202/429-7518) monthly, $80/annual nonmember subscription, free/members. About ten display ads for pharmaceutical scientists appear throughout.

Drug Store News (Lebhar–Friedman, 444 N. Michigan Ave., Chicago, IL 60611; phone: 813/664-6707) 22 issues/year, $95/annual subscription (U.S. and Canada), $125/elsewhere. About nine vacancies in health care management, suppliers, and marketing appear under "Job Mart."

Clinical Pharmacology & Therapeutics (Mosby Year Book, Journal Subscription Services, 11830 Westline Industrial Dr., St. Louis, MO 63146; phones: 800/325-4177, ext. 4351, 314/872-8370, ext. 4351) monthly, $92/annual subscription (U.S.), $47/student (U.S.), $123.44/Canada, $117/elsewhere. There are usually two or three display ads for job openings.

Pharmaceutical Technology (Aster Publishing Corp., 859 Willamette St., Eugene, OR 97440; phone: 503/343-1200) monthly, $54/annual subscription. "Recruitment—Career Opportunities" includes close to 30 ads for pharmaceutical engineers, formulations scientists, laboratory directors, research and development, quality control, chemists, sales, marketing, biostatisticians, technical evaluators, and regulatory affairs experts.

American Pharmacy (1288 Valley Forge Rd., Valley Forge, PA 19481; phone: 215/ 925-3301) monthly, $50/annual nonmember subscription, free/members. About three ads for pharmacists appear under "Classified—Help Wanted."

Pharmacy Times (80 Shore Rd., Port Washington, NY 11050; phone: 516/883-6350) monthly, $30/annual subscription, $18/pharmacists and students. The "Classifieds" feature three or four ads for pharmacists.

Job services

National Registry for Pharmaceutical Scientists (c/o Illinois Department of Employment Security, 401 S. State St., Chicago, IL 60605; phone: 312/793-4904) free. Operated in conjunction with the American Association of Pharmaceutical Scientists (601 King St., Alexandria, VA 22314; phone: 703/548-3000), this service keeps your resume application form on file for one year. Obtain the application form from the Chicago office. The Registry submits a copy of the forms of qualified applicants to employers who are seeking pharmaceutical scientists. Employers then contact them directly for an interview.

PharmNet—Career Opportunities (American Society of Hospital Pharmacists, 4630 Montgomery Ave., Bethesda, MD 20814; phone: 301/657-3000) free/job seekers; computer and modem essential. Call 800/848-8980 to obtain a local access number and then look for the C—Career Opportunities option on your PharmNet main menu. Job seekers can use this electronic bulletin board to browse job opportunities, generally with hospitals, before they appear in ASHP's *American Journal of Hospital Pharmacists* described above under "Job openings." Job seekers may also place their resume on the bulletin board—you can be listed without your name—for employers to browse and contact you if they are interested. This service just started in 1991.

Job Service (National Association of Retail Druggists, 205 Daingerfield Rd., Alexandria, VA 22314; phone: 703/683-8200) available only to members, $25/annual fee. Complete this job-matching service's resume form. Resumes are sent to appropriate employers who contact the job candidate directly. Positions covered include pharmacists, registered nurses, and i.v. services.

Directories

National Association of Chain Drug Stores Membership Directory (NACDS, 413 N. Lee St., Alexandria, VA 22314; phone: 703/549-3001) $500/nonmembers, free/members, published each January. Includes member chain drug stores, supplies, colleges of pharmacy, and state agencies.

Drug Store and HBA Chains (Chain Store Guide Information Services, 425 Park Ave., New York, NY 10022; phone: 212/371-9400, ext. 306) $239, published each December. Profiles 2,000 chains that operate 30,000 drug and health and beauty aid (HBA) stores. Includes 11,000 key executive, buying, and administrative personnel.

High Volume Independent Drug Stores (Chain Store Guide Information Services, 425 Park Ave., New York, NY 10022; phone: 212/371-9400, ext. 306) $269, published biennially in December. Describes 9,500 one-unit drug stores. Includes 15,000 key executive, buying, and administrative personnel.

Directory of Drug Stores & HBA Chains (Chain Store Guide Information Services, 425 Park Ave., New York, NY 10022; phone: 212/371-9400) $229 plus $5 shipping, issued each December. Includes 30,000 drug stores and health and beauty aid (HBA) stores in 2,000 drug store chains as well as drug wholesalers and 10,000 key personnel. Contact for information on regional editions.

Salary survey

ACCP Employment, Salary, and Compensation Survey (American College of Clinical Pharmacy, 3101 Broadway, Suite 380, Kansas City, MO 64111; phone: 816/531-2177), appears in the July issue of *ACCP Report*, contact for availability and costs. Provides details on clinical pharmacists in practice, teaching, and research settings.

Technical, medical assistants

Also see the job sources listed under "Nursing" earlier in this chapter.

Job openings

PAJF Employment Magazine (American Academy of Physician Assistants, 950 N. Washington St., Alexandria, VA 22314; 703/836–2272, ext. 3508) semimonthly, $50/two–month nonmember subscription, $20/two–month member subscription, $80/annual member subscription. Close to 200 jobs for physician assistants and some nurse practitioners fill this to the brim.

Journal of the American Academy of Physician Assistants (Mosby Year Book, Journal Subscription Services, 11830 Westline Industrial Dr., St. Louis, MO 63146; phones: 800/325–4177, ext. 4351, 314/872–8370, ext. 4351) ten issues/year, $35/annual subscription (U.S.), $52.45/Canada, $50/elsewhere. "JAAPA Classifieds" run about 40 job ads and ten display ads for physician assistants.

AARD Times (American Association for Respiratory Diseases, 11030 Ables Ln., Dallas, TX 75229; phone: 214/243–2272) monthly, $50/annual nonmember subscription, free/members. "Employment Opportunities" features 200 or more openings for respiratory therapists, perinatal pediatric specialists, cardiopulmonary technologists, and administrators.

Lab Tech Med Tech Professional Career Bulletin (Prime National Publishing Company, 470 Boston Post Rd., Weston, MA 02193; phones: 800/869–2700, 617/899–2702) monthly, $22/annual subscription (U.S.), $26/foreign. Display ads for 30 to 40 medical technologists, cytotechnolgists, and laboratory researchers appear throughout.

Clinician Reviews (Williams & Wilkins, 428 E. Preston St., Baltimore, MD 21202–3993; phone: 800/638–6423) nine issues/year, $40/annual subscription (U.S.), $25/students, $28/nurse practitioners, $65/foreign. Around ten positions for physicians assistants and nurse practitioners appear in display ads.

Journal of the American Society of Echocariography (Mosby Year Book, Journal Subscription Services, 11830 Westline Industrial Dr., St. Louis, MO 63146; phones: 800/325–4177, ext. 4351, 314/872–8370, ext. 4351) bimonthly, $56/annual subscription (U.S.), $32/student (U.S.), $70.92/Canada, $67/elsewhere. About 12 openings appear in display ads and under "Opportunities Available."

AAPA Newsletter (American Association of Pathologists Assistants, c/o Robert Blasek, Holland Hospital, Holland, MI 49423; phone: 616/394–3619) quarterly, free, available only to members. About 30 ads for pathologists' assistants appear under "Classified."

NAEMT News (National Emergency Medical Technicians Job-Matching Service, 9140 Ward Pkwy., Kansas City, MO 64114; phone: 816/444–3500) monthly, $25/annual nonmember subscription, free/members. As many as five ads for emergency medical technicians, paramedics, EMS administrators, and EMS instructors appear under "Positions Available." Also carries " Positions Wanted" ads from job seekers.

Radiologic Technology (American Society of Radiologic Technology, 15000 Central Ave,. SE, Albuquerque, NM 89123; phone: 505/298–4500) bimonthly, $45/annual nonmember subscription, free/members. The "Classifieds" overflow with around 50 job ads for radiographers, radiation therapists, sonographers, nuclear medicine technologists, MRI, and others in this field.

RS Wavelength (American Society of Radiologic Technologists, 15000 Central Ave, SE, Albuquerque, NM 87123; phone: 505/298–4500) free upon request. About 30 openings for radiographers, radiation therapists, sonographers, nuclear medicine technologists, MRI, CT technologists, and others appear under "Classified Advertising."

Job Listing (Society of Diagnostic Medical Sonographers, 12225 Greenville Ave., Suite 434, Dallas, TX 75243; phone: 214/235–7367) $75/annual subscription. As best we can determine, this list of job openings is sent out upon request; but you better contact them directly for details.

Applied Radiology: The Journal of Medical Imaging and Therapy (Anderson Publishing, 80 Shore Rd., Port Washington, NY 11050; phone: 516/883–6530) monthly, $55/annual subscription, free to qualified professionals. A few jobs for radiologists, ultrasound operators, administrators, and nuclear medicine professionals get advertised in the "Classified" section.

CP Digest (National Society for Cardiovascular Technology/National Society for Pulmonary Technology, 1101 14th St., NW, Suite 1100, Washington, DC 20005; phone: 202/371–1267) bimonthly, free/members, available only to members of either society. Two to five ads for broad range of cardiology or pulmonary technical or administrative positions appear under "Employment Opportunity."

Health Facilities Management (American Society for Hospital Engineering, 840 N. Lake Shore Dr., Chicago, IL 60611; phone: 312/280–6000) monthly, $30/annual subscription (U.S.), $46/foreign. Two to five positions for facilities managers, biomedical equipment technicians, and managers of engineering appear under "Classified."

Journal of Opthalmic Nursing & Technology (SLACK, Inc., 6900 Grove Rd., Thorofare, NJ 08086–9447; phones: 800/257–8290, 609/848–1000) bimonthly, $32/annual subscription (U.S.), $44/Canada, $61/elsewhere. About five opportunities in vision care appear under "Classified Marketplace."

Transfusion (1117 N. 19th St., Suite 600, Arlington, VA 22209; phone: 703/528–8200) nine issues/year. $98/annual subscription (U.S.), $113/foreign. Under "Classified," you'll find ten to 15 ads for medical blood technicians, blood bank directors, and medical technicians with specialties in transfusion medicine and blood banking.

Blood Bank Week (American Association of Blood Banks, 1117 N. 19th St., Suite 600, Arlington, VA 22209; phone: 703/528–8200) weekly, $128/annual nonmember subscription, $98/members. "Classified Advertising" will have about five jobs for medical technologists, donor recruiters, laboratory doctors, inventory managers, and administrators.

The Cytotechnologist's Bulletin (American Society of Cytology, 1015 Chestnut St., Suite 1518, Philadelphia, PA 19107; phone: 203/679–4215) bimonthly, free. Fifteen to 20 job announcements appear under "Positions Available."

AMT Events (American Medical Technologists, 710 Higgins Rd., Park Ridge, IL 60068; phone: 708/823–5169) eight issues/year, $35/annual subscription. Three or four job announcements appear under "Classified Ads."

Job services

National Medical Network—Technologists' Network (Boyds Branch Rd., Rt. 1, Box 1230, Manchester, TN 37355; phone: 800/752–1906) free. Tell them the type of work you seek and the geographic area in which you wish to work, and they'll send you a list of hospitals that are looking for RTTs, NMTs, MRIs, sonographers, dosimetrists, CT Scan, and other health care technologists like you. This is not a recruiting service.

Placement Service (American Medical Technologists, 710 Higgins Rd., Park Ridge, IL 60068; phone: 708/823–5169) free, available only to members, resumes kept on file four months. Participants complete this service's resume form. Job seekers are sent a list of available jobs on file and employers are sent a list of job candidates seeking medical technologist, technician, and assistants jobs.

Job Opportunities Bank (National Society for Cardiovascular Technology/National Society for Pulmonary Technology, 1101 14th St., NW, Suite 1100, Washington, DC 20005; phone: 202/371–1267) $150/nonmember annual fee, $10/members, $5/student members. You complete their detailed "Resume Form for Computer Matching"

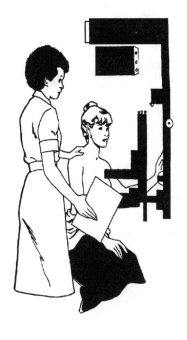

and narrative form (this is given to potential employers, so be neat) which are kept on file for 12 months. When matches are made, the employer contacts the job candidate. Even if matches are not made, reports on all registrants are sent to employers at least quarterly and a list of all jobs being handled by this service is sent to job seekers at least quarterly so you can contact potential employers directly. Covers positions in a broad range of cardiology or pulmonary technology and administration.

Job Opportunities 800 Number (National Society for Cardiovascular Technology/National Society for Pulmonary Technology, 1101 14th St., NW, Suite 1100, Washington, DC 20005; phone: 202/371-1267), free. Call 800/743-5627 for to hear a recording of several open positions in cardiology or pulmonary technology and administration.

Employers Employment Exchange Service (American Society of Electroneurodiagnostic Technologists, Sixth at Quint, Carroll, IA 51401; phone: 712/792-2978) $30/six–month nonmember fee, free/members. Complete this job–matching service's resume form. It will be circulated to employers seeking electroneurodiagnostic technologists in: EEG, evoked potential, sleep, and nerve conduction. Twice each month, you will be sent a listing of open positions and told whom to contact.

AARD Job Hotline (American Association for Respiratory Diseases, 11030 Ables Ln., Dallas, TX 75229; phone: 214/243-2272). Call 214/241-7249 24 hours a day for a recording of current employment opportunities in respiratory care. You select the positions that interest you and send your resume to the AARC. Updated on the first and fifteen of the month.

AAPA Job Hotline (American Association of Pathologists Assistants, c/o Thomas LeFoley, Pathology Dept., Wentworth Douglas Hospital, Dover, NH 03820; phone: 603/742-5252, ext. 557) free, available only to members. Member pathologists' assistants call the hotline to receive information about job openings. The job seeker then contacts the employer directly.

National Emergency Medical Technicians Job-Matching Service (NEMT, 9140 Ward Pkwy., Kansas City, MO 64114; phone: 816/444-3500). Submit a copy of your resume which is kept on file for six months. Companies list positions available and individuals' resumes are highlighted. Both parties contact the NEMT headquarters for further information.

New England Technologists Section Job Hotline (Society of Nuclear Medicine, 136 Madison Ave., New York, NY 10016; phone: 212/889-0717) free. Medical technologists can call 800/562-6387 to register. They are sent a list of vacancies from Tom Starno who operates this service which is funded by the Tech Physicians of New England. To reach Tom Starno for more information, call 207/945-7186. Vacancies are kept on the list for three months.

Directories

Directory of Radiologic Technologists (American Registry of Radiologic Technologists, 1255 Northland Dr., Mendota Heights, MN 55120; phone: 612/687-0048) free, available only to members, last issued in 1991.

National Society for Cardiovascular Technology/National Society for Pulmonary Technology Membership Directory (NSCT/NSPT, 1101 14th St., NW, Suite 1100, Washington, DC 20005; phone: 202/371-1267) free, available only to members, published each autumn.

ASET Membership Directory (American Society of Electroneurodiagnostic Technologists, Sixth at Quint, Carroll, IA 51401; phone: 712/792-2978) free, available only to members, issued each spring.

Directory of Community Blood Bank Centers (American Association of Blood Banks, 1117 N. 19th St., Suite 600, Arlington, VA 22209; phone: 703/528-8200) $35/nonmembers, $25/members, issued in July of odd-numbered years. Provides in-depth information on over 100 blood centers listed by state including a map of the service area, names of key personnel, services offered, and financial and governance details.

Salary survey

PAJF Employment Magazine (American Academy of Physician Assistants, 950 N. Washington St., Alexandria, VA 22314; 703/836-2272, ext. 3508) semimonthly, $50/two–month nonmember subscription, $20/two–month member subscription, $80/annual member subscription. The January issue often features the results of the AAPA's salary survey.

Therapy—mental

Also see the entries under "Therapy—physical," later in this chapter, and see the "Social services" chapter. Many of these sources under "Therapy–physical" include positions in mental therapy. Also see the Government Job Finder and the Non–Profit's Job Finder.

Job openings

The APA Monitor (American Psychological Association, 1200 17th St., NW, Washington, DC 20036; phone: 202/955–7690) $25/nonmember annual subscription (U.S.), $37/foreign, free/members. Jobs listed under "Position Openings." From 400 to 800 job ads for psychologists and psychiatrists, and support staff, grace the pages of a typical issue.

Psychiatric News (American Psychiatric Association, 1400 K St., NW, Washington, DC 20005; phone: 202/682–6250) semimonthly, $40/annual nonmember subscription (U.S.), $60/foreign, free/members. Display ads and the "Classified Notices" feature close to 400 job vacancies for staff psychiatrists and psychologists, administrative staff, and support staff.

The Guidepost (American Rehabilitation Counseling Association, 5999 Stevenson Ave., Alexandria, VA 22304; phone: 703/823–9800, ext. 234) 18 issues/year, $30/annual subscription. "Employment Classifieds" describe around 35 vacancies for psychologists and counselors in private practice, agencies, and universities.

American Journal of Psychiatry (American Psychiatric Association, 1400 K St., NW, Washington, DC 20005; phone: 202/682–6250) monthly, $56/annual nonmember subscription (U.S.), $86/foreign, free/members. About seven job openings appear in display ads.

Mother Goose and Grim is reprinted by permission of MGM L&M and Grimmy, Inc. Copyright 1991. All rights reserved.

Archives of General Psychiatry (American Medical Association, Circulation Dept., 515 N. State St., Chicago, IL 60610; phone: 312/464–0183) monthly, $58/annual subscription, $73 foreign (surface mail), special rates for residents and medical students. About 20 positions are listed under "Classified Advertising."

Psychiatric Annals (SLACK, Inc., 6900 Grove Rd., Thorofare, NJ 08086–9447; phones: 800/257–8290, 609/848–1000) monthly, $85/annual subscription (U.S.), $103/Canada, $121/elsewhere. Around two or three job openings and practices for sale appear under "Classified Marketplace."

Journal of Psychosocial Nursing (SLACK, Inc., 6900 Grove Rd., Thorofare, NJ 08086–9447; phones: 800/257–8290, 609/848–1000) monthly, $44/annual subscription (U.S.), $62/Canada, $80/elsewhere. Around two or three job openings appear under "Classified Marketplace."

Perspectives in Psychiatric Care (Nursecom, Inc., 1211 Locust St., Philadelphia, PA 19107; phone: 215/547-7222) quarterly, $35/annual subscription (U.S.), $45/foreign. About four ads for psychiatric nurses appear under "Classified."

American Academy of Child and Adolescent Psychiatry Newsletter (AACAP, 3615 Wisconsin Ave., NW, Washington, DC 20016; phones: 800/333-7636, 202/966-7300) quarterly, contact for availability and subscription rates. You'll generally find about six ads under "Positions" for practitioner and academic positions.

Family Therapy News (American Association for Marriage and Family Therapy, 1100 17th St., NW, Washington, DC 20036; phone: 202/452-0109) bimonthly, $25/annual subscription (U.S.), $35/foreign. "Classified Ads" has about 25 openings for marriage and family therapists including practitioners, researchers, pastoral counselors, faculty, and practices for sale.

ABA Newsletter (Association for Behavior Analysis, ATTEN: Sharon Myers, 258 Wood Hall, Western Michigan University, Kalamazoo, MI 49008-5052; phone: 616/387-4495) quarterly, $15/annual nonmember subscription (U.S. and Canada), $20/elsewhere, free/members. "Positions available" lists from five to ten openings for psychologists, therapists, consultants, and faculty.

Forthcoming Jobs Bulletin (National Association of Private Psychiatric Hospitals, 1319 F St., NW, Suite 1000, Washington, DC 20004; phone: 202/393-6700). Sometime in the first half of 1992, NAPPH will start publishing this as yet unnamed jobs bulletin that will be filled with announcements of job vacancies for physicians, nurses, psychologists, and administrators in both private and public psychiatric hospitals. It will be available to nonmembers. Contact Ms. Connie Schantz at NAPPH for details.

Newsletter of the American Art Therapy Association (AATA, 1202 Allanson Rd., Mundelein, IL 60060; phone: 708/949-6064) quarterly, $16/annual nonmember subscription (U.S. and Canada), $28/elsewhere, free/members. Four to six positions for art therapists in rehabilitation medical facilities and universities appear under "Opportunities."

Journal of Gerontological Nursing (SLACK, Inc., 6900 Grove Rd., Thorofare, NJ 08086-9447; phones: 800/257-8290, 609/848-1000) monthly, $34/annual subscription (U.S.), $52/Canada, $70/elsewhere. Around two or three job openings appear under "Classified Marketplace."

Job services

Psychiatric Placement Service (American Psychiatric Association, 1400 K St., NW, Washington, DC 20005; phone: 202/682-6108), free. Obtain an application form and submit it with your resume. When matched with a vacancy, both you and the employer are notified. Resumes are kept on file indefinitely.

Job Bank (American Association for Music Therapy, 4901 Henry Hudson Pkwy., #St-D, Riverdale, NY 10471; phone: 215/242-4450) $15 registration fee; only for certified or registered music therapists. You submit self-addressed stamped #10 business envelopes and the service sends you computer printouts of appropriate job vacancies. The job seeker then contacts the potential employer.

Psychology Society Placement Service (Psychology Society, 100 Beekman St., New York, NY 10038; 212/285-1872). Each time we called this number we got an individual who confirmed that this service exists, but refused, in a most snobbish way, to give us any information about it except to say that it is available only to members. He said that the society would not be interested in nonmembers learning about this service since it is only for Ph.Ds. He said that anybody in the field knows about this service, so why list it in our book? I assume that this gentleman does not represent the attitudes of most PS members, but his behavior certainly does not represent the society in a positive manner.

Directories

APA Membership Directory (American Psychological Association, 1200 17th St., NW, Washington, DC 20036; phone: 202/955-7690) $35/nonmembers, $22.50/members, published every four years. Most recent edition, 1991.

AMHA Membership Directory (Association of Mental Health Administrators, 60 Revere, Suite 500, Northbrook, IL 60062; phone: 708/480-9626) contact them for price. This directory of mental health administrators was first published in August 1991.

Association for Behavior Analysis Membership Directory (ABA, 258 Wood Hall, Western Michigan University, Kalamazoo, MI 49008-5052; phone: 616/387-4495) $10, issued each February, 80 pages. Lists the names, addresses, phones, fax numbers, and specialties for each of its 1,900 members.

Membership Directory of the American Art Therapy Association (AATA, 1202 Allanson Rd., Mundelein, IL 60060; phone: 708/949-6064) $50/individual nonmembers, $100/nonmember institutions, $10/members, new edition in December of even-numbered years, addendum published in odd-numbered years.

Therapy—physical

Also see the entries under "Therapy—mental," earlier in this chapter, and see the "Social services" chapter. Many of these sources under "Therapy-mental" include positions in physical therapy. Also see the Government Job Finder and the Non-Profit's Job Finder for additonal job sources.

Job openings

ASHA (American Speech-Language-Hearing Association, 10801 Rockville Pike, Rockville, MD 20852; phones: 800/638-8255, 301/897-5700) 11 issues/year, $90/annual nonmember subscription, free/members. Around 200 ads in the "ASHA Classifieds" describe openings for speech-language pathologists, audiologists, speech scientists, and speech and hearing professors.

Hearing Instruments (Edgell Communications, 1 E. First St., Duluth, MN 55802; phones: 800/346-0085, 218/723-9870) monthly; $35/annual subscription (U.S.); $60/Canada; $90/elsewhere. The "Marketplace—Help Wanted—Reps Wanted—For Sale—Business Opportunities" includes nearly 20 job ads for audiologists, speech therapists, hearing aid technicians and repair persons, sales and manufacturers' reps plus about ten hearing aid practices for sale. The May directory issue costs $15 by itself.

Physical Therapy (American Physical Therapy Association, 111 N. Fairfax St., Alexandria, VA 22314; phones: 800/999-2782, 703/684-2782) monthly, $55/annual nonmember subscription ($65 via first class mail), free/members. About 40 ads for physical therapists and assistants, faculty, and related positions appear under "Classified Advertising."

Occupational Therapist Weekly (164 Rollins Ave., Suite 301, Rockville, MD 20852: phone: 301/881-2490) weekly, free to qualified occupational therapists. Around 200 job openings for occupational therapists fill this tabloid.

PT/OT Job News (Prime National Publishing Company, 470 Boston Post Rd., Weston, MA 02193; phones: 800/869-2700, 617/899-2702) monthly, $22/annual subscription (U.S.) $26/foreign. Under different regional headings, you'll find about 20 jobs for physical therapists, occupational therapists, and rehabilitation therapists.

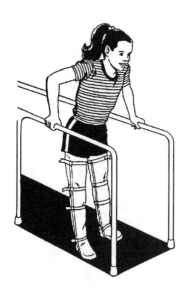

Journal of Cardiopulmonary Rehabilitation (American Association of Cardiovascular and Pulmonary Rehabilitation, 7611 Elmwood, Suite 201, Middleton, WI 53562; phones: 800/638-3030, 608/831-6989) bimonthly, $55/annual nonmember subscription. Just a few ads for cardiopulmonary rehabilitation services, exercise physiologists, and other medical personnel appear under "Professional Opportunities."

ASHT News (American Society of Hand Therapists, 1002 Vandora Springs Rd., Suite 101, Garner, NC 27529; phone: 919/779-2748) bimonthly, $25/six-month nonmember subscription, free/members. Five to ten openings for occupation or physical therapists who specialize on rehabilitating hands appear under "Job Placement."

Update (American Alliance for Health, Physical Education, Recreation and Dance, 1900 Association Dr., Reston, VA 22091; phone: 703/476–3400) eight issues/year, $45/annual nonmember subscription, free/members ($85/annual dues). While "Job Exchange" features 30 or more jobs with largely camps and universities as well as numerous graduate assistantships and grants, many of the positions involve physical therapist skills.

Journal PERD (American Alliance for Health, Physical Education, Recreation and Dance, 1900 Association Dr., Reston, VA 22091; phone: 703/476–3400) monthly, $65/annual nonmember subscription. The "Classifieds" feature vacancies for about five positions with camps and universities, some of which require physical therapist skills.

Massage Therapy Journal (American Massage Therapy Association, 1130 W. North Shore Ave., Chicago, IL 60626; phone: 312/761–2682) quarterly, $15/annual subscription (U.S. and Canada), $25/elsewhere. About five ads for massage therapists appear under "Classified—Business Opportunities."

Massage (Noah Publishing Company, 1772 Picasso Ave., Suite E, Davis, CA 95616; phone: 800/533–4263) bimonthly, $18/annual subscription (U.S.), $22/Canada, $30/elsewhere. Two to six job opportunities appear under "Classified Ads."

Job services

Employment Referral Service (American Speech–Language–Hearing Association, 10801 Rockville Pike, Rockville, MD 20852; phones: 800/638–8255, 301/897–5700) $45/four-month nonmember fee, $35/four-month member fee; can renew for longer period. Submit the service's application and each week it will run its matching program. Potential employers will contact the job seeker directly. The service is geared for speech–language pathologists, audiologists, speech scientists, and speech and hearing professors.

The Job Bank (164 Rollins Ave., Suite 301, Rockville, MD 20852: phone: 301/881-2490) contact for details. If you have a computer modem you can access this database to see about 650 jobs for occupational therapists.

AOTA—OT Source (American Occupational Therapy Association, 1383 Piccard Dr., Rockville, MD 20850-0822; phone: 948-9626) $150/nonmembers, $50/individual members (additional one-time $65 charge for Macintosh users for special software); computer and modem imperative. The "Job Bank," one of the many databases on this computerized information system, lists hundreds of occupational therapy-related vacancies nationwide. Operates 18 hours a day.

Directories

Physical Therapists Directory (American Business Directories, Inc., 5711 S. 86th Cr., Omaha, NE 68127; phone: 402/593-4600) $475, annual. Over 14,000 listings.

ASHA Membership Directory (American Speech-Language-Hearing Association, 10801 Rockville Pike, Rockville, MD 20852; phones: 800/638-8255, 301/897-5700) $60/nonmembers, $40/members, published in odd-numbered years.

Salary survey

1990 Member Data Survey: Summary Report (Occupational Therapy Association, Research and Evaluation Division, 1383 Piccard Dr., Rockville, MD 20850; phone: 301/948-9626) contact for price, published every three or four years. Based on returns from 50 percent of its 40,000 members, this report discloses details on member salaries, demographics, education, and types of jobs.

Chapter 18

Hospitality and food industries

Hospitality industry in general

Job openings

Opportunities in Hospitality (21250 Box Springs Rd., Suite 215, Moreno Valley, CA 92557; phone: 714/788–9099) biweekly, $45/12–issue subscription, $36/six–issue subscription. From 45 to 200 job openings in all aspects and levels of the hospitality industry fill this jobs bulletin: hotel, country club, resort, cruise, restaurant, golf club, yacht club management, occasionally chef positions.

Hospitality Careers Mart (c/o Dr. Fred Antil, Statler Hall, Cornell University, Ithaca, NY 14853; phone: 607/255–3945) biweekly, $15/Cornell Hotel School alumni only. Twenty to 25 job descriptions for positions in hospitality (hotel, restaurant, tourism, hospital patient services, teaching, and investment opportunities) fill the typical issue.

Hotel & Motel Management (Edgell Communications, 1 E. First St., Duluth, MN 55802; phones: 800/346-0085, 218/723-9870) monthly; $35/annual subscription (U.S.); $60/Canada; $110/elsewhere. The "Action Ads" section is chock full with nearly 20 ads for hotel and motel managers, chefs, and sales reps as well as over 100 hotels or motels for sale.

Directory

Directory of Executive Search Companies (Atlantic Enterprises, 21346 St. Andrews Blvd., Suite 212, Boca Raton, FL 33433) $29. Includes more than 200 executive search firms that specialize in the hospitality industry.

Salary survey

American Hotel and Motel Association Hospitality Industry Compensation Survey (AHMA, 1201 New York Ave., NW, Washington, DC 20005; phone: 202/289-3162) $190/nonmembers, $95/members, issued in June of odd-numbered years. Positions covered include general manager, resident manager, front office manager, reservations manager, controller, executive housekeeper, chief engineer, director of sales and marketing, sales managers, security director, personnel director, food and beverage director, executive chef, executive steward, and restaurant manager.

Lodging and travel industry

Job openings

Lodging Magazine (American Hotel and Motel Association, 1201 New York Ave., NW, Washington, DC 20005; phone: 202/289-3162) 11 issues/year, $35/annual nonmember subscription, free/members. About a dozen ads for management positions, marketing, accountants, safety/security, and related personnel in hotel/motel management are in "Lodging Classified."

Executive Career Services (Club Managers Association of America, 1733 King St., Alexandria, VA 22314; phone: 703/739-9500) weekly, $610/nonmembers, $100/members (think they're tying to make it worth your while to join?). Positions listed are for general managers of clubs.

Tour & Travel News (CMP Publications, 600 Community Dr., Manhasset, NY 11030; phone: 516/562-5000) 50 issues/year, $75/annual subscription (U.S., Canada), free to qualified travel agents who specialize in leisure travel, tour operators/wholesalers, incen-

"The staff was rude, the bed was hard, the food was inedible—and when we come back next year, I'm going to tell them so."

tive travel companies and qualified subscribers. About five job openings with tour operators and travel agencies are in the "Classified Recruitment/Marketplace" section.

Business Travel News (CMP Publications, 600 Community Dr., Manhasset, NY 11030; phone: 516/562-5000) 27 issues/year, $90/annual subscription (U.S., Canada), free to qualified corporate travel arrangers and to travel agencies specializing in business travel in the U.S. and Canada. "Business Travel Recruitment" runs ads for about ten management, sales, and travel specialist positions.

Travelware (Business Journals, 50 Day St., Norwalk, CT 06854; phone: 203/853-6015) nine issues/year, $32/annual subscription (U.S.), $42/Canada, $100/elsewhere. Four or five ads for sales representatives are in the "Classifieds."

Club Director (National Club Association, 3050 K St., NW, Suite 330, Washington, DC 20007; phone: 202/625-2080) monthly, $15/members only. As of late 1991, NCA was considering adding job advertisements to *Club Director* sometime in 1992.

Bottomline (International Association of Hospitality Accountants, P.O. Box 27649, Austin, TX 78755; phone: 512/346-5680) bimonthly, $50/annual nonmember subscription, free/members.

Published in alternating months with *The President's Log* described immediately below. "Job Opportunities" lists about ten jobs for accountants and comptrollers for hotels, resorts, and cruise lines.

The President's Log (International Association of Hospitality Accountants, P.O. Box 27649, Austin, TX 78755; phone: 512/346-5680) bimonthly, available only to members, included in dues. Published in alternating months with *Bottomline* described immediately above. "Job Opportunities" features about eight positions for accountants and comptrollers with hotels, resorts, and cruise lines.

Job service

International Society of Hotel Association Executives Job–Matching Service (ISHAE, 9415 Hull Rd., Suite B, Richmond, VA 23236; phone: 804/276-8614) contact for details. You submit your own resume which is then given to employers when there is job match.

Directories

The Travel Industry Personnel Directory (Fairchild Books, 7 E. 12th St., New York, NY 10003; phone: 800/247-6622) $25, published each spring, 545 pages. Includes over 20,000 entries of sales and executive personnel for U.S. and Canadian hotel representatives and the hotels they handle as well as domestic and regional airlines, shiplines, railroads, motorcoach and car rental companies and tour operators.

Who's Who in the Lodging Industry (American Hotel and Motel Association, 1201 New York Ave., NW, Washington, DC 20005; phone: 202/289-3162) $39.95, annual, over 1,000 pages. Also available as address labels. Lists over 40,000 key executives at lodging companies plus purveyors and consultants to the lodging industry.

Tours—Operators and Promoters (American Business Directories, 5711 S. 86th Cr., Omaha, NE 68127; phone: 402/593-4600) $215, published each January. Over 5,500 operators and promoters of vacation tours are described by state.

American Society of Travel Agents Membership Directory (ASTA, 1101 King St., Alexandria, VA 22314; phone: 800/828–2712) $125/nonmembers, free/members, most recent edition January 1992.

Institute of Certified Travel Agents Directory (ICTA, 148 Linden St., Wellesley, MA 02181; phones: 800/542–4282, 617/237–0280) contact for price, annual.

Who's Who in the Private Club Industry (National Club Association, 3050 K St., NW, Suite 330, Washington, DC 20007; phone: 202/625–2080) $395, free/members, annual.

Salary survey

Agency Salary and Benefits Survey (American Society of Travel Agents, 1101 King St., Alexandria, VA 22314; phone: 800/828–2712) $100/nonmembers, $50/members, issued in autumn of 1989 and every three years thereafter.

Restaurants and foodservice

Also see the entries under "Food production" in the "Manufacturing" chapter.

Nation's Restaurant News (Lebhar–Friedman, 425 Park Ave., New York, NY 10022; phone: 800/4447–7133) weekly, $89/annual subscription, $34.50/qualified foodservice operators, wholesalers, distributors, brokers, and dealers. "Foodservice Mart" includes about 40 job ads for all types of positions (mostly management) in the foodservice industry under "Help Wanted," 30 ads under "Business Opportunities," and 20 ads for restaurants under "For Sale."

Restaurant Business (633 Third Ave., New York, NY 10017; phone: 212/984–2299) 18 issues/year, $79/annual subscription, free/qualified foodservice professionals. "Foodservice Marketplace" carries ads for about six ownership or franchising opportunities.

Restaurants & Institutions (Cahners Publishing, 44 Cook St., Denver, CO 80206; phone: 800/637–6089) 31 issues/year, $104.95/annual subscription (U.S.), $179.95/Mexico, $192.55/Canada, $234.95/elsewhere. Around ten job openings in the foodservice industry as well as ownership opportunities are advertised under "Classified—Positions Available," "Franchise Opportunities," and "Business Opportunities."

Food Service Director (633 Third Ave., New York, NY 10017; phone: 212/984–2299) monthly, $35/annual subscription (U.S.), $45/Canada, $60/elsewhere, free to qualified food service personnel. About eight job ads in foodservice management and for chefs are in the "Classifieds."

International Food Service Executives Association (IFSEA, 1100 S. State Road 7, Suite 103, Margate, FL 33068; phone: 305/977–0767) contact for details. IFSEA expects to start running job ads in one of its publications during 1992.

Foodservice Equipment & Supplies (Cahners Publishing, 44 Cook St., Denver, CO 80206; phone: 800/637–6089) 14 issues/year, $99/annual subscription. About a dozen positions for foodservice equipment are advertised under "Marketplace—Recruitment/Classified."

Food Management (Edgell Communications, 1 E. First St., Duluth, MN 55802; phones: 800/346-0085, 218/723-9870) monthly, $35/annual subscription (U.S.), $60/Canada, $125/elsewhere. Three or four positions for chefs, food production managers, and commissary managers with private companies, schools, and amusement facilities are advertised under "Classified—Career Opportunities."

"It's health food. As long as you don't eat it, you'll be in good health."

National Culinary Review (American Culinary Federation, P.O. Box 3466, St. Augustine, FL 32084-3466; phone: 904/824-4468) monthly, $25/annual subscription. "Open Market" includes six to eight job openings for chefs and cooks for restaurants, clubs, resorts, and hotels as well listing restaurants for sale.

Bon Appetit (P.O. Box 7196, Red Oak, IA 51591-2196; phone: 800/876-3663) monthly, call for current subscription rate. A few job openings and business opportunities are listed in "The Marketplace."

The Foodservice Distributor (Penton Publishing, 1100 Superior Ave., Cleveland, OH 44114; phone: 216/696-7000) monthly; free to qualified professionals, call or write for application form; otherwise: $50/annual subscription (U.S.), $80/Canada, $90/elsewhere. "Employment Opportunities—Foodservice Distributor Opportunities" includes a handful of job ads, largely from recruitment firms.

American Automatic Merchandiser (Edgell Communications, 1 E. First St., Duluth, MN 55802; phones: 800/346-0085, 218/723-9870) monthly; $25/annual subscription (U.S.); $50/Canada; $100/elsewhere. About half a dozen ads appear under "Classified Ads—Help Wanted" for vending machine sales and dealers, and foodservice and vending management. The July *Buyers Guide* is available by itself for $25.

Bakery Production and Marketing (Gorman Publishing, 8750 W. Bryn Mawr Ave., Chicago, IL 60631; phone: 312/693-3200) 14 issues/year; $79/annual subscription (U.S.), $139/foreign. See the "Classified Marketplace—Employment Marketplace" for ads for over 15 positions for all aspects of the bakery industry including bakery plan engineers, equipment sales, management, production supervisors, and sanitation.

Job service

International Chefs' Association Placement Service (ICA, P.O. Box 1889, New York, NY 10116; phone: 201/825-8455) free/members only. This service refers member chefs who are seeking work to employers seeking chefs.

Directories

Chain Restaurant Operators (Chain Store Guide Information Services, 425 Park Ave., New York, NY 10022; phone: 212/371-9400, ext. 306) $239, published each May. Describes about 3,400 chain restaurant companies that operate more than 191,000 restaurants, drive-ins, cafeterias, hotels, motels, contract feeders/industrial feeders, and food units in drug chains, general merchandise and variety chains, discount stores, or department stores. Includes 12,000 key executive, buying, and administrative personnel.

High Volume Independent Restaurants (Chain Store Guide Information Services, 425 Park Ave., New York, NY 10022; phone: 212/371-9400, ext. 306) $249, published biennially in July. Profiles about 7,000 independent restaurant companies operating more than 8,500 restaurants in the U.S. Includes 18,500 key executive, buying, and administrative personnel.

Foodservice Industry Directory (National Restaurant Association, 1200 17th St., NW, Suite 800, Washington, DC 20036; phone: 800/424-8156) $50/nonmembers, free/members, published each August.

Directory of College and University Foodservice (Chain Store Guide Information Services, 425 Park Ave., New York, NY 10022; phone: 212/371-9400, ext. 306) $249, published biennially in October. Profiles over 3,300 two- and four-year college and universities as well as the top 300 foodservice management companies. Includes key executive, buying, and administrative personnel.

Foodservice Distributors (Chain Store Guide Information Services, 425 Park Ave., New York, NY 10022; phone: 212/371-9400, ext. 306) $219, published each June. Profiles about 3,500 major distributors who supply food, equipment, and supplies to restaurants and institutional accounts. Includes 15,000 key executive, buying, and administrative personnel.

Retailer Owned Cooperatives, Wholesale Sponsored Voluntaries & Wholesale Grocers (Chain Store Guide Information Services, 425 Park Ave., New York, NY 10022; phone: 212/371-9400, ext. 306) $229, published each November. Details about 1,350 headquarters and divisions for about 120 cooperatives serving 25,000 stores, over 350 voluntary groups, 420 nonsponsoring wholesalers, and 450 cash-and-carry warehouse operations. Includes 11,500 key executive, buying, and administrative personnel.

Supermarket, Grocery and Convenience Store Chains (Chain Store Guide Information Services, 425 Park Ave., New York, NY 10022; phone: 212/371-9400, ext. 306) $249, published each October. Profiles 2,200 supermarket and grocery store chains. Includes 18,000 key executive, buying, and administrative personnel.

Single Unit Supermarket Operators (Chain Store Guide Information Services, 425 Park Ave., New York, NY 10022; phone: 212/371-9400, ext. 306) $219, published biennially in December. Focuses on over 6,000 single units supermarket operators. Includes 15,000 key executive, buying, and administrative personnel.

Society for American Cuisine Membership Directory (SAC, 304 W. Liberty St., Suite 301, Louisville, KY 40202; phone: 502/583-3783) free/members only, annual.

International Military Club Executive Association Membership Directory (IMCEA, 1438 Duke St., Alexandria, VA 22314; phone: 703/548-0093) $200, published each May.

Salary surveys

Foodservice Equipment & Supplies Salary Survey (Cahners Publishing, 44 Cook St., Denver, CO 80206; phone: 800/637-6089) $10/single issue. Last published in November 1990 issue of *Foodservice Equipment & Supplies* magazine described above under "Job openings," this survey covers a wide variety of management and sales positions in the foodservice industry. This survey has been conducted in 1984, 1986, and 1990.

Chapter 19

Legal services

Legal services

Most, if not all, state and local bar associations publish magazines or newsletters that include ads for attorney positions, and often for paralegals, court reporters, and office support positions within their geographic area. Contact your local bar association for information. The job sources presented in this chapter are national in scope.

Job openings

Opportunities in Public Interest Law (ACCESS: Networking in the Public Interest, 50 Beacon St., Boston, MA 02108; phone: 617/720-5627) quarterly, $175/annual subscription. With 3,000 jobs from 600+ employers, this national job bulletin includes all sorts of private sector positions as well as government positions.

Position Report (David J. White & Associates, 809 Ridge Rd., Wilmette, IL 60091; phone: 800/962-4947) weekly, $42.50/four week subscription, $115/12 weeks. This is a collection of 500+ job ads for attorneys taken from over 100 newspapers and periodicals from across the country.

The American Lawyer (American Lawyers Media, 600 Third Ave., New York, NY 10016; phone: 212/973-2885) monthly, $135/annual individual's subscription, $495/annual law firm subscription. ''Classified Advertising—Employment for Attorneys'' includes dozens of positions from around the country. Jobs include attorneys, paralegals, legal secretaries, and managing partners. Also includes a "Positions Wanted" section and a directory of legal recruiters.

National and Federal Legal Employment Report (Federal Reports, Inc., Suite 408, 1010 Vermont Ave., NW, Washington, DC 20005; phone: 202/393-3311) monthly. Subscription rates for individuals: $32/three-month, $55/six-month, $99/annual subscription; rates for institutions: $40, $75, $130, respectively. The typical issue contains descriptions of 500 to 600 attorney and law-related positions primarily in the federal government, state and local government, and private employers in government-related fields, including legal aid offices. Includes legal positions outside the U.S.

National Law Journal (111 Eighth Ave., New York, NY 10011; phones: 800/274-2893, 212/741-8300) weekly, $88/annual subscription (U.S.), $108/foreign (surface mail). Under "Career Opportunities" you'll find about 40 to 60 ads for attorney positions plus ads from "headhunters."

Legal Times (1730 M St., NW, Washington, DC 20036; phone: 202/457-0686) weekly, $175/annual individual's subscription, $435/annual law firm subscription. The classifieds section contains job vacancies largely in the DC area, but also nationally, under these headings: "Attorney Employment," about 40 jobs; "Employment" has about ten jobs for paralegals and legal assistants and four for legal secretaries.

NABWA News (National Association of Black Women Attorneys, 3711 Macomb St., NW, Washington, DC 20016; phone: 202/966-9693) monthly, available only to members, included in dues. "Job Bank" lists about five jobs for attorneys, law firm managers, and paralegals.

NCRA Employment Referral Service Bulletin (National Court Reporters Association, 8224 Old Courthouse Rd., Vienna, VA 22182; phone: 703/281-4677) biweekly, $24/nonmember annual subscription, $12/members. Typical issue features 20 to 30 job announcements for both free-lance and more formal court reporter positions.

Manhattan Lawyer (American Lawyers Media, 600 Third Ave., New York, NY 10016; phones: 212/973–2810, 212/973–2885) monthly, $49.50/annual individual's subscription, $295/annual law firm subscription. "Classified Advertising—Employment for Attorneys" includes ten to 15 positions from around the country. Jobs include attorneys, paralegals, legal secretaries, managing partners, and even judgeships. Also includes a "Positions Wanted" section and a directory of legal recruiters.

Doonesbury

BY GARRY TRUDEAU

Lawyers Job Bulletin Board (Federal Bar Association, Suite 408, 1815 H St., NW, Washington, DC 20006; phone: 202/638–0252) monthly, $30/nonmember annual subscription, $20/members, $20/students. Typical issue features 25 job openings primarily with the federal government, although about 10 percent of the ads are for positions with District of Columbia area courts, private firms, and non–profits.

National Health Lawyers' Association Members Corner (NHLA, 1620 I St, NW, Suite 900, Washington, DC 20006; phone: 202/833–1100) monthly, $150/annual nonmember subscription, free/members. "Job Opportunities" lists six to ten vacancies for attorneys, risk managers, health care executives and academicians.

The Attorney–CPA (American Association of Attorney-Certified Public Accountants, 24196 Alicia Pkwy., Suite K, Mission Viejo, CA 92691; phone: 714/768–0336) five issues/year, $30/annual nonmember subscription, free to members. "Position Clearinghouse" will have as many as two or three jobs openings for attorney–CPAs.

Broward Review (American Lawyers Media, 600 Third Ave., New York, NY 10016; phones: 305/463-1432, 212/973-2885) daily, $265/annual law firm subscription, contact for individual's subscription rate. "Classified Advertising—Employment for Attorneys" includes ten to 15 positions from around the country, in addition to local positions in the Broward County, Florida area. Jobs include attorneys, paralegals, legal secretaries ,and managing partner. Also includes a "Positions Wanted" section and a directory of legal recruiters

Miami Review (American Lawyers Media, 600 Third Ave., New York, NY 10016; phones: 305/377-3721, 212/973-2885) daily, $265/annual law firm subscription, contact for individual's subscription rate. "Classified Advertising—Employment for Attorneys" includes ten to 15 positions from around the country, in addition to local positions in the Miami, Florida area. Jobs include attorneys, paralegals, legal secretaries, and managing partners. Also includes a "Positions Wanted" section and a directory of legal recruiters

Palm Beach Review (American Lawyers Media, 600 Third Ave., New York, NY 10016; phone: 212/973-2885) daily, $265/annual law firm subscription, contact for individual's subscription rate. "Classified Advertising—Employment for Attorneys" includes ten to 15 positions from around the country, in addition to local positions in the Palm Beach, Florida area. Jobs include attorneys, paralegals, legal secretaries, and managing partners. Also includes a "Positions Wanted" section and a directory of legal recruiters

Connecticut Law Tribune (American Lawyers Media, 600 Third Ave., New York, NY 10016; phones: 203/256-3600, 212/973-2885) weekly, $345/annual law firm subscription, contact for individual's subscription rate. "Classified Advertising—Employment for Attorneys" includes ten to 15 positions from around the country, in addition to local positions in the states of Connecticut and New York. Jobs include attorneys, paralegals, legal secretaries, and managing partners. Also includes a "Positions Wanted" section and a directory of legal recruiters

Fulton County Daily Report (American Lawyers Media, 600 Third Ave., New York, NY 10016; phones: 404/256–3600, 212/973–2885) daily, $425/annual law firm subscription, contact for individual's subscription rate. "Classified Advertising—Employment for Attorneys" includes ten to 15 positions from around the country, in addition to local positions in the Atlanta, Georgia area. Jobs include attorneys, paralegals, legal secretaries, and managing partners. Also includes a "Positions Wanted" section and a directory of legal recruiters

New Jersey Law Journal (American Lawyers Media, 600 Third Ave., New York, NY 10016; phones: 201/642–0075, 212/973–2885) weekly, $225/annual law firm subscription, contact for individual's subscription rate. "Classified Advertising—Employment for Attorneys" includes ten to 15 positions from around the country, in addition to local positions in the New Jersey—New York area. Jobs include attorneys, paralegals, legal secretaries, and managing partners. Also includes a "Positions Wanted" section and a directory of legal recruiters

The Recorder (American Lawyers Media, 600 Third Ave., New York, NY 10016; phones: 415/749–5400, 212/973–2885) daily, $390/annual law firm subscription, contact for individual's subscription rate. "Classified Advertising—Employment for Attorneys" includes ten to 15 positions from around the country, in addition to local positions in the San Francisco Bay area. Jobs include attorneys, paralegals, legal secretaries, and managing partners. Also includes a "Positions Wanted" section and a directory of legal recruiters

Texas Lawyer (American Lawyers Media, 600 Third Ave., New York, NY 10016; phones: 214/744–9300, 212/973–2885) weekly, $399/annual law firm subscription, contact for individual's subscription rate. "Classified Advertising—Employment for Attorneys" includes ten to 15 positions from around the country, in addition to local positions in Texas. Jobs include attorneys, paralegals, legal secretaries, and managing partners. Also includes a "Positions Wanted" section and a directory of legal recruiters.

Job services

Resume Bank (American Corporate Counsel Association, 1225 Connecticut Ave., NW, Suite 302, Washington, DC 20036; phone: 202/296-4522) $65/six-months nonmembers, $25/members. Complete this job-matching service's application form and submit it with five copies of your resume and fee. When a match is made, your resume is forwarded to the corporate employer who may contact you directly. If a referral is not made during your six-month period, your registration will be extended for two months for free.

American Lawyer JOBS Hotline (American Lawyers Media, 600 Third Ave., New York, NY 10016; phone: 212/973-2885). Call 800/753-5627 to reach this geographic database of attorney and related positions advertised in the various American Lawyers Media newspapers described above under "Job openings." You may listen to the introduction and instructions for using this service at no charge. However, once your search begins, you are charged a flat $10 fee for the first 20 minutes plus $5 for each ten minutes thereafter. You are able to define your search by geographic area, practice specialty, and job sector (law firm, corporate counsel, or government). Listings are updated daily.

Paralegal Placement Network (Paralegal Placement Network, Inc., P.O. Box 710, Solebury, PA 19009; phones: 215/938-1182, 215/297-8697) $15/registration fee, $10/National Paralegal Association members (NPA members should write check payable to NPA). Complete the detailed enrollment application, pay your registration fee, and you are in their database for two years. When matched with a job opening, this job-matching service will contact you directly.

NCRA Employment Referral Service (National Court Reporters Association, 8224 Old Courthouse Rd., Vienna, VA 22182; phone: 703/281-4677) $6/six-month nonmember registration, free to members. Obtain the "Employment Referral Data Sheet." Completed data sheets are kept on file for a six-month period. A copy of the data sheet is furnished to potential employers. NCRA recommends that you also contact your state court reporters association to see if it has a referral service. Contact NCRA for the address and phone of the association in your state.

CU Career Connection (University of Colorado, Campus Box 133, Boulder, CO 80309–0133; phone: 303/492–4127) $20/two–month fee entitles you to a "passcode" which unlocks this job hotline. You need a touch-tone phone to call and request the legal service jobs and the geographic area for which you want to hear job openings. The hotline is turned off Monday through Friday, 2 to 4 p.m. for daily updating. This hotline carries a good number of jobs in all aspects of the legal field.

Local Women's Bar Associations. A number of these operate job services. Contact the National Conference of Women's Bar Associations (P.O. Box 77, Edenton, NC 27932–0077; phone: 919/482–8202) for information.

Directories

Martindale–Hubbell Law Directory (Martindale–Hubbell, 121 Chanlon Rd., New Providence, NJ 07974; phone: 800/526–4902) $305 plus $32 shipping, 16 volumes, published annually. This is the big bopper, grand–daddy of all attorney directories with over 800,000 legal practitioners in the U.S., Canada, and worldwide. It includes a primary practice profile on virtually every attorney in the U.S. and Canada and detailed biographies of attorneys highly recommended by their colleagues. It also include in–house counsels of major corporations. This directory is also available on CD-ROM for $750 to $1295 depending on the purchaser's status (subscriber to the annual directory, library, law firm, individual, and whether purchasing the CD-ROM version for one year or longer). For details, call 800/323–3288 or write to the above address.

The American Lawyer Guide to Leading Law Firms (American Lawyer Media, 600 Third Ave., New York, NY 10016; phone: 212/956–3712) $749/full five–volume set plus $49.75 shipping, $245/individual volume (each of which contains several states) plus $9.95 shipping per volume, published annually. Provides eight to ten pages of details on law firms with 50 or more attorneys: number of lawyers (equity shareholders, partners, associates, of counsel, senior attorneys), paralegals, and support staff broken down by sex and ethnicity, hiring history, starting salaries, billing rates, administrative personnel (including recruiting director), minimum billable hours expected, review system—

everything you could want to know before you decide which firms you want to make part of your job search. Also includes governments, law schools, and corporate legal departments.

West's Legal Directory (West Publishing Company, 610 Opperman Dr., St.Paul, MN 55164; phone: 800/328-0109). This national directory of thousands of law firms and attorneys is accessed through the WESTLAW® computer database which is often available for use at law libraries—which usually charge for the privilege of using WESTLAW®—and law firms. Contact West Publishing for details on subscribing to the WESTLAW®service.

Law and Business Directory of Litigation Attorneys (Prentice Hall Law & Business, 270 Sylvan Ave., Englewood Cliffs, NJ 07632; phones: 800/223-0231, 201/894-8869) $350, $297.50/American Bar Association Litigation Section members, add your local sales tax; two volumes, published each autumn. 6,800 pages. Profiles in detail 12,000 law firms with 31,000 litigators in 90 areas of concentration.

NACDL Membership Directory (National Association of Criminal Defense Lawyers, 1110 Vermont Ave., NW, Suite 1150, Washington, DC 20005; phone: 202/872-8688) available only to members. Published each September.

FDL Directory (Food and Drug Law Institute, 1000 Vermont Ave., NW, Suite 1200, Washington, DC 20005; phone: 202/371-1420) free. Most recent edition published in 1991.

American Association of Attorney–Certified Public Accountants Membership Directory (AAA-CPA, 24196 Alicia Pkwy., Suite K, Mission Viejo, CA 92691; phone: 714/768-0336) $160/nonmembers, free/members, annual. Includes biographies of member CPA-attorneys.

National Association of Surety Bond Producers Membership Directory (NASBP, 55301 Wisconsin Ave., NW, Suite 450, Washington, DC 20015; phone: 202/686-3700) free, available only to members, issued each September.

Salary surveys

Legal Salary Survey (David J. White & Associates, 809 Ridge Rd., Wilmette, IL 60091; phone: 800/962–4947) $185, annual. Covers attorney positions.

Salary & Employment Survey (National Paralegal Association, P.O. Box 406, Solebury, PA 18963; phone: 215/297–8333) national edition: $50/nonmembers, $30/members, individual regional editions: $20/nonmembers, $10/members. Available as a national edition or in nine regional editions. Reports on average salaries, benefits, and demographic characteristics of paralegals.

Compensation of Legal & Related Jobs (non–law firms) (Abbott, Langer & Associates, 548 First St., Crete, IL 60417; phone: 708/672–4200) $475/entire set; Vol. 1: Supervisory and Managerial Attorneys, $195; Vol. 2: Non–supervisory attorneys, $195; Vol. 3: Legal Administrators/Paralegal Assistants/Legal Secretaries, $195; annual. Findings are presented by job type, geographic area, experience, education, size of firm, and more.

Chapter 20

Management and administration

Management and administration

Also see the general sources listed in Chapter 2 as well as sources within each specialty throughout this book.

Job openings

Position Report (David J. White & Associates, Suite 200, 809 Ridge Rd., Wilmette, IL 60091; phone: 708/256-8826) weekly, $42.50/four week subscription, $115/12 weeks, $220/24 weeks, $440/48 weeks. This is a collection of over 500 job ads in management extracted from more than 100 newspapers and periodicals nationwide.

CEO Job Opportunities Update (2011 I St., NW, Suite 600, Washington, DC 20006; phone: 202/331-3838) biweekly, $90/seven-issue subscription, $160/13-issue subscription, $300/annual subscription. Each issue contains close to 100 vacancy announcement for chief operating officers or executive directors for all sorts of associations as well as 70 vacancy announcements for senior staff.

Association TRENDS (Martineau Corp., 4948 St. Elmo Ave., Bethesda, MD 20814; phone: 301/652–8666) $65/annual subscription (U.S.), $98/foreign. The "Classifieds" section carries ads for about 15 jobs with associations for management, executive directors, editors, writers, and trade show or convention staff.

Association Management (American Society of Association Executives, 1575 I St., NW, Washington, DC 20005; phone: 202/626-2723) monthly; $30/annual subscription for non-members, $35/Canada, $40/elsewhere, free/members. The "ExecutiveSearch" section includes about three or four executive director positions with trade or professional associations. Includes "Position Wanted."

Job service

Jobseeker Service (Martineau Corp., 4948 St. Elmo Ave., Bethesda, MD 20814; phone: 301/652–8666) $52. Send ten copies of your resume (up to three pages long) and a 30–word classified ad. Your ad, with a box number, will run in three consecutive issues of *Association Trends*, described above under "Job Openings." Unless otherwise requested, your resume will be sent to all employers who ask for it. The employer is responsible for contacting you for an interview. A typical issue sports about a dozen of these ads under "Free Resumes."

ASAE Referral Service (American Society of Association Executives, 1575 I St., NW, Washington, DC 20005; phone: 202/626-2723) $80/nonmembers, $40/members. Submit fee with seven copies of your resume and a completed application form. Your resume will be kept on file for nine months. When the service matches you with an appropriate vacancy with an association, it sends your resume to the employer who is then responsible for contacting you.

ASAE Executive Search (American Society of Association Executives, 1575 I St., NW, Washington, DC 20005; phone: 202/626-ASAE) free. This is a genuine executive search service for higher level positions with associations.

Purchasing

Job openings

Employment Opportunity Listing (National Association of Purchasing Management, 2055 E. Centennial Cr., Tempe, AZ 85282; phone: 602/752–6276) monthly, distributed to NAPMS 168 affiliate offices. Twenty to 25 purchasing and materials management positions are in the usual issue.

Purchasing (Cahners Publishing, 44 Cook St., Denver, CO 80206–5000; phone: 303/388–4511) 21 issues/year, $84.95/annual subscription (U.S.), $124.95/Mexico, $133.70/Canada, $149.95/elsewhere. "Job Mart" features nearly 20 ads for purchasing agents, buyers, comptrollers, and management for manufacturers.

Purchasing World (29100 Aurora Rd., Solon, OH 44139; phone: 216/248–1125) monthly $65/annual subscription, $70/Canada, $120/elsewhere, free to qualified purchasing professionals. The "Marketplace" lists 20 vacancies.

"All I said was that you would see the
salesman who lowered his prices first."

Contract Management (National Contract Managers Association, 1912 Woodford Rd., Vienna, VA 22182; phones: 800/344-8096, 703/448-9231) monthly, $72/nonmember annual subscription, free/members. Typical issue has about 14 ads for contract managers, procurement, materials management, contractor negotiators, administrators, buyers, attorneys, and certified public accountants listed under "Job Watch" and in display ads in the "CM Final Edition" supplement.

Job services

NAPM Services, Inc.—Employment Services (National Association of Purchasing Management, 2055 E. Centennial Cr., Tempe, AZ 85282; phone: 602/752-6276) free, available only to members. The job seeker submits a copy of her resume with an informal cover letter that outlines her salary requirements, geographical preference, and three major areas of commodities expertise. When a match is found, the Employment Service contacts the job seeker to confirm her interest in the position and then sends the job seeker's resume to the employer who is responsible for contacting the potential employee for an interview.

Job Matching Service (American Purchasing Society, 11910 Oak Trail Way, Port Richey, FL 34668; phone: 813/862-7998) free. Send your resume to APS with a request that it be kept on file for job openings. When an employer submits a request for job candidates, APS sends a copy of the resumes of qualified persons to the employer who is responsible for contacting candidates for interviews. APS also sends a letter to each candidate when his resume has been sent to an employer to tell him the employer's name and address, and suggest that he contact the employer for more information about the job. Resumes are kept on file for three years.

NCMA's Job Referral Service (National Contract Managers Association, 1912 Woodford Rd., Vienna, VA 22182; phones: 800/344-8096, 703/448-9231) free. Complete the service's resume form and submit it with ten copies of your resume. The service forwards the resumes of qualified applicants to employers who are responsible for contacting the job hopeful. Resumes are kept on file for six months. The vast majority of positions are private sector.

Chapter 21

Manufacturing

Manufacturing in general

Also see entries in the chapters "Computers and electronics," "Management," "Sales," and "Science and engineering." This first set of sources is broad in scope. The sources that appear under "Manufacturing specialties" are more narrow in scope.

Job openings

Plant Engineering (Cahners Publishing Company, 44 Cook St., Denver, CO 80206; phone: 303/388-4511) semimonthly, $64.95/annual subscription (U.S.), $96.25/Canada, $184.95/elsewhere. About ten vacancies for manufacturing plant engineers, plant services managers, chemical engineers, maintenance and inspection, and manufacturers' representatives are advertised under "Classified."

American Machinist (Penton Publishing, 1100 Superior Ave., Cleveland, OH 44114; phone: 216/696-7000) monthly; free to qualified professionals, call or write for application form; otherwise: $65/annual subscription (U.S.), $80/Canada, $100/elsewhere. "Marketplace—Employment Opportunities" sports five ads for design engineers, machinists, and production foremen.

Machine Design (Penton Publishing, 1100 Superior Ave., Cleveland, OH 44114; phone: 216/696-7000) monthly; free to qualified professionals, call or write for application form; otherwise: $75/annual subscription (U.S.), $100/Canada, $140/elsewhere. Five ads for design and manufacturing engineers as well as management positions grace the "Design Engineer Search" pages.

Manufacturing Engineer (Society of Manufacturing Engineers, P.O. Box 930, Dearborn, MI 48121; phone: 313/271-1500) monthly, $60/annual nonmember subscription, free/members. Ten to 20 job ads for manufacturing engineers appear under "Opportunities."

Manufacturing Engineering (Society of Manufacturing Engineers, P.O. Box 930, Dearborn, MI 48121; phone: 313/271-1500) monthly, free/members only. Over 40 job vacancies for manufacturing and design engineers appear under "Opportunities." Includes "Position Wanted" ads.

Industrial Distribution (Cahners Publishing, P.O. Box 173377, Denver, CO 80217; phones: 800/323-4958, 303/388-4511) monthly, $64.95/annual subscription (U.S.), $99.95/Canada. Over a dozen jobs for manufacturers' representatives, purchasing managers, distributors, and salespeople are in the "Classified Marketplace."

Quality in Manufacturing (29100 Aurora Rd., Suite 200, Cleveland, OH 44139; phone: 216/248-1125) bimonthly, $75/annual subscription (U.S.), $95/Canada, $140/elsewhere, free to qualified professionals. The "Classifieds" carry about three ads from recruitment agencies for quality control assurance professionals in manufacturing companies. They expect to include many more ads from employers beginning in 1992.

Refrigeration Service and Contracting (P.O. Box 7021, Troy, MI 48007; phone: 313/362-3700) monthly, $36/annual subscription, free/members of the Refrigeration Service Engineers Society. Two or three job ads for air conditioning, heating, and refrigerator service technicians are in the "Classified Market Place."

Directories

U.S. Manufacturers Directory (American Business Directories, 5711 S. 86th Cr., Omaha, NE 68127; phone: 402/593-4600) $315, $195/one-year lease of the directory, annual. Listings for 120,000 manufacturers with 25 or more employees include address, phone, chief executive name and title, annual sales volume, number of employees, and up to three SIC codes to identify specialties.

MacRae's Blue Book (Business Research Publications, 817 Broadway, New York, NY 10003; phones: 800/622–7237, 212/673–4700) $120 plus $4.50 shipping, issued each March. Includes over 40,000 manufacturers. Volume 1 lists information about each company. Volumes 2 and 3 are product indexes.

Used Machinery Buyer's Guide (Machinery Dealers National Association, 1110 Spring St., Silver Spring, MD 20910; phone: 301/585–9494) free, annual. Lists information on 450 member firms that sell used manufacturing machinery.

Who's Who in IRI (Industrial Research Institute, 1550 M St, NW, Washington, DC 20005; phone: 202/872–6350) free/members only, constantly updated. Lists member industrial researchers.

Industrial Safety Equipment Association Membership Directory (ISEA, 1901 N. Moore St., Suite 808, Arlington, VA 22209; phone: 703/525–1695) free/members only, issued each June and December.

Salary survey

Compensation in Manufacturing (Abbott, Langer & Associates, 548 First St., Crete, IL 60417; phone: 708/672–4200) $350, annual. Surveying 225 manufacturing firms, this study reports on 39 manufacturing management and engineering jobs from CEO to foreman and production leadman.

Food production

Job openings

Grocery Marketing (Gorman Publishing, 8750 W. Bryn Mawr Ave., Chicago, IL 60631; phone: 312/693–3200, ext. 279) 22 issues/year, $65/annual subscription (U.S.), $130/foreign. About half a dozen job openings in the grocery industry, primarily management, are listed in the "Classified Marketplace."

SuperMarket News (7 W. 34th St., New York, NY 10001; phone: 212/630–4000) weekly, $175/annual subscription. About ten job ads are in "Help Wanted."

The Gourmet Retailer (Sterling Southeast, 1450 NE 123rd St., North Miami, FL 33161–6051; phone: 305/893–8771) monthly, $25/annual subscription. Job vacancies are listed under "Classified."

Food Engineering (Chilton Company, Chilton Way, Radnor, PA 19089; phone: 215/964–4443) monthly, free to qualified professionals in the food and beverage industry. Notices for more than 50 jobs for management, quality control, food engineers, warehouse personnel, and all other aspects of the food and beverage production industry appear under "Classified Marketplace—Employment Services" and "Employment Opportunities." These positions are mostly offered through recruiters. "Positions Wanted" also included.

National Purvisioner (15 W. Huron, Chicago, IL 60610; phone: 312/944–3380) biweekly, $38/annual subscription. Eight to 12 job ads in meat plants are under "Classified."

Coldfacts Newsletter (International Association of Refrigerated Warehouses, 7315 Wisconsin Ave., Bethesda, MD 20814; phone: 301/652–5674) five to seven issues/year, available only to members. Ten job ads for refrigerator warehouse positions, management, and sales are under "Classified."

Prepared Foods (Gorman Publishing, 8750 W. Bryn Mawr Ave., Chicago, IL 60631; phone: 312/693–3200, ext. 279) monthly, $80/annual subscription (U.S.), $135/foreign. "Classified" carries about 15 openings for food technologists, food scientists, and plant management.

Food Production/Management (CTI Publications, 2619 Maryland Ave., Baltimore, MD 21218; phone: 301/467–3338) monthly, $25/annual subscription (U.S.), $40/foreign. Two or three openings in food processing are under "Help Wanted."

Dairy Foods (Gorman Publishing, 8750 W. Bryn Mawr Ave., Chicago, IL 60631; phone: 312/693–3200, ext. 279) 22 issues/year, $78/annual subscription (U.S.), $138/foreign. Over 30 job openings in the dairy industry are listed under "Employment Opportunities."

Cheese Market News (Gorman Publishing, 8750 W. Bryn Mawr Ave., Chicago, IL 60631; phone: 312/693–3200, ext. 279) 22 issues/year, $59/annual subscription (U.S.), $94/foreign. About four job openings in the cheese industry are listed under "Classified Advertising—Help Wanted."

Bakery Production and Marketing (Gorman Publishing, 8750 W. Bryn Mawr Ave., Chicago, IL 60631; phone: 312/693–3200, ext. 279) monthly, $79/annual subscription (U.S.), $139/foreign. "Classified" runs ads for a dozen openings in food technology, marketing, and plant management.

Quick Topics (National Candy Wholesalers Association, 1128 16th St., NW, Washington, DC 20036; phone: 202/463–2124) 13 issues/year, free/members only. The last page carries two to eight openings for sales representatives, distributors, and brokers.

Snack Food (Edgell Communications, 1 E. First St., Duluth, MN 55802; phones: 800/346-0085, 218/723-9870) monthly; $30/annual subscription (U.S.); $55/Canada; $100/elsewhere. About a dozen ads appear under "Classifieds—Help Wanted—Reps Wanted—Business Opportunities—Distributors Wanted," primarily for manufacturers' and sales reps.

Poultry Processing (Edgell Communications, 1 E. First St., Duluth, MN 55802; phones: 800/346-0085, 218/723-9870) bimonthly; $15/annual subscription (U.S.); $30/Canada; $60/elsewhere. The "Classified—Help Wanted" section includes about five ads for anything in the poultry and egg related industries, particularly sales and manufacturers' reps. The October directory issue sells for $25 by itself.

Meat (P.O. Box 1059, Mill Valley, CA 94942; phone: 415/388–7575) monthly, $40/annual subscription. Three or four job ads are in the "Classifieds."

Meat Processing (Edgell Communications, 1 E. First St., Duluth, MN 55802; phones: 800/346-0085, 218/723-9870) monthly; $25/annual subscription (U.S.); $50/Canada; $100/elsewhere. There are about 15 job ads under "Classifieds—Help Wanted" for all aspects of the meat packing, sausage manufacturing, meat wholesaling, and poultry and seafood processing industries. The December directory costs $25 by itself.

National Fisherman (Journal Publications, P.O. Box 908, Rockland, ME 04841) 13 issues/year, $22.95/annual subscription (U.S.), $32.95/foreign. About three ads for fishermen and boat repair personnel are in the "Service Pages—Help Wanted."

Pacific Fishing (1515 NW 51st St., Seattle, WA 98107; phone: 206/842-7229) monthly, $19.95/annual subscription (U.S.), $25/Canada. "Help Wanted" carries five to ten ads for fishing people, deck hands, cooks, longliners, and engineers as well as "Positions Sought."

Health Foods Business (Howmark Publishing, 567 Morris Ave., Elizabeth, NJ 07208; phone: 908/353-7373) monthly, $30/annual subscription (U.S.), $34/Canada, $50/elsewhere. Several job ads for sales managers and sales representatives are under "Classified."

Vegetarian Times (PO Box 570, Oak Park, IL 60303; 800/435-9610, in Illinois call 800/435-0715, from outside the U.S. call 815/734-6309) monthly, $24.95/annual subscription for individuals, $29.95 for libraries and institutions, add $5 for Canada, add $10 for elsewhere. Over a dozen business opportunities and a few jobs are listed under "Classifieds."

Sugar Journal (4640 S. Carrollton Ave., New Orleans, LA 70119; phone: 504/482-3914) monthly, $27/annual subscription. Near the back you'll find two or three ads for management and food engineers.

Beverage World (150 Great Neck Rd., Great Neck, NY 11021; phone: 516/829-9210) monthly, $30/annual subscription (U.S., Canada), $40/elsewhere. Ten to 15 job openings in all aspects of beverage manufacturing, sales, plant management, and quality control are touted under "Help Wanted." Also includes "Positions Wanted."

Wines and Vines (1800 Lincoln Ave., San Rafael, CA 94901; phone: 415/453-9700) monthly, $27.50/annual subscription (U.S.), $33/Canada, $39/elsewhere. "Position Available" lists about three openings for winemakers, vineyard managers, and other production positions.

The Wine Spectator (P.O. Box 1960, Marion, OH 43306–1960; phone: 800/622–2062) 22 issues/year, $40/annual subscription, $50/Canada, $110/elsewhere. Over a dozen business opportunities and job openings for executives, sales, marketing, and vineyard management appear under "Classifieds." Also includes "Positions Wanted."

Directories

Prepared Foods Industry Sourcebook (Gorman Publishing, 8750 W. Bryn Mawr Ave., Chicago, IL 60631; phone: 312/693–3200, ext. 279) $65, annual, 400 pages. Includes leading food and beverage processors guide, manufacturers guide, economic development guide, architects and engineers guide, government agency guide, and product guide (equipment, ingredients, packaging materials, instruments, sanitation and maintenance, and services and supplies).

Grocer Manufacturers Association Directory (GMA, 1010 Wisconsin Ave., NW, Suite 800, Washington, DC 20007; phone: 202/337–6233) free, annual.

National Food Processors Association Membership Directory (NFPA, 1401 New York Ave., NW, Washington, DC 20005; phone: 202/639–5900) $150/nonmembers, free/members, published each March.

Food Processing Machinery and Supplies Association Buyers Guide and Membership Directory (FPMSA, 200 Daingerfield Rd., Alexandria, VA 22314; phone: 703/684–1080) $25, published in odd-numbered years.

Directory of Membership Products and Services (Dairy and Food Industries Supply Association, 6245 Executive Blvd., Rockville, MD 20852-3938; phone: 301/984-1444) contact for price, most recent edition was 1990/1991, 148 pages. Provides details on suppliers that serve the food, dairy, beverage, and related industries.

Dairy Food Market Directory (Gorman Publishing, 8750 W. Bryn Mawr Ave., Chicago, IL 60631; phone: 312/693-3200, ext. 279) $65, annual, 275 pages. Describes suppliers, distributors, and co-packers.

Cheese Market News Directory (Gorman Publishing, 8750 W. Bryn Mawr Ave., Chicago, IL 60631; phone: 312/693-3200, ext. 279) $21, annual, 100 pages. This includes a directory of suppliers, manufacturers, and marketers.

Bakery Red Book (Gorman Publishing, 8750 W. Bryn Mawr Ave., Chicago, IL 60631; phone: 312/693-3200, ext. 279) $249, annual, 380 pages. Includes a wholesale directory, distributors' directory, and the top 100 in-store bakery headquarters.

American Frozen Food Industry Directory (American Frozen Food Institute, 1764 Old Meadow Lane, McLean, VA 22102; phone: 703/821-0770) $50/nonmembers, free/members, annual.

International Frozen Food Association Membership Directory and Buyer's Guide (IFFA, 1700 Old Meadow Rd., McLean, VA 22102; phone: 703/821-0770) $100, annual.

National Association of Meat Purveyors Membership Directory (NAMP, 8365-B Greensboro Dr., McLean, VA 22102; phone: 703/758-1900) free/members only, issued every January.

The Bluebook (National Fisheries Institute, 1525 Wilson Blvd., Suite 500, Arlington, VA 22209) free/members only, annual. Lists member wholesalers and distributors of fish products.

National Confectioners Association of the United States Membership Directory (NCAUS, 7900 West Park Dr., Suite A-320, McLean, VA 22102; phone: 703/790-5750) free/members only, issued each January.

Peanut Industry Guide (National Peanut Council, 1500 King St., Suite 301, Alexandria, VA 22314; phone: 703/838-9500) $65/non-members, free/members, published in even-numbered years.

National Food Brokers Association Directory of Members (NFBA, 1010 Massachusetts Ave., NW, Washington, DC 20001; phone: 202/789-2844) $105/nonmembers, free/members, published each August. Gives details on each member company's product categories and trade called on. Includes key personnel.

Food Marketing Institute Membership Directory (FMI, 1750 K St., NW, Suite 700, Washington, DC 20006; phone: 202/452-8444) free/members only, annual.

Salary surveys

Food Engineering (Chilton Company, Chilton Way, Radnor, PA 19089; phone: 215/964-4443) monthly, free to qualified professionals in the food and beverage industry. The December issue includes the annual salary survey for positions in the food production industry. Positions covered range from purchasing agent, sanitation and maintenance mangers to packaging to company president. Median salaries are also presented by product produced.

Forest products

Also see the chapter "Forestry and horticulture."

Job openings

American Papermaker (Maclean Hunter, 6 Piedmont Center, Suite 300, Altanta, GA 30305; phones: 800/323-9335, 404/841-3339) 11 issues/year, $30/annual subscription (U.S.), $45/Canada, free to qualified professionals in the pulp, paper, and paperboard manufacturing industries; available in Great Lakes, Southern, Eastern, or Pacific editions. The "Classifieds" are chock full of 50 to 70 job ads for absolutely everything in the paper and pulp industries.

PIMA Magazine (Paper Industry Management Association, 2400 E. Oakton, Arlington Heights, IL 60005; phone: 708/956-0250) $50/annual subscription, $75/foreign, $25/mills, converters, and their personnel (U.S., Canada, Mexico), free/members, $60/annual dues. Over 30 paper industry jobs in production, technical, research, purchasing, and management are advertised in the "Classified Ads."

Paper Film & Foil Converter (Maclean Hunter, 29 N. Wacker Dr., Chicago, IL 60606; phone: 312/726-2802) monthly, $100/annual subscription (U.S., Canada), $140/elsewhere. About 20 ads for all facets of the packaging industry positions are in "Classified."

Forest Industries (500 Howard St., San Francisco, CA 94105; phones: 800/227-4675, 415/397-1881) ten issues/year, $55/annual subscription. About five positions, including labor, within the forest products industry are in "Classified Advertising."

Paper Age (400 Old Hook Rd., Westwood, NJ 07675; phone: 201/666-2262) monthly, $50/annual subscription (U.S.), $80/foreign. Three to five technical, management, and sales positions with paper manufacturers appear under "Classified...."

Paperboard Packaging (Edgell Communications, 1 E. First St., Duluth, MN 55802; phone: 800/346-0085) monthly, $30/annual subscription (U.S.), $55/Canada, $75/elsewhere. Three or four jobs in packaging, sales, recruitment, and management are under "Help Wanted" or "Reps Wanted."

Boxboard Containers (Maclean Hunter, 29 N. Wacker Dr., Chicago, IL 60606; phones: 312/726-2802) monthly, $26/annual subscription (U.S.), $35/Canada, $35/elsewhere. Under "The Industry Marketplace—Help Wanted" about 20 job ads for all aspects of the packaging industry appear.

Container News (Communication Channels, 6255 Barfield Rd., Atlanta, GA 30328; 404/256-9800) monthly, $34/annual subscription. Two or three ads for sales and manufacturers' representatives as well as marketing positions are in the "Classified" section.

Can Tube Bulletin (Composite Can and Tube Institute, 1818 N St, NW, Suite T-10, Washington, DC 20036; phone: 202/223-4840) monthly $50/annual nonmember subscription, free/members. Two or three ads for jobs in manufacturing paperboard packaging are in the "Classified Ads."

Hardwood Plywood and Veneer News (Hardwood Plywood Manufacturer's Association, P.O. Box 2789, Reston, VA 22090; phone: 703/435-2900) bimonthly, $30/annual nonmember subscription, free/members. Four or five jobs in wood technology, forestry, marketing, and management are advertised in the typical issue.

Panel World (P.O. Box 5613, Montgomery, AL 36103; phone: 205/834-1170) bimonthly, $12/annual subscription (U.S.), $20/Canada, $25/elsewhere. Job openings for seven to 15 positions in wood-based panel production and management are under "Employment Opportunities."

Wood & Wood Products (P.O. Box 1400, Lincolnshire, IL 60069; phone: 708/634-4347) monthly, free to qualified professional wood workers and manufacturers. Typical issue includes around ten classified and display ads for management, sales, and technical positions in the furniture, cabinet, and related wood products manufacturing and sales industry.

Fine Woodworking (Tauton Press, 63 S. Main Street, Newtown, CT 06470; phones: 800/283-7252, ext. 562, 203/426-8171) bimonthly, $25/annual subscription (U.S.), $30/foreign. Ads for about ten jobs in cabinet making (wood workers, designers, shops) plus business opportunities are in the "Classifieds."

Directories

Lockwood-Post's Directory of the Paper, Pulp, and Allied Trades (Miller Freeman, P.O. Box T, Gilroy, CA 95021-9968; phone: 408/848-5296) $147 plus $5/shipping (U.S.), $8.50/Canada, annual, over 1,000 pages. Provides information on 1,000 pulp and paper mills and executive offices, 4,000 converting plants, 3,000 paper merchants and distributors, 850 rag and paper stock dealers, and 24,000 industry officials, including personnel directors.

Directory of the Forest Products Industry (Miller Freeman, P.O. Box T, Gilroy, CA 95021–9968; phone: 408/848–5296) $177 plus $5/shipping (U.S.), $8.50/Canada, published in December of odd–numbered years, 730 pages. It includes listings for every aspect of the U.S. and Canadian forest industries: logging, pulpwood, lumber, plywood, and board. More than 7,500 independent and mill logging operations, pulpwood producers and dealers, and woodlands divisions of pulp and paper companies are included. Over 3,100 head and division offices of primary producers as well as 1,750 offices of wholesalers, jobbers, distributors, yards, and importers are also described. Over 18,000 key industry personnel (including personnel directors) are included.

International Pulp and Paper Directory (Miller Freeman, P.O. Box

T, Gilroy, CA 95021–9968; phone: 408/848–5296) $157 plus $5/shipping (U.S.), $8.50/Canada, annual, 950 pages. Includes entries for 5,430 pulp and paper mills and executive offices in 86 countries, 8,000 key executives (including personnel directors), 750 European paper merchants, 330 North American paper importers and exporters, 200 companies than produce market pulp, and 2,000 supplier who export.

PIMA Membership Directory (Paper Industry Management Association, 2400 E. Oakton, Arlington Heights, IL 60005; phone: 708/956–0250) $50/nonmembers, free/members, published each October, 156 pages. Lists individual and company members.

PIMA Catalog (Paper Industry Management Association, 2400 E. Oakton, Arlington Heights, IL 60005; phone: 708/956–0250) $50/nonmembers, free/members, issued each March, 200+ pages. This detailed buyers guide gives you information on manufacturers and suppliers of paper industry equipment, materials, supplies, and chemicals, plus consultants, and trade services.

National Hardwood Lumber Association Membership Directory (NHLA, P.O. Box 34518, Memphis, TN 38384; phone: 901/377-1818) $75/nonmembers, free/members, annual. Includes saw mills, furniture manufacturers, and related businesses.

International Container Directory (Edgell Communications, 233 N. Michigan Ave., Chicago, IL 60601; phone: 312/938-2300) $95/U.S. plus $3.50 shipping, $145/foreign plus $5 shipping. Provides details on packaging plants outside the U.S., grouped by country, under corrugated container plants and folding carton plants.

Paperboard Packaging Council Directory (PPC, 1101 Vermont Ave,. NW, Washington, DC 20005; phone: 202/289-4100) free/members only, annual.

Flexible Packaging Association Membership Directory (FPA, 1090 Vermont Ave., NW, Suite 500, Washington, DC 20005; phone: 202/842-3880) free/members only, annual.

HPMA Buyers Guide and Directory: Where to Buy Hardwood, Plywood, and Veneer (Hardwood Plywood Manufacturer's Association, P.O. Box 2789, Reston, VA 22090; phone: 703/435-2900) $5/nonmembers, free/members, issued each February. Lists manufacturers, their products, and sales agents.

Panel World Directory/Buyers' Guide (P.O. Box 5613, Montgomery, AL 36103; phone: 205/834-1170) $5, published each January, 110+ pages. Describes manufacturers and products of wood veneer, plywood, composites, and laminates, including veneer and panel mills worldwide.

Industry Directory (Composite Can and Tube Institute, 1818 N St, NW, Suite T-10, Washington, DC 20036; phone: 202/223-4840) $75/nonmembers, free/members, published every January. Includes manufacturers and their suppliers in the U.S., Canada, and elsewhere of composite cans, tubes, cores, and related items.

Salary survey

Wages and Benefits Survey (Composite Can and Tube Institute, 1818 N St, NW, Suite T-10, Washington, DC 20036; phone: 202/223–4840) $300, $175/members, free/member companies that participated in the survey, every January. Covers manufacturers in the U.S., Canada, and elsewhere of composite cans, tubes, cores, and related items.

Manufacturing by specialty

Job openings

Glass Digest (310 Madison Ave., New York, NY 10017; phone: 212/682–7681) monthly, $25/annual subscription (U.S., Canada), $35/elsewhere. ''Positions Available'' typically includes three to ten openings for salespeople, estimators, project managers, and manufacturers' representatives.

Glass (National Glass Association, 8200 Greensboro Dr., Suite 302; Mc Lean, VA 22102; phone: 703/442–4890) monthly, $34.95/annual nonmember subscription (U.S.), $44.95/foreign, free/members. Three or four openings for sales representatives appear under ''Classified.''

Glass Industry (310 Madison Ave., New York, NY 10017; phone: 212/682–7681) monthly, $30/annual subscription (U.S.), $45/foreign. A few ads for technicians, designers, and engineers appear under ''Positions Available.''

Paperboard Packaging (Edgell Communications, 1 E. First St., Duluth, MN 55802; phone: 800/346–0085) monthly, $25/annual subscription (U.S.), $50/Canada, $75/elsewhere. ''Classified—Help Wanted'' includes over ten ads for packaging professionals of all sorts.

Fenestration (310 Madison Ave., New York, NY 10017; phone: 212/682–7681) bimonthly, $15/annual subscription (U.S., Canada), $21/elsewhere. A few jobs for sales representatives and other positions in the fenestration industry (doors and windows) are advertised under ''Positions Available.''

Modern Casting (American Foundrymen's Society, 505 State St., Des Plaines, IL 60616; phone: 708/824–0181) monthly, $35/annual subscription (U.S., Mexico, Canada), $45/elsewhere. Over 60 positions are advertised in "Classified Advertising" under "Help Wanted," "Reps Wanted," and "Employment." Positions include all aspects of the metals industry including metallurgists, foundry maintenance, engineers, plant management, sales and manufacturers' representatives, and anything else related to the industry.

Finishers' Management (4350 DiPaolo Center, Glenview, IL 60025; phone: 708/699–1700) ten issues/year, $28/annual subscription (U.S.), $35/Canada, $50/elsewhere. The "Market Place" carries six to ten ads for plating and painting plant management.

The Fabricator (Fabricators and Manufacturers Association Member Resource, 5411 E. State St., Rockford, IL 61108; phone: 815/399–8700) ten issues/year, $30/annual subscription (U.S.), $125/foreign, free to individuals and companies in the metal forming and fabricating industry. Five to ten openings for manufacturing engineers and other steel fabrication professionals (foreman, estimators, superintendents, detailers, draftspeople, quality control managers, and project managers) appear in "Classified—Recruitment." Also lists "Positions Wanted."

Stamping Quarterly (Fabricators and Manufacturers Association Member Resource, 5411 E. State St., Rockford, IL 61108; phone: 815/399–8700) quarterly, $15/annual subscription (U.S.), $54/foreign, free to qualified professionals in the steel stamping industry. "Classified—Help Wanted" handles one or two ads for stamping engineers and other positions.

TPQ (Fabricators and Manufacturers Association Member Resource, 5411 E. State St., Rockford, IL 61108; phone: 815/399–8700) quarterly, $15/annual subscription, free to qualified workers in the tube and pipe industries. Two or three openings for manufacturers' representatives and other industry positions appear under "Classified."

American Metal Market (825 Seventh Ave., New York, NY 10019; phone: 212/887–8560) daily, $495/annual subscription (U.S.), $580/Canada, $910/elsewhere. "Classified—Help Wanted" carries over ten ads for metal industry personnel, mostly executives.

Metal Finishing (655 Avenue of the Americas, New York, NY 10010; phone: 212/633-3950) monthly, $32/annual subscription. A few jobs for manufacturers' representatives and plant managers in the metals industry appear under "Situations Open."

Wire Journal International (Wire Association International, 1570 Boston Post, Guildford, CT 06749; phone: 203/453-2777) monthly, $60/annual nonmember subscription, free/members. A look at "Career Opportunities" and "Classifieds" will yield five to ten ads for metallurgical engineers, sales and account representatives, production, and management, plus a section for "Positions Wanted."

Wire Technology (Initial Publications, 3869 Darrow Rd., Suite 101, Stow, OH 44224; phone: 216/686-9544) bimonthly, $30/annual subscription (U.S., Canada), $55/elsewhere. A few job ads for wire industry engineers and sales people appear under "Classified."

Welding Design & Fabrication (Penton Publishing, 1100 Superior Ave., Cleveland, OH 44070; phone: 216/696-7000) monthly, $45/annual subscription (U.S.), $65/Canada, $80/elsewhere. Five positions for welding designers and engineers, plant, production, maintenance, and operating managers show up under "Employment Opportunities."

Playthings (51 Madison Ave., New York, NY 10010-1675; phone: 212/689-4411) monthly, $22/annual subscription (U.S., Canada), $42/elsewhere. Ten to 15 ads for positions with toy manufacturers, importers, licensing agents, designers, inventors, suppliers, consultants, and manufacturers' representatives are in the "Classified Advertising."

Supply House Times (Cahners Publishing, 7574 N. Lincoln Ave., Skokie, IL 60077; phone: 312/273-2787) monthly, $50/annual subscription (U.S.), $65/foreign. Five openings for operations managers, sales, and department managers are in the "Classifieds."

Ceramic Industry (95900 Harper Rd., Suite 109, Solon, OH 44139-1835; phone: 216/498-9214) monthly, $50/annual subscription (U.S.), $65/Mexico and Canada, $120/elsewhere (air mail). "Positions Available" carries ads for three or five ceramic and materials engineers, production management, plant managers, foremen, and supervisors.

Rubber World (1867 W. Market St., Akron, OH 44334; phone: 216/864-2122) monthly, $29/annual subscription (U.S.),m $34/Canada, $45/elsewhere. A few rubber industry positions are advertised under "Classified."

Non-Wovens Industry (Rodman Publishing, P.O. Box 555, Ramsey, NJ 07446; phone: 201/825-2552) monthly, $48/annual subscription (U.S.), $52/Canada, $64/elsewhere. Seven to 15 positions in technical engineering, production, and management are advertised under "Classified."

Fastener Technology (Initial Publications, 3869 Darrow Rd., Suite 101, Stow, OH 44224; phone: 216/686-9544) bimonthly, $30/annual subscription (U.S.), $40/Canada, $55/elsewhere. Around three or four job ads for engineers, sales people, and management in the fasteners field appear in "Classified."

Job service

Tooling & Manufacturing Association Job Referral Service (TMA, 1177 S. Dee Rd., Park Ridge, IL 60068; phone: 708/825-1120) free to any person not already employed by a TMA member company. Job seekers can come to TMA's offices and copy job openings out of TMA's Referral Book of job vacancies with many of the 1,476 precision metalworking firms in the seven-county Chicago metropolitan area that belong to TMA. This must be done in person. Call to arrange a weekday appointment. Job seekers can also submit a resume to include in TMA's "Applicant Available" book that the member firms examine for prospective employees. The employer contacts the job seeker for the next step in the hiring process.

Directories

Gas Appliance Manufacturers Association Member Directory (GAMA 1901 N. Moore St., Suite 1100, Arlington, VA 22209; phone: 703/525-9596) $5/nonmembers, free/members, annual.

American Boiler Manufacturers Association Membership Directory (ABMA, 950 N. Glebe Rd., Suite 160, Arlington, VA 22203; phone: 703/522-7350) $250/nonmembers, free/members, annual (quarterly updates available only to members). Lists all active and associate members along with each one's product or service, names of principal representatives, address, and phone and fax numbers.

National Electrical Manufacturers' Representatives Directory (NEMR, 222 Westchester Ave., White Plains, NY 10604; phone: 914/428-1307) $200/nonmembers, free/members, published each spring. Lists member manufacturers and representatives in the U.S. and Canada.

American Gear Manufacturers Association Membership Directory (AGMA, 1500 King St., Suite 201, Alexandria, VA 22314; phone: 703/684-0211) free/members only, issued each August.

American Hardware Manufacturers Association Membership Directory (AHMA, 801 N. Plaza Dr., Schaumburg, IL 60173; phone: 708/605-1025) free/members only, released each April.

Health Industry Manufacturers Association Membership Directory (HIMA, 1030 15th St., NW, Suite 1100, Washington, DC 20005; phone: 202/452-8240) free, available only to members, published annually. Includes contact names at manufacturers of health care items.

The Membership Directory (Health Industry Distributors Association, 225 Reinekers Ln., Suite 650, Alexandria, VA 22314; phone: 202/452-8240) $35, annual. Provides details on distributors of medical products.

Investment Casting Industry Directory (Investment Casting Institute, 8350 N. Central Expressway, Suite M1110, Dallas, TX 75206; phones: 800/338-0264, 214/368-8896) $145/nonmembers, $95/members; plus shipping. Includes key personnel of investment casters and industry suppliers as well as members of the Investment Casting Institute. Includes the U.S. and over 25 other countries.

Fabricators and Manufacturers Association Member Resource Directory (FMA, 5411 E. State St., Rockford, IL 61108; phone: 815/399-8700) $65/nonmembers, free/members, issued each January, 175 pages. Provides information on member firms in the FMA, Tube and Pipe Fabricators Association, American Tube Association, and the Society for Computer–Aided Engineering. Names key personnel, technical specialty, and products/services for each company listed.

Tooling & Manufacturing Association Purchasing Guide (TMA, 1177 S. Dee Rd., Park Ridge, IL 60068; phone: 708/825-1120) contact for price, free/members, published in May of even-numbered years. Lists members' products and services in metalworking in the seven-county Chicago area.

American Concrete Pipe Association Directory (ACPA, 8200 Boone Blvd., Suite 400, Vienna, VA 22182; phone: 703/821-1990) free, issued each July. Lists member companies.

National Corrugated Steel Pipe Association Membership Directory (2001 I St., NW, Suite 500, Washington, DC 20006; phone: 202/223-2217) free/members only, issued semiannually. Lists member firms that fabricate steel pipe.

Porcelain Enamel Institute Membership Directory (PEI, 1101 Connecticut Ave., NW, Suite 700, Washington, DC 20036; phone: 202/857-1134) free, annual. Lists information on manufacturers.

Ceramic Source (American Ceramic Society, 757 Brooksedge Plaza Dr., Westerville, OH 43081; phone: 614/890-4700) $85/nonmembers, free/members, issued each autumn. Describes companies in the ceramic industry. Also includes a products directory.

Soap and Detergent Association Directory (SDA, 475 Park Ave., New York, NY 10016; phone: 212/725-1262) free, strictly available only to members, annual.

Who Makes It (Playthings, 51 Madison Ave., New York, NY 10010-1675; phone: 212/689-4411) $22, published each June. Provides information on the toy industry: toy manufacturers, importers, licensing agents, designers, inventors, suppliers, consultants, and manufacturers' representatives.

Chapter 22

The media

Also see the chapters on "The arts," "Entertainment," "Computers and electronics," and "Telecommunications." The first group of job sources beginning immediately below is largely for journalists. However, it also includes a wide array of othe media specialties.

Job openings

Medialine (National Black Media Coalition, 38 New York Ave, NE, Washington, DC 20002; phone: 202/387–8155) monthly, arrives around the first of the month, $25/annual nonmember subscription, free/members. Subscription rate includes subscription to *Jobline* described immediately below. Four to eight pages of "Career Alternatives" list openings in all aspects of print and broadcast journalism, production, public relations, and sales.

Jobline (National Black Media Coalition, 38 New York Ave, NE, Washington, DC 20002; phone: 202/387–8155) monthly, arrives in the middle of the month, $25/annual nonmember subscription, free/members. Subscription rate includes subscription to *Medialine* described immediately above. The typical issue bursts with more job ads than the typical *Medialine* issue.

The Quill (Society of Professional Journalists, P.O. Box 77, Greencastle, IN 46135; phone: 317/653-3333) nine issues/year, $25/annual nonmember subscription, included in dues package. The "Classifieds" section has six or seven positions in all aspects of the print and broadcast media, including faculty.

Job Information Letter (National Association of Government Communicators, 669 S. Washington St., Alexandria, VA 22314; phone: 703/519-3902) biweekly, $50/nonmember annual subscription (no subscription fee to members) plus send NAGC 26 self-addressed stamped #10 envelopes (2 ounce postage) for NAGC to mail the issues to you. Typical issue lists about 30 to 35 federal government positions plus photocopies of 50 or more classified ads for private sector editorial and art positions for several metropolitan areas. Also identifies over a dozen job hotlines and referral services.

The Professional Communicator (Women in Communications, Inc., 2101 Wilson Blvd., Suite 417, Arlington, VA 22201; phone: 703/528-4200) $18.50/annual nonmember subscription, free/members. The "Classifieds" list from five to ten positions for communications professionals in print and broadcast journalism, public relations, advertising, marketing, and education.

Job Hotline (Asian American Journalists Association, 1765 Sutter St., Suite 1000, San Francisco, CA 94115; phone: 415/346-2051) weekly, $10/ten-week subscription. About 80 announcements for print and broadcast journalists, photographers, news directors and producers, public relations, and journalism faculty appear in each issue. This is essentially a compilation of jobs listed in the AAJA's phone-in *Job Hotline* described below under "Job services."

National Association of Black Journalists Job Listing (NABJ, 11600 Sunrise Valley Dr., Reston, VA 22091; phone: 703/648-1270) biweekly, free, available only to members. Each issue is filled with 30 to 50 jobs for reporters and editors in print and broadcasting, as well as a few positions in public relations, sales, and university faculty.

Medium Rare (Native American Journalists Association, Macky Auditorium, Room 121, University of Colorado, Boulder, CO 80309; phone: 303/492-7397) quarterly, free, available only to members. About 30 positions in all aspects of broadcast and print journalism are listed under "jobs."

NAHJ Newsletter (National Association of Hispanic Journalists, National Press Building, Suite 1193, Washington, DC 20045; phone: 202/662-7145) monthly, free, available only to members. About 20 positions in all aspects of print and broadcast journalism are listed under "Job Opportunities."

El Sol (California Chicano News Media Association, 727 W. 27th St., Los Angeles, CA 90007; phone: 213/743-7158) monthly, free, available only to members. Ten to 20 positions in all aspects of print and broadcast journalism appear under "CCNMA Job Bank."

Job services

Employment Resource Center (National Black Media Coalition, 38 New York Ave, NE, Washington, DC 20002; phone: 202/387-8155) free. Submit three copies of your resume and a cover letter that explains what sort of work you are seeking and the geographic area in which you wish to work. When a job match is found, the employer contacts the job seeker. This service covers all aspects of broadcast and print journalism (including production), public relations, and sales.

In addition, the center offers consulting services for job seekers. Nonmembers pay $25 per consulting session which can be held in person on the phone with the center's director on Mondays through Wednesdays, 10 a.m. to 4:30 p.m.

Jobs for Journalists (Society of Professional Journalists, P.O. Box 77, Greencastle, IN 46135; phone: 317/653-3333) $25/six-month fee, available only to members. A registrant completes a resume form and submits it with copies of her resume and clips and/or tapes. Registrants matched with a job opening are contacted by the potential employer for an interview. Resumes are kept on file for six-month periods.

WICI National Job Hotline (Women in Communications, Inc., 2101 Wilson Blvd., Suie 417, Arlington, VA 22201; phone: 703/528-4200) free, available only to members. WICI maintains a toll-free number members can call to hear a listing of openings. For detailed information on positions, they call the WICI office for complete job specifications. Fields covered include print and broadcast journalism, public relations, advertising, marketing, and education.

Job Bank (National Association of Black Journalists, 11600 Sunrise Valley Dr., Reston, VA 22091; phone: 703/648-1270) free, available only to members. The job seeker completes the service's form which is kept on file for as long as the job seeker wishes. When matched with an opening, your "resume" is sent to the employer who then is responsible for contacting promising applicants. Covers reporters and editors in print and broadcast, as well as public relations, sales, and university faculty.

Jobphone (Editorial Freelance Association, 36 E. 23rd St., 9th floor, New York, NY 10110; phone: 212/677-3357). Anybody can call the "Jobphone," 212/260-6470, to hear a recording that briefly describes about 40 freelance writing, editing, proofreading, and translating opportunities. Listings are updated weekly. Only EFA members who subscribe to this service can call another phone number to get details (such as pay and whom to contact) on the listed jobs. Members can subscribe to "Jobphone" for $20/year. Write for membership rates (they're too complicated to explain here).

NAHJ/Job Exchange (National Association of Hispanic Journalists, National Press Building, Suite 1193, Washington, DC 20045; phone: 202/662-7145) free, available only to members. About 20 positions in print and broadcast journalism are listed on this job hotline which is updated weekly.

Asian American Journalists Association Job Bank (Asian American Journalists Association, 1765 Sutter St., Suite 1000, San Francisco, CA 94115; phone: 415/346-2051) free, available only AAJA members; for print and broadcast positions in news (including writing, directing, and producing), photography, and public relations. Complete the detailed job bank application and submit it with ten copies of your resume. Do not send clips, tapes, or photos. When matched with a job opening, the employer will contact you. Registrants are kept in the database for six–month periods.

Job Hotline (Asian American Journalists Association, 1765 Sutter St., Suite 1000, San Francisco, CA 94115; phone: 415/346-2051). To hear a recording of job openings for print and broadcast journalists, photographers, news directors and producers, public relations, internships, and journalism faculty, call 415/346-2261. Job fairs and fellowship opportunities are also announced on the hotline. Updated weekly.

Job Referral Service (Native American Journalists Association, Macky Auditorium, Room 121, University of Colorado, Boulder, CO 80309; phone: 303/492-7397) free, available only to members and to nonmember Native Americans. This informal service has you submit you resume. When a match is made, both the potential employer and job seeker are notified. Covers all aspects of print and broadcast journalism.

Jobline (National Federation of Press Women, P.O. Box 99, Blue Springs, MO 64015; phone: 816/229-1666) $25/nonmember registration fee, $15/members. Five to 12 positions in all aspects of broadcast and print journalism, public relations, and teaching are listed on the job hotline which is updated every two weeks. When you pay your fee, you also submit 10 resumes. When you call the hotline and hear a description of a job to which you'd like to apply, you leave a message for the service to send your resume to that job. Once all ten of your resumes have been sent out, you have to register again.

Jobs for Journalists (Society of Professional Journalists, P.O. Box 77, Greencastle, IN 46135; phone: 317/653-333) available only to members, $25/six-month fee. The job seeker submits ten copies of his resume and cover letter plus clips or audition tapes as well as the service's completed resume form. When the service matches a registrant with a job vacancy, it sends the resume to the employer and a post card to the job seeker so he can contact the employer himself if he wishes. This service covers all aspects of the print and broadcast media including university faculty and public relations.

JOBank (California Chicano News Media Association, 727 W. 27th St., Los Angeles, CA 90007; phone: 213/743-7158) $35/member fee, $10/student member fee, available only to members. The registrant submits his resume which is kept on file as long as he likes. When matched to a job, the registrant is contacted by the potential employer.

Job Hotline (California Chicano News Media Association, 727 W. 27th St., Los Angeles, CA 90007; phone: 213/743-7158) monthly, free, available only to members. About 20 positions in all aspects of print and broadcast journalism are listed on the hotline which is updated weekly.

Directories

All-In-One (Gebbie Press, P.O. Box 1000, New Paltz, NY 12561; phone: 914/255-7560) $73/prepaid; published annually. Over 500 pages that include information on more than 21,000 daily and weekly newspapers, radio and television stations, general consumer magazines, business papers, trade press, African American press, Hispanic press, farm publications, and news syndicates. Although intended for use by public relations folk, this directory is a good, affordable source for anyone trying to identify individual media for a job search.

This directory is also available in three separate sets on computer disk ($90/prepaid for each set, available in standard ASCII code on MS–DOS 5.25" or 3.5" disks [in variable length, comma–delimited fields, or fixed length fields], and on Macintosh 3.5" disks [in tab or comma delimited forms]); arranged by geographic area or zip code order: (1) daily, weekly, African American, and Hispanic newspapers; (2) television, radio, Black and Hispanic television and radio; (3) consumer magazines, business publications, and farm press.

WICI Membership and Resource Directory (Women in Communications, Inc., 2101 Wilson Blvd., Suite 417, Arlington, VA 22201; phone: 703/528–4200) $100/nonmembers, free/members, published in January of odd–numbered years. Members are in all aspects of media and communications including print and broadcast journalism, public relations, advertising, and marketing.

Gale Directory of Publications and Broadcast Media (Gale Research, Inc., 835 Penobscot Bldg., Detroit, MI 48226–4094; phone: 800/877–4253) $265, annual, 3,441 pages in three volumes. Includes listings of more than 10,000 radio and television stations and cable companies as well as over 20,000 newspapers and magazines.

The Christian Media Directory (James Lloyd, P.O. Box 3, Ashland, OR 97520; phone: 503/488–1405) $35 prepaid only. Lists over 3,500 producers, publishers, recording labels, studios, all–Christian music and radio stations, film and video companies, television stations, and more—all with a Christian slant.

New Careers: A Directory of Jobs and Internships in Technology and Society (Student Pugwash USA, 1638 R St., NW, Suite 32, Washington, DC 20009; phone: 202/328–6555) $18, $10/students (add $3 shipping). Offers full details on where and how to apply for internships and entry–level jobs in communications. Published in even–numbered years.

Madison Avenue Handbook: The Image Makers Source (Peter Glenn Publications, 17 E. 48th St., 6th floor, New York, NY 10017; phones: 800/223–1254, 212/688–7940) $45, published every April. This directory is a most thorough compendium of information for New York City, and nationally to the extent indicated, in the following areas: production (national and international), post–

production (New York, Los Angeles, Chicago), music and sound (New York, Chicago, Los Angeles, Detroit, Toronto, Florida), equipment/studios and stages (some national), props, locations/film commissions (national and international), model and talent agencies (national and international), print business, advertising (national), public relations, marketing, media, and the fashion and beauty industry.

Satellite Industry Directory & Buyers Guide (Satellite Communications, 6300 S. Syracuse Way, Suite 650, Englewood, CO 80111; phone: 303/220-0600) $19.95, $250/on MS–DOS computer disk in ASCII format or on labels; published each November. Describes hundreds of satellite communications businesses listed in alphabetical order. Includes a detailed subject index.

Salary surveys

WICI Job & Salary Survey Results (Women in Communications, Inc., 2101 Wilson Blvd., Suie 417, Arlington, VA 22201; phone: 703/528-4200) published in the April/May issue of *The Professional Communicator*, $4/single issue. Includes salary levels in print and broadcast media, corporate, non–profit, advertising and public relations, government, education, and free–lance.

Journalism Career and Scholarship Guide (Dow Jones Newspaper Fund, P.O. Box 300, Princeton, NJ 08543-0300; phone: 609/452-2820) first copy free, $3/each additional copy; published each December. Reports on entry–level salaries for journalists with newspapers, radio, television, and in advertising and public relations.

Broadcasting and film

Also see the entries under "Film industry" in the "Entertainment" chapter. Many of those entries, which are oriented toward entertainment rather than the more serious side of the business, include jobs in television and video.

Job openings

Broadcasting (Cahners Publishing Company, 1705 DeSales St., NW, Washington, DC 20036; phone: 202/659-2340) weekly, $85/annual subscription (U.S.), $125/foreign. The "Classifieds" typically carry over 90 ads for virtually everything in radio and television: management, on-air positions, sales, technical, programmers, and production. Also includes stations for sale.

Electronic Media (Crain Communications, 965 Jefferson Ave., Detroit, MI 48207-3185; phone: 800/678-9595) weekly, $59/annual subscription. Job vacancies for nearly everything in radio and television (mostly TV)—on-air positions, production, editors, engineers, directors, sales, research, station managers, etc.—appear in two places: "Jobs" where about a dozen positions are described, and "Classified Advertising—Help Wanted," where 20 to 30 additional vacancies are advertised.

Radio-Television News Directors Association Job Information Service (RTDA, c/o Howard Back, Chairman, RTNDA Job Information Service, c/o National Television News, Suite 201A, 23480 Park Sorrento, Calabasas Park, CA 91302; phone: 818/883-6121; for membership information: RTDA, 1717 K St., NW, Washington, DC 20006; phone: 202/659-6510) semimonthly, $16/two-month subscription, free to members. Twenty to 30 job announcements for television news photographers, producers, directors, anchors, reporters, and editors, plus several "situations wanted" fill this newsletter.

Television Broadcast (PSN Publications, 2 Park Ave., Suite 1820, New York, NY 10016; phone: 212/779-1919) $38/annual subscription. Includes about three ads for broadcast engineers under "Classifieds."

ITN (International Television Association, 6311 N. O'Connor Rd., LB51, Irving, TX 75039; phone: 214/869-1112) monthly, available only to members. The typical issue includes one or two display ads for all type of positions in corporate television (writers, editors, directors, producers) plus several "positions wanted" ads.

Street Sound (174 Spadina Ave., Suite 506, Toronto, Ontario, Canada M5T 2C2; phone: 416/369–0070) monthly, $42/annual subscription (U.S. air mail, Canada ground mail), $30/U.S. (surface mail), $75/elsewhere. Up to five ads will appear under ''Classifieds—Talent Wanted'' for radio disk jockeys.

Guide to Volunteer and Internship Programs in Public Broadcasting (Corporation for Public Broadcasting, 901 E St., NW; Washington, DC 20004; phone: 202/879–9600) free, published every 18 months, most recently in January 1991 and September 1992. Describes internship opportunities (some with stipends) with public broadcasting stations.

SMPTE Journal (Society of Motion Picture and Television Engineers, 595 W. Hartsdale, Ave., New York, NY 10607; phone: 914/761–1100) monthly, $75/annual nonmember subscription (U.S.), $85/elsewhere, free to members ($50/annual membership dues). About six ads for film and television technical, lighting, sales, and production positions appear under ''Classified.''

Television Broadcast (PSN Publications, 2 Park Ave., Suite 1820, New York, NY 10016; phone: 212/779–1919) monthly, $38/annual subscription. Includes about three ads for broadcast engineers under ''Classifieds.''

Videography (PSN Publications, 2 Park Ave., Suite 1820, New York, NY 10016; phone: 212/779–1919) monthly, $25/annual subscription. Includes about three ads for broadcast engineers under ''Classifieds.''

Pro–Sound News (PSN Publications, 2 Park Ave., Suite 1820, New York, NY 10016; phone: 212/779–1919) monthly, $30/annual subscription. Includes about three ads for broadcast engineers under ''Classifieds.''

Government and Military Video (PSN Publications, 2 Park Ave., Suite 1820, New York, NY 10016; phone: 212/779–1919) monthly, free. Includes about three ads for broadcast engineers, generally in the private sector, under ''Classifieds.''

Communications Engineering and Design (600 S. Cherry, Suite 400, Denver, CO 80222; phone: 303/393–7449) monthly, $48/annual subscription for members of the industry (U.S.), $69/foreign. About ten ads for technical positions in cable television appear

DENNIS THE MENACE

"I WONDER HOW PEOPLE KNEW WHAT TO BUY
BEFORE THEY HAD TELEVISION?"

under "Career Marketplace." Each August there is a story on management, engineering, and technical jobs in the cable television industry.

Community Radio News (National Federation of Community Broadcasters, 666 11th St., NW, Suite 805, Washington, DC 20001; phone: 202/393-2355) monthly, $75/annual nonmember subscription, free/members. The "Message Pad" section features about seven ads for radio station managers, on-air personnel, audio engineers, fundraisers, and producers.

FMedia! newsletter (FM Atlas-Publishing and Electronics, 241 Anderson Rd., Esko, MN 55733-9413; phone: 218/879-7676) monthly, $25/annual subscription, $2/sample issue. About five jobs for broadcast announcers, engineers, managers, etc. appear under "From the Classifieds."

QST (American Radio Relay League, 225 Main St., Newington CT 06111; phone: 203/666-1541) monthly, $30/annual subscription includes membership in ARRL. At the end of the "Ham Ads" section comes "Jobs for Hams" which advertises three to five positions for radio operators, engineers, and electronics instructors.

Documentary Editing (Association for Documentary Editing, c/o Indiana Historical Society, 315 W. Ohio St., Indianapolis, IN 46202-3299; phone: 317/232-6546) quarterly, available only to members, free. Four or five jobs for documentary editors appear under "Positions Available."

The Independent (Association for Independent Video and Film, 625 Broadway, New York, NY 10012; phone: 212/473-3400) ten issues/year, individual issues available at newsstands for $3.50, subscription available only to members, included in dues ($45/annual dues, $25/students). The "Notices-Opportunities-Gigs" section lists five positions in video/television direction, marketing, curators, media artists—anything to do with film and video.

AV Video (Montage Publishing, 25550 Hawthorne Blvd., Torrance, CA 90505) monthly, $36/annual subscription (U.S.), $40/Canada, $75/elsewhere. About three positions for audio-video technicians, sales marketing, and management appear under "Merchandiser—Position Available."

Job services

National Association of Broadcasters Employment Clearinghouse (NAB, 1771 N St., NW, Washington, DC 200036; phone: 202/429-5300) free, resumes kept on file for six months. You submit your own resume and the clearinghouse matches you to openings. It contacts job seekers to let them know when they are selected for an interview. This service covers all aspects of the television industry: switchboard operators, engineers, management—everything!

Noble Search (326 S. Wille Ave., Wheeling, IL 60090; phone: 708/541-3547). Call 900/933-3456, extension 33, on a touch-tone phone ($1.95/minute; the average call lasts seven minutes; charged directly to your phone bill). This job hotline lists positions in film, video, and broadcast production (including secretarial positions). When you call you'll be asked to choose which of the 11 regions for which you wish to hear vacancies: Southern California, Northern California, New York/New Jersey, Chicago, Florida, Texas, Minnesota, Ohio, Georgia, Tennessee, or Arizona. Jobs are further broken down by when they are available right now, whether it is an on-going position, or whether it is a frequently-needed free-lance position. For each position, you are told the nature of the job, when it starts, salary, and whom to contact. You can rewind, speed ahead, and check out more than one region. Updated daily. Job seekers may also list themselves on Noble Search's "Producer's Search Service."

MediaLine (P.O. Box 51909, Pacific Grove, CA 93950; phones: 800/237-8073, 408/648-5200) $42.50/six-week subscription to one phone line, $62.50/13-week subscription to one phone line. In contact with 800 television stations across the nation, this service features about 23 job openings each day among its five phone lines that are updated daily. Each line requires a separate subscription wherein you are given an access code to use when you call the job hotline. These are all in television news: (1) news production and promotion; (2) news anchors and reporters; (3) management; (4) sports and weather; (5) videographers (videotape and photographers).

Corporation for Public Broadcasting Job Hotline (CPB, 901 E St., NW; Washington, DC 20004; phone: 202/879-9600) free; open to the general public. Call 800/582-8220 or 202/393-1045 for detailed descriptions of jobs on public broadcasting. The 125+ listings on this service are updated weekly. Have your pencil and paper ready when you call and use a touch-tone telephone. You'll get to choose between hearing a very brief description of every job listed for the week and a radio or television specialty (programming and production; engineering and technical; general management and administration; promotion and fundraising; and CPB, PBS, and NPR and situations wanted. After you choose a specialty, you'll be told how to select a multi-state region. Then you'll hear a brief description of each job available in that region and specialty. You'll be told how to hear the description again and how to hear a much more detailed description that includes instructions on how to apply for the job.

Job Hotline (International Television Association Membership Directory (ITA, 6311 N. O'Connor Rd., LB51, Irving, TX 75039; phone: 214/869-1112) free, available only to members. Submit a copy of your resume. Resumes are forwarded to potential employers who are responsible for contacting job seekers. Covers all positions in corporate television (writing, editing, directing, producing).

Job Bank (American Sportscasters Association, 5 Beekman St., Suite 528, New York, NY 10038; phone: 212/227-8080) available only to members, $40/annual fee. When a job opening is submitted to the ASA, it sends a description of it to members. About ten to 15 sportscasting jobs are listed at any one time.

Job Service (Broadcast Designers Association, 251 Kearney St., Suite 611, San Francisco, CA 94108; phone: 415/788-2324) available only to members. A graphic designer member submits his own resume which is kept on file up to 12 months. When matched to a vacancy, the potential employer will contact him.

Job Service (Broadcast Promotion and Marketing Executives, 6255 Sunset Blvd., Suite 524, Los Angeles, CA 90028; phone: 213/465-3777) free, available only to members. You submit your resume which is kept on file for six months. You are notified when you are matched to a job opening and are responsible for contacting the potential employer yourself.

Directories

AV Market Place (R. R. Bowker, P.O. Box 31, New Providence, NJ 07974-9903; phone: 800/521-8110) $99.95 plus 5 percent shipping, published annually. This 1,336-page tome includes descriptions of 19,000 companies and individuals in audio, audio visual, computer systems, film, video, and programming. Also included are equipment dealers, "AV" manufacturers, producers, and corporate and government professionals.

Broadcasting® & Cable Market Place (R. R. Bowker, P.O. Box 31, New Providence, NJ 07974-9903; phone: 800/521-8110) $159.95 plus 5 percent shipping, first published March 1992. Formerly *The Broadcasting Yearbook*, this tome provides comprehensive listings for all radio, television, and cable stations in the U.S. and Canada with details on equipment, programs, personnel, and more. It also lists broadcasting equipment manufacturers and distributors. Attorneys who specialize in communications litigation are also listed.

Public Broadcasting Directory (Corporation for Public Broadcasting, 901 E St., NW; Washington, DC 20004; phone: 202/879-9600) $10, brought out each March. Provides information on public television and radio stations: managers, department heads, phone, and address.

International Television and Video Almanac (Quigley Publishing Co., 159 W. 53rd St., New York, NY 10019; phone: 212/247-3100) $77, published each January. Essentially a "Who's Who in Motion Pictures, Television, and Home Video," this directory provides addresses and phone numbers for television networks and stations, major program producers, major group station owners, cable television companies, distributors, casting agencies, literary agencies, advertising and publicity representatives, and firms that service the television and home video industries.

Who's Who in the Television Industry (Packard Publishing, P.O. Box 2187, Beverly Hills, CA 90213; phone: 213/854-0276) $19.95, published each January. Gives address, phone, and credits for directors, producers, writers, cinematographers, and executives. For the networks, production companies, and distribution companies, this directory also names their officers.

International Television Association Membership Directory (ITA, 6311 N. O'Connor Rd., LB51, Irving, TX 75039; phone: 214/869-1112) available only to members, issued each May. Lists members, their jobs, and work address and phone.

New York TV Directory (National Academy of Television Arts and Sciences, 111 W. 57th St., Suite 1020, New York, NY 10019; phone: 212/768-7050) $15, published in even-numbered years. Lists information on members and associations affiliated with it.

SMPTE Membership Directory (Society of Motion Picture and Television Engineers, 595 W. Hartsdale, Ave., New York, NY 10607; phone: 914/761-1100) free, available only to members, published each April.

Members of National Association of Telecommunications Officers and Advisors (NATOA, 6th Floor, 1301 Pennsylvania Ave., NW, Washington, DC 20004; phone: 202/626-3250) published monthly; included in membership package. Lists local cable television and telecommunications managers.

International Radio and Television Society Roster Yearbook (IRTS, 420 Lexington Ave., Suite 531, New York, NY 10170; phone: 212/876-6650) available only to members, published each February.

Broadcast Promotion and Marketing Executives Membership Directory (BPME, 6255 Sunset Blvd., Suite 524, Los Angeles, CA 90028; phone: 213/465-3777) free, available only to members. Published each August.

National Federation of Community Broadcasters Membership Directory (NFCB, 666 11th St., NW, Suite 805, Washington, DC 20001; phone: 202/393-2355) $50/nonmembers, $25/members, published each autumn. Provides information on participating member radio stations including names of the station manager and other officials.

National Association of Sportscasters and Sportswriters Membership Directory (NASS, P.O. Box 559, Salisbury, NC 28144; phone: 704/633-4275) $50/nonmembers, included in membership package, published in autumn of odd-numbered years.

North American Telecommunications Association Telecom Source (NATA, 2000 M St., NW, Washington, DC 20036; phones: 800/538-6282, 202/296-9800) $53/nonmembers, first copy free to members, published each November. Lists about 1,200 headquarter and branch offices of member telecommunications firms.

Salary survey

International Television Association Salary Survey (ITA, 6311 N. O'Connor Rd., LB51, Irving, TX 75039; phone: 214/869-1112) $50, annual. Also published each August in *ITN*, the association's newsletter. Based on a random sample of about half the membership. Salaries are reported upon for 22 professional categories (aerospace, broadcast/cable, energy, finance, hospitality, etc.) and by major departments (public relations, personnel, communications, administrative, marketing, other).

Print media

Also be sure to go back to the job sources listed in this chapter under "Media in general." Most of those sources are primarily for journalists.

Job openings

Editor & Publisher (11 W. 19th St., New York, NY 10011; phone: 212/675-4380) weekly; $45/annual subscription in U.S. and Canada, $86/elsewhere. The "Help Wanted" section of "Classified Advertising" features about 50 to 75 ads in all facets of publishing: academic, advertising, circulation, data processing, editorial, marketing, photography, production, and sales. Includes "Positions Wanted."

Publishers Weekly (Bowker Magazine Group, P.O. Box 1979, Marion, OH 43302; phone: 800/842-1669) weekly, $119/annual subscription (U.S.), $177/Canada, $260/elsewhere (air mail). "Weekly Exchange—Positions Open" lists over 20 vacancies in all aspects of book publishing as well as "positions wanted."

New England Newspaper Association Bulletin (NENA, 70 Washington St., Salem, MA 01970; phone: 508/744-8940) monthly, free, available only to members. About 10 ads for all types of positions with newspapers appear under "Classified."

Employment Roundup (American Business Press, 201 E. 42nd St., Suite 400, New York, NY 10017; phone: 212/661-6360) monthly, free, available only to members. Features positions in all aspects of publishing except secretarial support staff.

Writer's Digest (F & W Publications, P.O. Box 2123, Harlan, IA 51593; phone: 800/333-0133) monthly, $21/annual subscription (U.S.), $25/foreign (surface mail), $50/foreign (air mail). Over 30

HAGAR the HORRIBLE is reprinted by special permission of King Features
Syndicate, Inc. Copyright © 1991. All rights reserved.

jobs and writing opportunities are advertised under "Writer's Mart—Literary Services—Writers Wanted" and under "Classifieds." Positions include writing books, articles, business writers and song writers.

American Medical Writers Job Market Sheet (American Medical Writers Association, 9650 Rockville Pike, Bethesda, MD 20814; phone: 301/493-0003) bimonthly, available only to members. Between ten and 30 announcements of full-time and free-lance writing positions in medical communications appear in a typical issue. Includes "positions wanted."

Magazine Design and Production (South Wind Publishing, 8340 Mission Rd., Suite 106, Prairie Village, KS 66206; phone: 913/642-6611) monthly, $48/annual subscription (U.S.), $58/Canada, $150/elsewhere. As many as five positions in magazine design and production are in the typical issue.

Publishers' Auxiliary (National Newspaper Association, 1627 K St., NW, Washington, DC 20006; phone: 202/466-7200) biweekly, $50/annual nonmember subscription, included in membership package. Under "Help Wanted" you'll find about half a dozen positions for editors, writers, sales, circulation, financial, newspaper management, and university faculty.

Magazine & Bookseller (North American Publishing Company, 401 N. Broad St., Philadelphia, PA 19108; phone: 215/238–5300) monthly, $49/annual subscription (U.S.), $71/foreign. The "Classified" section has two or three ads for sales representatives for books and magazines.

Poets & Writers (72 Spring St., New York, NY 10012; phone: 212/226–3586) bimonthly, $18/annual subscription. "Classifieds" features calls for manuscripts for anthologies, books, and magazines, contests, and a few job openings.

The Newsletter on Newsletters (The Newsletter Clearinghouse, 44 W. Market St., Rhinebeck, NY 12572; phone: 914/876–2081) semi-monthly, $120/annual subscription. The "Newsletter Services Directory" section has two to five or more "newsletters wanted", "newsletters for sale," and "situations available." Also see the last page or two where you can find a few available newsletters under "For Sale."

Hotline (Newsletter Association, 1401 Wilson Blvd., Suite 403, Arlington, VA 22209; phone: 703/527–2333) biweekly, available only to members. "Notes in the News" features two to five newsletters for sale and acquisitions wanted.

Job services

E & P Voice Classified Service (Editor & Publisher, 11 W. 19th St., New York, NY 10011; phone: 212/675–4380) free, touch-tone phone required. This service essentially lets you place yourself in a job bank from which newspaper and magazine publishers select job candidates to interview. For a recorded demonstration of this service, call 212/230–2225.

The job seekers calls this still nascent service and answers job specific questions about herself in sort of a "telephone resume." She is then given a personal resume i.d. number.

This telephone resume is kept recorded on tape for one week. Employers who use the service scan these telephone resumes and leave a message for the job seekers they wish to interview.

As early as 48 hours after a job seeker records his telephone resume, he can call back to hear messages from any employers who are interested in him and learn the next step in the job search process: whether an employer wants him to call to schedule an interview, or if he should send in a written resume, or if no employer is interested at this time.

Job ANPA (American Newspaper Publishers Association, 11600 Sunrise Valley Dr., Reston, VA 22091; phone: 703/648-1072) free. Call 800/562-2672, 24-hours a day, for a national telephone job bank recording, updated every two weeks, for positions in all aspects of newspapers: editing and reporting, marketing, personnel, computer programming, engineering, operations, advertising, circulation, business administration, and accounting. Even if you don't have a touch-tone phone, you can still access this job hotline because operator assistance will be provided.

Western Publications Association Job Bank (WPA, 5000 Van Nuys Blvd, Suite 300, Sherman Oaks, CA 91403; phone: 818/995-7338) free. For all aspects of magazine publishing (editorial, art, circulation, sales, etc.), job seekers furnish a two- to three-paragraph summary of the type of job they seek and their basic qualifications. Employers are responsible for contacting job seekers for an interview. "Resumes" are kept on file for three months.

New England Newspaper Association Job Bank (NENA, 70 Washington St., Salem, MA 01970; phone: 508/744-8940) free, available only to members. The job seeker submits her own resume which is kept on file for six months at a time. Employers contact job seekers directly. Covers all aspects of newspapers from writing to management and production.

Dial-a-Writer Referral Service (American Society of Journalists and Authors, 1501 Broadway, Suite 302, New York, NY 10036; phone: 212/997-0947) commission paid on jobs secured, available only to members. After you register with this service, your name is among those given to publishers seeking professional free-lance fiction writers. If you obtain an assignment, you pay a commission to the service.

Job Service (Black Women in Publishing, P.O. Box 6275 F.D.R. Station, New York, NY 10150; phone: 212/772-5951) free. The job seeker submits her own resume and is contacted by potential employers for an interview or further submission. Covers all aspects of the print media: editorial, reporters, information systems, etc.

GENIE, The Well (Computer Press Association, 1260 25th Ave., San Francisco, CA 94122; phone: 415/681–5364) available only to members. From five to ten jobs for editors, free-lance writers, and publishers appear on this computer bulletin board which is accessed by modem. Users pay only for on-line time.

Directories

Novel & Short Story Writer's Market (Writer's Digest Books, 1507 Dana Ave., Cincinnati, OH 45207; phone: 800/289–0963) $18.95 plus $3 shipping, issued annually. Its 624 pages describe 1,900 fiction publishers including submission requirements, pay rates, and helpful hints so you submit to the right person.

Children's Writers & Illustrator's Market (Writer's Digest Books, 1507 Dana Ave., Cincinnati, OH 45207; phone: 800/289–0963) $16.95 plus $3 shipping, issued annually. Over 300 book and magazine publishers are described: writing and illustration needs, submission procedures and requirements, payment terms, and tips to help you target your work.

Humor & Cartoon Markets (Writer's Digest Books, 1507 Dana Ave., Cincinnati, OH 45207; phone: 800/289–0963) $16.95 plus $3 shipping, issued annually. Provides details on submitting cartoons and humor to over 500 magazine, greeting card, newsletter, and comic book publishers, plus advertising agencies (for jingles and slogans), animation studios, radio disk jockeys who use humorous material, and syndicates.

The Professional Free-Lance Writers Directory (Associated Business Writers of America, 1450 S. Havana, Suite 620, Aurora, CO 80012; phone: 303/751–7844) $14/nonmembers, free/members, issued each March.

Publishers, Distributors, & Wholesalers of the United States (R.R. Bowker, 245 W. 17th St., New York, NY 10011; phone: 800/521–8110) $124.95 plus 5 percent for shipping, published annually. Provides contact information for 53,300 publishers, distributors, wholesalers, museum and association publishing programs, software producers and manufacturers, and audio cassette producers and distributors across the country. Also available on CD–ROM. Also available online on DIALOG, file number 450, $66/hour search time plus nominal charge for display; updated monthly.

Literary Marketplace (R.R. Bowker, 245 W. 17th St., New York, NY 10011; phone: 800/521–8110) $134.95 plus 5 percent for shipping, published each November, about 1,700 pages. With 13,700 major listings and over 40,000 names in all, this is publishing's definitive contact directory to find publishers, printers and book manufacturers, distributors, wholesalers, advertising and promotion agencies, and literary agents.

International Literary Marketplace (R.R. Bowker, 245 W. 17th St., New York, NY 10011; phone: 800/521–8110) $124.95 plus 5 percent for shipping, published annually. Over 13,000 publishing, literary, printing, and library organizations in over 160 countries are listed.

Western Publications Association Directory (WPA, 5000 Van Nuys Blvd, Suite 300, Sherman Oaks, CA 91403; phone: 818/995–7338) $25, released annually. This is a directory of magazine publishers who belong to the WPA.

Black Women in Publishing Member Directory (BWP, P.O. Box 6275 F.D.R. Station, New York, NY 10150; phone: 212/772–5951) free, available only to members ($50/annual membership, $25/students), published annually. Covers members in all aspects of the print media.

Journalism Career and Scholarship Guide (Dow Jones Newspaper Fund, P.O. Box 300, Princeton, NJ 08543–0300; phone: 609/452–2820) first copy free, $3/each additional copy; published each December. Includes internship opportunities and training programs with newspapers and magazines.

Ulrich's International Periodicals Directory (R. R. Bowker, P.O. Box 31, New Providence, NJ 07974–9903; phone: 800/521–8110) $339.95, published each August, about 6,000 pages in three volumes. Lists 120,000 regularly and irregularly published periodicals with addresses for nearly 65,000 publishers in 188 countries. Also includes a listing of over 360 serials available on CD–ROM and CD–ROM producers. Includes newsletter and toll–free hotline for serials research assistance.

Ulrich's PLUS™ (R. R. Bowker, P.O. Box 31, New Providence, NJ 07974–9903; phone: 800/521–8110) $465/annual subscription, updated quarterly. This CD–ROM places *Ulrich's International Periodical's Directory*, described immediately above, on your computer.

Ulrich's Online™ (R. R. Bowker, P.O. Box 31, New Providence, NJ 07974–9903; phone: 800/521–8110). This service makes the contents of *Ulrich's International Periodical's Directory*, described immediately above, available by modem on DIALOG, file number 480, for $60/hour search time, plus a nominal charge for display. Updated monthly.

Ulrich's on Microfiche™ (R. R. Bowker, P.O. Box 31, New Providence, NJ 07974–9903; phone: 800/521–8110) $325, quarterly. This service gives you *Ulrich's International Periodical's Directory*, described immediately above, on microfiche. It also includes all deceased titles.

Standard Periodical Directory (Oxbridge Communications, 150 Fifth Ave., New York, NY 10011; phones: 800/955–0231, within New York: 212/741–0231) $425, last issued in 1991. Details on over 75,000 North American periodicals fill these 1,832 pages.

Standard Periodical Directory (Gale Research, Inc., 835 Penobscot Bldg., Detroit, MI 48226–4094; phone: 800/877–4253) $425, 1991, 1,782 pages. Includes listings on 65,000 periodicals published in the U.S. and Canada arranged under 230 major subject areas.

Magazines for Libraries™ (R.R. Bowker, 245 W. 17th St., New York, NY 10011; phone: 800/521–8110) $139.95 plus 5 percent for shipping, published each March. Offers detailed profiles of 6,500 periodicals under 145 subject areas.

National Directory of Magazines (Oxbridge Communications, 150 Fifth Ave., New York, NY 10011; phones: 800/955–0231, within New York: 212/741–0231) $295, most recent edition in 1991. Extensive descriptions of large and small North American magazines, including staff, circulation, and publication information.

Directory of Members and Industry Suppliers (The Newsletter Association, 1401 Wilson Blvd., Suite 403, Arlington, VA 22209; phone: 703/527-2333) $45, released each September. These 200 pages offer a detailed description of newsletter publishers and the newsletters they publish.

Hudson's Subscription Newsletter Directory (The Newsletter Clearinghouse, 44 W. Market St., Rhinebeck, NY 12572; phone: 914/876-2081) $118, $98/libraries or subscribers to *The Newsletter on Newsletters*; published annually. In 514 pages, this directory describes 4,570 subscription newsletters.

Oxbridge Directory of Newsletters (Oxbridge Communications, 150 Fifth Ave., New York, NY 10011; phones: 800/955-0231, within New York: 212/741-0231) $295, published annually. Over 1,200 pages provide full editorial and subscription information on 21,000 U.S. and Canadian newsletters in more than 200 subject categories.

Newsletters in Print (Gale Research, Inc., 835 Penobscot Bldg., Detroit, MI 48226-4094; phone: 800/877-4253) $175, 1990, 1,397 pages. Furnishes information on over 10,000 newsletters.

American Book Trade Directory (R. R. Bowker, P.O. Box 31, New Providence, NJ 07974-9903; phone: 800/521-8110) $189.95, annual, 1,900 pages. Over 25,000 bookstores and antiquarian book dealers plus 14,000 book and magazine wholesalers, distributors, and jobbers are presented by state and city. Retailers are also indexed by bookselling category.

Publishers Directory (Gale Research, Inc., 835 Penobscot Bldg., Detroit, MI 48226-4094; phone: 800/877-4253) $235, 1991, 1,794 pages. Gives details on over 20,000 U.S. and Canadian publishing firms as well as small independent presses and 550 distributors.

Cassell and the Publishers Association Directory of Publishing (Oryx Press, 4041 N. Central, Phoenix, AZ 85012; phone: 800/279-6799) $55.50, annual, 443 pages. Describes over 1,100 English-language publishers from 19 countries and over 100 authors; agents from five countries.

Directory of Directory Publishers (Gale Research, Inc., 835 Penobscot Bldg., Detroit, MI 48226–4094; phone: 800/877–4253) $125, 1990, 530 pages. Furnishes key facts on over 7,000 directory publishers worldwide.

Photography

See also entries under "Models" and "Print media" in this chapter.

Job openings

Photo District News (49 E. 21st St., New York, NY 10010; phone: 212/677–8418) ten issues/year, $36/annual subscription. Available in regional editions. "Classifieds" section features about 15 job openings under "Help Wanted" and about 12 under "Reps Wanted," plus "Position Wanted" and "Assistants Available." Jobs include still photographers, photographic illustrators, film processors, studio managers, and assistants.

National Press Photographers Association (National Press Photographers Association, 3200 Crosdaile Dr., Salem, NC 27705; phone: 919/383–7246) monthly, available only to members. About 15 job announcements for still photographers fill this newsletter.

Professional Photographer (PPA Publications, 1090 Executive Way, Des Plaines, IL 60018; phone: 708/299–8161) monthly, $24.50/annual subscription (U.S.), $40/Canada, $60/elsewhere. Five to ten ads for still photographers and studio management appear under "Classifieds—Help Wanted."

The News Photographer (National Press Photographers Association, 3200 Crosdaile Dr., Salem, NC 27705; phone: 919/383–7246) monthly, $28/annual nonmember subscription, included in dues package. Up to five ads for still photographers appear under "Classifieds." Vacancies for television news camera operators and graphic art directors also appear.

Shutterbug (5211 S. Washington Ave., Titusville, FL 32780; phone: 407/268-5010) monthly, $16/annual subscription, elsewhere: $40 by surface mail, $100 by air mail. Typical issue contains about three jobs under "Help Wanted" and about ten "Photo Business for Sale/Wanted."

Job services

Job Bank (National Press Photographers Association, 3200 Crosdaile Dr., Salem, NC 27705; phone: 919/383-7246) free, available only to members. Members send in a self-addressed, stamped envelop to receive a six to 12 page listing of current job vacancies for still photographers, television camera operators, graphic artists, and studio management. The listing is updated weekly.

Directory

National Press Photographers Association Membership Directory (NPPA, 3200 Crosdaile Dr., Salem, NC 27705; phone: 919/383-7246) $40/nonmembers, free/members, published each September. Lists still photographers.

Graphic arts and print production

Job openings

American Printer (Maclean Hunter, 29 N. Wacker Dr., Chicago, IL 60606; phones: 312/726-2802) monthly; $50/annual subscription (U.S.); $60/Canada; $100/elsewhere (surface mail), $180 (air mail). "Printer's Marketplace—Help Wanted" has just three to ten ads for prepress, pressroom, bindery, sales, and graphic arts positions.

New England Printer and Publisher (P.O. Box 810, Newburyport, MA 01950; phone: 508/462-9461) monthly, $11/annual subscription. About seven ads for graphic arts specialists, printers, and printing sales appear under "Help Wanted" in addition to ten ads under "Business Opportunities."

DESIGNperspectives (Industrial Designers Society of America, 1142 Walker Rd., Great Falls, VA 22066; phone: 703/759–0100) monthly, $30/annual nonmember subscription, free/members. Ten ads for industrial designers, product designers, and graphic artists are under "Employment." Also includes "Position Wanted" ads.

Guild News (Graphic Artists Guild, 11 W. 20th St., New York, NY 10011; phone: 212/463–7730) quarterly, available only to members. Three or four positions for graphic artists appear under "Job Opportunities."

The Artist's Magazine (F & W Publications, P.O. Box 2120, Harlan, IA 51593; phone: 800/333–0444) monthly, $24/annual subscription (U.S.), $28/foreign (surface mail), $59/air mail. About six jobs for graphic artists appear under "Classified—Artists Wanted."

Graphic Arts Product News (Maclean Hunter, 29 N. Wacker Dr., Chicago, IL 60606; phones: 312/726–2802) bimonthly; $40/annual subscription (U.S.); $50/Canada; $75/elsewhere (surface mail), $125 (air mail). There's usually only a handful of graphic arts positions listed under "Printer's Marketplace—Help Wanted."

Print (104 Fifth Ave.; New York, NY 10011; phone: 212/463–0600) bimonthly, $50/annual subscription, $62/Canada. A typical issue includes three to five ads for graphic artists under "Art Services Marketplace."

Messages (Society of Environmental Graphic Designers, 47 Third St., Cambridge, MA 02141; phone: 617/577–8225) quarterly, available only to members. About seven positions in graphic design and architecture appear under "Job Openings."

Signs of the Times (407 Gilbert, Cincinnati, OH 45202; phone: 513/421–2050) monthly, $30/annual subscription (U.S.), $50/Canada, $55/elsewhere. "Opportunity Exchange" carries 40 to 50 job ads for everything in the sign industry: sales representatives, neon tube benders, sheetmetal sign fabricators, sign and billboard installers, screen printers, etc. The December issue features an extensive directory of sign supply distributors.

SIGNCRAFT (1938 Hill Ave., Fort Meyers, FL 33906; phone: 813/939–4644) bimonthly, $24/annual subscription (U.S.), $31/foreign. About three to six ads for sign designers and painters appear under "Classified—Employment."

Screen Printing (407 Gilbert, Cincinnati, OH 45202; phone: 513/421–2050) monthly, $30/annual subscription (U.S.), $50/Canada, $55/elsewhere. "Opportunity Exchange" carries 15 to 20 ads for graphic artists, production and plant managers, screen printers, and sales and marketing.

Graphic Arts Monthly (Cahners Publishing, 249 W. 17th St., New York, NY 10011; phone: 800/637–6079) monthly, $79.95/annual subscription (U.S.), $155.10/Canada, $159.95/elsewhere. The "Marketplace" section has about eight ads for positions in the printing industry: printers, pressmen, scanmen, electricians, plant superintendents, customer service representatives, direct sales, etc.

Creative Register (American Center for Design, 233 E. Ontario, Chicago, IL 60611; phone: 312/787–2018) monthly, $15/annual nonmember subscription, free/members. Ten to 20 job announcements in communications design fill this jobs newsletter: graphics designers, entry level to art directors, sales representatives for print houses.

The Typographer (Typographers International Association, 2233 Wisconsin Ave, NW, Suite 235, Washington, DC 20007; phone: 202/965–3400) monthly, $24/annual subscription, free to qualified professionals. Just one or two ads for jobs or business opportunities appear under "Classified."

Job service

The Jobline (Printing Industries of America, 100 Dangerfield Rd., Alexandria, VA 22314; phone: 703/519–8100) free. Call 800/621–8973, weekdays only, 8 a.m. to 4 p.m. Eastern time, to state your job qualifications. PIA member employers contact job seekers directly. Employers are seeking to fill about 60 jobs at any one time. Positions are in the commercial printing and graphics communications industries: graphic artists, pre-press work, sales, production, management, etc.

Directories

Graphic Arts Blue Book (A. F. Lewis & Co., 79 Madison Ave., New York, NY 10016; phone: 212/679-0770) $80/edition, published each April in six regional editions. Lists information on printers, trade shops, and suppliers.

Directory of Industrial Designers (Industrial Designers Society of America, 1142 Walker Rd., Great Falls, VA 22066; phone: 703/759-0100) $50/nonmembers, free/members, annual. Lists IDSA members by specialty, region, employer, and alphabetically.

American Center for Design Membership Directory (ACD, 233 E. Ontario, Chicago, IL 60611; phone: 312/787-2018) free, available only to members, issued annually. Members include graphic artists and designers, photographers, interior, industrial, and lighting designers.

The Design Firm Directory: Graphics and Industrial Design (Wefler & Associates, Inc., P.O. Box 1591, Evanston, IL 60204; phone: 312/454-1940) $52, annual, most recent edition November 1991. Covers 1,600 firms in this field.

Society of Illustrators Membership Directory (Society of Illustrators, 128 E. 63rd St., New York, NY 10021; phone: 212/838-2560) $30, issued every summer.

National Computer Graphics Association Membership Directory (NCGA, 2722 Merrilee Dr., Fairfax, VA 22031; phone: 703/698-9600) available only to members, most recent edition released in 1990.

National Electric Sign Association Membership Directory (NESA, 801 N. Fairfax St., Suite 205, Alexandria, VA 22314; phone: 703/22314) $40/nonmembers plus 10 percent shipping, free to members, published each April. Provides details on over 1,100 sign companies, product manufacturers, and suppliers.

Binding Industries of America Membership Directory (BIA, 60 E. Lake St., Chicago, IL 60601; phone: 312/372-7606) free, available only to members, most recent edition published in December 1991.

Salary surveys

Sales Compensation Computer Package (National Association of Printers and Lithographers, 780 Palisade Ave., Teaneck, NJ 07666; phone: 201/342-0706) $100/nonmembers, $65/members, order must be in writing on company letterhead signed by a key officer; most recently issued in spring 1991. Based on a survey of 600 graphic arts firms, this computer program with database reports on salaries, commissions, and benefits for salespeople in the graphic arts industry. Available only on MS–DOS floppy disks, 5.25–inch and 3.5–inch.

Executive and Key Personnel Compensation Study (National Association of Printers and Lithographers, 780 Palisade Ave., Teaneck, NJ 07666; phone: 201/342-0706) $100/nonmembers, first copy free to members, order must be in writing on company letterhead signed by a key officer; 133 pages. Reports on compensation packages for top printing executives covering 28 job titles.

Models

Also see listings in the "Apparel and accessories" chapter.

Job openings

MPA Buyline (Models and Photographers of America, P.O. Box 25099, Colorado Springs, CO 80936–5099; phone: 719/597–8106) free, available only to members; $36/annual associate dues. Around a dozen detailed requests for photographic models appears in a typical issue of this irregular publication.

Job services

MPA Talentsource Databank (Models and Photographers of America, P.O. Box 25099, Colorado Springs, CO 80936–5099; phone: 719/597–8106) free, available only to members; $36/annual associate member dues. This is a national registry of models and photographers available for local, regional, or national assign-

ments. You complete a detailed registration form and submit a sample of non–returnable pictures for each of your modeling or photographic specialties (along with photocopies of model releases covering the pictures submitted). The Databank notifies registered models and photographers of a match leaving the parties to contact each other directly.

Directories

Models and Photographers of America Showcase (Models and Photographers of America, P.O. Box 25099, Colorado Springs, CO 80936–5099; phone: 719/597–8106) free, available only to members; $36/annual associate dues. This "industry hotline talent directory" is a national directory of advertising directories; associations; backdrops; photographic equipment; fashion, glamour, and figure photo markets; film commissions; photographic production services; props; modeling agencies; publications; studio rentals, and more. In addition, models and photographers can purchase listings in the talent directory section.

International Directory of Model & Talent Agencies (Peter Glenn Publications, 17 E. 48th St., 6th floor, New York, NY 10017; phones: 800/223–1254, 212/688–7940) $29.50, published each September. Features over 2,000 listings of model and talent agencies and schools, associations, and pageant information in the U.S., Canada and overseas.

New York City Model Agency Directory (Peter Glenn Publications, 17 E. 48th St., 6th floor, New York, NY 10017; phones: 800/223-1254, 212/688-7940) $10.95. This pocket-sized directory identifies the types of models each of the New York City model agencies handle as well as the special interests they serve.

Advertising and public relations

Be sure to revisit the job sources at the beginning of this chapter under "Media in general"— many of them include a good number of job openings for people in public relations and advertising.

Job openings

Advertising Age (740 N. Rush St.; Chicago, IL 60611; phone: 800/678-9595) weekly. $79/annual subscription, foreign: $133/surface, $205/air. Ten to 20 job ads appear in the typical issue under "Advertising Marketplace."

Adweek (PO Box 700; Brewster, NY 10598-9943; phone: 800/722-6658, 312/467-6500) weekly; $79/annual subscription, $214/foreign (by airmail). Around 20 job ads grace the "Employment Opportunities" section each week. Although this magazine appears in regional editions (East, New England, Southeast, Southwest, West, and Midwest), the job advertisements are usually identical in all six editions. The identical job ads also appear in *Adweek's Marketing Week* (weekly; $75/annual subscription, $210/foreign by airmail) and *Mediaweek* (weekly; $65/annual subscription).

O'Dwyers PR Marketplace (J.R. O'Dwyer Co., 271 Madison Ave., New York, NY 10016; phone: 212/679-2471) biweekly, $24/annual subscription. Twenty to 25 ads for all types of public relations jobs fill this jobs newsletter. It also includes business opportunities and a "Talent Available" section.

The Counselor (1120 Wheeler Way, Langhorn, PA 19047; phone: 215/752-4200) monthly, $55/annual subscription. About eight job openings for ad specialists appear in display ads and under "Classifieds."

Doonesbury BY GARRY TRUDEAU

Public Relations Journal (Public Relations Society of America, 33 Irving Pl., New York, NY 10003; phone: 212/995–2266) monthly, $45/annual nonmember subscription, included in dues package. "Fast Close Classified" features about 12 ads for the higher level executive positions in public relations and marketing.

PR Marcom Jobs West (Rachel P.R. Services, 513 Wilshire Blvd., Suite 238, Santa Monica, CA 90401; phone: 213/326–2661) semi-monthly, $25/three–month subscription (first class mail), $35/three–month subscription (by fax). About 20 job announcements, virtually all for positions in California, fill this newsletter.

Marketing News (American Marketing Association, 250 S. Wacker Dr., Suite 200, Chicago, IL 60606–5819; phone: 312/648–0536) bi-weekly, $50/annual nonmember subscription, $25/members. The "Marketplace" features 25 jobs in marketing and marketing research including university faculty.

Alert (2189 Silas Dean Highway, Suite 5, Rockyhill, CT 06067; phone: 203/257–4008) ten issues/year, $25/annual subscription. Two or three jobs in marketing research and field management are advertised under "Classified."

The Marketer (Society for Marketing Professional Services, 99 Canal Plaza, Suite 320, Alexandria, VA 22314; phones: 800/292–7677, 703/549–6117) available only to members, included in $210 annual dues. About 12 jobs for marketing directors with design and construction companies appear under "Positions/Positions Wanted."

Direct Marketing (224 Seventh Ave., Garden City, NJ 11530; phone: 516/746–6700) monthly, $52/annual subscription. Two or three ads for marketing positions in lower management appear in display ads or in the "Classifieds."

IDEAS (International Newspaper Marketing Association, 11600 Sunrise Valley Dr., Reston, VA 22091; phone: 703/648–1094) 11 issues/year, free, available only to members. One or two ads for newspaper marketing jobs appear under "Classifieds."

Newspaper Marketing (International Newspaper Advertising and Marketing Executives, 11600 Sunrise Valley Dr., Reston, VA 22091; phone: 703/648–1098) monthly, $50/annual nonmember subscription, included in member dues. One or two ads for newspaper advertising directors appear under "Classifieds."

Job services

Job Hotline (Public Relations Society of America, 33 Irving Pl., New York, NY 10003; phone: 212/995–2266). Call 212/995–0476 to hear a recording of job vacancies and for instructions on how to submit your resume. If interested in a job, you inform the service which arranges for forwarding your resume to the employer(s) you request. Nonmembers are charged $25 for each resume forwarded; members pay $8.

PR Newswire Job Bank (PR Newswire, 900 Wilshire Blvd., Suite 1222, Los Angeles, CA 90017; phones: 800/321–8169, 213/862–4700) free. Send one copy of your resume and cover letter. Your resume will be forwarded to companies with vacancies that match your qualifications. Jobs are in public relations, largely in the Los Angeles area.

Direct Marketing Association Job Bank (DMA, 11 W. 42nd St., New York, NY 10036; phone: 212/768–7277, ext. 429) free. Send in your resume which will be kept on file for three months. When a job match is made, the employer, if interested, will contact the job seeker. Jobs are mostly on the east coast.

Directories

Creative Black Book (Macmillan Creative Services Group, 115 Fifth Ave., New York, NY 10003; phone: 212/254–1330) $100 plus $7/shipping, published each January. Includes 20,000 model and advertising agencies, art suppliers, photographers, color labs, printers, illustrators, designers, television directors and producers, and others whose products are used in advertising and public relations.

Standard Directory of Advertising Agencies (National Register Publishing Company, 3004 Glenview Rd., Wilmette, IL 60091; phones: 800/323–6772, 708/441–2210) $267 plus $9.45 shipping, published each February. Lists key management, creative, account, and production people at over 5,000 advertising agencies plus breakdowns of billings by media.

American Association of Advertising Agencies Roster and Organization (AAAA, 666 Third Ave., New York, NY 10017; phone: 212/682–2500) free, most recent edition 1991–1992. Geographical and alphabetical listings; includes branch offices.

International Advertising Association Worldwide Membership Directory (IAA, 342 Madison Ave., Suite 2000, New York, NY 10017; phone: 212/557–1133) $350/nonmembers, included in dues, published every February.

Macmillan Directory of International Advertisers and Agencies (National Register Publishing Company, 3004 Glenview Rd., Wilmette, IL 60091; phones: 800/323–6772, 708/441–2210) $267 plus $8.45 shipping, annual. Over 800 pages reporting on 1,900 foreign ad agencies and 1,600 foreign advertisers.

Directory (League of Advertising Agencies, 333 Rector Pl., New York, NY 10280; phone: 212/945–4314) write for details.

O'Dwyer's Directory of Public Relations Firms (J.R. O'Dwyer Co., 271 Madison Ave., New York, NY 10016; phone: 212/679–2471) $110, annual. This 414–page directory provides details on over 1,800 U.S. and 500 overseas public relations firms and their branch offices. Firms are indexed geographically and by 17 specialties in public relations.

O'Dwyer's Directory of Corporate Communications (J.R. O'Dwyer Co., 271 Madison Ave., New York, NY 10016; phone: 212/679-2471) $110, annual. Over 6,700 corporate public relations executives with their direct-dial phone numbers and addresses fill this 417-page tome. Extensive details on the public relations departments are provided.

O'Dwyer's Directory of Public Relations Executives (J.R. O'Dwyer Co., 271 Madison Ave., New York, NY 10016; phone: 212/679-2471) $70, annual. Included biographies of 5,000 business public relations executives with more than five years experience.

The Source (Rachel P.R. Services, 513 Wilshire Blvd., Suite 238, Santa Monica, CA 90401; phone: 213/326-2661) $45, published annually with quarterly updates included; 26 pages. Says it provides details on 300 job sources in public relations, journalism, advertising, and marketing: job banks, trade publications, job hotlines, free-lance cooperatives, executive recruiters, employment agencies, and associations.

International Newspaper Marketing Association Membership Directory (INMA, 11600 Sunrise Valley Dr., Reston, VA 22091; phone: 703/648-1094) available only to members, published each February.

International Newspaper Advertising and Marketing Executives Membership Roster (INAME, 11600 Sunrise Valley Dr., Reston, VA 22091; phone: 703/648-1098) available only to members, issued each January.

Society for Marketing Professional Services Membership Directory (SMPS, 99 Canal Plaza, Suite 320, Alexandria, VA 22314; phones: 800/292-7677, 703/549-6117) free, available only to members, published annually.

Salary Surveys

Compensation Survey of Public Affairs Positions (Foundation for Public Affairs, 1019 19th St., NW, Suite 200, Washington, DC 20036; phone: 202/872-1750) $250, issued in autumn of even-numbered years. Reports on salaries and perquisites for corporate public affairs staff positions: senior public affairs executive; top positions within federal government relations, state government relations, community relations, and corporate contributions functions; regional state government relations manager; and state government relations representative.

Washington Office Salary Survey (Foundation for Public Affairs, 1019 19th St., NW, Suite 200, Washington, DC 20036; phone: 202/872-1750) $250, issued in autumn of odd-numbered years. Reports on salaries and perquisites of corporate public affairs staff positions in the nation's capitol: executive head of office; deputy head of office; legislative counsel/lobbyist; research assistant; executive secretary; and secretary.

Translators

Job openings

ATA Chronicle (American Translators Association, 109 Croton Ave, Ossining, NY 10562; phone: 914/941-1500) 11 issues/year, $35/annual nonmember subscription (U.S., Canada), $45/elsewhere, free/members. About ten job openings for translators appear in display ads and the "Classifieds."

Directories

Membership List of Interpreters (American Society of Interpreters, P.O. Box 9603, Washington, DC 20016; phone: 703/998-8636) free, annual.

Directory of Translators (Association of Professional Translators, 3 Mellon Bank Center, Suite 2523, Pittsburgh, PA 15259; phone: 412/234-4590) $1/nonmembers, free/members, published irregularly.

Chapter 23

Museums and libraries

For additional sources of library positions, also see the much more extensive set of job sources under "Library services" in the Government Job Finder.

Job openings

American Libraries (American Library Association, 50 E. Huron St., Chicago, IL 60611; phones: 800/545-2433 (outside Illinois), 800/545-2444 (Illinois only), 800/545-2455 (Canada only), 312/280-4211) 11 issues/year; $50/annual subscription for libraries, subscription included in membership package. Jobs listed under "Career Leads." Typical issues features 75 to 100 job ads.

Job notices can be obtained three weeks prior to publication in *American Libraries* in *Career Leads Express* which is a copy of the uncorrected galleys of job notices that will appear in the next issue of *American Libraries. Career Leads Express* is available to nonmembers and members alike for $1/issue, prepaid only. With your check, send a self-addressed stamped (two ounces postage) #10 envelope to AL Leads Express, 50 E. Huron, Chicago, IL 60611." Typical issue includes 75 or more positions.

Library Journal (Bowker Magazine Group, P.O. Box 1977, Marion, OH 43305–1077; phones: 800/669–1002, 614/382–3322) 20 issues/year, $74/annual subscription (U.S.), $99/Canada, $130/elsewhere (air mail). Jobs listed under "Classified Advertising." Fifty to 70 ads for librarian positions grace the pages of a typical issue.

Wilson Library Bulletin (The H. H. Wilson Company, 950 University Ave., Bronx, NY 10452; phones: 800/367–6770 ext. 2245, 212/588–2245) ten issues/year, $46/annual subscription. Typically, about two ads for librarians, information brokers, or library consultants appear under "Library Services Directory."

Jobline (American Society for Information Science, 8720 Georgia Ave., Suite 501, Silver Spring, MD 20910–3602; phone: 301/495–0900) monthly, available to nonmembers upon request, included in membership package.

Rural Libraries Jobline (Center for the Study of Rural Librarianship, Department of Library Science, Clarion University of Pennsylvania, Clarion, PA 16214; phone: 814/226–2383) monthly, $1/issue.

Specialist (Special Libraries Association, 1700 18th St., NW, Washington, DC 20009; 202/234–4700) monthly, $48/annual subscription, $58/foreign. From five to ten jobs are listed under "Positions Open."

Canadian Association of Special Libraries and Information Services, Ottawa Chapter Jobline (Job Bank Coordinator, CASLIS, 54 Mason Terrace, Ottawa, Ontario K1S 0K9 Canada) Call 613/237–3688 for a recording of job openings.

Newsletter (American Association of Law Libraries, Suite 940, 53 W. Jackson, Chicago, IL 60604; phone: 312/939–4764) ten issues/year, $50/nonmember annual subscription, free to members. Jobs listed under "Career Hotline." Over 20 job ads appear in the typical issue. Advance copies of job ads are available for $2.50/month prepaid. The advance copies include job ads two to four weeks before they are published in the *Newsletter* and ads not published in the *Newsletter.*

Job Database (American Association of Law Libraries, Dept. 77-6021, Chicago, IL 60678–6021; phone: 312/939–4764) monthly, $25/annual subscription. This is a monthly compilation of all jobs listed on the AALA's *Job Database Service* and *Career Hotline* described later under "Job services." Expect to see 25 to 35 positions in an issue.

The Women's Review of Books (828 Washington St., Wellesley, MA 02181; phone: 617/431-1453) 11 issues/year, $16/annual subscription for individuals and $30 for institutions, add $3 for Canada, elsewhere add $20 for airmail, $5 for surface mail. "Classified" features two or three ads for jobs, generally in education or library work.

Job services

Grapevine Job Database (American Library Association, 50 E. Huron St., Chicago, IL 60611; phones: 800/545-2433 (outside Illinois), 800/545-2444 (Illinois only), 800/545-2455 (Canada only), 312/280-4214). Contact the ALA's Deputy *Grapevine* System Manager for details on how to use this computer database of jobs that is updated every Monday. Includes some jobs that do not appear in *Career Leads Express* or *American Libraries*, both of which are discussed above under "Job openings."

Resume Referral Service (Special Libraries Association, 1700 18th St., NW, Washington, DC 20009; 202/234-4700) fee for six-month listing: $75/nonmember $50/members, $25/student members. Exclusively for library/information professionals seeking positions in the U.S. or Canada, this service has the job seeker submit ten copies of her resume and a completed application form detailing your job, salary, and geographical preferences. When a match is found, your resume is forwarded to the potential employer who chooses whom to interview.

Career Hotline (American Association of Law Libraries, Suite 940, 53 W. Jackson, Chicago, IL 60604) Call 312/939-7877 for a tape of job listings for law libraries. Recording is changed every two weeks. Five or more jobs on each recording.

SpeciaLine Employment Clearinghouse Job Hotline (Special Libraries Association, 1700 18th St., NW, Washington, DC 20009; 202/234-4700) Call 202/234-3632 for 24-hour tape recording of jobs with special libraries.

American Library Association Job Hotline (American Library Association, 50 E. Huron St., Chicago, IL 60611; phones: 800/545-2433 (outside Illinois), 800/545-2444 (Illinois only), 800/545-2455 (Canada only), 312/280-4211). If you want to work for the ALA, call 312/280-2464 to hear a recording of job openings at the ALA. 24-hours, seven days a week.

Career Hotline/Job Database Service (American Association of Law Libraries, Suite 940, 53 W. Jackson, Chicago, IL 60604; phone: 312/939-4764). Call the 24-hour Career Hotline, 312/939-7877, for a recording of brief job descriptions of law librarian positions and where to apply. This is the index to the AALL's *Job Database Service* which is updated weekly by Friday noon. AALL members can request a free printout of all job listings by calling 312/939-4764 or faxing a request to 312/431-1097. Nonmembers can obtain a printout for $5 (send to: AALL, Dept. 77-602, 53 W. Jackson, Chicago, IL 60678-6021). There are typically 10 to 15 jobs listed at any one time.

Directories

AALL Directory and Handbook (American Association of Law Libraries, Suite 940, 53 W. Jackson, Chicago, IL 60604; phone: 312/939-4764). This annual directory of government and private law libraries is available only to members.

Who's Who in Special Libraries (Special Libraries Association, 1700 18th St., NW, Washington, DC 20009; 202/234–4700) $25/non-members, included in membership package. Includes alphabetical and geographical lists of special libraries. Published annually in the autumn.

Directory of Special Libraries and Information Centers (Gale Research, Inc., 835 Penobscot Bldg., Detroit, MI 48226; phone: 800/233–4253) $380, in two parts, 1991. Provides comprehensive information on 18,600 information centers, archives, and special and research libraries in the U.S., Canada, and elsewhere. Includes subject index.

Subject Directory of Special Libraries (Gale Research, Inc., 835 Penobscot Bldg., Detroit, MI 48226; phone: 800/233–4253) $675/three volumes, 1990. These volumes contain the same material as the *Directory of Special Libraries and Information Centers*, which is described immediately above, but rearranged into 14 subject areas in three volumes, available individually: Business, Government, and Law Libraries, $250; Computers, Engineering, and Science Libraries, $250; Health Sciences Libraries, $250.

New Special Libraries (Gale Research, Inc., 835 Penobscot Bldg., Detroit, MI 48226; phone: 800/233–4253) $335; 1990. Furnishes comprehensive information on special libraries in the U.S., Canada, and elsewhere.

Museums

For a much more extensive set of sources for curator and other museum positions, see the job sources described in the Non–Profits' Job Finder.

Directories

The Official Museum Directory and Products and Services Guide (National Register Publishing Company, 3004 Glenview Rd., Wilmette, IL 60091; phones: 800/323–6772, 708/441–2210) $194, $112/members of the American Association of Museums, plus $8.25 shipping, annual. Provides details on 6,700 U.S. museums: art associations, art museums and galleries, arts and crafts museums, folk art museums, children and junior museums, college and university museums, company museums, general museums, planetariums, zoos, aquariums, arboreta, and 60 other types of institutions.

Art in America (Brant Art Publications, 575 Broadway, New York, NY 10012; phones: 800/247–2160, 212/941–2800) $39.95/U.S., $59.95/Canada, $69.95/elsewhere, published each month. Contains an alphabetical list, by city and state, of museums, galleries, non–profit exhibition spaces, corporate consultants, private dealers, and print dealers. Provides basic information plus a short description of the type of art shown and artists presented.

Records management and archival

Job openings

News Notes and Quotes (Association of Records Managers and Administrators, Suite 215, 4200 Somerset Dr., Prairie Village, KS 66208; phone: 913/341–3808) bimonthly, available only as part of membership package. Jobs listed under "Job Opportunities." About six to 12 job ads per issue.

SAA Newsletter (Society of American Archivists, Suite 504, 600 S. Federal, Chicago, IL 60605; phone: 312/922–0140) published in alternating months with *SAA Employment Bulletin*, available only to members. Jobs listed under "Employment Opportunities." About 25 job ads per issue.

SAA Employment Bulletin (Society of American Archivists, Suite 504, 600 S. Federal, Chicago, IL 60605; phone: 312/922–0140) published in alternating months with *SAA Newsletter*, available to members for $24/year; nonmembers can purchase individual issues for $6. Lists only jobs. About 25 job ads per issue.

AIC Newsletter (American Institute for Conservation of Historic and Artistic Works,, Suite 340, 1400 16th St., NW, Washington, DC 20036; phone: 202/232–6636) bimonthly, available to members only. Jobs listed under "Positions Available." Around 20 job ads per issue, largely for conservators.

Job services

Career Placement Service (Association of Records Managers and Administrators, Suite 215, 4200 Somerset Dr., Prairie Village, KS 66208; phone: 913/341–3808) $25/available to members only. Places candidate's resume in the Career Placement Registry on the DIALOGUE on–line computer service.

Directories

AIC Directory (American Institute for Conservation of Historic and Artistic Works, Suite 340, 1400 16th St., NW, Washington, DC 20036; phone: 202/232–6636) $43/nonmembers, free/members, published each August. Members listed alphabetically, geographically, and by specialty.

If you're having trouble finding job sources for your specialty, you probably should refresh your memory on how to use this book most effectively. Please read Chapter 1 which explains how to get the most out of the *Professional's Job Finder*.

Chapter 24

Parks, recreation, and sports

Camps and camp grounds

Also see entries in this chapter under "Coaching" and the "Forestry and horticulture" chapter.

Job openings

Summer Camp Employment Booklet (American Camping Association, 5000 State Road 67 North, Martinsville, IN 46151; phones: 800/428–2267, 317/342–8456) free, annual. This is a pretty comprehensive nationwide listing of over 100 vacancies for day and overnight (resident) camps complete with detailed descriptions, salary ranges, and employment benefits. Includes counselors, activity specialists, instructors, lifeguards, and nurses.

Camping Magazine (American Camping Association, 5000 State Road 67 North, Martinsville, IN 46151; phones: 800/428–2267, 317/342–8456) bimonthly, $18.95/annual nonmember subscription (U.S.), $25/Canada, $31.50/elsewhere, free/members. About 20 job vacancies for camp directors, counselors, activity specialists, instructors, lifeguards, and nurses appear under "Classifieds—Help Wanted" plus ads for camp planners and ads for camps for sale or lease.

Job's Clearinghouse (Association for Experiential Education, University of Colorado, Box 249, Boulder, CO 80309; phone: 303/492-1547 **TDD:** 303/492-0526) monthly, $25/nonmember annual subscription, $15/members. Dozens of job ads for camp counselors are among the 30-plus pages of opportunities in a typical issue.

Scholastic Coach (P.O. Box 3025, Southeastern, PA 19398; phone: 212/505-4902) ten issues/year, $23.95/annual nonmember subscription, $17.95/members. "Help Wanted" features 15 plus job openings for coaches, largely at camps.

Workamper News (201 Hiram Rd., Heber Springs, AR 72543; phone: 800/446-5627) bimonthly, $18/annual subscription. Lists over 100 different employers who are actively seeking employees for public parks and campgrounds as well as commercially-operated parks, resorts, campgrounds with positions available at all levels, from housekeeping and grounds maintenance to upper management.

Highways (The Good Sam Club, P.O. Box 500, Agoura, CA 91376; phones: 800/234-3450, 818,991-4980) monthly, $6/annual nonmember subscription, free/members. About 15 jobs in campground maintenance and office work, gift shops, public relations, entertainment, and camp grounds promotion are listed under "Help Wanted." Many of these jobs seek couples with a recreational vehicle to live in.

Trailer Life (TL Enterprises, P.O. Box 51644, Boulder, CO 80321; phones: 800/234-3450, 818/991-4980) monthly, $14.98/annual subscription. Two to five job ads for campground positions (maintenance, office work) are in "Help Wanted."

Motorhome (TL Enterprises, P.O. Box 51644, Boulder, CO 80321; phones: 800/234-3450, 818/991-4980) monthly, $14.98/annual subscription. About three job ads for campground positions (maintenance, office work) are in "Help Wanted."

"Sure it's 'your' park. When I suggest you keep it
clean—just think of me as your mommy."

Coaching

Job openings

Athletics Employment Weekly (RDST Enterprises, Route 1, Box 103, Basco, IL 62313; phone: 217/357-3615) weekly, $40/six-month subscription, $65/annual subscription. A typical issue features 50 to 75 coaching, training, and administrative positions in athletics, primarily with universities.

NSCA Bulletin (National Strength and Conditioning Association, P.O. Box 81410, Lincoln, NE 68501; phone: 402/472-3000) free, available only to members. About ten to 20 jobs at a time are advertised under "Positions Available." Positions include strength coaches and exercise specialists in corporate fitness.

Update (American Alliance for Health, Physical Education, Recreation and Dance, 1900 Association Dr., Reston, VA 22091; phone: 703/476-3400) eight issues/year, $45/annual nonmember subscription, included in $85/annual membership. "Job Exchange" features 30 or more jobs largely with camps and universities as well as numerous graduate assistanceships and grants.

Journal PERD (American Alliance for Health, Physical Education, Recreation and Dance, 1900 Association Dr., Reston, VA 22091; phone: 703/476-3400) monthly, $65/annual nonmember subscription. The "Classifieds" feature about five positions, primarily coaching, with camps and universities.

Job services

National Strength and Conditioning Association Job Hotline (NSCA, P.O. Box 81410, Lincoln, NE 68501; phone: 402/472-3000) free, available only to members. About 20 jobs at a time are listed on this hotline for strength and conditioning positions including strength coaches and exercise specialists in corporate fitness.

Directories

National Directory of College Athletics (Men) (Roy Franks Publishing Ranch, P.O. Box 7068, Amarillo, TX 79109; phone: 806/355-6417) $16, published each August. Provides details on over 2,100 senior and junior college men's athletic departments in the U.S. and Canada.

National Directory of College Athletics (Women) (Roy Franks Publishing Ranch, P.O. Box 7068, Amarillo, TX 79109; phone: 806/355-6417) $12, published each August. Provides details on over 2,000 senior and junior college women's athletic departments in the U.S. and Canada.

National Directory of High School Coaches (Athletic Publishing Company, P.O. Box 931, Montgomery, AL 36101; phone: 205/263-4436) $39.95 plus $3 shipping, issued every September. Lists more than 186,000 high school coaches at 22,600 high schools.

Clell Wade Coaches Directory (P.O. Box 177, Cassville, MO 65625; phone: 417/847-2783) $7.95/state or regional edition, prepaid, published each September. Published in 30 state or regional editions, this series of directories covers high school and college athletic programs and their personnel.

NCAA Directory (National Collegiate Athletic Association, P.O. Box 1906, Mission, KS 66201; phone: 913/384–3220) $6, released every October. Includes key personnel at 1,000 NCAA member schools.

Parks and recreation

Also see entries in the chapters on "Environment" and "Forestry and horticulture."

Job openings

Park and Recreation Opportunities Job Bulletin (National Recreation and Park Association, 3101 Park Center Dr., Alexandria, VA 22302; phone: 703/820–4940) 22 issues/year, individual copies available to nonmembers and members for $5 prepaid; annual subscription available only to members, $30. Typical issue includes 40 to 60 U.S. and foreign jobs listed by geographic area.

Park Maintenance (P.O. Box 1936, Appleton, WI 54913; phone: 414/733–2301) monthly, $16/annual subscription (U.S.), $20/Canada, $24/elsewhere. Two or three ads for administrators of large outdoor grounds such as parks, golf courses, and campuses appear under "Classifieds."

1992 Summer Employment Directory of the United States (Petersons Guides, PO Box 2123, Princeton, NJ 08543–2123; phone: 800/338–3282) $14.95. Published annually in the autumn. Its 200+ pages list over 75,000 summer job openings at resorts, camps, amusement parks, national parks, and government.

Golf Course Management (Golf Course Superintendents Association of America, 1421 Research Park Dr., Lawrence, KS 66049–3859; phones: 800/422–6383, 913/832–4466) monthly; $30/annual subscription, included in dues. Jobs listed under "Classifieds." About eight ads including municipal golf courses, appear in a typical issue.

Employment Referral Service (Golf Course Superintendents Association of America, 1421 Research Park Dr., Lawrence, KS 66049-3859; phones: 800/422-6383, 913/832-4466) Available only to members for $10/six months. Typical issue lists ten job openings in golf course management and landscape architecture.

Parks and Grounds Management (P.O. Box 1936, Appleton, WI 54913-1936; phone: 414/733-2301) monthly, $16/annual subscription. A handful of ads in management of public parks and college campuses appear under "Classified."

Backpacker (33 E. Minor St., Emmaus, PA 18098; phone: 215/967-5171) eight issues/year, $24/annual subscription, $29/Canada. "Classified Advertising" features five to ten jobs openings each issue.

Job services

JOBSource (Computerized Employment Systems, Inc., 1720 W. Mulberry, Suite B9, Fort Collins, CO 80521; phones: 800/727-5627, 303/493-1779) There are three services available using an extensive database of over 700 positions, mostly in the environmental arena (fisheries, natural resources, wildlife, forestry, biology, and especially parks and recreation). For individuals, the most useful is JOBSource's in-house search program. Obtain a resume application form from JOBSource. Within two weeks of receiving your completed form, JOBSource will conduct a job search of its database for you. JOBSource guarantees from six to 25 matches per search. The cost is $30. If fewer than six matches are found, JOBSource will run a second search the next month for free. If the second run turns up fewer than six matches, there is a $5 charge for that second run.

However, if you have a computer and modem, you can download the entire database onto your computer for $20 plus your phone call. It takes 20 to 40 minutes to download the three files. To update, you need to download just one file which takes about 20 minutes and costs $15. The database is updated every Thursday. A growing number of universities and colleges are subscribing to JOBSource. They receive the database and user programs around the 24th of each month and can conduct their own job searches. Subscriptions are available for a year ($495), the nine months of September through May ($375), or for the three months of January, April, and November ($189).

NRPA/SCHOLE Network (National Recreation and Park Association, 3101 Park Center Dr., Alexandria, VA 22302; phone: 703/820–4940) $75/annual subscription for nonmember individuals, $225/nonmember agencies, $50/member individuals, $150/member agencies. This computer information and communications network includes NRPA's *Park and Recreation Opportunities Job Bulletin*. Updated biweekly.

Directories

Compendium of Special Recreation (Special Recreation, Inc., 362 Koser Ave., Iowa City, IA 52246-3038; phone: 219/337-7578) $49.95/nonmembers. Lists organizations that deal with recreation for people who have disabilities. New edition expected in 1992.

Who's Who in Golf Course Management (Golf Course Superintendents Association of America, 1421 Research Park Dr., Lawrence, KS 66049–3859; phones: 800/422–6383, 913/832–4466) free, available only to members, issued each March. This directory of members includes salary data for golf course superintendents.

Golf Course Builders of America Yearbook (GCB, 920 Airport Rd., Suite 210, Chapel Hill, NC 27514; phone: 919/942-8922) contact for cost, if any; annual. Provides details on member companies involved in building golf courses.

Association of Physical Fitness Centers Roster of Reciprocal Centers (APFC, 600 Jefferson St., Suite 202, Rockville, MD 20852; phone: 301/424-7744) free/members only, issued every January and July. Lists member health clubs.

Sports

Job openings

Career Services Bulletin (American College of Sports Medicine, 401 W. Michigan St., Indianapolis, IN 46202–3233; phone: 317/637-9200) monthly, $20/annual nonmember subscription, $10/members. Around 50 positions in sports medicine and exercise science, including positions with wellness and fitness centers, appear throughout.

Golf Illustrated (PO Box 420057, Palm Coast, FL 32142; phone: 800/829-9134) 10 issues/year, $15/annual subscription, $21/Canada, $23/elsewhere. The ''Classifieds'' section sports about three jobs and three business opportunities each issue.

On Track (PO Box 8509, Fountain Valley, CA 92728; phone: 714/966-1131) biweekly, $62.50/annual subscription in U.S., Canada, and Mexico, $112.50/foreign surface mail, $152.50/foreign airmail. Fifteen to 20 job ads for auto racers/drivers, mechanics, instructors, crews, and fabricators appear under ''Classifieds.''

IDEA Today (Association for Fitness Professionals, 6190 Cornerstone Court East, Suite 204, San Diego, CA 92121–3773; phones: 800/999-9332, 619/535-8979) available only to members, $58/annual member subscription. About ten ads for fitness professionals including aerobics instructors and directors, health club personnel, and personal trainers.

The Sporting Goods Dealer (1212 N. Lindbergh Blvd., St. Louis, MO 63132; phones: 800/669-5700, 314/997-7111) weekly, $82.50/annual subscription. Two or three ads for athletic directors and other sports–related positions appear in the ''Classifieds.''

Skiing Trade News (2 Park Ave., New York, NY 10016; phone: 212/779-5019) eight issues/year, $20/annual subscription. One or two jobs for ski instructors subsist under "Classified."

Job services

Sports Careers Hotline. Call 900/420-3005 to hear descriptions of over 200 vacancies in sports journalism, administration, marketing, representation, and business ventures. This is not a free call. Call the first minute costs $2 with additional per minute charges.

Directories

Blue Book of College Athletics for Senior, Junior and Community Colleges (Rohrich Corp., 903 E. Tallmadge Ave., Akron, OH 44310; phone: 216/633-1711) $20, published each September. Provides details on over 1,800 colleges and universities with athletic programs, athletic conferences, and related associations in the U.S. and Canada, with some in Mexico and Puerto Rico.

National Bowling Congress Membership Directory (NBC, 2300 Claredon Blvd., Suite 1107, Arlington, VA 22201; phone: 202/659-9070) free, available only to members, annual.

Directory of Golf (National Golf Foundation, 1150 South U.S. Highway 1, Jupiter, FL, 334477; phone: 407/744-6006) $35/non-members, free/members, issued two or three times each year. Lists members of the NGF.

Water–based recreation

Job openings

Motor Boating & Sailing (PO Box 7158, Red Oak, IA 51591; phone: 800/888-9123) monthly, $15.97/annual subscription, $33.97/foreign. About five job ads or business opportunities are in each issue under "Classifieds: The Nautical Marketplace."

Boat Journal (PO Box 2091, Knoxville, IA 50198; phone: 404/955-5656) bimonthly, $17.95/annual subscription, $19.95/foreign. The "Classifieds" section features around three business opportunities.

Power and Motoryacht (PO Box 173306, Denver, CO 80217; phone: 800/637-6076) monthly, $29.97/annual subscription, $44.97/foreign surface mail, $104.97/foreign airmail. Each issue has a few businesses for sale and services advertisements under "Ship's Store."

Sail (PO Box 56397, Boulder, CO 80321; phone: 800/745-7245) monthly, $19.95/annual subscription, $24.95/Canada, $29.95/elsewhere. About six jobs in sailing appear under "Classified."

WoodenBoat: The Magazine for Wooden Boat Owners, Builders, and Designers (PO Box 492, Mt. Morris, IL 61054; phone: 800/435-0715) bimonthly, $22.95/annual subscription. The "Classifieds" section features about nine jobs for captains, cooks, boat builders, etc. under "Positions" and another two or three ads under "Business Opportunities."

Boating Industry (Communication Channels, 6255 Barfield Rd., Atlanta, GA 30328; phone: 404/256-9800) monthly, contact for subscription rates. "Marketplace" contains three or four ads under "Personnel & Positions," largely for salespeople, and almost 20 "Business Opportunities" with marinas and marine businesses for sale.

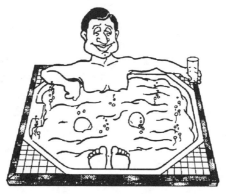

Swimming Pool/Spa Age (Communication Channels, P.O. Box 1147, Skokie, IL 60076; phone: 708/647–7124) 13 issues/year, $38/annual subscription (U.S.), $58/foreign. About ten job openings and business opportunities appear in the "Classifieds." Include sales, production, management, and ownership opportunities.

Spa and Pool News (Leisure Publications, 3923 W. Sixth St., Los Angeles, CA 90020; phone: 213/385–3926) semimonthly, available to qualified professionals. Four or five job ads for management, production, and sales are in the "Classifieds."

Aqua Magazine (555 Anton Blvd., Suite 820, Costa Mesa, CA 92626; phone: 714/530–7383) monthly, $25/annual subscription. As many as three ads for pool sales representatives are in the "Classifieds."

Aquatics (Communication Channels, P.O. Box 1147, Skokie, IL 60076; phone: 708/647–7124) bimonthly, $30/annual subscription (U.S.), $50/foreign. One or two positions for sales and manufacturers' representatives for such goods as aquatic fitness items are in "Classifieds—Employment Opportunities."

Marine Technology Society Currents (Marine Technology Society, 1825 K St., NW, Suite 218, Washington, DC 20006; phone: 202/775–5966) bimonthly, $10/annual subscription, included in dues. Two or three ads for such positions as fish hatchery managers appear near the back of the newsletter.

Job services

Captains and Crews (Route 5, No. 11–Long Bay, St. Thomas, Virgin Islands 00802; phone: 809/776–2395) $15 registration fee plus 20 percent of first month's pay if hired or plus $25 if hired to go cruising or deliver a yacht. You complete this service's resume form and are matched to available positions ranging from crew (deck hands, stewards and stewardesses, cooks, etc.) to captains for cruise boats and charter yachts. Resume forms for captains are kept on file indefinitely; forms for crew stay active for a year.

Chapter 25

Personnel and human resources

Also see the chapter on "Social services."

Job openings

HR News (Society for Human Resource Management, 606 N. Washington St., Alexandria, VA 22314; phone: 703/548-3440) monthly, $39/nonmember subscription, included in membership package. Jobs listed under " HR News Employment Service." Contains 30 to 35 job ads in a typical issue.

HR Magazine (Society for Human Resource Management, 606 N. Washington St., Alexandria, VA 22314; phone: 703/548-3440) monthly, $49/nonmember subscription, included in membership package. In the back of the magazine are two to three dozen positions in personnel management, mostly in display ads placed by executive search firms.

Personnel Journal (A. C. Croft, Inc., Suite B-2, 245 Fischer Ave., Costa Mesa, CA 92626; phone: 714/751-1883) monthly; $50/annual subscription. Jobs listed under "Classified." Typical issue features five to 12 jobs ads.

Spotlight (College Placement Council, 62 Highland Ave., Bethlehem, PA 18042; phones: 800/544–5272, 215/868–1421) 21 issues/year, $65/annual nonmember subscription, included in membership package. Under "Jobwire" there are usually five to ten openings for personnel directors, recruiters, and career counselors.

Recruiter Service (International Personnel Management Association, 1617 Duke St., Alexandria, VA 22314; phone: 703/549–7100) monthly $21/nonmember annual subscription, included in dues. Four to six personnel positions appear in the typical issue.

IPMA News (International Personnel Management Association, 1617 Duke St., Alexandria, VA 22314; phone: 703/549–7100) monthly, $21/nonmember annual subscription, included in membership package. Jobs listed under "Recruiter Service." Typical issue carries about 12 job ads for personnel.

CUPA News (College and University Personnel Association, 1233 20th St., NW, Washington, DC 20036; phone: 202/429–0311, ext. 23) semimonthly, $75/nonmember, $50/member. Two to four jobs for human resource professionals are listed under "Classified."

ACA NEWS (American Compensation Association, 14040 N. Northsight Blvd., Scottsdale, AZ 85260; phone: 602/951–9191) monthly, available to members only, included in membership. About ten to 20 ads for compensation analysts appear under "CAREER Network."

Employment Management Association Job Placement Service (EMA, 4101 Lake Boone Trail, Suite 102, Raleigh, NC 27607; phone: 919/787–6010) free/members only. Each month listings of about ten to 15 positions in human resources are sent to EMA members. "Positions Wanted" also included.

Training Magazine (50 S. 9th St., Minneapolis, MN 55402; phone 612/333–0471) monthly, $54/annual subscription, $64/Canada, $75/foreign. Four ads for corporate training professionals (human resource development specialists) are under "Classified."

Training and Development Journal (American Society for Training and Development, 1640 King St., Alexandria, VA 22313; phone: 703/683–8100) monthly, $75/nonmember annual subscription(U.S.), $110/foreign, free/members. About five ads for instructional designers, trainers, and training directors are under "Classified."

Career Planning and Adult Development Network Newsletter (CPADN, 4965 Sierra Rd., San Jose, CA 95132; phone: 408/559-4946) monthly, $40/annual subscription (U.S.), $50/foreign. About three ads for career counselors and career development specialists appear under "Employment."

Job services

CU Career Connection (University of Colorado, Campus Box 133, Boulder, CO 80309-0133; phone: 303/492-4127) $20/two-month fee entitles you to a "passcode" which unlocks this job hotline. You need a touchtone phone to call and request the field in which you are interested and geographic area in which you want to hear job openings. The hotline is turned off Monday through Friday, 2 to 4 p.m. for daily updating.

Placement Referral Service (National Employee Services and Recreation Association, 2400 S. Downing Ave., Westchester, IL 60153; phone: 708/562-8130) available to members only, $20/12-month member registration. Submit five copies of your resume and your registration fee. When a match is made, your resume is sent to the potential employer who is responsible for contacting you. Positions are largely in management: employee services, fitness programs, recreation, employee stores, and travel programs.

E-R-C's Relocation Career Hotline (Employee Relocation Council, 1720 N St., NW, Washington, DC 20036; phone: 202/659-0857) free/pay only for the cost of the phone call. Call 202/857-0842 24-hours a day, seven days a week, to hear a recording of available job openings for relocation specialists. Five to eight jobs are listed at a time. Updated every Monday.

Directories

Who's Who in Human Resources (Society for Human Resource Management, 606 N. Washington St., Alexandria, VA 22314; phone: 703/548-3440) available only to members, included in dues. Published annually.

"I realize that you're not getting what you're worth—but the government won't let me pay you any less."

IPMA Membership Directory (International Personnel Management Association, 1617 Duke St., Alexandria, VA 22314; phone: 703/549–7100) $150/nonmembers, included free in membership. Published annually.

National Directory of Personnel Consultants (National Association of Personnel Consultants, 3133 Mt. Vernon Ave., Alexandria, VA 22305; phone: 703/684–0180) $22.95/nonmembers, free/members, published each April, 500 pages. Over 2,200 personnel consultants are listed.

Training and Development Organizations Directory (Gale Research, Inc., 835 Penobscot Bldg., Detroit, MI 48226–4094; phone: 800/877–4253) $310, most recently published in 1991, 750 pages. Provides detailed information on training organizations that provide the special training your staff may need. This directory also describes workshops, seminars, videos, and other training programs.

Employment Management Association Annual Membership Directory (EMA, 4101 Lake Boone Trail, #102, Raleigh, NC 27607; phone: 919/787-6010) $150/nonmember, free/member. Published each June.

National Employee Services and Recreation Association Membership Directory (NESRA, 2400 S. Downing Ave., Westchester, IL 60153; phone: 708/562-8130) free/members only, issued each April. Members are management in charge of employee services, fitness programs, recreation, employee stores, and travel programs.

Who's Who in Training and Development (American Society for Training and Development, 1640 King St., Alexandria, VA 22313; phone: 703/683-8100) $50/nonmembers, $40/members, issued every spring. Lists ASTD members.

The Buyer's Guide (American Society for Training and Development, 1640 King St., Alexandria, VA 22313; phone: 703/683-8100) $40/nonmembers, $30/members, released each December. Lists products and services available to human resource development professionals.

CUPA Directory (College and University Personnel Association, 1233 20th St., NW, Washington, DC 20036; phone: 202/429-0311, ext. 23) $150/nonmembers, $25/members, issued in odd-numbered years. Lists personnel administrators at universities and colleges.

Salary survey

Compensation in the Human Resources Field (Abbott, Langer & Associates, 548 First St., Crete, IL 60417; phone: 708/672-4200) $450/entire set, 1,000 pages; Part 1: Recruitment/Selection/Employment Jobs, $100; Part 2: Compensation and Benefits Jobs, $100; Part 3: Training and Organizational Development Jobs, $100; Part 4: Human Resources Management, Personnel Management, Labor Relations, Employee Relations Jobs, $100; Part 5: Remaining Human Resources Jobs, $100; biennial. Salaries and benefits are reported for over 125 job categories.

Salary Budget Survey Report (American Compensation Association, 14040 N. Northsight Blvd., Scottsdale, AZ 85260; phone: 602/951-9191) $50/nonmembers, $40/members, published each September.

Employment recruiting

Directories

Directory of Executive Recruiters (Kennedy Publications, 20 Templeton Rd., Fitzwilliam, NH 03477; phone: 603/585-6544) $39.95, annual, 792 pages. Over 2,100 executive recruiting firms are described; 5,300 key personnel identified; cross-indexed by function, industries served, and geography. Also included is an excellent 100-page introduction to executive searches and how the system works. Addresses are given, but phone numbers are not.

Directory of Executive Recruiters, Corporate Edition (Kennedy Publications, 20 Templeton Rd., Fitzwilliam, NH 03477; phone: 603/585-6544) $79.95, annual, 800 pages, hardcover. This is a expanded version of the *Directory of Executive Recruiters* described immediately above. It includes longer descriptions, phone numbers, and listed specialties for each firm.

Executive Employment Guide (American Management Association, 135 W. 50th St., New York, NY 10020; phone: 212/586-8100) $20/nonmembers, free/members, updated monthly. Lists around 140 AMA member firms conduct executive searches, recruiting, or outplacement. Specifies geographic area covered and minimum salary levels of positions for which each firm conducts searchs.

50 Leading Search Firms (Kennedy Publications, 20 Templeton Rd., Fitzwilliam, NH 03477; phone: 603/585-6544) $10, 8 pages. Lists executive search firms, large and small, with profiles and key contact information for each one.

40 Largest Search Firms (Kennedy Publications, 20 Templeton Rd., Fitzwilliam, NH 03477; phone: 603/585-6544) $10, 8 pages. Gives key contact persons for each of the 40 largest employment search firms in the U.S.

Chapter 26

Pest control

Job openings

Pest Control (Edgell Communications, 1 E. First St., Duluth, MN 55802; phone: 800/346-0085) monthly, $22/annual subscription. Twelve to 24 ads for exterminators, managers, and salespersons are in the "Classifieds" section.

Directories

Directory of Pesticide Control Officials (Association of American Pesticide Officials, P.O. Box 1249, Hardwick, VT 05843; phone: 802/472-6956) $15/nonmembers, free/members, published each March. Lists members, meeting summaries, and association officers. These are government officials.

Chapter 27

Planning and economic development

Community and economic development

Also see the more extensive listings of job sources in the Government Job Finder under "Community and economic development" and "Planning," some of which include private sector as well as government job vacancies.

Job openings

Chamber Jobwatch (Association of Chamber of Commerce Executives, 4232 King St., Alexandria, VA 22302; phone: 703/998–0072) semimonthly, $99/annual nonmember subscription, $49/members. Each issue is packed with 20 to 30 job ads for executives and management personnel for chambers of commerce, including executive directors, government relations staff, marketing, community development, and communications.

Council News (American Economic Development Council, 9801 W. Higgins, Suite 540, Rosemont, IL 60018; phone: 708/692–9944) 10 issues/year, available to members only, annual membership: $265, plus $15 processing fee first year only; $140, plus $15 processing fee first year only, when another person in your office is already a member. Jobs listed under "Career Opportunities." About 10 job ads per issue.

Economic Developments (National Council for Urban Economic Development, 1730 K St., NW, Suite 915, Washington, DC 20006; phone: 202/223-4735) 24 issues/year, available only to members; membership costs $275/year). Jobs listed under "Job Mart." Typical issue sports three to ten job ads.

Resources for Community-Based Economic Development (National Congress for Community Economic Development, Suite 523, 1875 Connecticut Ave., Washington, DC 20009; phone: 202/659-8411) quarterly, $39/annual subscription. Two to five jobs are listed under "The Checklist."

The Center City Report (International Downtown Association, 915 15th St., NW, Suite 900, Washington, DC 20005; phone: 202/783-4963) bimonthly, $50/annual subscription. Three or four openings for executive directors of downtown organizations and businesses are listed under "Classified."

Job services

Resume Referral Service (American Economic Development Council, 9801 W. Higgins, Suite 540, Rosemont, IL 60018; phone: 708/692-9944) $100/nonmembers for 12 months, free to members. Return form with 10 copies of your resume. AEDC lets you know when it matches your qualifications with a potential employer, but it is up to the employer to contact you for the interview.

Directories

Private Sector Development Organizations: A Directory (National Council for Urban Economic Development, 1730 K St., NW, Suite 915, Washington, DC 20006; phone: 202/223-4735) $20/nonmembers, $17.50/members. Profiles of organizations led, initiated, and supported by community business and corporate leaders.

CUED Directory (National Council for Urban Economic Development, 1730 K St., NW, Suite 915, Washington, DC 20006; phone: 202/223–4735) $25/nonmembers, free/members. Published annually. Lists all private corporate members of National Council for Urban Economic Development.

Who's Who in Economic Development (American Economic Development Council, 9801 W. Higgins, Suite 540, Rosemont, IL 60018; phone: 708/692–9944) available only to members, included in dues. Published each August. Geographical and alphabetical listings of members throughout the world. Also includes geographical and alphabetical lists of certified industrial/economic developers.

NCCED Membership Directory (National Congress for Community Economic Development, Suite 523, 1875 Connecticut Ave., Washington, DC 20009; phone: 202/659–8411) $10. Published in odd–numbered years.

The New ICC World Directory of Chambers of Commerce (Gale Research, Inc., 835 Penobscot Bldg., Detroit, MI 48226–4094; phone: 800/877–4253) $140, annual, 551 pages. Gives details on chambers of commerce throughout the world.

Planning

Job openings

JobMart (American Planning Association, 1313 E. 60th St., Chicago, IL 60637; phone: 312/955–9100) 22 issues/year, annual subscription rates: $25/first class mail, $35/Canada, $65/elsewhere, $15/bulk rate (U.S. only); available only to members; also available as part of reduced–cost package deal with *Planners Referral Service* discussed below under "Job services." Write to APA for salary–based dues structure. Spring issues include job ads for summer internships. With over 1,200 public agency and consulting firm jobs listed annually, the typical issue features from 25 to 50 ads itemized by state.

Planning (American Planning Association, 1313 E. 60th St., Chicago, IL 60637; phone: 312/955-9100) monthly, $40/annual subscription (U.S.), $50/elsewhere, included free in membership package. Write for salary-based dues schedule. Growing number of display ads featuring job announcements, usually for higher-level positions in public agencies—generally three to eight ads per issue. Note that most of APA's state chapters publish newsletters that include timely job announcements. Many of these chapters allow nonmember subscriptions or chapter-only membership which includes the chapter newsletter. Many chapters also publish rosters of planners within their state. Contact APA for names, addresses, and phone numbers of the presidents of the state chapters you wish to contact.

ACSM Bulletin (American Congress on Surveying and Mapping, 5410 Grosvenor Ln., Bethesda, MD 20814; phone: 301/493-0200) bimonthly, $70/annual nonmember subscription (U.S.), $80/foreign, free to members. About six openings for land surveyors, cartographers, and geographic information system specialists appear under "Professional Directory."

GIS World (2629 Redwing Rd., Suite 280, Fort Collins, CO 80526; phone: 303/223-4848) nine issues/year, $60/annual subscription, $39/government employees. Under "Classified Ads—Positions Available" appear seven to 11 job vacancies for geographic information system operators, managers, and engineers.

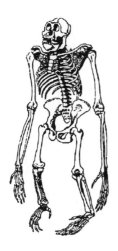

Photogrammetric Engineering and Remote Sensing (American Society for Photogrammetry and Remote Sensing, 5410 Grosvernor Ln., Suite 210, Bethesda, MD 20814; phone: 301/493-0290) monthly, $120/annual nonmember subscription (U.S.), $140/foreign, free/members. Around 30 ads for GIS specialists, biometricians, photogrammetists, stereoplotter operators, aerial photographers, and cartographers are listed under "Classifieds—Positions Open."

Practicing Anthropology (Society for Applied Anthropology, P.O. Box 24083, Oklahoma City, OK 73124; phone: 405/843-5113) quarterly, $14/nonmember annual subscription (U.S.),

$40/foreign; included in dues. Two or three display ads for anthropologists and sociologists including planning positions are in the typical issue.

Bulletin of the SAA (Society for American Archaeology, 808 17th St., NW, Suite 200, Washington, DC 20006; phone: 202/223-9774) five or six issues/year, $15/annual nonmember subscription, included in dues. About six ads for archaeologists and anthropologists are listed under "Positions Open."

Job services

Planners' Referral Service (American Planning Association, 1313 E. 60th St., Chicago, IL 60637; phone: 312/955-9100) $25/annual registration fee; available only to members; also available in reduced–cost package deal with *JobMart* discussed above under "Job ads:" get both for $40/*JobMart* sent via first class mail (U.S.), $50/Canada, $80/elsewhere, $32/*JobMart* sent by bulk rate mail (U.S. only). Resumes are kept in computer file for one year. Six–month renewals are available. An employer requests APA to search its computer file for qualified applicants. Employers contact applicants directly to arrange interviews.

Directories

American Planning Association Membership Directory (American Planning Association, 1313 E. 60th St., Chicago, IL 60637; phone: 312/955-9100) $31.95 plus $3.95 shipping. Alphabetical listing of 26,000 professional planners and planning commissioners plus geographical index and specialty index. First published in 1990, there may be a new edition in 1992.

AICP Roster (American Institute of Certified Planners, c/o American Planning Association, 1776 Massachusetts Ave., NW, Washington, DC 20036; phone: 202/872-0611) $30/nonmember, $20/APA member, included in AICP membership package. AICP is an institute within the American Planning Association. This directory lists the 7,000+ AICP members alphabetically and by city within state. Although AICP membership is achieved by passing a demanding test, it does not indicate that AICP members are better qualified or more competent than other professional planners.

Since titles are listed, this is a good source to identify directors of municipal and county planning departments and related departments. Published in even-numbered years.

American Society of Consulting Planners Directory of Firms ASCP, c/o 1015 15th St., NW, Suite 500, Washington, DC 20005) contact for price, most recent edition: winter 1992. Lists member planning consulting firms. This list contains a fraction of the hundreds of planning consultants in the country. Members, though, are generally larger firms. If you have trouble reaching these folks—they have moved their office several times in recent years—try asking the American Planning Association for an address or phone number for ASCP.

The 1987 APA Planning Consultant Roster (Planners Bookstore, c/o American Planning Association, 1313 E. 60th St., Chicago, IL 60637; phone: 312/955-9100) $8 plus shipping. Lists nearly 400 planning consultants alphabetically. Includes geographic index. A bit long in the tooth, this is the only directory of its sort.

ACSM Membership Directory (American Congress on Surveying and Mapping, 5410 Grosvenor Ln., Bethesda, MD 20814; phone: 301/493-0200) available only to members for $31. Most recent edition published in 1991.

ASPRS Directory of Mapping Sciences (American Society for Photogrammetry & Remote Sensing, 5410 Grosvenor Ln., Suite 210, Bethesda, MD 20814-2160; phone: 301/493-0290) $25/nonmembers, free/members. Published each June.

Salary survey

Planners' Salaries and Employment Trends, 1991 (American Planning Association, 1313 E. 60th St., Chicago, IL 60637; phone: 312/955-9100) $20/general public and APA members, $10/subscribers to APA's Planning Advisory Service, issued in December of odd-numbered years.

Chapter 28

Real estate and construction

Real estate in general

Also see the chapter on "Architecture."

Job openings

Employment Newsletter (National Association of Corporate Real Estate Executives, 440 Columbia Dr., Suite 100, West Palm Beach, FL 33409; phone: 407/683-8111) monthly, free/members only. Twelve to 35 ads for corporate real estate executives fill this jobs bulletin.

Placement Newsletter (International Institute of Corporate Real Estate Executives, 440 Columbia Dr., Suite 100, West Palm Beach, FL 33409; phone: 407/683-8111) monthly, free/members only. "Job Opportunity" sports ads for 15 corporate real estate executive positions.

National Real Estate Investor (Communication Channels, 6255 Barfield Rd., Atlanta, GA 30328; phone: 404/256-9800) 13 issues/year, $70/annual subscription (U.S.), $80/foreign. ""National Marketplace—Business Opportunities" carries ads for several real estate investment opportunities. Occasionally ads for management positions appear under "Position Available." "Position Wanted" ads are also run.

Multi-Housing News (Gralla Publications, 1515 Broadway, New York, NY 10036; phone: 212/869-1300) $65/annual subscription, free to qualified individuals involved in building, designing, developing, or financing multi-family housing. "Classified Advertising" runs two or three job ads under "Positions Available" and "Business Opportunities."

Directories

National Roster of Realtors® (National Association of Realtors®, 430 N. Michigan Ave., Suite 500, Chicago, IL 60611; phones: 800/874-6500, 312/329-8200) $75/nonmembers, $50/members, published each June. Lists all Realtors® by local board affiliation.

CRB/CRS Roster of Designees (Real Estate Brokerage Council/Realtors National Marketing Institute®, 430 N. Michigan Ave., Chicago, IL 60611; phone: 800/621-7035) free/members only, last revised in 1989. Lists brokerage managers and sales associates with either or both the CRB® or CRS® designations.

CRE® Member Directory (ASREC, 430 N. Michigan Ave., Chicago, IL 60611; phone: 312/329-8257) free/members only, annual. Lists CRE® members with counseling specialties such as properties or services.

National Directory of Instructors (National Association of Realtors, 430 N. Michigan Ave., Chicago, IL 60611; phone: 800/874-6500) $5/members only, most recent edition is 1991. Lists top real estate instructors across the country.

Realtors® Land Institute Roster of Members (RLI, 430 N. Michigan Ave., Chicago, IL 60611; phones: 800/441-5263, 312/329-8440) $10/nonmembers, free/members, released each October, 30 pages. Listed members are specialists in marketing, exchanging, developing, and appraising all aspects of land.

Roster of Accredited Land Consultants (Realtors® Land Institute, 430 N. Michigan Ave., Chicago, IL 60611; phones: 800/441-5263, 312/329-8440) contact for price, annual, 24 pages.

CRB–CRF Roster (Realtors National Marketing Institute, 430 N. Michigan Ave., Suite 500, Chicago, IL 60611; phone: 312/670–3780) free/members only, issued each January.

I.I. of C.R.F.E. Membership Directory (International Institute of Corporate Real Estate Executives, 440 Columbia Dr., Suite 100, West Palm Beach, FL 33409; phone: 407/683–8111) $1,000/non-members, free/members, annual.

Registry of Members (International Real Estate Institute, 8388 E. Evans Rd., Scottsdale, AZ 85260; phone: 602/998–8267) free/members only, released every January.

National Multi–Housing Council Membership Directory (NMHC, 1250 Connecticut Ave., NW, Suite 620, Washington, DC 20036; phone: 202/659–3381) free/members only, monthly. Lists members.

The Executive Guide to Specialists in Industrial and Office Real Estate (Society of Industrial and Office Realtors, 777 14th St., NW, Suite 400, Washington, DC 20005; phone: 202/383–1150) $52/non-members, free/members, published every April, 211 pages. Includes more than 1,800 SOIR members by office or industrial specialty, alphabetically, and geographically.

Salary survey

Compensation and Benefit Survey for Corporate Real Estate Executives (National Association of Corporate Real Estate Executives, 440 Columbia Dr., Suite 100, West Palm Beach, FL 33409; phone: 407/683–8111) $150/nonmembers, $40/members, published in odd–numbered years.

Appraisers

Job openings

Appraiser News (Appraisal Institute, 875 N. Michigan Ave., Suite 2400, Chicago, IL 60611; phone: 312/819–2466) semimonthly, $15/annual nonmember subscription, free/members. The "Job Search" section features 20 to 30 positions.

Real Estate Appraisal Newsletter (National Association of Real Estate Appraisers, 8383 E. Evans Rd., Scottsdale, AZ 85260-3614; phone: 602/948-8000) quarterly, available only as part of membership package. Jobs listed under "Appraiser Job Mart." Four to ten positions in typical issue.

IAAO Update (International Association of Assessing Officers, 1313 E. 60th St., Chicago, IL 60637; phone: 312/947-2048) monthly, available only to members. Write for membership information. Lists jobs under "Opportunities." Two to seven job ads per issue.

Newsline (American Society of Appraisers, 535 Herdon Parkway, Suite 150, Herdon, VA 22070; phone: 703/478-2228) bimonthly, free/members only. Two to four job ads for real estate appraisers appear throughout under the headline "Employment Opportunities."

Appraiser–Gram (National Association of Independent Fee Appraisers, 7501 Murdoch, St. Louis, MO 63119; phone: 314/781-6688) monthly, $20/annual nonmember subscription, included in dues. Jobs listed under "Career Opportunities." Few job ads.

FMRA News (American Society of Farm Managers and Rural Appraisers, Inc., Suite 500, 950 Cherry, Denver, CO 80222; phone: 303/758-3513) bimonthly, available only as part of membership package. Jobs listed under "Job Mart." Usually two to four job ads per issue, but some issues have no ads.

Job services

NAMA Member Referral Program (National Association of Master Appraisers, 303 W. Cypress, San Antonio, TX 78212; phones: 800/531-5333, 512/225-2897) free, available only to members. Your resume is placed on file. Employers request resumes of qualified candidates. Employer contacts candidate directly.

NAREA Job Referral Service (National Association of Real Estate Appraisers, 8383 E. Evans Rd., Scottsdale, AZ 85260-3614; phone: 602/948-8000) free, available only to members. This is a very informal member service where the NAREA puts job candidates in touch with potential employers.

NAMA Internship Program (National Association of Master Appraisers, 303 W. Cypress, San Antonio, TX 78212; phones: 800/531–5333, 512/225–2897) free, available only to members. New appraisers can request free list of agencies and firms that offer internships. Candidate is responsible for contacting possible internship employers.

Directories

The Real Estate Sourcebook (National Register Publishing Company, 3004 Glenview Rd., Wilmette, IL 60091; phones: 800/323–6772, 708/441–2210) $288 plus $10.65 shipping, annual. Lists real estate brokers in the U.S. and Canada as well as real estate investors.

Appraisal Institute Directory of Members (Appraisal Institute, 875 N. Michigan Ave., Suite 2400, Chicago, IL 60611; phone: 312/819–2466) free. Contains business information on 13,000 members. Published each spring.

NAMA Membership Directory (National Association of Master Appraisers, 303 W. Cypress, San Antonio, TX 78212; phones: 800/531–5333, 512/225–2897) free. Published each February.

IAAO Membership Directory (International Association of Assessing Officers, 1313 E. 60th St., Chicago, IL 60637; phone: 312/947–2069) $25/nonmembers, included in membership package. Published annually. Lists member real estate assessors and appraisers.

Accredited and General Membership Directory (American Society of Farm Managers and Rural Appraisers, Inc., Suite 500, 950 Cherry, Denver, CO 80222; phone: 303/758–3513) write for price.

American Institute of Real Estate Appraisers Directory of Members (AIREA, 430 N. Michigan Ave., Chicago, IL 60611; phone: 312/329–8537) free/members only. Lists MAI®s and RM®s.

Construction

Job openings

The Estimator (American Society of Professional Estimators, 11141 Georgia Ave., Suite 412, Wheaton, MD 20902; phone: 301/929-8849) bimonthly, free/members only. In the back of each issue are four or five ads for estimators in construction, building, plumbing, and electricity.

Newsdigest (Construction Specifications Institute, 601 Madison St., Alexandria, VA 22314; phone: 703/684-0300) monthly, free/members only. "Employment Watch" runs two to five job ads for architects, engineers, specifiers, and manufacturers' representatives in the construction industry.

The Construction Specifier Magazine (Construction Specifications Institute, 601 Madison St., Alexandria, VA 22314; phone: 703/684-0300) monthly, $36/annual subscription. Display ads for architects, engineers, specifiers, and manufacturers' representatives in the construction industry are scattered throughout.

Professional Builder (Cahners Publishing, 44 Cook St., Denver, CO 80206; phone: 303/388-4511) 21 issues/year, $129/annual subscription, $169.95/Canada and Mexico. $185/elsewhere. "Builders' Marketplace" includes many business opportunities and ads from placement services.

Manufactured Home Merchandiser (203 N. Wabash, Suite 800, Chicago, IL 60601; phone: 312/236-3528) monthly, free to qualified professionals. Eight jobs in the manufactured housing and related industries are under "Personnel."

Concrete Product (Maclean Hunter, 29 N. Wacker Dr., Chicago, IL 60606; phones: 312/726-2802) monthly; $50/annual subscription (U.S. and Canada); $75/elsewhere. "Classified Advertising—Help Wanted" features about a dozen positions in all aspects of the concrete industry

Concrete Trader (Cahners Publishing, 1350 E. Touhy, Des Plaines, IL 60018; phone: 708/635-8800) monthly, free to qualified professionals. Three or four ads for sales and management are in the typical issue under "Classified."

Concrete Construction (Aberdeen Group, 426 S. Westgate, Addison, IL 60101; phone: 708/543–0870) $21/annual subscription. One or two ads for concrete contractors are under "Classified."

Ready Mix (Edgell Communications, 1 E. First St., Duluth, MN 55802; phones: 800/346-0085, 218/723-9870) bimonthly; $25/annual subscription (U.S.); $50/Canada; $100/elsewhere. "Classifieds—Business Opportunities—Help Wanted" include about three ads for concrete plant managers.

Masonry Construction (Cahners Publishing, 1350 E. Touhy, Des Plaines, IL 60018; phone: 708/635–8800) monthly, $24/annual subscription. One or two ads for masons, engineers, and management are in "Classified."

Constructor (Associated General Contractors of America, 1957 E St., NW, Washington, DC 20006; 202/393–2040) monthly, $135/annual nonmember subscription, $35/members. Two or three ads for general contractors are in the "Classifieds" or display ads.

NAWIC Image (National Association of Women in Construction, 327 S. Adams, Fort Worth, TX 76104; phones: 800/552-3506, 817/877–5551) bimonthly, $15/nonmember annual subscription, free/members. One or two ads for construction jobs are in the "Classified Ads."

Fine Homebuilding (63 S. Main Street, Newtown, CT 06470; phones: 800/283-7252, 203/426-8171) seven issues/year, $29/annual subscription. One or two ads for professional house builders are in "Classifieds."

Doors and Hardware Magazine (Door and Hardware Institute, 14170 Newbrook Dr., Chantilly, VA 22021; phone: 703/227–2010) monthly, $40/annual subscription (U.S.), $65/Canada, $75/elsewhere. "Marketplace" contains ads for roughly 30 positions in the door and hardware industry and architecture.

Flooring (Edgell Communications, 1 E. First St., Duluth, MN 55802; phones: 800/346-0085, 218/723-9870) monthly; $20/annual subscription (U.S.); $45/Canada; $90/elsewhere. About five ads for sales representatives for flooring, ceramic tiles, or carpeting appear under "Classifieds—Reps Wanted—Business Opportunities." The October directory issue is available by itself for $20.

Roofing/Siding/Insulation (Edgell Communications, 1 E. First St., Duluth, MN 55802; phones: 800/346-0085, 218/723-9870) monthly; $25/annual subscription (U.S.); $50/Canada; $100/elsewhere. Over a dozen ads for sales, roofing personnel, estimators, foam mechanics appear under "Classified—Personnel Wanted—Business Opportunities." The April directory issue is available by itself for $20.

American Painting Contractor (American Paint and Coatings Journal Company, 2911 Washington Ave., St. Louis, MO 63103; phone: 314/534–0301) monthly, free to qualified professionals. Four to ten positions in the paint industry are advertised under "Opportunities."

Job services

NAWIC Job Connection (National Association of Women in Construction, 327 S. Adams, Fort Worth, TX 76104; phones: 800/552–3506, 817/877–5551). Sent monthly to 228 NAWIC chapters, this bulletin is chock full of ads for everything in construction from apprenticeships through executive positions. Each chapter posts or distributes these job services to members.

Directories

Membership Directory of ASPE (American Society of Professional Estimators, 11141 Georgia Ave., Suite 412, Wheaton, MD 20902; phone: 301/929–8849) free/members only, issued each September. Details on companies and individuals in construction estimating.

Manufactured Home Merchandiser Producers Directory (203 N. Wabash, Suite 800, Chicago, IL 60601; phone: 312/236–3528) $7.50, issued each December. Includes companies that build manufactured or factory–built housing.

National Association of Women in Construction Membership Directory (NAWIC, 327 S. Adams, Fort Worth, TX 76104; phones: 800/552-3506, 817/877-5551) free/members only, released each June.

Associated Builders and Contractors Membership Directory (ABC, 729 15th St,. NW, Washington, DC 20005; phone: 202/637-8800) $150/nonmembers, free/members, published every October.

National Erectors Association Membership Directory (NEA, 1501 Lee Highway, Suite 202, Arlington, VA 22209; phone: 703/841-9707) $100/nonmembers, free/members, annual.

Guide to America's Finest Professional Insulation Contractors (Insulation Contractors Association of America, 15819 Crabbs Branch Way, Rockville, MD 20855; phone: 301/590-0030) $6/nonmembers, free/members, annual.

Roofing Contractors Directory (American Business Directories, 5711 S. 86th Cr., Omaha, NE 68127; phone: 402/593-4600) $865, prepaid, annual.

SMACNA Membership Directory (Sheet Metal and Air Conditioning Contractors' National Association, P.O. Box 221230, Chantilly, VA 22022-1230; phone: 703/803-2989) $75/nonmembers, free/members, issued each January, 230 pages.

Air Conditioning Contractors of America Membership Directory (ACCA, 1513 16th St., NW, Washington, DC 20036; phone: 202/483-9370) free/members only, annual.

National Association of Plumbing, Heating, Cooling Contractors Membership Directory (NAPHCC, 180 S. Washington St., Falls Church, VA 22046; phone: 703/237-8100) $25/nonmembers, free/members, most recently published in 1991.

Independent Electrical Contractors Directory (IEC, P.O. Box 10379, Alexandria, VA 22310; phone: 703/549-7351) $75/nonmembers, free/members, released each March.

Inspections

Job openings

Building Standards Magazine and *Building Standards Newsletter* (International Conference of Building Officials, 5360 S. Workman Mill Rd., Whittier, CA 90601; phone: 213/699–0541) published in alternating months, $21/nonmember annual subscription to the magazine, the newsletter is available only in the membership package. Jobs listed under "Job Opportunities." About 9 to 12 job ads appear in the usual issue.

Directories

SBCCI Membership Directory (Southern Building Code Congress, International, 900 Montclair Rd., Birmingham, AL 35213–1206; phone: 205/591–1853) $15. Published each January.

IAEI Membership Directory (International Association of Electrical Inspectors, 901 Waterfall Way, Richardson, TX 75080) $25. Published annually.

Property management

Job openings

CPM® Aspects® (Institute of Real Estate Management, 430 N. Michigan Ave., Chicago, IL 60611; phone: 312/329–6000) seven issues/year, available only to members. Write or call for membership information. Jobs listed under "JOBS*Bulletin*." About 60 to 75 job ads for property managers appear in the typical issue. Also lists "Positions Wanted" ads from members seeking employment.

ARM® News (Institute of Real Estate Management, 430 N. Michigan Ave., Chicago, IL 60611; phone: 312/329-6000) eight issues/year, available only to members, included in dues. About ten positions for property mangers and site managers of residential real estate are included under "Jobs Bulletin." ARM® program participants may place "Position Wanted" ads.

FMRA News (American Society of Farm Managers and Rural Appraisers, Inc., Suite 500, 950 Cherry, Denver, CO 80222; phone: 303/758-3513) bimonthly, available only as part of membership package. Jobs listed under "Job Mart." Usually two to four job ads per issue, but some issues have no ads.

Developments (American Resort and Residential Development Association, 1220 L St., NW, Washington, DC 20005; phone: 202/371-6700) 11 issues/year, $25/annual nonmember subscription (U.S.), $35/elsewhere, free/members. Among the three to seven positions listed under "Classifieds" are management, sales, and business opportunities.

Common Ground (Community Associations Institute, 1630 Duke St., Alexandria, VA 22314; phone: 703/548-8600) bimonthly, available only to members, price depends on membership category. Jobs listed under "CAI Classifieds." About five ads per issue for managers of community and condominium associations, and planned unit developments. When you join CAI, you automatically become a member of a local chapter and receive the local chapter's directory of members.

Shopping Centers Today (International Council of Shopping Centers, 665 Fifth Ave., New York, nY 10022; phone: 212/421-8181) monthly, $50/annual nonmember subscription (U.S.), $85/Canada, $35/members. Twenty-five ads for job openings in marketing, leasing, management, sales, and law as well as business opportunities are in "SCT Classified."

Shopping Center World (Communication Channels, 6255 Barfield Rd., Atlanta, GA 30328; phone: 404/256-9800) 13 issues/year, $60/annual subscription (U.S.), $80/foreign. Ads placed by recruiting firms advertise about ten openings for shopping center management, marketing, leasing, construction, and development executives under "Executive Search."

Directories

Accredited Management Organization® Directory (Institute of Real Estate Management, 430 N. Michigan Ave., Chicago, IL 60611; phone: 312/329–6000) nonmembers: submit written request for a copy, free/members. This geographical listing of accredited management organization® firms is published every April.

IREM Membership Directory (Institute of Real Estate Management, 430 N. Michigan Ave., Chicago, IL 60611; phone: 312/329–6000) nonmembers: submit written request for a copy, included in membership package. This geographical listing of certified property managers® and accredited management organizations® in the U.S., Canada, and overseas, is published each April.

Accredited Residential Manager Directory (Institute of Real Estate Management, 430 N. Michigan Ave., Chicago, IL 60611; phone: 312/329–6000) nonmembers: submit written request for a copy; free/members. This geographical listing of accredited residential managers in the U.S. and Canada is published every April.

Accredited and General Membership Directory (American Society of Farm Managers and Rural Appraisers, Inc., Suite 500, 950 Cherry, Denver, CO 80222; phone: 303/758–3513) write for price.

Salary surveys

CPM® Profile and Compensation Study (Institute of Real Estate Management, 430 N. Michigan Ave., Chicago, IL 60611; phone: 312/329–6000) $17.95/nonmembers, $16.16/members. Published in 1989 and every three years thereafter.

Accredited Residential Manager® Profile and Compensation Study (Institute of Real Estate Management, 430 N. Michigan Ave., Chicago, IL 60611; phone: 312/329–6000) $18.95/nonmembers, $17.06/members, 1990 and every three years thereafter.

Chapter 29

Retailing

Also see the entries in the chapter "Sales."

Job openings

Discount Store News (3922 Coconut Palm Dr., Tampa, FL 33619; phone: 813/664-6700) semimonthly, $79/annual subscription (U.S.), $89/Canada, $175/elsewhere. "Discount Mart—Help Wanted" runs about 20 ads for store management and sales representatives.

Convenience Store News (7 Penn Plaza, New York, NY 10001; phone: 800/223-9638) 15 issues/year, $48/annual subscription (U.S.), $60/Canada, $100/elsewhere. Under "CSNews Classified—Help Wanted" and "Business Opportunities" you'll find a dozen ads for sales, marketing, and management.

Stores (National Retail Federation, 100 W. 31st St., New York, NY 10001; phone: 212/244-8780) monthly, $49/annual nonmember subscription, free/members. One or two jobs in retail management are under "Classified."

VM & SD: Visual Merchandising and Store Design (ST Publications, 407 Gilbert Ave., Cincinnati, OH 45202; phone: 513/421-2050) monthly, $30/annual subscription (U.S.), $50/Canada, $55/elsewhere.

About eight ads for sales representatives for display products manufacturers and for store planners and visual merchandisers in retail stores are in "Opportunity Exchange."

Display and Design Ideas (Shore Publishing, 180 Allen Rd., NE, Atlanta, GA 30328; phone: 404/252-8831) monthly, distributed free to retailers. Four or five ads for retailer representatives and design specialists are in the "Classifieds."

Modern Tire Dealer (Bill Communications, P.O. Box 3599, Akron, OH 44309; phone: 216/867-4401) monthly, $55/annual subscription (U.S.) $90/Canada, $180/elsewhere. Ten to 20 jobs for service directors, general managers, store managers, sales representatives, and consultants in the automotive retail field are in the "Classified" section.

Aftermarket Today (Automotive Service Industry Association, 444 N. Michigan Ave., Chicago, IL 60611; phone: 312/836-1300) monthly, $40/annual nonmember subscription, free/members. "Business and Employment Opportunities" carries about 11 ads for sales managers, parts managers, accounts managers, salespeople, and marketing managers in the automotive parts and service industry.

Jobber Retailer (Bill Communications, P.O. Box 3599, Akron, OH 44309; phone: 216/867-4401) monthly, $60/annual subscription (U.S., Canada), $75/elsewhere. Two to four jobs for store managers, sales representatives, service directors, and automotive consultants—primarily for automotive parts retailers—are in the "Classifieds."

Monitor: The Magazine of Shopping Center Retailing (4 Stamford Forum, Stamford, CT 06901; phones: 800/252-2530, 203/325-3500) bimonthly, $75/annual subscription. One or two openings for leasing coordinators and shopping center management are in the "Classifieds."

Hardware Age (Chilton Company, Chilton Way, Radnor, PA 19089; phone: 215/964-4275) monthly, $14/annual subscription (U.S.), $75/Canada. Ten to 15 job ads for hardware store and manufacturers management positions and sales representatives appear under "Classified Advertising."

National Home Center News (Lebhar-Friedman, P.O. Box 31185, Tampa, FL 33631; phone: 813/664-6707) semimonthly, $79/annual subscription (U.S.), $89/Canada, $239/elsewhere (air mail only), free to qualified retailers and wholesalers of lumber and building supplies and hardware. Fifteen to 20 positions for merchandise buyers, salespeople, managers, lumber traders, and executives with building supply, lumber, and hardware stores are advertised under "Home Center Mart."

Building Supply Home Centers (Cahners Publishing, 44 Cook St., Denver, CO 80206; phone: 303/388–4511) monthly, $64.95/annual subscription (U.S.), $96.25/Canada, $89.95/elsewhere. The "Classified" section carries about six job openings in sales and management.

Sports Trend (Shore Publishing, 180 Allen Rd., NE, Atlanta, GA 30328; phone: 404/252–8831) monthly, free to qualified retailers. About six ads for representatives of sporting good manufacturers are in the "Classified" section.

Directories

Directory of General Merchandise, Variety/Specialty Chains & Specialty Stores (Chain Store Guide Information Services, 425 Park Ave., New York, NY 10022; phone: 212/371–9400, ext. 306) $219, published each March. Profiles about 880 of these companies that operate a total of 22,000 stores. Includes names and titles for 17,500 key executive, buying, and administrative personnel.

National Association of Convenience Stores Membership Directory (NACS, 1605 King St., Alexandria, VA 22314; phone: 703/684–3600) $200/nonmembers, $50/members, issued each January.

Associate Directory (National Retail Federation, 100 W. 31st St., New York, NY 10001; phone: 212/244–8780) $20/nonmembers, free/members, issued each January. Lists retail store management personnel.

Discount Department Stores (Chain Store Guide Information Services, 425 Park Ave., New York, NY 10022; phone: 212/371–9400, ext. 306) $219, published each March. Profiles over 200 discount store chains with 8,400 self–service type stores. Includes 10,000 key executive, buying, and administrative personnel.

Department Stores (Chain Store Guide Information Services, 425 Park Ave., New York, NY 10022; phone: 212/371–9400, ext. 306) $239, published each November. Profiles over 750 department store companies that operate 6,300 stores. Includes 10,000 key executive, buying, and administrative personnel.

Directory of Recreational Marine Product Dealers (Chain Store Guide Information Services, 425 Park Ave., New York, NY 10022; phone: 212/371–9400, ext. 306) $249, published each October. Profiles 5,700 marine dealers, marine equipment supply stores, boat dealers, and marinas. Includes 11,000 key executive, buying, and administrative personnel.

SHOE reprinted by permission of Tribune Media Services. All rights reserved.

Hardlines Distributors (Chain Store Guide Information Services, 425 Park Ave., New York, NY 10022; phone: 212/371–9400, ext. 306) $189, published biennially in March. Describes 2,250 hardware, paint, electrical, heating, cooling, plumbing, lumber, and building supplies distributors. Includes 8,800 key executive, buying, and administrative personnel.

Home Center Operators & Hardware Chains (Chain Store Guide Information Services, 425 Park Ave., New York, NY 10022; phone: 212/371–9400, ext. 306) $229, published each July. Describes 6,500 home centers, warehouses, and lumber, and building material companies as well as hardware chains that operate over 16,000 stores, 200 specialty paint chains with over 5,000 stores, and 100 farm and home store chains with nearly 700 stores. Includes 20,000 key executive, buying, and administrative personnel.

Home Furnishings Retailers (Chain Store Guide Information Services, 425 Park Ave., New York, NY 10022; phone: 212/371-9400, ext. 306) $269, published each August. Details on 5,500 furniture and horizontal home furnishing retail companies that operate over 14,000 stores. Includes 14,700 key executive, buying, and administrative personnel.

VM & SD: Visual Merchandising and Store Design Buyers' Guide (ST Publications, 407 Gilbert Ave., Cincinnati, OH 45202; phone: 513/421-2050) February issue each year, $25. Includes entries of manufacturers, sales, and services for animations, architectural elements, audio-visual equipment, ceilings, display decoratives and props, fixtures and components, floor and wall covering, furniture, interior lighting, mannequins and forms, materials, interior signage and graphics, and supplies and equipment used in retail store displays. Also includes descriptions of educational programs in merchandising and store design as well as a list of associations in the field.

Salary surveys

National Association of Convenience Stores Compensation Survey (NACS, 1605 King St., Alexandria, VA 22314; phone: 703/684-3600) $225/nonmembers, $150/members, issued every August. Includes salaries and benefits for all positions from cashiers to chief executive officers.

Chapter 30

Safety

Job openings

JobLine Bulletin (American Society of Safety Engineers, 1800 E. Oakton St., Des Plaines, IL 60018-2187; phone: 708/692-4121, ext. 33) monthly, $80/nonmembers for six-month subscription, $25/members, free/unemployed members. Special issues are published occasionally upon employer request. About 30 safety and health job openings in construction, communications, insurance, manufacturing, utilities, and transportation appear throughout the typical issue.

Professional Safety (American Society of Safety Engineers, 1800 E. Oakton St., Des Plaines, IL 60018-2187; phone: 708/692-4121, ext. 13) monthly, $43/nonmember annual subscription (U.S., Canada, and Mexico), $50/elsewhere surface mail, $102/elsewhere by air mail; free/members. About 25 safety and health job openings in construction, communications, insurance, manufacturing, utilities, transportation, and the petrochemical industries as well as university faculty opportunities are listed under "Personnel Center."

Occupational Hazards (Penton Publishing, 1100 Superior Ave., Cleveland, OH 44114; phone: 216/696-7000) monthly; free to qualified professionals, call or write for application form; otherwise: $45/annual subscription (U.S.), $65/Canada, $80/elsewhere. "Opportunities" lists about seven positions for industrial hygienists and sales people.

The NCCEM Bulletin (National Coordinating Council on Emergency Management, Unit N, 7297 Lee Highway, Falls Church, VA 22042; phone: 703/533-7672) monthly, available only to members ($75/annual dues, membership open to anyone). Jobs listed under "Personnel Corner." About one job ad every three months.

Directories

Industrial Safety Equipment Association Membership Directory (ISEA, 1901 N. Moore St., Suite 808, Arlington, VA 22209; phone: 703/525-1695) free/members only, issued each June and December.

The NCCEM Membership Directory (National Coordinating Council on Emergency Management, Unit N, 7297 Lee Highway, Falls Church, VA 22042; phone: 703/533-7672) $10, published every January.

Chapter 31

Sales

Also see the entries in the chapters "Manufacturing" and "Retailing."
See the entry "Sales" in the Index for other job sources located elsewhere
in this book that include job openings for salespeople.

Job openings

Agency Sales Magazine (Manufacturers' Agents National Association, 23016 Mill Creek Rd., Laguna Hills, CA 92654-3467; phone: 714/859-4040) monthly, $37.50/annual subscription (U.S.), $40/foreign, included in dues. Nearly 200 ads for all types of products appear "Manufacturers' Agents Wanted." Under "Miscellaneous Sales, Services—Agency Opportunities" are about 15 ads to sell sales agencies.

UAMR Bulletin (United Association Manufacturers' Representatives, 133 Terrace Trail West, Lake Quivira, KS 66106; phone: 913/268-9466) monthly, $48/nonmember annual subscription, free/members. Around 75 opportunities for manufacturers' representatives including product lines to represent for all sorts of products are advertised in the typical issue.

Sales and Marketing Management (Bill Communications, P.O. Box 1025, South Eastern, PA 19398; phone: 215/630–1549) 15 issues/year, $48/annual subscription. "Sales Mart—Positions Available" runs one or two ads for sales executives.

Executive Female (National Association of Female Executives, 127 W. 24th St., New York, NY 10011; phone: 212/645–0770) bimonthly, free/members only. Two or three ads for sale managers are in "Help Wanted."

Salesworld (Professional Salespersons of America, 3801 Monaco, NE, Albuquerque, NM 87111; phone: 505/275–0857) quarterly, contact for subscription information. This is a new association that will start running job ads for salespeople in January 1992. *Salesworld* will come out more frequently as PSA's membership increases.

Job services

Career Op Bank (National Network of Women in Sales, 10613 Depot, Fort Worth, TX 60482; phone: 800/321–6697) free/members only. Each month the central office sends a set of job descriptions for sales vacancies to its, at present, six chapters (Texas, North Carolina, and four in the midwest). These are posted at each chapter's regular meeting. There are usually around 50 or more jobs in each listing.

Women in Sales Association Job Bank (Women in Sales Association, 8 Madison Ave., P.O. Box M, Valhalla, NY 10595; phone: 514/546–3802) free/members only. A member's resume is kept on file for six months. Employers submit job specifications which are distributed to chapters. Sales positions range from entry–level sales to upper management.

Directories

MANA Directory of Manufacturers' Sales Agencies (Manufacturers' Agents National Association, 23016 Mill Creek Rd., Laguna Hills, CA 92654–3467; phone: 714/859–4040) $85/U.S. nonmembers, $105/Canada, $117/elsewhere, free/members, published every June, 920 pages. The alphabetic listing that describes each of the 10,000 top manufacturers' agents agencies is supplemented with product

"If your product is so good that it sells
itself, what do you need me for?"

and geographic indices. Covers 93 product classifications. The associate member section includes manufacturers and other businesses that work within the manufacturer/agency profession.

Sales & Marketing Management Magazine (Bill Communications, P.O. Box 1024, Southeastern, PA 19398; phone: 215/630–1549) monthly, $48/annual subscription (U.S.), $62/Canada, $77/elsewhere. Three or four ads for sales and marketing positions are in "Positions Available."

Salary surveys

Income in Sales/Marketing Management (Abbott, Langer & Associates, 548 First St., Crete, IL 60417; phone: 708/672–4200) $275, annual. Gives salaries and benefits for 16 managerial jobs in the sales and marketing field from top management executives to district sales managers to market research managers.

Sales Force Compensation (Abbott, Langer & Associates, 548 First St., Crete, IL 60417; phone: 708/672–4200) $159.50, annual, 355 pages. Provides data by 39 different types of employer.

Furniture

Job openings

Furniture/Today (200 S. Main St., High Point, NC 27261; phones: 800/395-2329, 919/889-0113) weekly, $69.95/annual subscription (U.S.), $85/Canada, $225/elsewhere. The 40 to 80 ads in "Classifieds/Today" under "Buyers Wanted," "Help Wanted," and "Lines Offered" include sales positions as well as management and furniture and floral designers.

Furniture Today (Cahners Publishing, P.O. Box 1424, Riverton, NJ 08077; phone: 800/395-2329) weekly, $69.96/annual subscription (U.S.), $85/Canada, $225/elsewhere. The "Classifieds" carry ads for 15 positions such as sales management, director of delivery services, and director of design.

Directory

American Society of Furniture Designers Official Directory (P.O. Box 2688, High Point, NC 27261; phone: 919/884-4074) $40/non-members, free/members, published every April.

Home fashions

Job openings

Wallcoverings Windows & Interior Fashion (Publishing Dynamics, 15 Bank St., Suite 101, Stamford, CT 06901; phone: 203/357-0028) monthly, $18/annual subscription (U.S.), $70/foreign. Four to ten vacancies in sales of wall coverings, windows, and interior fashion are advertised in the "Classified" section.

Walls & Ceilings (8602 N. 40th St., Tampa, FL 33604; phone: 813/989-9300) monthly, $24/annual subscription (U.S.), $29/Canada. One or two ads for manufacturers' representatives and distributors are in "Classified."

"I've heard several rumors that you're setting the sales
quotas too high—keep up the good work."

Fenestration (310 Madison Ave., New York, NY 10017; phone: 212/682-7681) bimonthly, $15/annual subscription (U.S., Canada), $21/elsewhere. A few jobs for sales representatives and other positions in the fenestration industry (doors and windows) are advertised under "Positions Available."

Kitchen and Bath Business (Gralla Publishing, 1515 Broadway, New York, NY 10035; phone: 212/869-1300) monthly, $29/annual subscription (U.S.), $67/Canada, $90/elsewhere. Thirty to 35 job ads for sales representatives and executives in the kitchen and bath business are under "Help Wanted," "Reps Wanted," and "Positions Available."

Home Textiles Today (Cahners Publishing, P.O. Box 1424, Riverton, NJ 08077; phone: 800/395-2329) biweekly, $59.95/annual subscription (U.S.), $75/Canada, $95/elsewhere. "Classifieds" runs about four ads for directors of design, research and development directors, stylists, salespeople, and buyers in the home fashions industry.

Tile & Decorative Surfaces (20335 Ventura Blvd., Suite 400, Woodland Hills, CA 91364; phone: 818/704–5555) monthly, $45/annual subscription (U.S.), $55/foreign. Two to 12 ads for sales people are in "Classified."

Floor Covering News/U.S.A. (Altron Communications, 30—20 Thomas Ave., Long Island City, NY 11101; phone: 718/706–7830) biweekly, $20/annual subscription (U.S.), $50/Canada. "Classified" has ads for two or three vacancies for salespeople and manufacturers' representatives for floor tiles and carpeting. "Position wanted" ads also are carried.

Directories

Residential & Contract Directory (Publishing Dynamics, 15 Bank St., Suite 101, Stamford, CT 06901; phone: 203/357–0028) $25, published in the May and September issues of *Wallcoverings, Windows & Interior Fashion* described above under "Job openings."

Tile & Decorative Surfaces Directory and Buyers Guide (20335 Ventura Blvd., Suite 400, Woodland Hills, CA 91364; phone: 818/704–5555) $20, December issue each year.

Luggage and leather

Job openings

Showcase (Luggage and Leather Manufacturers Association of America, 350 Fifth Ave., New York, NY 10118; phone: 212/695–2340) bimonthly, $35/annual subscription. Twelve ads for salespeople for luggage and leathers are under "Classified."

Travelware (Business Journals, 50 Day St., Norwalk, CT 06854; phone: 203/853–6015) ten issues/year, $30/annual subscription (U.S.), $42/Canada, $65/elsewhere. About four ads for sales representatives for leather accessories, luggage, and other goods are in "Trade Mart."

Office Products

Job openings

Industry Report (National Office Products Association, 301 N. Fairfax St., Alexandria, VA 22314; phones: 800/542-6672, 703/549-9040) biweekly, $36/annual nonmember subscription, free/members. Ten to 15 job vacancies, mostly for salespeople and manufacturers' representatives, are in the "Classifieds."

Office Products Dealer (Hitchock Publishing, 191 S. Gary Ave., Carol Stream, IL 60188; phone: 708/665-1000) monthly, $55/annual subscription (U.S.), $70/foreign. Five jobs for salespeople are in the "Classifieds."

Geyer's Office Dealers (Geyer-McAllister Publishing, 51 Madison Ave., New York, NY 10010; phone: 212/289-2300) monthly, $20/annual subscription (U.S., Canada), $40/elsewhere. A few jobs for sales mangers, product managers, and sales representatives are in "Classified."

Directories

NOPA Membership Directory & Buyer's Guide (National Office Products Association, 301 N. Fairfax St., Alexandria, VA 22314; phones: 800/542-6672, 703/549-9040) $75/nonmembers, free/members, annual. Includes an alphabetical and geographical listing of members as well as a buyer's guide of products and services to the office products industry.

Miscellaneous products

Gifts and Decorative Accessories (Geyer-McAllister Publishing, 51 Madison Ave., New York, NY 10010; phone: 212/289-2300) monthly, $35/annual subscription (U.S., Canada), $80/elsewhere. A few ads for sales managers appear occasionally.

Art Material Trade News (Communication Channels, 6255 Barfield Rd, Atlanta, GA 30328; phone: 404/256–9800) monthly, $40/annual subscription (U.S.), $60/foreign. ''Classified—Manufacturers Reps Wanted'' carries five or six job ads in art supplies and photographic product sales.

Contracting Business (Penton Publishing, 1100 Superior St., Cleveland, OH 44115; phone: 216/696–7000) monthly, $45/annual subscription. Two or three ads for manufacturers' reps and sales persons are in the typical issue under ''Classifieds.''

If you're having trouble finding job sources for your specialty, you probably should refresh your memory on how to use this book most effectively. Please read Chapter 1 which explains how to get the most out of the *Professional's Job Finder*.

Chapter 32

Science and engineering

Science and engineering in general

Also see the chapters on "Computers and electronics" and "Manufacturing." Although some of these sources include positions in academia and research, you'll find many more sources of academic and research positions in the Non–Profits' Job Finder.

Job openings

High Technology Careers (Westech Publishing, 4701 Patrick Henry Dr., Suite 1901, Santa Clara, CA 95054; phone: 408/970–8800) bimonthly, $29/annual subscription, free to residents of northern California. From 500 to 700 positions in engineering, technology, and computers fill each issue.

Science (American Association of the Advancement of Science, 1333 H St., NW, Washington, DC 20005; phone: 202/326–6539) 51 issues/year, $82/annual subscription (U.S.), $128/foreign ($172/air mail). "Personnel Placement" overflows with around 200 advertisements for scientists of all types, although most ads seem to be for biologists in academia.

New Scientist (IPC Magazines, Ltd., Freepost 1061, Hawwards Heath, England RH16 3ZA) weekly, $130 (U.S. dollars)/annual subscription via air mail to the U.S., $170 (Canadian dollars)/annual subscription via air mail to Canada, £110/United Kingdom annual subscription. Over 100 positions in Great Britain are listed throughout, including many private sector positions.

Nature (P.O. Box 1733, Riverton, NJ 08077-9733; phone: 800/524-0384) weekly, $135/annual subscription. Job ads for about 80 scientists of all sorts appear in "Classified."

Natural History (P.O. Box 3030, Harlan, IA 51593-2091; phone: 800/234-5252) monthly, $22/annual subscription, $29/elsewhere. You'll find about 10 ads for jobs or job services in "The Market."

AWIS Magazine (Association for Women in Science, 1522 K St., NW, Suite 820, Washington, DC 20005; phone: 202/408-0742) bimonthly, $55/annual nonmember subscription, included in member dues. From 15 to 20 ads for life, physical, social, and mathematical sciences and engineering appear under "Help Wanted—Employment Advertisements."

Popular Science (P.O. Box 51824, Boulder, CO 80321-1824; phone: 212/779-5000) monthly, $13.94/annual subscription for U.S. and possessions, $20.94/Canada, $21.94/elsewhere. The "Classified Opportunity Mart" is chock full of business opportunities and a few help wanted ads.

Tappi Journal (Technical Association of the Pulp and Paper Industry, P.O. Box 105113, Atlanta, GA 30348; phones: 800/332-8686, 404/446-1400) monthly, $96/annual nonmember subscription, $60/members. Around 15 ads for engineers and scientists appear in the "Classified Ads." Members can place "Position Wanted" ads for free.

Occupational Hazards (Penton Publishing, P.O. Box 95759, Cleveland, OH 44115; phone: 216/696-7000) monthly, $45/annual subscription (U.S.), $65/Canada, $80/elsewhere. A couple of ads for industrial hygienists and safety engineers are in the "Opportunities" section.

Elevator World (354 Morgan Ave., Mobile, AL 36609; phone: 205/479-4514) monthly, $52/annual subscription. Two to six ads for elevator engineers appear in the "Classifieds."

Journal of Imaging Technology (Society for Imaging Science and Technology, 7003 Kilworth Ln., Springfield, VA 22151; phone: 703/642-9090) bimonthly, $80/annual nonmember subscription, $90/foreign, $60/members. More than six job ads plus "Positions Wanted" are listed under "Placement Services."

OE Reports (SPIE, P.O. Box 10, Bellingham, WA 98227-0010; phone: 206/676-3290) monthly, free to qualified professionals and to members. Twenty to 30 job ads for engineers in optics, holography, optoelectronics, lasers, research and development, and related fields appear under "Employment Opportunities/Placement Exchange." Job seekers may place ads to find jobs.

Optics and Photonics News (Optical Society of America, 2010 Massachusetts Ave., NW, Washington, DC 20036; phones: 800/582-0416, 202/223-8130) monthly, $99/annual nonmember subscription, $60/members. A few job ads for optical engineers, research scientists, and professors are in the typical issue.

Sky & Telescope (Sky Publishing Corp., P.O. Box 9111, Belmont, MA 02178; phone: 617/864-7360) monthly, $24/annual subscription (U.S.), $34/Canada, $42/elsewhere. About three ads for astronomers, planetarium directors, and opticians are scattered throughout.

Agricultural Engineering (American Society of Agricultural Engineers, 2950 Niles Rd., St. Joseph, MI 49085; phone: 616/429-0300) bimonthly, $36.50/annual nonmember subscription, free/members. Eight to ten ads for agricultural engineers appear under "Personnel Services." "Position Wanted" ads are also printed. *Also see the chapter on "Farming and ranching."*

Within ASAE (American Society of Agricultural Engineers, 2950 Niles Rd., St. Joseph, MI 49085; phone: 616/429-0300) bimonthly, free, available only to members. Eight to ten ads for agricultural engineers appear under "Personnel Services." "Position Wanted" ads are also printed. *Also see the chapter on "Farming and ranching."*

Drug & Cosmetic Industry (Edgell Communications, 1 E. First St., Duluth, MN 55802; phones: 800/346-0085, 218/723-9870) monthly, $20/annual subscription (U.S.), $45/Canada, $90/elsewhere. Under "Professional Services—Reps wanted" you'll find fewer than five ads for jobs in cosmetics, pharmaceuticals, medicines, and flavor and allied packaged chemical products. The July directory issue costs $30 by itself.

LD+A (Illuminating Engineering Society of North America, 345 E. 47th St., New York, NY 10017; phone: 212/705-7926) monthly, $35/annual nonmember subscription (U.S.), $50/foreign, free/members. Three job vacancies for lighting designers and applications engineers appear under "Classified."

Plating and Surface Finishing (American Electroplaters and Surface Finishers Society, 12644 Research Parkway, Orlando, FL 32826; phone: 407/281-6441) monthly, $40/annual nonmember subscription (U.S., Canada), $55/elsewhere, free/members. The "Classifieds" carry around ten ads for surface finishing managers, engineers, and chemists.

Products Finishing (6600 Clough Pike, Cincinnati, OH 45214; phone: 513/231-8020) monthly, $18/annual subscription (U.S.), $24/Canada, $48/elsewhere. Four or five ads for finishing engineers, chemists, and specialists are in the "Classified Advertising."

Weatherwise (4000 Albemarle St., NW, Washington, DC 20016; 800/365-9753, 202/362-6445) bimonthly, $25/annual subscription for individuals, $42 for institutions, elsewhere are $9. Two to five job openings appear in "The Weather Network" section.

Technology Review (P.O. Box 489, Mount Morris, IL 61054; phones: 800/435-0715; 815/734-6309) eight issues/year, $24/annual subscription. The "Classifieds" carry two or three ads for engineers and development scientists and engineers.

Job services

SAE Resume Database (SAE International: The Engineering Society for Advancing Mobility Land Sea Air and Space, 400 Commonwealth Dr., Warrendale, PA 15096; phone: 412/776-4841, ext. 369) $30/nonmember fee for three months, free/members. The job candidate completes the service's "Resume Database System" information form. Employers subscribe to this database system and are able to search it with up to 40 search criteria. They are responsible for contacting the job seeker for an interview. Among the thousands of job candidates listed are mechanical, civil, electrical, aeronautical, and chemical engineers, physicists, chemists, and others who work closely with engineers.

Directories

Job Opportunities for Engineering, Science, and Computer Graduates (Peterson's P.O. Box 2123, Princeton, NJ 08543–2123; phones: 800/338–3282, 609/243–9111) $20.95 plus $4.75 shipping, issued each August for the following year. This is essentially a directory of more than 1,000 firms that actively recruit in these fields. Actual vacancies cannot be guaranteed, but this serves as a good directory of firm descriptions.

ACIL Directory: A Guide to the Leading Independent Testing, Research, and Inspection Laboratories of America (American Council of Independent Laboratories, 1725 K St., NW, Washington, DC 20006; phone: 202/887–5872) $25/nonmembers, $5/members, biennial, most recent edition 1990–91. Describes over 350 member companies plus 1,000 facilities throughout the U.S. and abroad.

TAPPI Membership Directory (Technical Association of the Pulp and Paper Industry, P.O. Box 105113, Atlanta, GA 30348; phones: 800/332–8686, 404/446–1400) $112/nonmembers, free/members, issued each October.

Sky & Telescope's Astronomy Resource Guide (Sky Publishing Corp., P.O. Box 9111, Belmont, MA 02178; phone: 617/864–7360) September issue of *Sky & Telescope*, $2.95. Lists U.S. and Canadian planetariums, museums, and observatories plus astronomy dealers and manufacturers.

Products Finishing Directory (6600 Clough Pike, Cincinnati, OH 45214; phone: 513/231–8020) November issue each year, contact for single issue price. Includes companies that supply factories that apply paint or electroplates.

Agricultural Engineering Guide to Products and Services (American Society of Agricultural Engineers, 2950 Niles Rd., St. Joseph, MI 49085; phone: 616/429–0300) $30/nonmembers, free/members, last issued in 1990.

Products Finishing (6600 Clough Pike, Cincinnati, OH 45214; phone: 513/231–8020) monthly, $18/annual subscription (U.S.), $24/Canada, $48/elsewhere. Four or five ads for finishing engineers, chemists, and specialists are in the "Classified Advertising."

Salary surveys

Summary of Salaries of Scientists, Engineers, and Technicians (Commission on Professionals in Science and Technology, 1500 Massachusetts Ave., NW, Suite 831, Washington, DC 20005; phone: 202/223–6995) $75, annual.

Compensation in Research & Development (Abbott, Langer & Associates, 548 First St., Crete, IL 60417; phone: 708/672–4200) $495/entire set, 748 pages; Part I: Directors/Managers/Supervisors, $915; Part II: Engineers/Scientists/Technologists, $195; Part III: Technicians, $195. Sponsored by the Society of Research Administration, the entire set covers 17 job categories.

Careers in Biotechnology (Industrial Biotechnology Association, 1625 K St., NW, Washington, DC 20006; phone: 202/857–0244) contact for price, most recently published in 1990. In addition to explaining this emerging field in some detail, this directory describes the training needed, sources of additional information, relevant associations, sample job ads and job descriptions, a guide to recruiters for biotechnology jobs, and results of a salary survey. Specialties included in biotechnology are chemists, chemical engineers, physicists, engineers, biologists, and geneticists.

Employee Wage and Salary Survey (American Council of Independent Laboratories, 1725 K St., NW, Washington, DC 20006; phone: 202/887–5872) $300/nonmembers, $100/members, issued in February of even–numbered years. Gives data by job description, technical area, education and experience, and firm size and geographic location.

Biological sciences

Job openings

ASM News (American Society of Microbiologists, 1325 Massachusetts Ave., NW, Washington, DC 20005; phone: 202/737-3600) monthly, $19/annual nonmember subscription, free/members. You'll find between 22 to 50 job opportunities for biologists, molecular biologists, and microbiologists under "Employment."

The FASEB Journal (Federation of American Societies for Experimental Biology, 9650 Rockville Pike, Bethesda, MD 20814-3998; phone: 301/530-7020) monthly, contact for subscription rates. About 20 ads for life science positions, mostly at the doctoral level, appear under "Employment Opportunities." An equal number of "Position Desired" ads also appear.

Bio/Technology (Nature Publishing Company, P.O. Box 1721, Riverton, NJ 08077-7321; phone: 800/524-0328) monthly, $59/annual subscription (U.S., Canada). Around 20 job ads are under "Classified."

ASC Bulletin (American Society of Cytology, 1015 Chestnut St., Suite 1518, Philadelphia, PA 19107; phone: 215/922-3880) bimonthly, free, available only to members. Around 17 positions for cyto-technologists are in the "Classifieds."

ESA Newsletter (Entomological Society of America, 9301 Annapolis Rd., Suite 300, Lanham, MD 20706; phone: 301/731-4535) monthly, $20/nonmember annual subscription, free/members. "Opportunities" lists ten to 15 jobs for entomologists, biologists, geneticists, and toxicologists.

EMS Newsletter (Environmental Mutagen Society, Business Office, 1600 Wilson Blvd., Suite 905, Arlington, VA 22209; phone: 703/525-1191) twice/year, free, available only to members. "Genetic Toxicology Placement Service" lists six to ten positions in genetic toxicology and drug safety evaluation.

SOT Newsletter (Society of Toxicology, 1101 14th St., NW, Suite 1100, Washington, DC 20005; phone: 202/293-5935) bimonthly, free, available only to members. "Placement Service" typically has about eight job ads for toxicologists.

"Somehow I don't think a wee tiny condom
will be the world's best mousetrap."

American Journal of Botany (Botanical Society of America, 1735 Neil Ave., Columbus, OH 43210; phone: 203/486-4322) monthly, $145/annual subscription (U.S.), $155/Canada, $170/elsewhere. Four to eight ads for botanists and biologists appear under "Positions Available." Four times a year, *Plant Science Bulletin* is included free; it also has job ads in it.

BioScience (American Institute of Biological Sciences, 703 11th St., NW, Washington, DC 20001-4521; phone: 202/628-1500) 11 issues/year, $43.50/annual subscription. "Professional Opportunities" features about three ads for biologists.

SIM News (Society for Industrial Microbiology, P.O. Box 12534, Arlington, VA 22209; phone: 703/941-5373) bimonthly, $90/18-month nonmember subscription, free/members. One or two ads for microbiologists are in "Placement."

Genetic Engineering News (1651 Third Ave., New York, NY 10128; phone: 212/289-2300) ten issues/year, $190/annual subscription. Only one or two ads for biochemists, bioengineers, and biologists appear under "Classified."

Job services

FASEB Placement Service (Federation of American Societies for Experimental Biology, 9650 Rockville Pike, Bethesda, MD 20814–3998; phone: 301/530–7020) $10/annual registration fee. If you register before January 22, you'll be included in the annual *Candidates*, a bound collection of current registrations published and distributed each February to about 300 potential employers. All registrants are entitled to place a "Position Desired" ad in one issue of the *FASEB Journal* (described earlier under "Job Openings"). You can place additional "Position Desired" ads for $15 each. Employers may also see your registration "resume" form when they review registrants at the FASEB office. FASEB staff refer about 1,400 registrants each year to employers with whom they match position qualifications. You also receive a copy of copy of the *Positions*, published each March, in which vacancies are listed. You can also use the interview scheduling services, but you must report in person at the Placement Service at the annual meeting to initiate this last service.

American Society for Microbiology Placement Service (ASM, 1325 Massachusetts Ave., NW, Washington, DC 20005; phone: 202/737–3600) $100/nonmember annual fee, $35/members. You fill out their registry form. When there is a match, your form is sent to the employer who is responsible for contacting you.

SIM Placement Service (Society for Industrial Microbiology, c/o Jim Kowowski, Abbot Laboratories, D47P Building AP9A, Abbot Park, IL 60064–3500; phone: 708/937–7967) free. You submit your own resume. When a job match is made, you are notified and are responsible for contacting the potential employer. Positions include microbiologists, quality assurance, fermentation, bioremediation, process control, and research.

BioTron (American Institute of Biological Sciences, 703 11th St., NW, Washington, DC 20001–4521; phone: 202/628–1500) free. Using your computer modem, call 202/628–2427 anytime to access job vacancies. The communications configuration is 300, 1200, or 2400 baud, 8 data bits, 1 stop bit, no parity, full duplex, Xon/Xoff active, carriage return (ASCII 13) at end of lines. Received text may be stopped and started by pressing Control-S/Q.

Directories

SAE Roster of Members (SAE International: The Engineering Society for Advancing Mobility Land Sea Air and Space, 400 Commonwealth Dr., Warrendale, PA 15096; phone: 412/776–4841, ext. 369) free/members only, issued each March. Members include mechanical, civil, electrical, aeronautical, and chemical engineers, physicists, chemists, and others who work closely with engineers.

Society of Toxicology Membership Directory (SOT, 1101 14th St., NW, Suite 1100, Washington, DC 20005; phone: 202/293–5935) free, available only to members, issued each June.

SIM Membership Directory (Society for Industrial Microbiology, P.O. Box 12534, Arlington, VA 22209; phone: 703/941–5373) free, available only to members, issued each March.

Membership Directory (Genetics Society of America, 9650 Rockville Pike, Bethesda, MD 20877; phone: 301/571–1825) free, available only to members, issued in the spring of even–numbered years. Includes members of GSA, American Society of Human Genetics, and the American Board of Medical Genetics.

Botanical Society of America Directory (BSA, 1735 Neil Ave., Columbus, OH 43210; phone: 203/486–4322) $10/nonmembers, free/members, published in the spring of even–numbered years.

Salary surveys

Salaries of Scientists, Engineers, and Technicians (American Association of the Advancement of Science, 1500 Massachusetts Ave., NW, Suite 831, Washington, DC 20036; phone: 202/326–6539) $75/nonmembers, $50/members, annual. Reports the results of about 50 salary surveys.

Chemists

Also see listings under "Engineers" in this chapter.

Job openings

Chemical Engineering Progress (American Institute of Chemical Engineers, 345 E. 47th St., New York, NY 10017; phone: 212/705-7663) monthly, $60/annual nonmember subscription (U.S.), $73/foreign, free/members. Between 70 and 90 job ads for chemical engineers grace the "Classified Advertising."

Chemical & Engineering News (American Chemical Society, 1155 16th St., NW, Washington, DC 20036; phones: 800/227-5558, 202/872-4363) weekly, $95/annual nonmember subscription, free/members. "Classifieds" contain around 25 to 30 private sector positions as well as another 25 to 30 positions in academia.

Chemical Engineering (McGraw-Hill, 1221 Avenue of the Americas, New York, NY 10020; phone: 609/426-7070) monthly, $29.50/annual subscription (U.S.), $46/Canada. You'll find 15 to 20 vacancies for chemical, process, mechanical, and environmental engineers under "Employment Opportunities."

American Paint and Coatings Journal (2911 Washington Ave., St. Louis, MO 63103; phone: 314/534-0301) weekly, $25/annual subscription (U.S.), $47/Canada, $52/elsewhere. The typical issue includes 12 to 17 painting industry "Opportunities" for chemists, salespeople, and managers.

Modern Paint and Coatings (Communication Channels, 6255 Barfield Rd., Atlanta, GA 30328; phone: 404/256-9800) monthly, $42/annual subscription, $62/foreign. The "Classifieds" carry around 12 job vacancies and recruiter firms, including sales representatives.

Adhesives Age (Communication Channels, 6255 Barfield Rd., Atlanta, GA 30328; phone: 404/256-9800) 13 issues/year, $42/annual subscription, $62/foreign. About ten job openings are listed in the "Classifieds," including sales representatives.

Household and Personal Products Industry (P.O. Box 555, Ramsey, NJ 07446; phone: 201/825-2552) monthly, $48/annual subscription (U.S.), $52/Canada, $64/elsewhere. Five to ten positions for chemists and management are in "Classified."

Textile Chemists and Colorist (American Association of Textile Chemists and Colorists, P.O. Box 12215, Research Triangle Park, NC 27709; 919/549-8141) monthly, $30/annual nonmember subscription, free/members. "Personnel Available/Opportunities Available" list about ten jobs for the wet processing industry.

CHEMJOBS USA (American Chemical Society, 1155 16th St., NW, Washington, DC 20036; phones: 800/227-5558, 202/872-4363; press code "4") weekly, contact for nonmember and member rates. This bulletin includes abstracts of job ads for chemists from several major U.S. publications. It is also accessible by computer modem via ACS ECOM for a small fee. Contact ASC for details.

Chemical Processing (Putman Publishing, 301 E. Erie St., Chicago, IL 60611; phone: 312/644-2020) monthly, free to qualified professionals. Two or three positions for chemists and management in food processing appear under "Classified."

Job Listing (Society of Cosmetic Chemists, 1995 Broadway, Suite 1701; New York, NY 10023; phone: 212/874-0600) bimonthly, free. About ten openings for chemists in cosmetics, pharmaceuticals, and lab technicians fill this jobs bulletin.

Clinical Chemistry News (American Association for Clinical Chemistry, 2029 K St., NW, Suite 700, Washington, DC 20006; phones: 800/892-1400, 202/857-0717) monthly, $30/annual nonmember subscription, free/members. About six positions for clinical chemists and clinical laboratory personnel are printed under "Classified." "Positions Wanted" ads also appear.

Elastometics (Communication Channels, 6255 Barfield Rd., Atlanta, GA 30328; phone: 404/256-9800) monthly, $42/annual subscription, $62/foreign. Only one or two ads for chemists are in the "Classifieds—Employment Opportunities."

Analytical Chemistry (American Chemical Society, 1155 16th St., NW, Washington, DC 20036; phones: 800/227-5558, 202/872-4363) semimonthly, $289/annual nonmember subscription, $31/members. Ads for private sector and academia are included.

CHEMTECH (American Chemical Society, 1155 16th St., NW, Washington, DC 20036; phones: 800/227-5558, 202/872-4363) monthly, $325/annual nonmember subscription, $41/members. Includes job ads.

Job services

Year–Round Professional Data Bank (American Chemical Society, 1155 16th St., NW, Washington, DC 20036; phones: 800/227-5558, 202/872-4363, press code four) free, available only to members. Complete the "Professional Information Summary Form" which is then entered into ACS's Professional Data Bank. When a job match is made, your entry is sent to the employer who is responsible for contacting you. Each month all registrants' forms are sent to participating employers.

Confidential Employment Listing Service (American Chemical Society, 1155 16th St., NW, Washington, DC 20036; phones: 800/227-5558, 202/872-4363; press code four) available only to members, fee charged. This is a part of the ACS's *Year–Round Professional Data Bank*. You provide a list of employers who should *not* receive your qualifications. The information sent to employers does not include your name or other personal information. Interested employers contact ACS which then contacts you. If you are interested, you contact the employer.

American Association for Clinical Chemistry Employment Service (AACC, 2029 K St., NW, Suite 700, Washington, DC 20006; phones: 800/892-1400, 202/857-0717) $45/annual nonmember fee, $25/members; add $25 for AACC to type your form for you. You complete the AACC Candidate Registration Form which is then placed in the AACC's *Resume Book* which is distributed to over 100 employers at the annual national meeting and throughout the year. Interested employers contact you directly. Interviewing is available at the annual meeting held at the end of July. In addition, registrants receive the AACC *Jobs Packet* which gives details on up to 250 job openings. Throughout the year, until April, you will be sent new position postings as AACC receives them.

Job Referral Service (American Institute of Chemical Engineers, 345 E. 47th St., New York, NY 10017; phone: 212/705-7525) $70/nonmembers, $35/currently employed members, $25/currently unemployed members. This service is for serious job seekers, not those who simply want to test the waters. You complete this service's resume forms and are matched with specific openings. You are notified to send the potential employer your resume.

American Association of Cereal Chemists Placement Service (AACC, 3340 Pilot Knob Rd., St. Paul, MN 55121; phone: 612/454–7250) $35/annual nonmember fee, free/members. You submit your resume or fill out their form. Resumes are given to employers at the AACC's annual meeting. During the year, job notices will be sent to you if you request this service.

Society of Cosmetic Chemists Placement Service (ACC, 1995 Broadway, Suite 1701; New York, NY 10023; phone: 212/874–0600) free, available only to members. You submit you resume which is kept on file for 12 to 18 months. When a job match is made for a position in cosmetics, pharmaceuticals, and lab technicians, your resume is given to the potential employer who is responsible for contacting you.

Directories

American Institute of Chemists Professional Directory (AIC, 7315 Wisconsin Ave., NW, Bethesda, MD 20814; phone: 301/652–2447) $50/nonmembers, free/members, issued each October.

Chemical Engineering Catalog (Penton Publishing, 1100 Superior Ave., Cleveland, OH 44114; phone: 216/696-7000) monthly; free to qualified professionals, call or write for application form; otherwise: write for price. This annual directory lists products and manufacturers and sales offices, and includes an equipment index and product directory. It's a good source to identify manufacturers in chemical engineering.

Directories of Chemical Producers—U.S.A. (SRI International, 333 Ravenswood Ave., Menlo Park, CA 94025–3493; phone: 415/859–4771) $1,300, issued each May. Provides extremely detailed information on chemical manufacturers and their products. Other volumes are for Canada ($560), East Asia ($1,560), and Western Europe ($1,720).

National Organization for Black Chemists and Chemical Engineers Directory (NBCCE, P.O. Box 5, Howard University, Washington, DC 20059; phone: 202/667–1699) free/members, issued each June.

Membership Directory (American Association of Textile Chemists and Colorists, P.O. Box 12215, Research Triangle Park, NC 27709; 919/549–8141) $53/nonmembers, $33/members, issued each July.

Formaldehyde Institute Directory (FI, 1330 Connecticut Ave., NW, Suite 300, Washington, DC 20036; phone: 202/659–0060) free/members, available only to members, annual.

Institute of Makers of Explosives Member Companies (IMA, 1120 19th St., NW, Suite 310, Washington, DC 20036; phone: 202/429–9280) free, updated frequently, four pages.

Salary surveys

Salaries (American Chemical Society, 1155 16th St., NW, Washington, DC 20036; phones: 800/227–5558, 202/872–4363) $170, annual. Results of salary survey of ACS members.

Chemists' & Chemical Engineers' Salaries (Abbott, Langer & Associates, 548 First St., Crete, IL 60417; phone: 708/672–4200) $170, annual. Based on a survey of over 39,000 chemists and chemical engineers, this study reports on salary by work function, experience, education, and geographic location.

Engineers

Also see the entries listed under "Chemicals," "Physics," "Plastics," and "Utilities" in this chapter, and those listed under "Construction" in the "Real estate and construction" chapter.

Job openings

ENR—Engineering News Record (McGraw–Hill, 1221 Avenue of the Americas, New York, NY 10020; phones: 800/257–9402, 212/512–3549) weekly; $51/annual subscription (U.S. and possessions),

$59/Canada, $128/Europe, $144/elsewhere. Jobs listed under "Positions Vacant." Typical issue prints 50 to 100 job ads plus "Positions wanted.".

Prism (American Society for Engineering Education, 11 DuPont Cr., Suite 200, Washington, DC 200036; phone: 202/293-7080) ten issues/year, $75/annual nonmember subscription, free/members. Around 75 vacancies in private industry and academia are published under "Classified."

Minority Engineer (Equal Opportunity Publications, 44 Broadway, Greenlawn, NY 11740; phone: 516/261-8899) quarterly, $17/annual subscription, free/minority engineering professionals and minority college students within two years of graduation (must complete detailed form). Around 40 vacancies for engineers are scattered throughout. Readers can submit their resumes to the magazine's free resume service which then forwards it to advertising employers the job seeker names—for free.

Graduating Engineer (16030 Ventura Blvd., Suite 560, Encino, CA 91436; phone: 818/789-5293) monthly, $5/copy. About 30 or so display ads for all disciplines of engineers are in the typical issue.

Equal Opportunity (Equal Opportunity Publications, 44 Broadway, Greenlawn, NY 11740; phone: 516/261-8899) three issues/year, $13/annual subscription, free to female engineering college graduates (or within two years of graduating) and women professional engineers. Over 25 display ads throughout this magazine feature positions in all areas of engineering. A readers can submit her resume to the magazine which then forwards it to advertising employers the job seeker names—for free.

Woman Engineer (Equal Opportunity Publications, 44 Broadway, Greenlawn, NY 11740; phone: 516/261-8899) quarterly, $17/annual subscription. Over 20 display ads throughout this magazine feature positions in all areas of engineering. A reader can submit her resume to the magazine which then forwards it to advertising employers the job seeker names—for free.

U.S. Woman Engineer (Society of Women Engineers, 345 E. 47th St., New York, NY 10017; phone: 212/705-7855) bimonthly, $20/nonmember annual subscription, free/members. Five to 25 ads for all types of engineers appear under "Classified/Recruitment Advertising."

Engineering Times (National Society of Professional Engineers, 1420 King St., Alexandria, VA 22314; phone: 703/684-2800) monthly, $30/nonmember annual subscription, $48/foreign, $10/member annual subscription. Jobs listed under "Engineering Times Career Mart." A typical issue carries about ten to 15 job ads.

Civil Engineering–ASCE (American Society of Civil Engineers, 345 E. 47th St., New York, NY 10017; phone: 212/705-7288 or 7276) monthly, $72/nonmember annual subscription, $101/foreign, included in membership package. Jobs listed under "Engineering Market Place." About 100 job ads in a typical issue.

ASCE News (American Society of Civil Engineers, 345 E. 47th St., New York, NY 10017; phone: 212/705-7288 or 7276) monthly, $33/nonmember annual subscription, $48/foreign, included in membership package. Jobs listed under "Engineering Market Place." About 100 job ads in a typical issue.

NSBE Magazine (National Society of Black Engineers, 344 Commerce St., Alexandria, VA 22314; phone: 703/549-2207) five issues/year; $10/nonmember annual subscription, included in membership package. From 35 to 75 engineering positions are advertised in every issue.

Mechanical Engineering (American Society of Mechanical Engineers, 345 E. 47th St., New York, NY 10017; phone: 212/705-7722) monthly, $45/nonmember annual subscription, $8/member annual subscription. Jobs listed under "Jobs Open." About 50 job ads appear in the average issue.

ASHRAE Journal (American Society of Heating, Refrigerating and Air Conditioning Engineers, 1792 Tullie Cr., NE, Atlanta, GA 30329; phone: 404/636-8400) monthly, $39/annual subscription (U.S.), $53/Canada, $107/elsewhere. Five pages of ads for about 60 vacancies are in the typical issue.

Telephony (Intertect Publishing, P.O. Box 12948, Overland Park, KS 66212; phone: 800/972-5858) weekly, $45/annual subscription (U.S.), $80/foreign. Around 50 vacancies for engineers and OSP personnel are published in the "Classified Ads."

Nuclear News (American Nuclear Society, 555 N. Kensington Ave., La Grange Park, IL 60525; phone: 708/352-6611) 15 issues/year, $180/annual subscription (U.S.), $180/Canada, $226/elsewhere)

"Employment" runs about 60 job vacancy announcements for nuclear engineers, quality assurance engineers, and mechanical engineers.

InTech (Instrument Society of America, 67 Alexander Dr., Research Triangle Park, NC 27709; phone: 800/334–6391) monthly, free, available only to members. "Special Classifieds" include 20 to 30 job ads for engineers.

Microwaves and RF (Penton Publications, 1100 Superior Ave., Cleveland, OH 44114; phone: 216/696–7000) 13 issues/year, $55/annual subscription, free to qualified professionals. Three to ten display ads for engineers, primarily in microwave technology and instrumentation (some management) appear throughout.

Control Engineering (Cahners Publishing Company, 1350 E. Touhy Ave., Des Plaines, IL 60018; phone: 708/635–8800) monthly, $74.95/annual subscription (U.S.), $117.65/Canada, $134.95/elsewhere. Four to ten ads for process automation engineers and chemical and electrical engineers are under "Classified."

Plant Engineering (Cahners Publishing Company, 44 Cook St., Denver, CO 80206; phone: 303/388–4511) semimonthly, $64.95/annual subscription (U.S.), $96.25/Canada, $184.95/elsewhere. About ten vacancies including manufacturing plant engineers, plant services managers, and chemical engineers, are advertised under "Classified."

Career Net Job Bulletin (American Institute of Plant Engineers, 3975 Erie Ave., Cincinnati, OH 45208; phone: 513/561–6000) monthly, $35/three-month nonmember subscription, free/members. Many vacancies for plant and facilities engineers, power plant managers, and manufacturing supervisors are advertised in the typical issue.

AIPE Facilities (American Institute of Plant Engineers, 3975 Erie Ave., Cincinnati, OH 45208; phone: 513/561–6000) bimonthly, $34/annual nonmember subscription, $19/members. Two to five ads for power plant managers, facilities engineers, and manufacturing supervisors are described under "Professional Opportunities."

Machine Design (Penton Publishing, 1100 Superior Ave., Cleveland, OH 44114; phone: 216/696-7000) bimonthly, $100/annual subscription (U.S.), $140/Canada, $160/elsewhere. Ten to 15 job openings for mechanical, electric, rubber, and materials engineers, plant supervisors, and managers are described under "Design Engineer Search."

American Machinist (Penton Publishing, 1100 Superior Ave., Cleveland, OH 44114; phone: 216/696-7000) monthly; free to qualified professionals, call or write for application form; otherwise: $65/annual subscription (U.S.), $80/Canada, $100/elsewhere. "Marketplace—Employment Opportunities" sports five ads for design engineers, machinists, and production foreman.

Manufacturing Engineer (Society of Manufacturing Engineers, P.O. Box 930, Dearborn, MI 48121; phone: 313/271–1500) monthly, $60/annual nonmember subscription, free/members. Ten to 20 job ads for manufacturing engineers appear under "Opportunities."

Manufacturing Engineering (Society of Manufacturing Engineers, P.O. Box 930, Dearborn, MI 48121; phone: 313/271–1500) monthly, free/members only. Over 40 job vacancies for manufacturing and design engineers appear under "Opportunities." Includes "Position Wanted" ads.

Welding Design & Fabrication (Penton Publishing, 1100 Superior Ave., Cleveland, OH 44070; phone: 216/696–7000) monthly, $45/annual subscription (U.S.), $65/Canada, $80/elsewhere. Five positions for welding designers and engineers, plant, production, maintenance, and operating managers show up under "Employment Opportunities."

Welding Journal (American Welding Society, 550 NW Le Jeune Rd., Miami, FL 33126; phones: 800/443-9353, 305/443-9353) monthly, $60/annual nonmember subscription (U.S.), $90/foreign, $46/members. About three ads for welding engineers or inspectors and manufacturers' representatives are under "Classified—Employment Opportunities."

Welding Distributor (Penton Publishing, P.O. Box 95759, Cleveland, OH 44114; phone: 216/696–7000) bimonthly, $30/annual subscription (U.S.), $40/Canada, $50/elsewhere. Under "Opportunities" you'll find ads for around ten sales and store manager positions in the industrial gas and welding supply industry.

"I had this design down pat until he came over and
explained how he thought it should be."

Industrial Engineering (Institute of Industrial Engineers, 25 Technology Park, Atlanta, GA 30092; phone: 404/449–0460) monthly, $48/annual nonmember subscription, free/members. Ten to 20 positions for industrial engineers are advertised in the typical issue.

Machine Design (Penton Publishing, 1100 Superior Ave., Cleveland, OH 44114; phone: 216/696-7000) monthly; free to qualified professionals, call or write for application form; otherwise: $75/annual subscription (U.S.), $100/Canada, $140/elsewhere. Five ads for design and manufacturing engineers as well as management positions grace the "Design Engineer Search" pages.

Design News (Cahners Publishing, 44 Cook St., Denver, CO 80206; phone: 800/323–4958) 25 issues/year, $89.95/annual subscription (U.S.), $110/Canada, $140/elsewhere. Fifteen to 20 vacancies for design, and other, engineers are advertised in "Engineering Job Mart."

Non–Wovens Industry (Rodman Publishing, P.O. Box 555, Ramsey, NJ 07446; phone: 201/825–2552) monthly, $48/annual subscription (U.S.), $52/Canada, $64/elsewhere. Seven to 15 positions in technical engineering, production, and management are advertised under "Classified."

Ceramic Industry (95900 Harper Rd., Suite 109, Solon, OH 44139-1835; phone: 216/498-9214) monthly, $50/annual subscription (U.S.), $65/Mexico and Canada, $120/elsewhere (air mail). "Positions Available" carries ads for three or five ceramic and materials engineers, production management, plant managers, foremen, and supervisors.

Ceramic Bulletin (American Ceramic Society, 757 Brooksedge Plaza Dr., Westerville, OH 43081; phone: 614/890-4700) monthly, $25/annual nonmember subscription, free/members. "Classified— Help Wanted" runs 15 to 20 ads for ceramic engineers, materials scientists and engineers, sales, and laboratory personnel.

ASME News (American Society of Mechanical Engineers, 345 E. 57th St., New York, NY 10017; phone: 212/705-7782) monthly, free, available only to members. Around two positions for mechanical engineers appear in "Opportunities."

Consulting-Specifying Engineer (Cahners Publishing, 44 Cook St., Denver, CO 80206-5800; phone: 303/388-4511) 15 issues/year, $69.95/annual subscription, $80/Canada and Mexico, $100/elsewhere (surface mail), $150/elsewhere (air mail). Jobs listed under "Job Opportunities." Typical issue includes about eight job ads for mechanical, civil, and project engineers.

Automotive Engineering Magazine (SAE International: The Engineering Society for Advancing Mobility Land Sea Air and Space, 400 Commonwealth Dr., Warrendale, PA 15096; phone: 412/776-4841) monthly, contact for subscription rates. About ten vacancies primarily for engineers in all aspects of the mobility field are advertised in the typical issue.

SAE UPdate (SAE International: The Engineering Society for Advancing Mobility Land Sea Air and Space, 400 Commonwealth Dr., Warrendale, PA 15096; phone: 412/776-4841) monthly, free/members only. About ten ads primarily for engineers in all aspects of the mobility field appear under "Engineering Career Resources."

Cost Engineering (American Association of Cost Engineers, P.O. Box 1557, Morgantown, WV 26507-1557; phone: 304/296-8444) monthly, $42/nonmember annual subscription, free/members. Scattered throughout are four to eight ads for cost engineers, control managers, and cost estimators and controllers.

Packaging Magazine (Cahners Publishing, P.O. Box 5594, Denver, CO 80217; phone: 800/323–4958) monthly, $84.95 (U.S.), $114.95/Canada, $149.95/elsewhere, free to qualified professionals in the packaging industry. "Recruitment/Classified Advertising" carries ads for a dozen job vacancies for packaging engineers and designers, package development engineers, and project engineers.

Journal of the Air Pollution Control Association (P.O. Box 2861, Pittsburgh, PA 15230; phone: 412/232–3444) monthly; annual subscription: $88/non–profit libraries and institutions, $150/others, add $10/Europe, add $15/Asia. Jobs listed under "Classified."

The Diplomate (American Academy of Environmental Engineers, Suite 100, 130 Holiday Ct., Annapolis, MD 21401; phone: 301/266–3311) quarterly, $20/annual subscription (U.S. and Canada), $30/elsewhere. Typical issue features two to four display ads for jobs.

Electronics (Penton Publishing, 1100 Superior Ave., Cleveland, OH 44114; phone: 216/696-7000) monthly; free to qualified professionals, call or write for application form; otherwise: $60/annual subscription (U.S.), $70/Canada, $125/elsewhere. About six job ads appear in "Marketplace—Employment Opportunities" for research and development engineers and for quality assurance engineers.

National Engineer (National Association of Power Engineers, 2350 E. Devon Ave., Suite 115, Des Plaines, IL 60018; phone: 708/298-0600) monthly, $18/annual nonmember subscription, free/members. Only one or two ads for mechanical, heating, maintenance, or architectural engineers are in the "Classifieds."

See also Airport Report described in the "Transportation" chapter.

Job services

Professional Engineering Employment Registry (Career Technologies Corp., Suite 6, 44 Nashua Rd., Londonderry, NH 03053; phone: 603/437-7337) free service/members of American Society of Civil Engineers (345 E. 47th St., New York, NY 10017; phone: 202/705-7288 or 7276). ASCE members submit their resume (in their own format) to PEER which places it in its computer database which potential employers access via modem to identify job candidates to interview. Resumes are viewed without the job candidate's name, address, and phone, and are coded to prevent a current employer from ever seeing any portion of a current employee's resume. PEER never discloses a job candidate's identity. PEER contacts the job candidates whom employers wish to interview. Job candidates then can contact the employer directly.

CU Career Connection (University of Colorado, Campus Box 133, Boulder, CO 80309-0133; phone: 303/492-4127) $20/two-month fee entitles you to a "passcode" which unlocks this job hotline. You need a touch-tone phone to call and request the engineering jobs and the geographic area for which you want to hear job openings. The hotline is turned off Monday through Friday, 2 to 4 p.m. for daily updating. This service includes a large number of engineering and other science vacancies.

SOLE Electronic Job Referral Service (Society of Logistics Engineers, 8100 Professional Pl., Suite 211, New Carrollton, MD 20785; phones: 800/695-7653, 301/459-8446) free. Armed with a modem and communications software, use your computer to call 800/331-3808 (settings: 1200/2400 Baud, 8-N-1) and you'll be connected to a national bulletin board. If you run into difficulty, call Dick Spinner at 301/584-3697 or SYSOP at 800/331-6026. A free printout of the job listings is available from Sam Hahn (9720 Redd Rambler Dr., Philadelphia, PA 19115; phone: 215/464-4442).

Design News Data Bank (Placement Services, Ltd., 265 S. Main St., Akron, OH 44308; phone: 216/762-0279) free. Obtain the service's form in an issue of *Design News* discussed above under "Job openings" or send in your resume. When matched with a specific job, the employer will contact you for an interview. Resumes are kept on file for 12 months.

American Association of Cost Engineers Resume Service (AAAC, P.O. Box 1557, Morgantown, WV 26507-1557; phone: 304/296-8444) free/members only. A members submits his resume which is kept on file indefinitely. When a match is made, the resume is given to the potential employer who is responsible for contacting the job candidate.

Employment Marketplace (Optical Society of America, 2010 Massachusetts Ave., NW, Washington, DC 20036; phones: 800/582-0416, 202/223-8130) free/members only. Members complete this service's forms. A summary of each resume is given a code number (and the candidate's name removed) and is sent to employers who may then request the full resume.

WIRE: Welding Industry Referral for Employment (American Welding Society, 550 NY Le Jeune Rd., Miami, FL 33126; phones: 800/443-9353, ext. 281, 305/443-9353, ext. 281) $65/six-month nonmember fee, $10/members. Complete the detailed application form which can be found in AWS's *Welding Journal*, described above under "Job openings." You have the option to keep your name from being submitted to particular companies. When a match is made, your resume is sent to the employer who is responsible for contacting you. Types of jobs include welder/operator, research and development, inspector/tester, supervisor/foreman, technician, engineering, sales and marketing, and education.

Placement Exchange (SPIE, P.O. Box 10, Bellingham, WA 98227-0010; phone: 206/676-3290) free. Submit your resume to be put in resume books available to employers at SPIE's symposia. Resumes are kept in the books for two symposia (about four months). Jobs are in optics, optoelectronics, lasers, holography, research and development, and related fields.

Resume Referral Service (Instrument Society of America, 67 Alexander Dr., Research Triangle Park, NC 27709; phone: 800/334-6391) free, available only to members. The resume service form you complete is kept on file for three months. When a match is achieved, you are contacted. Positions included are engineers, technicians, and salespeople.

Placement Service (American Nuclear Society, 555 N. Kensington Ave., La Grange Park, IL 60525; phone: 708/352-6611) $35/nonmembers, $25/members. Fill out this service's form and your resume will be on file for six months. When a match is made, this service contacts you to see if you are interested in interviewing for the job and you are responsible for contacting the potential employer.

Informal Resume Service (Society for the Advancement of Material and Process Engineering, 1161 Parkview Dr., Covina, CA 91724; phone: 818/331-0616) free, members only. This is a very informal service where a member submits her resume and the staff will send it to an employer who informally asks them for prospects. The employer is responsible for contacting the job seeker.

Clearing Service (American Society of Design Engineers, c/o James Rogers, P.O. Box 931, Arlington Heights, IL 60006; phone: 708/259-7120) free, available only to members, $100/annual dues. This is an informal service that provides job counseling and job search assistance to fired or laid off design engineers.

Directories

Who's Who in Engineering (American Association of Engineering Societies, 1111 19th St., NW, Suite 608, Washington, DC 20036-5703; phones: 800/658-8897, 202/296-2237) $200/nonmembers, $120/members. 900+ pages. Lists more than 14,000 engineers. Most recently published in September 1991.

Directory of Engineering Societies and Related Organizations (American Association of Engineering Societies, 1111 19th St., NW, Suite 608, Washington, DC 20036-5703; phones: 800/658-8897, 202/296-2237) $150/nonmembers, $90/members. 263 pages. Provides information on 350 organizations in the U.S. and 350 overseas. Last published in 1989.

Directory of Engineering Societies and Related Organizations, 1990-1991 Supplement (American Association of Engineering Societies, 1111 19th St., NW, Suite 608, Washington, DC 20036-5703; phones: 800/658-8897, 202/296-2237) $85/nonmembers, $48/members. Adds another 350 organizations to the 1989 edition which is described immediately above. If purchasing both the 1989 edition and the supplement, the total cost is $200/nonmembers, $125/members.

ASCE Membership Directory (American Society of Civil Engineers, 345 E. 47th St., New York, NY 10017; phone: 212/705-7288 or 7276) $100/nonmembers, $25/members.

SOLE Membership Directory and Handbook (Society of Logistics Engineers, 8100 Professional Pl., Suite 211, New Carrollton, MD 20785; phones: 800/695-7653, 301/459-8446) free, printed each April.

The Biotechnology Directory (Stockton Press, 15 E. 26th St., New York, NY 10160-0077; phones: 800/221-2123 (outside New York state), 212/481-1334) $195 plus $3 shipping. Includes the often hard-to-find government departments engaged in biotechnology as well as over 8,800 companies, research centers, and academic institutions involved in the field. The most recent edition was released in 1991.

National Association of Power Engineers Membership Directory (NAPE, 2350 E. Devon Ave., Suite 115, Des Plaines, IL 60018; phone: 708/298-0600) available only to members. Last edition issued in 1989; new edition expected in 1992.

American Consulting Engineers Council Directory (ACEC, 1015 15th St., NW, Washington, DC 20005; phone: 202/347-7474) $140/nonmembers, $20/members, annual. Describes over 5,000 member firms by state.

Directory of Women and Minority-Owned Consulting Engineering Firms (American Consulting Engineers Council, 1015 15th St., NW, Washington, DC 20005; phone: 202/347-7474) $15, last published in 1991.

International Engineering Directory (American Consulting Engineers Council, 1015 15th St., NW, Washington, DC 20005; phone: 202/347-7474) $50/nonmembers, $25/members, last issued in 1989. Describes activities of international engineering consulting firms.

Holography Directory and Resource Guide (SPIE, P.O. Box 10, Bellingham, WA 98227-0010; phone: 206/676-3290) contact for cost, annual. Includes companies and individuals who work in optics and holography.

Salary surveys

Professional Income of Engineers (American Association of Engineering Societies, 1111 19th St., NW, Suite 608, Washington, DC 20036-5703; phones: 800/658-8897, 202/296-2237) $97/nonmembers, $59.50/members, published annually in July, 130+ pages. Includes data for federal, state, and local government engineers as well as broad industry groups.

Engineers' Salaries: Special Industry Report (American Association of Engineering Societies, 1111 19th St., NW, Suite 608, Washington, DC 20036-5703; phones: 800/658-8897, 202/296-2237) $287.50/nonmembers, $169/members, published each July, 230 pages. Extremely detailed breakdown of engineering salaries according to industry type and geographic location, company size, years of experience, highest degree held, and supervisory status.

Compensation of Professional Engineers (Abbott, Langer & Associates, 548 First St., Crete, IL 60417; phone: 708/672-4200) $100, annual. Based on data from 12,400 members of the National Society of Professional Engineers, this study covers every major branch of engineering.

American Association of Cost Engineers Salary Survey (AAAC, P.O. Box 1557, Morgantown, WV 26507-1557; phone: 304/296-8444) appears in the September or October issue of *Cost Engineering*, described above under "Job openings."

National Association of Minority Engineering Program Administrators Membership Directory (NAMEPA, 500 N. Michigan Ave., Suite 1400, Chicago, IL 60611) free, available only to members, published each January.

Annual Salary Survey by Engineering Manpower Consortium (American Society of Mechanical Engineers, 345 E. 57th St., New York, NY 10017; phone: 212/705-7782) free, available only to members, printed each July.

Design News Salary Survey (Cahners Publishing, 44 Cook St., Denver, CO 80206; phone: 800/323-4958) $10/single issue. The mid-December issue tends to carry the results of the magazine's annual employment survey that identifies the top 100 firms that employ design engineers and recites, in some detail, for each company the job outlook, entry salary levels, five+ year salary, specialties in demand, major benefits, and number of engineers. Also included is the name and address of the personnel official to contact about possible employment.

Compensation of Industrial Engineers (Abbott, Langer & Associates, 548 First St., Crete, IL 60417; phone: 708/672-4200) $130, annual. Sponsored by the Institute of Industrial Engineers, this study reports on salaries of over 6,200 individuals involved in industrial engineering.

Profile of Plant Engineers in *AIPE Facilities* (American Institute of Plant Engineers, 3975 Erie Ave., Cincinnati, OH 45208; phone: 513/561-6000) bimonthly, $34/annual nonmember subscription, $19/members, most recent survey published in January/February 1991 issue. Every few years AIPE conducts a random sample salary and benefits survey of its members and nonmembers and publishes the results in *AIPE Facilities*. Another survey was conducted in 1991 for publication in 1992.

Geology, materials, and metallurgy

Also see the job sources described under "Utilities" later in this chpater.

Job openings

Modern Casting (American Foundrymen's Society, 505 State St., Des Plaines, IL 60616; phone: 708/824-0181) monthly, $35/annual subscription (U.S., Mexico, Canada), $45/elsewhere. Over 60 positions are advertised in "Classified Advertising" under "Help Wanted," "Reps Wanted," and "Employment." Positions include all aspects of the metals industry including metallurgists, foundry maintenance, engineers, plant management, sales and manufacturers' representatives, and anything else related to the industry.

Pit & Quarry (Edgell Communications, 1 E. First St., Duluth, MN 55802; phones: 800/346-0085, 218/723-9870) monthly, $35/annual subscription (U.S.), $70/Canada, $110/elsewhere. Over 30 positions for managers, engineers, and sales personnel in mining, quarrying, and processing of non-metallic minerals appear under "Wanted."

Rock Products (Maclean Hunter, 29 N. Wacker Dr., Chicago, IL 60606; phones: 312/726-2802) monthly, $50/annual subscription (U.S. and Canada), $87.50/elsewhere. "Classified advertising—Employment Opportunities" has about 25 job openings for engineers, sand and gravel operations, quarry foremen, sales, maintenance, and plant management.

Mining Engineering Magazine (Society for Mining, Metallurgy, and Exploration, P.O. Box 625002, Littleton, CO 80162–5002; phone: 303/973–9550) $60/annual nonmember subscription (U.S., Canada), $67/elsewhere, free/members. Under "Employment Service" and "Classifieds" you'll find about half a dozen openings for mining engineers, metallurgy, and related positions plus a dozen "Positions Wanted."

GSA Today (Geological Society of America, P.O. Box 9140, Boulder, CO 80301; phones: 800/472–1988, 303/447–2020) monthly, $30/annual nonmember subscription, free/members. Four or five openings in the earth sciences appear under "Classifieds—Positions Open."

Coal (Maclean Hunter, 29 N. Wacker Dr., Chicago, IL 60606; phones: 312/726-2802) monthly, $62.50/annual subscription (U.S. and Canada), $100/elsewhere. "Coal Classified Advertising—Employment Opportunities" features about six positions in all aspects of the industry.

Engineering and Mining Journal (Maclean Hunter, 29 N. Wacker Dr., Chicago, IL 60606; phones: 312/726-2802) monthly, $50/annual subscription (U.S. and Canada), $75/elsewhere. "Classified Advertising—Employment Opportunities" includes about 15 positions in all aspects of the industry.

Skillings' Mining Review (130 W. Superior, Suite 728, Duluth, MN 55802; phone: 218/722–2310) weekly, $30/annual subscription (U.S.), $50/foreign. One to three display ads for geologists, mechanical and other engineers, and other mining industry positions are in the typical issue.

Dimensional Stone (20335 Ventura Blvd., Suite 400, Woodland Hills, CA 91364; phone: 818/704–5555) monthly, $40/annual subscription (U.S.), $50/foreign. Under "Classified Ads" you'll find two or three ads for jobs at stone quarries and for sales representatives for marble or stone companies.

Advanced Materials and Processes (ASM International, 9639 Kinsman, Materials Park, OH 44073–0002; phone: 216/338–5151) monthly, $103/annual subscription (U.S.), $128/foreign. From six to 20 ads for metallurgists and materials engineers are under "Classified."

Modern Materials Handling (Cahners Publishing, 44 Cook St., Denver, CO 80206; phone: 303/388–4511) 14 issues/year, $65/annual subscription (U.S.), $75/Mexico and Canada, $85/elsewhere. "Classified" features about eight job vacancies for systems and sales engineers, material handling engineers, and management.

Materials Performance (National Association of Corrosion Engineers, P.O. Box 218340, Houston, TX 77218; phone: 713/492–0535) monthly, $50/annual nonmember subscription (U.S.), $65/foreign, free/members. Ten openings for corrosion engineers, metallurgists, and sales are in the "Classifieds."

M.R.S. Bulletin (Material Research Society, 9800 McKnight Rd., Pittsburgh, PA 15237; phone: 412/367–3003) monthly, $95/annual nonmember subscription, free/members. About ten positions for post–doctoral research are in the "Classified" section.

33Metalproducing (Penton Publishing, 1100 Superior Ave., Cleveland, OH 44114; phone: 216/696-7000) monthly; free to qualified professionals, call or write for application form; otherwise: $50/annual subscription (U.S.), $65/Canada, $80/elsewhere. About two ads for metallurgists and engineers appear under "Classified—Employment Opportunities."

JOM (Minerals, Metals, and Materials Society, 420 Commonwealth Dr., Warrendale, PA 15086; phone: 412/776–9080) monthly, $50/annual nonmember subscription, free/members. Ten to 20 job vacancies in metallurgy and materials science appear under "Classified." Also lists "Positions Wanted."

Materials Engineering (Penton Publishing, 1100 Superior Ave., Cleveland, OH 44114; phone: 216/696-7000) monthly; free to qualified professionals, call or write for application form; otherwise: $45/annual subscription (U.S.), $65/Canada, $80/elsewhere. Only a handful of job ads appear under "Classifieds—Employment Opportunities."

Career Watch Bulletin (Society for the Advancement of Material and Process Engineering, 1161 Parkview Dr., Covina, CA 91724; phone: 818/331-0616) usually bimonthly, but a bit irregular, free, available only to members. The editors collect job ads for material and process engineers from other publications and reassemble them as want ads here.

ASM News (ASM International, 9639 Kinsman, Materials Park, OH 44073-0002; phone: 216/338-5151) monthly, free/members only. You'll find about five job ads for metallurgists and materials engineers under "Classified."

Wire Journal International (Wire Association International, 1570 Boston Post, Guildford, CT 06749; phone: 203/453-2777) monthly, $60/annual nonmember subscription, free/members. A look at "Career Opportunities" and "Classifieds" will yield five to ten ads for metallurgical engineers, sales and account representatives, production, and management plus a section for "Positions Wanted."

Wire Technology International (3869 Darrow Rd., Suite 101, Stowe, OH 44224; phone: 216/686-9544) bimonthly, $30/annual subscription (U.S.), $40/foreign, free to qualified people in the wire industry. About three jobs in the industry make it into "Classified."

Job services

Employment Matching Service (Geological Society of America, P.O. Box 9140, Boulder, CO 80301; phones: 800/472-1988, 303/447-2020) $60/annual nonmember fee, $30/members. Registrants complete a form and include a two-page resume. Employers receive printouts of these forms throughout the year and are responsible for contacting applicants directly.

Directories

GSA Membership Directory (Geological Society of America, P.O. Box 9140, Boulder, CO 80301; phones: 800/472-1988, 303/447-2020) available only to members, $35, issued each May.

American Coal Ash Association Membership Directory (ACAA, 1000 16th St., NW, Suite 507, Washington, DC 20036; phone: 202/659-2303) free/members only, published irregularly.

Salary survey

Compensation & Benefits in Engineering Firms in the Geotechnical Field (Abbott, Langer & Associates, 548 First St., Crete, IL 60417; phone: 708/672-4200) $300, annual, 238 pages. Covers numerous managerial, engineering, scientific, and "sub-professional" jobs in consulting engineering firms that practice in the geosciences.

Mathematics

Job openings

AMSTAT News (American Statistical Association, 1429 Duke St., Alexandria, VA 22314-3402; phone: 703/684-1221) monthly, available only to members. The number of job ads for statisticians, biostatisticians, and educators that are printed in "Professional Opportunities" typically varies between 30 and 100.

SIAM News (Society for Industrial and Applied Mathematics, 3600 University City Science Center, Philadelphia, PA 19104-2688; phone: 215/382-9800) bimonthly, $18/annual nonmember subscription, free/members. Fifty to 60 job ads for mathematics and engineering professionals appear under "Professional Opportunities."

Employment Information of the American Mathematical Society (AMS, 201 Charles St., Providence, RI 02904; phones: 800/321-4267, 401/455-4000) bimonthly, $146/annual subscription. Dozens upon dozens of job vacancies for mathematics-related positions in industry, research, and universities fill this newsletter.

Directories

Directory of Members (American Statistical Association, 1429 Duke St., Alexandria, VA 22314-3402; phone: 703/684-1221) $125/nonmembers, free/members, published in May of 1991 and every three years thereafter. Includes members of the ASA, Biometric Society (Eastern and Western North American Regions), Institute of Mathematical Statistics, and Statistical Society of Canada.

Physics

Also see the entries under "Engineers" earlier in this chapter.

Job openings

Physics Today (American Institute of Physics, MASS Division, 500 Sunnyside Blvd., Woodbury, NY 11797; phone: 212/661-9404) monthly, $95/annual nonmember subscription (U.S.), $110/Canada and Mexico, free/members. Around 70 job openings for physicists appear under "Information Exchange."

Job services

Teratology Society Placement Service (Teratology Society, c/o Dr. Stanley Kaplan, Anatomy and Cellular Biology, Medical College of Wisconsin, 8701 Watertown Plank Rd., Milwaukee, WI 53226; phone: 414/257-8473) $10/annual fee. Complete the service's resume form. This service sends your form to all registered employers. It is kept on file for a year or until you find a new job, whichever comes first. Positions are for physicians and scientists who do clinical work or research on birth defects.

Directories

Listing of Members (American Physical Society, Publication Billing Dept., 225 Executive Dr., Plainview, NY 11803; phone: 516/399-5810) contact for nonmember price, free/members. This is an issue of the *Bulletin of the American Physical Society*. This directory of member physicists is published in December of odd-numbered years.

Salary survey

Salary Report (American Institute of Physics, Education and Employment Division, 335 E. 45th St., New York, NY 10017; phone: 212/661-9404) free; most recent survey published in 1990.

Plastics and rubber

Job openings

Plastics World (Cahners Publishing, 44 Cook St., Denver, CO 80206; phone: 303/388–4511) 13 issues/year, $75/annual subscription (U.S.), $118/Canada, $130/elsewhere, free to qualified professionals. Twenty to 30 jobs in plastics engineering appear under "Positions Available."

Modern Plastics (McGraw–Hill, P.O. Box 602, Hightstown, NJ 08520; phone: 800/257-9402) monthly, $41.75/annual subscription (U.S.), $53/Canada. "Employment Opportunities" features ten to 15 job ads for design engineers, plant managers, technical positions, and sales representatives.

Rubber & Plastics News (Crain Communications, 965 E. Jefferson Ave., Detroit, MI 48207–3185; phone: 800/678-9595) 27 issues/year, $48/annual subscription (U.S.), $54/foreign. Fifteen job openings for tool design engineers, rubber chemists, plant managers, and sales—all primarily in tire manufacturing—appear under "Rubber & Plastics News' Classifieds–Help Wanted."

Plastics Engineering (14 Fairfield Dr., Brookfield Center, CT 06804–0403; phone: 203/775–0471) monthly, $40/annual subscription (U.S., Mexico, Canada), $55/elsewhere. About ten to 15 positions for plastics engineers appear in the "Classifieds." Also includes extensive set of "Position Wanted" ads.

Plastics News (Crain Communications, 965 E. Jefferson Ave., Detroit, MI 48207–3185; phone: 800/678-9595) weekly, $25/annual subscription (U.S.), $84/foreign. Six to ten positions for engineers, production managers, and sales agents are under "Plastics News Classifieds."

Job services

Rubber, Plastics & Chemical Opportunities (R.P.C. Search, Inc., 3250 W. Market St., Suite 100, Akron, OH 44333; phone: 216/867-1199) free. Submit your resume and employers will contact you directly when a match is made. Serves chemists, engineers, managers, quality control, and research and development positions.

Utilities and energy

Also see the entries listed under "Engineers" in this chapter.

Job openings

Power (McGraw-Hill, P.O. Box 524, Hightstown, NJ 08520; phones: 800/257-9402, 609/426-7070) monthly, $20/annual subscription (U.S.), $23/Canada, $90/elsewhere, free to qualified executives and engineering and supervisory personnel in electric utilities, process utilities, and other manufacturing industries in the U.S. and U.S. possessions. Around 30 jobs, mostly for power plant and electric utility engineers, are advertised under "Employment Opportunities."

EL&P—Electric Light and Power (PennWell Publishing, 1421 S. Sheridan Rd., Tulsa, OK 74112; phone: 918/835-3161) monthly, $42/annual subscription (U.S.), $73/foreign. Ten to 20 jobs for engineers in the power industry are advertised in the "Utility Mart."

Electrical World (McGraw-Hill, P.O. Box 524, Hightstown, NJ 08520; phones: 800/257-9402, 609/426-7070) monthly, $20/annual subscription (U.S.), $23/Canada, $90/elsewhere, free to qualified executives, engineering, and supervisory personnel in electric utilities (U.S. only). Around a dozen positions for electrical and civil engineers, journeymen–lineworkers, administrators, and plant managers are posted under "Employment Opportunities."

Rural Electrification (National Rural Electric Cooperative Association, 1800 Massachusetts Ave., NW, Washington, DC 20036; phone: 202/797-5441) monthly, $18/annual subscription. Fifteen to 20 job vacancies for general managers, marketing, engineers, and management are listed in "Classified/Help Wanted."

Solar Today (American Solar Energy Society, 2400 Central Ave., Suite B-1, Boulder, CO 80301; phone: 303/443-3130) bimonthly, $25/annual subscription (U.S.), $32/foreign. About two job ads appear in the "Classified Ads."

Public Utilities Fortnightly (Public Utilities Reports, Inc., Suite 200, 2111 Wilson Rd., Arlington, VA 22201; phone: 703/243-7000) biweekly; $92/annual subscription. Few job ads.

Public Power (American Public Power Association, 2301 M. St., NW, Washington, DC 20037; phone: 202/467-2970) bimonthly, $35/nonmember annual subscription, included in dues. Four to 12 jobs are advertised under "Classified."

Journal of Petroleum Marketing (Petroleum Marketers Association of America, 1120 Vermont Ave., NW, Washington, DC 20005; phone: 202//331-1198) monthly, free to qualified professionals. A few ads in utilities management appear under "Help Wanted."

Journal of Petroleum Technology (Society of Petroleum Engineers, P.O. Box 833836, Richardson, TX 75083-3836; phone: 214/669-3377) monthly, $30/annual nonmember subscription, $15/members. A number of government positions are among the 35 jobs for petroleum engineers, drilling engineers, and oil field production engineers listed under "Positions Open." Also lists "Positions Wanted."

AEE Energy Insight (Association of Energy Engineers, 4025 Pleasantdale Rd., Suite 420, Atlanta, GA 30340; phone: 404/447-5083) quarterly, available only to members, included in dues. Two or three ads for energy engineers appear under "AEE Referral Service."

APGA Newsletter (American Public Gas Association, P.O. Box 11094D, Vienna, VA 22183; phone: 703/352-3890) biweekly, available only to members, included in dues. Jobs listed under "Position Available." Few job ads; job ads not in every issue.

LP/Gas (Edgell Communications, 1 E. First St., Duluth, MN 55802; phone: 800/346-0085) monthly, $15/annual subscription. Six ads for management, operations, sales, and drivers in the liquid propane gas industry appear under "Classified."

Oil and Gas Journal (Pennwell Publishing, 1421 S. Sheridan Rd., Tulsa, OK 74112; phones: 800/331-4463, 918/835-3161) weekly, $52/annual subscription to qualified industry members, $98/others. Over 30 positions for engineers, project managers, and other pipeline personnel in all aspects of the pipeline, oil, gas, and refining industry appear in "Classified."

American Gas (American Gas Association, 1515 Wilson Blvd., Arlington, VA 22209; phone: 703/841–86860 monthly, $39/annual subscription (U.S., Canada) $70/elsewhere. "Employment Service" lists 20 to 25 positions in the natural gas industry.

Energy User News (Chilton Company, 1 Chilton Way, Radnor, PA 19087; phones: 800/247–8080, 215/964–4145) monthly, $69.50/annual subscription. Energy engineers, HCAC department managers, operations managers, designers, and technicians can find about ten job vacancies under "Help Wanted."

Journal of American Oil Chemists (American Oil Chemists Society, P.O. Box 3489, Champaign, IL 61826; phone: 217/359–2344) monthly, available only to members, $85/annual dues. About seven positions in a wide range of environmental maintenance are under "Classified Advertising."

Pipeline & Gas Journal (Edgell Communications, 1 E. First St., Duluth, MN 55802; 218/723–9477) monthly, $15/annual subscription to professionals in the gas field, $75/annual subscription for others. About five or six job ads for engineers, pipeline contractors, and sales and marketing representatives appear in the "Classifieds."

Gas Industries (Gas Industries and Appliance News, Inc., P.O. Box 558, Park Ridge, IL 60068; phone: 312/693-3682) monthly, $20/annual subscription (U.S., Mexico, Canada), $90/elsewhere. One or two openings for pipeline jobs like drillers and measuring engineers are in "Classified."

Petroleum Engineer International (Energy Publications, P.O. Box 1589, Dallas, TX 75221-1589; phone: 214/691-3911) monthly, $42/annual subscription to qualified members of the industry, $75/others. Two or three positions for petroleum engineers and management in all aspects of the oil industry are under "Classified."

World Oil (Gulf Publishing, P.O. Box 2608, Houston, TX 77353; phones: 800/231-6275, 713/529-4301) monthly, $24/annual subscription, free to qualified management. Three or four ads for all types of positions in the petroleum industry appear under "Classified."

Pipeline Industry (Gulf Publishing, P.O. Box 2608, Houston, TX 77353; phones: 800/231-6275, 713/529-4301) monthly, $20/annual subscription, free to qualified management. Three or four ads for all types of positions in the petroleum industry appear under "Classified."

Hydrocarbon Processing (Gulf Publishing, P.O. Box 2608, Houston, TX 77353; phones: 800/231-6275, 713/529-4301) monthly, $20/annual subscription, free to qualified management. Three or four ads for all types of positions in the petroleum industry appear under "Classified."

Ocean World (Gulf Publishing, P.O. Box 2608, Houston, TX 77353; phones: 800/231-6275, 713/529-4301) monthly, $20/annual subscription, free to qualified management. Three or four ads for all types of positions in the petroleum industry appear under "Classified."

Petroleum Engineer International Month (Hearst Publications, P.O. Box 1917, Denver, CO 80201; phone: 800/832–1917) monthly, $42/annual subscription (U.S.), $55/Canada, $60/elsewhere. "Help Wanted" and "Business Opportunities" list a few positions different positions in the oil industry.

Western Oil World (Hearst Publications, P.O. Box 1917, Denver, CO 80201; phone: 800/832–1917) monthly, $36/annual subscription. "Help Wanted" and "Business Opportunities" list a few different positions in the oil industry.

MidContinental Oil World (Hearst Publications, P.O. Box 1917, Denver, CO 80201; phone: 800/832–1917) bimonthly, $24/annual subscription. "Help Wanted" and "Business Opportunities" list a few different positions in the oil industry.

Southwest Oil World (Hearst Publications, P.O. Box 1917, Denver, CO 80201; phone: 800/832–1917) bimonthly, $24/annual subscription. "Help Wanted" and "Business Opportunities" list a few different positions in the oil industry.

Northeast Oil World (Hearst Publications, P.O. Box 1917, Denver, CO 80201; phone: 800/832–1917) monthly, $36/annual subscription. "Help Wanted" and "Business Opportunities" list as many as five positions for geologists and others involved in oil exploration.

Gulf Coast Oil World (Hearst Publications, P.O. Box 1917, Denver, CO 80201; phone: 800/832–1917) monthly, $36/annual subscription. "Help Wanted" and "Business Opportunities" list a few different positions in the oil industry.

Oil and Gas Investor (Hearst Publications, P.O. Box 1917, Denver, CO 80201; phone: 800/832–1917) monthly, $132/annual subscription (U.S.), $228/foreign. "Help Wanted" and "Business Opportunities" carry a few vacancies for executive positions in the oil industry.

Equipment Maintenance Council Newsletter (EMC, 113 Highland Lake Rd., Lewisville, TX 75067; phone: 214/317–6188) bimonthly, $75/annual subscription. "Job Shop" features about ten openngs for construction and transportation workers in the mining and oil fields.

Job services

Rural Electric Skills Bank (National Rural Electric Cooperative Association, 1800 Massachusetts Ave., NW, Washington, DC 20036; phone: 202/797-5441) contact Carol Pickerel, 3333 Quebec, Suite 8100, Denver, CO 80207 for fee structure. Your resume is kept on file for up to three years as this service matches you with job vacancies. The employer is responsible for contacting the job seeker.

Directories

Roughneck Rooker—The Intermountain Referral Service Guide to Obtaining Employment in the Oil and Gas Fields of the Western United States (Intermountain Publishing, 703 S. Broadway, Suite 100-B0, Denver, CO 80209; phone: 303/988-6707) $9, $5/subscribers to any edition of the *Rocky Mountain Employment Newsletter* which is described at the beginning of Chapter 2 among the general job sources.

Public Power Directory (American Public Power Association, 2301 M. St., NW, Washington, DC 20037; phone: 202/467-2970) $75/nonmember, included in membership package. Published in the January–February issue of *Public Power*.

Publicly Owned Natural Gas System Directory (American Public Gas Association, P.O. Box 11094D, Vienna, VA 22183; phone: 703/352-3890) $17/nonmember, free/members, published annually.

Directory of the Solar Thermal Industry (Solar Energy Industries Association, 777 N. Capitol St., NE, Suite 805, Washington, DC 20002; phone: 703/524-6100) $15/nonmembers, $12/members, published irregularly. Describes manufacturers.

Directory of the U.S. Photovoltaic Industry (Solar Energy Industries Association, 777 N. Capitol St., NE, Suite 805, Washington, DC 20002; phone: 703/524-6100) $15/nonmembers, $12/members, published irregularly. Describes manufacturers.

Annual Membership Issue of the *Journal of Petroleum Technology* (Society of Petroleum Engineers, P.O. Box 833836, Richardson, TX 75083-3836; phone: 214/669-3377) $100/nonmembers, $25/members. This is the May issue. It's obviously less expensive to just subscribe as described above under "Job openings."

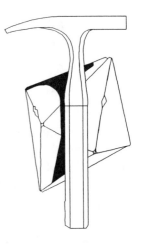

The Geophysical Directory (The Geophysical Directory, Inc., P.O. Box 130508, Houston, TX 77219; phone: 713/529-8789) $40/U.S. (Texas residents add 8.25 percent sales tax), $55/foreign (via air mail). Includes government agencies that utilize geophysics.

Brown's Directory of North American and International Gas Companies (Edgell Communications, 1 E. First St., Duluth, MN 55802; 218/723-9200) $225/U.S. and Canada plus $3.50/shipping, $235/foreign plus $5/shipping. Includes a company and city index of its listings of gas companies and municipal systems serving cities. Also includes gas holding companies and recent mergers and acquisitions.

Electrical World Directory of Electric Utilities (McGraw-Hill, 11 W. 19th St., New York, NY 10011; phone: 212/337-4068) $390 includes sections on U.S. and Canada, $25 includes only Canada section; add your state sales tax to all orders; annual. Available as bound or unbound volume. Gives personnel, addresses, phone and fax numbers for over 17,000 key utility executives and managers in over 3,500 utilities in the U.S. and Canada. Also provides details on each company, top consulting firms, and industry associations and commissions.

Electrical World Annual Buyers' Guide (McGraw-Hill, P.O. Box 524, Hightstown, NJ 08520; phones: 800/257-9402, 609/426-7070) $10, annually in June. Includes a "Generation Buyers' Guide" of companies, products, and services in electrical power generation and a "T&D Buyers' Guide" of companies, products, and services in transmission and distribution of electrical power.

Oil & Gas Directory (P.O. Box 130508, Houston, TX 77219; phone: 713/529–8789) $60/prepaid (U.S.), $75/prepaid (foreign). This massive 800-page directory includes listings of over 20,000 companies and 43,300 personnel in the oil and gas industry including exploration, drilling, and producing. It includes all aspects of the industry including suppliers.

Energy User News Directory of Manufacturers, Consultants Directory, Product Guide Collection (Chilton Company, 1 Chilton Way, Radnor, PA 19087; phones: 800/247–8080, 215/964–4145) $15, published each April, May, and December.

The Whole World Oil Directory (National Register Publishing Company, 3004 Glenview Rd., Wilmette, IL 60091; phones: 800/323–6772, 708/441–2210) $209 plus $8.50 shipping, annual, 720 pages. Covers 10,500 U.S. and Canadian oil and gas companies and the companies that produce equipment and supplies for them. Includes geologists, geophysicists, petroleum engineers, oil field specialists, and other professionals. Business categories covered also include: drilling contractors, oil field equipment and pipe and tubular manufacturers, oil well services and oil field specialties, consulting services, refineries, transmission pipelines, marine/offshore, and transportation.

Equipment Maintenance Council Newsletter (EMC, 113 Highland Lake Rd., Lewisville, TX 75067; phone: 214/317–6188) free/members only, annual. Members are engaged in construction and transportation jobs in mining and oil fields.

National Directory and Information Guide (National Utility Contractors Association, 1235 Jefferson Davis Highway, Suite 606, Arlington, VA 22202; phone: 703/486–2100) $50/nonmembers, free/members, issued each August.

Chapter 33

Security

Job openings

NELS—National Employment Listing Service (Criminal Justice Center, Sam Houston State University, Huntsville, TX 77341-2296; phones: 409/294-1692, 409/294-1690) monthly, individuals: $30/annual subscription, $37.50/foreign, $17.50/six–month subscription; institutions and agencies: $65/annual subscription (U.S.), $85/foreign; Texas residents must include 8.25 percent sales tax; tax–exempt institutions must include proof of tax exempt status. Each issue describes 100 to 200+ positions in five categories: Law enforcement and security (police officers, document examiners, print examiners, criminologists); Community services and corrections (correctional trainees, psychologists, social workers, physicians, speech pathologists, communications, clerical, counselors); Courts (pretrial service officers); Institutional corrections (correctional officers, psychologists, nurses, chaplains, cooks, therapists, pharmacists, trades and laborers); and Academics and research.

PSIC Listing (Protective Services Information Center, P.O. Box 1562 Decatur, IL 62525) monthly, $57.95/annual subscription, $16.95/three–month subscription. Display ads for entry–level to supervisory security and law enforcement positions are found throughout this magazine.

The Eagle (International Security and Detective Alliance, P.O. Box 6303, Corpus Christi, TX 78466; phone: 512/888–6164) tri-monthly, $7.95/annual nonmember subscription, free/members. Two or three security investigation positions appear under "Classifieds."

Security Management (American Society for Industrial Security, 1655 N. Fort Myer Dr., Suite 1200, Arlington, VA 22209; phone: 703/522–5800) monthly, $36/annual nonmember subscription (U.S.), $94/foreign, free/members. This newsletter typically has two to five ads for positions in security management under "Professional Notices."

Installation News (Bobits Publishing Co., P.O. Box 1939, Marion, OH 43306–2039; phone: 800/325–6751) monthly, $32/annual subscription (U.S.), $60/foreign, free/members. From five to seven ads for jobs in the security alarm installation industry appear under "Classified."

Security Sales (Bobits Publishing Co., P.O. Box 1939, Marion, OH 43306–2039; phone: 800/325–6751) monthly, $32/annual subscription (U.S.), $60/foreign, free/members. Two or three ads for jobs in the security alarm installation industry appear under "Classified."

Security Distributing & Marketing (Cahners Publishing, 44 Cook St., Denver, CO 80206) monthly, $69.95/annual nonmember subscription (U.S.), $178.35/Canada, $119.95/elsewhere, free/members. Around five ads for installation and service subcontractors, directors of sales, and chief technicians are listed under "SDM Classified."

Access Control (Communication Channels, 6255 Barfield Rd., Atlanta, GA 30328; phone: 404/256–9800) 13 issues/year, $39/annual subscription (U.S.), $59/foreign (surface mail), $102/foreign (air mail). Two or three positions for security systems salespeople and manufacturers' representatives appear under "Classifieds—Employment Opportunity." Also runs "Positions Wanted" ads.

Job services

Law Enforcement and Security Hot Line (National Association of Chiefs of Police, 3801 Biscayne Blvd., Miami, FL 33137; phone: 305/573–0202) $15/year. Calls are accepted weekdays from 9 a.m. to 4 p.m. The list of vacancies includes positions with private firms. When you call you get a live person, not a recording. Vacancies are available by geographical area and qualifications.

ASIS Placement Service (American Society for Industrial Security, 1655 N. Fort Myer Dr., Suite 1200, Arlington, VA 22209; phone: 703/522–5800) free/members only. The job seeker completes the "Positions Data Form" and submits two copies of his own resume which is kept on file for six months. This service is strictly confidential. Your name is removed from your resume and replaced with your ASIS member number. When a match is made, ASIS contacts you by phone to ask you to contact the employer with whom you have been matched. Positions are for security management professionals, not guards. Security functions include anti–terrorism, asset protection, audits, classified information, computer security, disaster management, executive protection, investigations, nuclear security, physical security, risk management, safety, surveillance, truth verification, warehouse/distribution, security systems, and more.

National Association of Security Dealers Job Hotline (NASD, 9513 Key West Ave., Rockville, MD 20850; phone: 202/728–8000), contact for availability and cost. About 15 positions in security sales are listed. Updated weekly.

Executive Protection Institute (Nine Lives Association Executive Protection Institute, Arcadia Manor, Route 2, Box 3645, Berryville, VA 22611; phone: 703/955–7128). Nine Lives helps to set up interviews for graduates of the Executive Protection Institute. Positions are for people who provide security to business executives.

Directories

Dynamics Directory (American Society for Industrial Security, 1655 N. Fort Myer Dr., Suite 1200, Arlington, VA 22209; phone: 703/522–5800) free/members, issued each March.

Nine Lives Associates Directory (Nine Lives Association Executive Protection Institute, Arcadia Manor, Route 2, Box 3645, Berryville, VA 22611; phone: 703/955–7128) free/members only, published every June.

ACCESS CONTROL Annual Directory (Communication Channels, 6255 Barfield Rd., Atlanta, GA 30328; phone: 404/256–9800) $29.95, annual. Includes manufacturers and suppliers to the security systems industry.

Salary survey

Compensation in Security/Loss Prevention Fields (Abbott, Langer & Associates, 548 First St., Crete, IL 60417; phone: 708/672–4200) $225, $185/members of the American Society for Industrial Security, annual. Sponsored by the American Society for Industrial Security, this study cover 21 job categories based on 50,000 employees.

Chapter 34

Social services

Also see the much more extensive sets of entries under "Social services" in the Government Job Finder and the Non–Profits' Job Finder.

Job openings

Occupational Therapist Weekly (164 Rollins Ave., Suite 301, Rockville, MD 20852; phone: 301/881–2490) weekly, free to qualified professionals. About 200 positions fill the pages of this newsletter.

Hospital and Community Psychiatry (American Psychiatric Association, 1400 K St., NW, Washington, DC 20005; phone: 202/682–6228) monthly, $37/annual subscription (U.S.), $57/foreign. Jobs listed under "Classified Advertising." Typical issue runs around 75 job ads.

Special Recreation Digest (Special Recreation, Inc., 362 Koser Ave., Iowa City, IA 52246–3038; phone: 219/337–7578) quarterly, $39.95/annual subscription. From 10 to 25 activity or recreation positions such as therapists, coordinators, and administrators appear under "Recreation."

Journal of Rehabilitation (National Rehabilitation Association, 633 S. Washington St., Alexandria, VA 22314; phone: 703/836–0850) quarterly, $35/annual subscription (U.S.), $40/Canada, $50/elsewhere, free/members. About ten openings are touted under "Classified."

Medical Rehabilitation Review (National Association of Rehabilitation Facilities, P.O. Box 17675, Washington, DC 20041; phone: 703/648–9300) weekly, available only as part of membership package. Jobs listed under "Employment Exchange." About five to ten job ads per issue.

Vocational/Developmental Rehabilitation Review (National Association of Rehabilitation Facilities, P.O. Box 17675, Washington, DC 20041; phone: 703/648–9300) weekly, available only as part of membership package. Jobs listed under "Employment Exchange." About five to ten job ads per issue.

Rehabilitation Management Review (National Association of Rehabilitation Facilities, P.O. Box 17675, Washington, DC 20041; phone: 703/648–9300) monthly, available only as part of membership package. Jobs listed under "Employment Exchange." About five to ten job ads per issue.

NRA Newsletter (National Rehabilitation Association, 633 S. Washington St., Alexandria, VA 22314; phone: 703/836–0850) eight issues/year, free/members only. Three or four openings are advertised under "Classified."

Medical Rehabilitation Review (National Association of Rehabilitation Facilities, P.O. Box 17675, Washington, DC 20041; phone: 703/648–9300) free/members only. You'll find about six openings for administrative and management positions in rehabilitation at hospitals and vocational centers listed under "Employment Exchange."

Vocational/Developmental Rehabilitation Review (National Association of Rehabilitation Facilities, P.O. Box 17675, Washington, DC 20041; phone: 703/648–9300) free/members only. Just two or three ads for higher level executives in medical and vocational rehabilitation are in "Employment Exchange."

Job's Clearinghouse (Association for Experiential Education, University of Colorado, Box 249, Boulder, CO 80309; phone: 303/492–1547, **TDD:** 303/492–0526) monthly, $25/nonmember annual subscription, $15/members. Many openings for outdoor therapists are among the 30–plus pages of opportunities in a typical issue.

EAP Digest (Performance Resource Press, P.O. Box 6112, Syracuse, NY 13217; phone: 313/588–7733) bimonthly, $36 for U.S., $39 other countries. About five ads for employee assistance personnel are listed under "Classified—Job Openings."

Student Assistance Journal (Performance Resource Press, P.O. Box 6282, Syracuse, NY 13217–9926; phone: 313/588–7733) bimonthly, $32/annual nonmember subscription (U.S.), $35/foreign, free/members of National Association of Leadership for Student Assistance Programs. Two or three ads for student assistance professionals appear under "Classified—Job Openings."

The Family Therapy Networker (8528 Bradford Rd., Silver Spring, MD 20901; phone: 301/589–6536) bimonthly, $20/annual subscription. One or two ads for clinical social workers and in mental health are under "Classified—Employment."

Job services

CU Career Connection (University of Colorado, Campus Box 133, Boulder, CO 80309–0133; phone: 303/492–4127) $20/two–month fee entitles you to a "passcode" which unlocks this job hotline. You need a touch-tone phone to call and request the jobs in social services and the geographic area for which you want to hear job openings. The hotline is turned off Monday through Friday, 2 to 4 p.m. for daily updating.

Career Guidance and Placement Service (Special Recreation, Inc., 362 Koser Ave., Iowa City, IA 52246–3038; phone: 219/337–7578) free. Submit your resume and this service will match you with appropriate activity or recreation coordinator, specialist, or therapist positions.

The Job Bank (Occupational Therapist Weekly, 164 Rollins Ave., Suite 301, Rockville, MD 20852; phone: 301/881-2490). This is an on-line database that you can reach via computer modem to learn about 650 job vacancies in occupational therapy. Contact for details.

Directories

Drug, Alcohol, and Other Addictions: A Directory of Treatment Centers and Prevention Programs Nationwide (Oryx Press, 4041 N. Central, Phoenix, AZ 85012; phone: 800/279-6799) $65, 1989, 784 pages. Includes 18,000 programs, many of which are in the private sector.

NARF Membership Directory (National Association of Rehabilitation Facilities, P.O. Box 17675, Washington, DC 20041; phone: 703/648-9300) contact for price and availability.

Directory of Medical Rehabilitation Programs (Oryx Press, 4041 N. Central, Phoenix, AZ 85012; phone: 800/279-6799) $95, 1190, 376 pages. Describes nearly 1,500 hospital-sponsored departments, private hospitals, and free-standing clinics.

Salary survey

A National Salary Survey of Rehabilitation Facility Staff (National Association of Rehabilitation Facilities, P.O. Box 17675, Washington, DC 20041; phone: 703/648-9300) $95/nonmembers, $65/members, 84 pages. Covers more than 40 full-time positions common to medical, vocational, and residential facilities.

Day care

Job services

National Academy of Nannies, Inc., Referral Service (NANI, 1681 S. Dayton St., Denver, CO 80231; phones: 800/222-6264, 303/333-6264) free/students and alumni of this school only.

ACNews (American Council of Nanny Schools, Delta College, University Center, MI 48710; phone: 517/686–9543) semiannual, $5/annual subscription. While this newsletter does not contain any job openings, it does list colleges that offer nanny programs and have placement services for nannies.

Directories

American Council of Nanny Schools List (ACNS, Delta College, University Center, MI 48710; phone: 517/686–9543) free. This lists schools that are members of the American Council of Nanny Schools. Many of these operate placement programs.

Start Your Own at–Home Child Care Business (Child Care., P.O. Box 555, Worcester, PA 19490; phone: 215/364–1945) $12.95 plus $2/shipping. Provides guidance for setting up a child day care center in your home. Be sure to also check your local zoning ordinance and any state or local licensing requirements.

So You Want to Open a Profitable Day Care Center (Child Care., P.O. Box 555, Worcester, PA 19490; phone: 215/364–1945) $12.95 plus $2/shipping. Provides guidance for setting up a child day care center in your home. Be sure to also check your local zoning ordinance and any state or local licensing requirements.

Long–term care

Job openings

Contemporary Long–Term Care (Bill Communications, P.O. Box 3599, Akron, OH 44398; phone: 216/867–4401) monthly, $29/annual subscription (U.S.), $75/Canada, $185/elsewhere. The "Classifieds" runs ads for around 30 positions for administrators, managers, marketing, sales representatives, and nursing directors.

Long–Term Care Administrator (American College of Health Care Administrators, 325 S. Patrick St., Alexandria, VA 22314; phone: 703/739–7913) monthly, $45/annual nonmember subscription, free/members. Two to five openings for long–term care administrators at nursing homes and hospices are advertised under "Professional Referral Service."

Journal of Long-Term Care Administration (American College of Health Care Administrators, 325 S. Patrick St., Alexandria, VA 22314; phone: 703/739-7913) quarterly, $70/annual nonmember subscription, free/members. An occasional display ad for nursing home administrators, directors of nursing, and medical directors makes it into an issue.

Job services

Compumatch (American College of Health Care Administrators, 325 S. Patrick St., Alexandria, VA 22314; phone: 703/739-7910) $125/six-month nonmember fee, $100/nonmember students, free/members. Complete this service's form and submit it with copies of your resume. When a job march is made, your resume is sent to the potential employer who contacts you. The service also contacts you to let you know that your resume has been sent to an employer, but it does not tell you who the employer is. Serves administrative positions in long-term care at nursing homes, hospices, and retirement communities.

Job Bank (National Association of Activity Professionals, 1225 I St., NW, Suite 300, Washington, DC 20005; phone: 202/289-0722) free. Your resume is kept on file for a year. When a match is made, a copy is sent to the employer who is responsible for contacting you. Jobs include activity directors and their assistants, largely at nursing homes.

Services for senior citizens

Job openings

AAHA Provider News (American Association of Homes for the Aging, 1129 20th St., NW, Suite 400, Washington, DC 20036; phone: 202/296-5960) monthly, free/members only. "Job Mart" carries about ten ads for administrative positions for residential facilities for senior citizens plus five or six "Positions Wanted."

Gerontology News (Gerontological Society of America, 1275 K St., NW, Washington, DC 20005; phone: 202/842–1275) monthly, $50/annual nonmember subscription, free/members. About five to eight positions for geriatric social workers appear under "Jobs."

Aging Today (American Society on Aging, 833 Market St., Suite 512, San Francisco, CA 94103; phone: 415/882–2910) bimonthly, $25/annual nonmember subscription, free/members, $80/annual dues. Two to four display ads for positions in caring for older people are in a typical issue.

Directories

Directory of Nursing Homes (Oryx Press, 4041 N. Central, Phoenix, AZ 85012; phone: 800/279–6799) $225, published in odd–numbered years, 1,512 pages. Rather extensive directory with details on nursing homes, nursing home chains, and corporate headquarters.

National Directory of Retirement Facilities (Oryx Press, 4041 N. Central, Phoenix, AZ 85012; phone: 800/279–6799) $195, published each January, 1,208 pages. Provides details on over 22,000 retirement facilities.

Membership Directory of the Gerontological Society of America (GSA, 1275 K St., NW, Washington, DC 20005; phone: 202/842–1275) $15/nonmembers, $9/members, most recently issued in 1991.

Salary surveys

Compensation Report—Management Employees in Hospital and Nursing Home Management Companies (Hospital Compensation Service, 69 Minnehaha Blvd., Oakland, NJ 07436; phone: 201/405–0075) $245 prepaid, annual. Reports on salary and bonus payments for 19 nursing home management company positions, both nationally and by region.

Nursing Home Salary and Benefits Report (Hospital Compensation Service, 69 Minnehaha Blvd., Oakland, NJ 07436; phone: 201/405–0075) $190 prepaid, annual. Reports on salary and bonus payments for 25 exempt positions and 14 nonexempt nursing, therapy, and other positions, both nationally and by region.

Chapter 35

Telecommunications

Also see the chapter on the "Media."

Job openings

Telocator Bulletin (2000 M St. NW, Suite 230, Washington, DC 20036; phone: 800/326–8638) weekly, $397/nonmember subscription, $125/members. Around five to ten management, technical, and marketing positions in mobile communications, namely cellular phones, are under "Classified—Help Wanted."

Communications Week (CMP Publications, 600 Community Dr., Manhasset, NY 11030; phone: 516/562–5000) weekly, $130/nonmembers (U.S.) and Canada, free to qualified management and professional personnel companies involved in communications."Career Opportunities" lists around eight ads for sales managers and network managers and technicians.

Communications Magazine (Cardiff Publishing, 6300 S. Syracuse Way, Suite 650, Englewood, CO 80111; phone: 303/220–0600) monthly, $26/annual subscription (U.S.), $35/Canada and Mexico, $39/elsewhere. From six to ten ads for sales, management, and technical telecommunications positions are listed in "Marketplace—Help Wanted."

Cellular Marketing (Cardiff Publishing, 6300 S. Syracuse Way, Suite 650, Englewood, CO 80111; phone: 303/220-0600) monthly, free/qualified professionals in the cellular phone industry. The "Classifieds" tend to carry two or three ads from executive search and recruiting firms under "Help Wanted."

Telephone Engineer & Management (Edgell Communications, 1 E. First St., Duluth, MN 55802; phones: 800/346-0085, 218/723-9870) twice monthly; $27/annual subscription (U.S.); $50/Canada; $90/elsewhere. Just a few ads for management positions appear under "TE&M Classifieds—Help Wanted."

Communications Industries Report (International Communications Industries Associations, 2150 Spring St., Fairfax, VA 22031; phone: 703/27-7200) monthly, free/members only. One or two audio-visual and computer-audio positions are listed under "Classified."

Job services

Armed Forces Communications and Electronics Association (AFCEA International Headquarters, 4400 Fair Lakes Court, Fairfax, VA 22033-3899; phone: 703/631-6100) free for retiring or separating military personnel who seek communication positions in the private sector; members only. Participants submit a two-page resume or a resume and membership application if not already a member. Each month, all resumes are sent to over 50 corporate subscribers who are responsible for directly contacting promising job candidates.

Directories

Telephone Industry Directory and Sourcebook (Philips Publishing, 7811 Montrose Rd., Potomac, MD 20854; phone: 301/340-2100) $159, issued each January.

Telecommunications Directory (Gale Research, Inc., 835 Penobscot Bldg., Detroit, MI 48226–4094; phone: 800/877–4253) $310, published 1991, 1,300 pages. Detailed descriptions and contact information are provided for over 2,300 national and international communications systems and services, voice and data communication services, local area networks, teleconferencing facilities, videotex and teletext operations, electronic mail services, telegram and telex services, interactive cable television, satellite services, and electronic transactional services.

Telephone Engineer & Management Directory (Edgell Communications, 1 E. First St., Duluth, MN 55802; phones: 800/346-0085, 218/723-94710) $86 plus $3.50/shipping (U.S.), $5.00/shipping (foreign), annual, 500+ pages. Includes a buyers guide with 35,000 listings, plus separate directories for the regional Bells and their 22 telcos and 1,300 independents with key personnel, cellular operators, distributors and supply houses, 2,600 manufacturers, 800 intercos, and local sources.

ICIA Membership Directory (International Communications Industries Associations, 2150 Spring St., Fairfax, VA 22031; phone: 703/273–7200) $100/nonmembers, free/members, annual.

The Mobile Communications Directory (2000 M St. NW, Suite 230, Washington, DC 20036; phone: 800/326–8638) $159, published each April. This directory lists all cellular telephone and paging companies in the U.S.

NABER Membership Directory (National Association of Business and Educational Radio, 1501 Duke St. Alexandria, VA 22314; phone: 703/739–0300), annual. Lists members, dealers, and manufacturers of cellular phones and pagers.

Association of Telemessaging Services, International (ATSI, 1150 S. Washington St., Suite 150, Alexandria, VA 22314; phone: 703/684–0016) $100, published every March.

Chapter 36

Trades

Trades

Be sure to also consult the Table of Contents and the Index because many of the job sources listed elsewhere in this book include trade positions within the specialty.

Job openings

American Salon (Edgell Communications, 1 E. First St., Duluth, MN 55802; phones: 800/346-0085, 218/723-9870) monthly, $24/annual subscription (U.S.), $55/Canada, $75/elsewhere. "Classifieds" features close to 10 job ads and businesses for sale.

W.I.T. (Step–Up for Women, 1 Prospect Ave., St. Johnbury, VT 05819; phone: 802/748-3308) quarterly, first issue free. Two or three job vacancies are advertised under "Jobs."

Trade Trax Newsletter (Tradeswomen, Inc., P.O. Box 40664, San Francisco, CA 94140; phone: 415/821–7334) monthly, $15/annual nonmember subscription, $20/Canada, $25/elsewhere, free to members. Four or five skilled trade jobs and apprenticeships, primarily in the San Francisco Bay Area, appear under "Employment."

Job services

Job–Matching Service (Step–Up for Women, 1 Prospect Ave., St. Johnbury, VT 05819; phone: 802/748–3308) free. Job seeker submits resume and service forwards it to potential employers who are responsible for contacting the job aspirant.

Salary surveys

Salaries & Bonuses in the Service Department (Abbott, Langer & Associates, 548 First St., Crete, IL 60417; phone: 708/672–4200) $225, annual. Sponsored by the National Association of Service Managers, this report covesr 42 job categories by type of employer.

Chapter 37

Transportation

Job openings

The Private Carrier (National Private Truck Council, 1320 Braddock Pl., Suite 720, Alexandria, VA 22314; phone: 703/683–1300) monthly, free. About ten ads for private fleet managers, safety experts, transportation managers, logistics managers, and distribution managers are in the "Job Clearinghouse."

Defense Transportation Journal (National Defense Transportation Association, 50 S. Pickett St., Suite 220, Alexandria, VA 22304; phone: 703/751–5011) bimonthly, $35/annual subscription (U.S., Canada), $45/elsewhere. "Job Bank" carries 15 to 20 job openings in the defense transportation industry.

SAE UPdate (SAE International: The Engineering Society for Advancing Mobility Land Sea Air and Space, 400 Commonwealth Dr., Warrendale, PA 15096; phone: 412/776–4841) monthly, free/members only. About ten ads primarily for engineers in all aspects of the mobility field appear under "Engineering Career Resources."

M & S Times (National Moving and Storage Association, 1500 N. Beauregard St., Alexandria, VA 22311; phone: 703/671–8813) biweekly, $50/annual nonmember subscription, $30/members. "Help Wanted" runs an even dozen ads for moving company executives, claims managers, branch managers, accountants, and salespeople.

American Mover (American Movers Conference, 1611 Duke St., Alexandria, VA 22314; phone: 703/683–7410) monthly, $35/annual nonmember subscription (U.S.), $45/Canada, $70/elsewhere, free/members. Each issue includes one to three ads for moving salespersons and business opportunities.

Job services

SAE Resume Database (SAE International: The Engineering Society for Advancing Mobility Land Sea Air and Space, 400 Commonwealth Dr., Warrendale, PA 15096; phone: 412/776–4841, ext. 369) $30/nonmember fee for three months, free/members. The job candidate completes the service's "Resume Database System" information form. Employers subscribe to this database system and are able to search it with up to 40 search criteria. They are responsible for contacting the job seeker for an interview. Among the thousands of job candidates listed are people involved in all facets of the transportation industry including mechanical, civil, electrical, aeronautical, and chemical engineers, physicists, chemists, and others who work closely with engineers.

Directories

Traffic Management Buyer's Guide (Cahners Publishing, 44 Cook St., Denver, CO 80206; phone: 800/622–7776) $25/U.S., $35/foreign. This is the March issue of *Traffic Management*. It includes a list of major North American port authorities, shipper associations and agents; manufacturers of highway and rail–flat equipment; railroads and intermodel services; airfreight services; motor carrier services; and steamship and barge services.

SAE Roster of Members (SAE International: The Engineering Society for Advancing Mobility Land Sea Air and Space, 400 Commonwealth Dr., Warrendale, PA 15096; phone: 412/776–4841, ext. 369) free/members only, issued each March. Members include mechanical, civil, electrical, aeronautical, and chemical engineers, physicists, chemists, and others who work closely with engineers.

ARTBA Membership Directory and Buyers' Guide (American Road and Transportation Builders Association, 501 School St., SW, Washington, DC 20024; phone: 202/488–2722) $50/nonmembers, free/members, published each January. This directory features details on the organization's 4,000 plus members as well as a buyers' guide of industry supplies.

Car and Locomotive Repair Directory (Simmons–Boardman Publishing, 345 W. Hudson St., New York, NY 10014; phones: 800/228–9670, 212/620–7200) $4. This is the July issue of *Railway Age*.

The Travel Industry Personnel Directory (Fairchild Books, 7 E. 12th St., New York, NY 10003; phone: 800/247–6622) $25, published each spring, 545 pages. Includes over 20,000 entries of sales and executive personnel for domestic and regional airlines, shiplines, railroads, motorcoach and car rental companies and tour operators.

National Moving and Storage Association Membership Directory and Buyers' Guide (NMSA, 1500 N. Beauregard St., Alexandria, VA 22311; phone: 703/671–8813) free/members only, annual,, 160 pages. Lists NMSA members and suppliers to the industry.

Salary surveys

Compensation & Benefits in the Trucking & Busing Field (Abbott, Langer & Associates, 548 First St., Crete, IL 60417; phone: 708/672–4200) $295, annual. Sponsored by *Commercial Carrier Journal*, this 250–page report presents salary and benefits data by 24 job functions from equipment specialist, fleet maintenance foreman, to owner or senior partner.

Compensation and Fringe Benefit Survey (National Moving and Storage Association, 1500 N. Beauregard St., Alexandria, VA 22311; phone: 703/671–8813) $80, annual, 25 pages. This is an in–depth report on salary and benefits by region.

Automotive industry

Job openings

Automotive News (Crain Communications, 965 E. Jefferson, Detroit, MI 48207-3185; phone: 800/678-3185) weekly, $70/annual subscription (U.S.), $108/Canada. The "Classifieds" carry ads for over 30 job openings in all facets of auto manufacturing and dealer sales under "Help Wanted" plus 50 ads for "Dealerships Available." Also carries "Positions Wanted" and "Dealerships Wanted" ads.

Automotive Engineering Magazine (SAE International: The Engineering Society for Advancing Mobility Land Sea Air and Space, 400 Commonwealth Dr., Warrendale, PA 15096; phone: 412/776-4841) monthly, contact for subscription rates. About ten vacancies primarily for engineers in all aspects of the mobility field are advertised in the typical issue.

AIA Update (Auto International Association, P.O. Box 4910, Diamond Bar, CA 91765; phone: 714/396-0289) bimonthly, free/members only. The "Classifieds" carries five to 15 job ads for auto parts salespeople, marketing, sales managers, and auto parts store managers. Also carried "Position Wanted" ads.

RV Business (29901 Agoura Rd., Agoura, CA 91301; phone: 818/991-4980) $48/annual subscription (U.S.), $96/foreign. Twelve to 40 vacancies for management personnel, service technicians, body shop repair people, salespeople, in the recreational vehicle industry appear in "Classified Advertising—Help Wanted." Also carries "Positions Wanted."

Aftermarket Today (Automotive Affiliated Representatives, 444 N. Michigan Ave., Chicago, IL 60611; phone; 312/836-1300) monthly, $40/annual nonmember subscription, free/members. Ten jobs for automotive specialists, particularly salespeople, are in "Business & Employment Opportunities." Twice as many ads for "Position Wanted," "Business for Sale," and "Acquisition Wanted" also appear.

Aftermarket Business (Edgell Communication, 1 E. First St., Duluth, MN 55802; phone: 800/346–0085) monthly, $30/annual subscription. Three jobs for sales representatives and distributors of auto parts are in "Classified."

Auto Rental News (2512 Artisia Blvd., Redondo Beach, CA 90278; phones: 800/325–6751, 213/376–8788) monthly, $27/annual subscription. Two or three openings for auto rental agency managers are in the "Classifieds."

Auto Trim and Restyling News (Shore Publishing, 180 Allen Rd., NE, Atlanta, GA 30328; phone: 404/252–8831) monthly, $23/annual subscription. Four ads for auto detailers and upholsterers grace the "Classifieds."

Motor Service (950 Lee St., Des Plaines, IL 60016; phone: 708/296–0770) monthly, $36/annual subscription (U.S.), $45/Canada. Two or three positions for auto mechanics and management in the automobile service industry appear in "Help Wanted" and "Personnel."

Automotive Body Repair News (Chilton Company, 201 King of Prussia Rd., Radnor, PA 19089; phones: 800/345–1214, 215/964–4231) monthly, $48/annual subscription (U.S.), $60/Canada, $90/elsewhere, free to qualified key personnel with managerial responsibilities at automotive body repair shops, at PBE jobbers, and at warehouse distributors. Two or three positions for sales representatives and body shop managers are in "Classified Advertising."

Auto, Inc. (Automotive Service Industry Association, 1901 Airport Freeway, Suite 100, Bedford, TX 76095; phone: 817/283-6205) monthly, free/members only. "Classified" has two or three ads for independent auto repair shop workers and managers.

Auto Glass (National Glass Association, 8200 Greenboro Dr., Suite 302, McLean, VA 22102; phone: 703/442-4890) seven issues/year $19.95/annual nonmember subscription (U.S.), $29.95/foreign, free/members. Two or three ads for sales representatives are in "Classified."

Tire Business (Crain Communications, 965 E. Jefferson, Detroit, MI 48207-3185; phone: 800/678-3185) biweekly, $39/annual subscription (U.S.), $54/foreign. Five ads for tire salespeople, store managers, and tire distributorships are in "Classified."

Tire Review (Babcox Publications, 11 S. Forge St., Akron, OH 44304; phone: 216/535-6117) monthly, $42/annual subscription, free to qualified professionals. As many as six jobs, largely for sales representatives, are in "Classified Advertising—Personnel."

Job services

Executive Referral Service (Automotive Parts and Accessories Association, 4600 East-West Highway, Bethesda, MD 20814; phone: 301/654-6664) free/members only. A member submits her own resume which is kept on file for three months. Contact for details. About five to ten positions are on file at any one time. Positions are upper-level sales, marketing, and management positions.

Directories

Automotive Aftermarket Supplies (Chain Store Guide Information Services, 425 Park Ave., New York, NY 10022; phone: 212/371-9400, ext. 306) $209, published biennially in September. Detailed company profiles on 1,300 firms that operate 15,000 stores plus 960 warehouse distributors that serve 65,000 stores. Includes 6,500 key executive, buying, and administrative personnel.

Automotive Parts Rebuilders Association Membership Directory (APRA, 6849 Old Dominion Dr., Suite 352, McLean, VA 22101; phone: 790-1050) $225/nonmembers, free/members, issued each April.

RV Business Directory (29901 Agoura Rd., Agoura, CA 91301; phone: 818/991-4980) $19.95, published every February. Lists companies and suppliers in the recreational vehicle business.

Membership Directory of the American Automotive Leasing Association (AALA, 1001 Connecticut Ave., NW, Suite 1201, Washington, DC 20036; phone: 202/223-2600) free/members only, annual.

Automotive Service Industry Association Membership Directory (ASA, 1901 Airport Freeway, Suite 100, Bedford, TX 76095; phone: 817/283-6205) free/members only, issued each June.

NTDRA Dealer News (National Tire Dealers and Retreaders Association, 1250 I St., NW, Suite 400, Washington, DC 20005; phone: 202/789-2300) January issue: $50/nonmembers, free/members. The January issue is a membership directory.

Aviation and aerospace

Also see listings under "Engineering."

Job openings

Air Jobs Digest (P.O. Box 70127, Dept. JF, Washington, DC 20088; phone: 301/984-4172) monthly, $96/annual subscription (U.S. and Canada), $59/six-month subscription, $39/three-month subscription, $18/single issue, $140.04/foreign annual subscription (air mail). The 500 to 1,000 job vacancies described include pilots, flight service station personnel, accident investigators, aviation safety instructors, avionics, technicians, engineers, and management and administration.

Aviation Employment Monthly (P.O. Box 8286, Saddle Brook, NJ 07662; phones: 800/543-5201, 201/794-6725) monthly, $49.95/three-month subscription, $79.95/six-month subscription, $99.95/annual subscription. The typical issue overflows with more than 300 jobs for pilots, mechanics, aviation and aerospace technicians and engineers.

"At home he can't even operate the VCR."

ALEA Job Opportunity Bulletin (Air Line Employees Association, 5600 S. Central Ave., Chicago, IL 60638–3797; phone: 312/767–3333) monthly, $40/annual subscription. About 20 job openings for just about everything in aviation (pilots, flight attendants, mechanics, customer service, ramp agents, clerical, reservationists, and more) fill this jobs bulletin.

Professional Pilot (3014 Colvin St., Alexandria, VA 22314; phones: 800/222–3212, 703/370–0606) monthly, $36/annual subscription. "Positions Available" features ads for ten vacancies for pilots, mechanics, technicians, engineers, avionics, administration, marketing, airport management, and flight instructors.

Private Pilot (P.O. Box 55064, Boulder, CO 80323; phone: 303/447–9330) monthly, $21.97/annual subscription (U.S.), $29.97/Canada, $33.97/elsewhere. Ten job ads appear in "Classified Flyer—Employment Information."

Pilot Job Reports (Future Aviation Professionals of America, 4959 Massachusetts Blvd., Atlanta, GA 30037; phones: 800/538–5627, 404/997–8097) monthly, $96/annual subscription also includes *Career Pilot* (monthly), free/members. A good number of ads for pilots are in the typical issue.

Flight Attendant Job Reports (Future Aviation Professionals of America, 4959 Massachusetts Blvd., Atlanta, GA 30037; phones: 800/538–5627, 404/997–8097) monthly, available only in membership package, $59/six–month membership. Membership also includes one copy of the *Flight Attendant Salary Survey/Directory of Employers* and *Flight Attendant Employment Guide*. Many job ads for flight attendants fill this jobs bulletin.

Flying (P.O. Box 53647, Boulder, CO 80302; phone: 800/678–0797, 303/447–9330) monthly, $21.94/annual subscription, $26.94/Canada, $29.94/elsewhere. About 17 ads for open positions and job services appear in the "Flying Marketplace" under "Employment Opportunities."

US Aviator (Airedale Press, 3000 21st St., NW, Winter Haven, FL 33881; phone: 813/294–6396) monthly, $25/annual subscription (U.S.), $35/Canada, $60/elsewhere. Five jobs for pilots; mechanics; aviation writers, photographers, and advertising reps are advertised under "Classified Ads—Help Wanted."

Air Progress (Challenge Publications, 7950 Deering Ave., Canoga Park, CA 91304; phone: 818/887–0550) monthly, $26.50/annual subscription (U.S.), $32.50/foreign. Six ads for pilots and technicians rest in "Classifieds—Employment."

Business and Commercial Aviator Magazine (Murdock Publications, 4 International Ave., Rye Brook, NY 10573; phone: 914/939–0300) monthly, $45/annual subscription. Under "Classified—Employment Opportunities" you will find 7 to 21 ads for pilots, mechanics, and other aviation professionals.

Flight Training (National Association of Flight Instructors, 405 Main St., Parkville, MO 64152; phone: 816/741–1165) monthly, $20/annual subscription, free/current FAA student pilot certificate holders. "Classified" carries ads for one to three jobs openings.

Air Cargo World (Communication Channels, 6255 Barfield Rd., Atlanta, GA 30328; phone: 404/256–9800) monthly, $42/annual subscription (U.S.), $62/foreign. Five or six management and business opportunities are in the "Classifieds" section.

Commuter Air International (Communication Channels, P.O. Box 1147, Skokie, IL 60076; phone: 708/647–7124) monthly, $42/annual subscription (U.S.), $62/foreign. Five or six job ads for mechanics, maintenance, avionics management, and others are in the "Classifieds—Employment Opportunities."

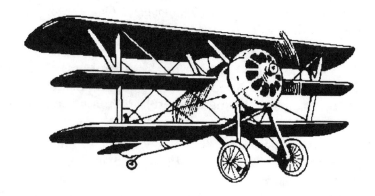

Aviation Week & Space Technology (McGraw Hill, 1221 Avenue of the Americas, New York, NY 10020; phones: 800/525–5003, 609/426–7070) 51 issues/year, $72/annual subscription. About six job ads appear under "Classified–Recruitment."

Plane and Pilot (Warner Publications, 16000 Ventura Blvd., Suite 800, Enrico, CA 91436; phones: 800/283–4330, 818/986–8400) monthly, $18.95/annual subscription. Among the six ads under "Help Wanted" are aviation–related positions in law enforcement.

Rotor and Wing (P.O. Box 1797, Peoria, IL 61656; phone: 800/777–5006) monthly, $36/annual subscription (U.S.), $44/elsewhere. "Market Place" carries three to five ads for pilots, mechanics, technicians, engineers, and more in the helicopter industry.

Agricultural Aviation News (National Agricultural Aviation Association, 1005 E St., SE, Washington, DC 20003; phone: 202/546–5722) ten issues/year, $20/annual subscription (U.S.), $30/foreign. Up to four ads for pilots are under "Classified."

Airport Highlights (Airport Associations Council International, 1220 19th St., NW, Suite 200, Washington, DC 20036; phone: 202/293–8500) 24 issues/year, $110/nonmember annual subscription (U.S.), $150/elsewhere; included in membership package. About ten positions are listed under "Employment Opportunities."

Airport Report (American Association of Airport Executives, 4212 King St., Alexandria, VA 22302; phone: 703/824–0500) biweekly, available to members only, included in membership package. Jobs listed under "Positions Open." Typical issue carries announcements of about ten positions for airport managers, airport operations, and support staff (noise abatement, public affairs, engineers).

Airport Report Express (American Association of Airport Executives, 4212 King St., Alexandria, VA 22302; phone: 703/824–0500) biweekly, subscription price depends on size of subscribing airport. Entire issue consists of job openings for airport managers, airport operations, and support staff (noise abatement, public affairs, engineers). This newsletter, which usually features about 10 job openings, is delivered by fax rather than mail.

Airport Executive (Communication Channels, 6255 Barfield Rd., Atlanta, GA 30328; phones: 800/241–9834, 404/256–9800) monthly, $42/annual subscription. Usually ten ads appear under "Employment Opportunities."

Airline Executive International (Communication Channels, P.O. Box 1147, Skokie, IL 60076; phone: 708/647–7124) monthly, $42/annual subscription (U.S.), $62/foreign. The "Classifieds" carry two or three ads for management airline positions.

Airport Services (Johnson Hill Press, 1233 Janesville Ave., Fort Atkinson, WI 53538; phone: 414/563–6388) bimonthly, $24/annual subscription, free to qualified professionals. Job vacancies are touted under "Classified Advertising."

National Defense (American Defense Preparedness Association, 2101 Wilson Blvd., Suite 400, Arlington, VA 22201-3061; phone: 703/522–1820) monthly, $35/annual nonmember subscription, $30/members. Five or so positions for engineers, researchers, and management in the defense and aerospace industries are listed under "Job Opportunities."

Air Traffic Control Journal (Air Traffic Control Association, 2300 Clarendon Blvd., Suite 711, Arlington, VA 22201; phone: 703/522-5717) quarterly, $36/nonmember annual subscription, included in membership package. A few positions are scattered throughout the magazine, although not in every issue, primarily for air traffic controllers in the U.S. and abroad, and for system engineers.

Job services

Aviation Maintenance Services (Future Aviation Professionals of America, 4959 Massachusetts Blvd., Atlanta, GA 3037; phones: 800/538-5627, 404/997-8097), available to members only, $72/annual membership fee. This service is for airplane mechanics and technicians. This service includes participation in the FAPA's computerized *Aviation Job Bank*. You complete the service's resume form and your resume is kept on file in the database for a year. When a match is made, your resume is sent to the employer who is responsible for contacting you for an interview.

Included in this membership are up to 12 calls to the ''Jet-Line Computer Telephone Interview Briefing'' service, a copy of FAPA's *Maintenance Employment Guide*, a subscription to the monthly *Job Reports* newsletter which lists job vacancies, the *Aviation Maintenance Salary Survey*, and a copy of the *Directory of Employers* with updates. FAPA also offers ''Career Day Seminars'' where you can meet representatives of the major airlines and obtain job applications. Call 800/538-5627, extension 120 for details and costs.

Career Pilot Services (Future Aviation Professionals of America, 4959 Massachusetts Blvd., Atlanta, GA 3037; phones: 800/538-5627, 404/997-8097), available to members only, $182/annual membership fee. This service is for airplane pilots. It includes participation in the FAPA's computerized *Aviation Job Bank*. You complete the service's resume form and your resume is kept on file in the database for a year. When a match is made, your resume is sent to the employer who is responsible for contacting you for an interview.

Included in this membership are up to 12 calls to the ''Jet-Line Computer Telephone Interview Briefing'' service, six calls to the FAPA's counseling/information center, a copy of FAPA's *Pilot*

Employment Guide, a subscription to the monthly *Pilot Job Reports* newsletter which lists job vacancies, the *Pilot Salary Survey* (annual), and a copy of the *Directory of Employers* (annual). FAPA also offers ''Pilot Career Day Seminars'' where you can meet representatives of the major airlines and obtain job applications. Call 800/538-5627, extension 120 for details and costs.

National Pilot Placement Service (Vertical Flight Center, P.O. Box 444, Faribault, MN 55021; phone: 800/926-7837) $140/annual fee. You complete their resume form and when a match is made, your resume is sent to the employer who is responsible for contacting you for an interview. Serves pilots largely for commuter airlines and corporate planes. Focuses heavily on helicopter pilots.

Directories

The Aviation and Aerospace White Pages (P.O. Box 8286, Saddle Brook, NJ 07662; phones: 800/543-5201, 201/794-6725) $10, biennial. Lists over 500 major, commuter, freight carrier, and air-taxi airlines; over 200 helicopter operators; over 250 major aerospace manufacturers, and over 550 FAA approved repair stations.

Domestic Airline Guide for Pilots (Specialty Products, P.O. Box 176, Allison Park, PA 15101) $7, published each August. Describes domestic commuter and major airlines, general job qualifications, how to apply, job descriptions, and average salaries.

2019: SPACE PROBE LANDS ON PLUTO

Mother Goose and Grim reprinted by permission of MGM L&M and Grimmy, Inc.
Copyright 1991. All rights reserved.

Foreign Airline Guide for Pilots (Specialty Products, P.O. Box 176, Allison Park, PA 15101) $7, published each August. Describes foreign commuter and major airlines, general job qualifications, how to apply, job descriptions, and average salaries.

Australian Employment Guide for Pilots (Specialty Products, P.O. Box 176, Allison Park, PA 15101) $7, published each August. Describes Australian commuter and major airlines, general job qualifications, how to apply, job descriptions, and average salaries.

Directory of Employers & Salary Survey (Future Aviation Professionals of America, 4959 Massachusetts Blvd., Atlanta, GA 3037; phones: 800/538-5627, 404/997-8097) annual, $22/nonmembers, free/members. Lists major turbojet national and regional airlines and contact names. Gives information on each company's aircraft fleet, flight attendant crew bases, benefits, and minimum qualifications for employment.

ALEA's Directory of Airline Colleges and Training Schools (Air Line Employees Association, 5600 S. Central Ave., Chicago, IL 60638-3797; phone: 312/767-3333) free/members only, $40/annual membership, published each January and July.

Aeronautical Repair Station Association Membership Directory (ARSA, 1612 K St., NW, Suite 1400, Washington, DC 20006; phone: 202/293-2511) free, issued twice a year.

Who's Who in Airport Management (American Association of Airport Executives, 4212 King St., Alexandria, VA 22302; phone: 703/824-0500) available to members only, included in membership package, published annually.

AOCI Member Directory (Airport Associations Council International, 1220 19th St., NW, Suite 200, Washington, DC 20036; phone: 202/293-8500) $35/members only, annual.

Helicopter Annual (Helicopter Association International, 1619 Duke St., Alexandria, VA 22314; phone: 703/683-4646) $43/nonmembers, annual. Includes a buyers guide.

American Helicopter Society International Membership Directory (AHSI, 217 N. Washington St., Alexandria, VA 22314; phone: 703/684-6777) $10, issued each summer.

National Air Transport Association Membership Directory (NATA, 4226 King St., Alexandria, VA 22302; phone: 703/845-9000) free/members only, released each June.

National Business Aircraft Association Membership Directory (NBAA, 1200 18th St., NW, Washington, DC 20036; phone: 202/783-9000) free/members only, annual.

National Aircraft Finance Association Membership Directory (NAFA, 500 E St., SW, Suite 930, Washington, DC 20024; phone: 202/554-5570) free/members only, issued each May.

Aviation Distributors and Manufacturers Association Membership Directory (ADMA, 1900 Arch St., Philadelphia, PA 19103; phone: 215/5645-3484) free/members only, annual.

Salary surveys

Directory of Employers & Salary Survey (Future Aviation Professionals of America, 4959 Massachusetts Blvd., Atlanta, GA 30037; phones: 800/538-5627, 404/997-8097) annual, $22/nonmembers, free/members. Provides comprehensive salary and benefits information including free and reduced fare transportation privileges, uniform expenses, and more.

National Business Aircraft Association Salary Survey (NBAA, 1200 18th St., NW, Washington, DC 20036; phone: 202/783-9000) $50 to $100, contact for details, biennial.

Also see **Career Pilot Services** *and* **Aviation Maintenance Services** *described above under "Job services" for salary surveys that are included in these packages, and the* **Domestic Airline Guide for Pilots**, **Foreign Airline Guide for Pilots**, *and the* **Australian Employment Guide for Pilots** *described above under "Directories."*

Fleet/facilities management

Job openings

Automotive Fleet (Bobit Publishing, 2512 Artesia Blvd., Redondo Beach, CA 90278; phone: 213/376–8788) 13 issues/year, $24/annual subscription. Jobs listed under "Classifieds." About three to six job ads in typical issue. Many more "Positions Wanted" ads appear in each issue.

NAFA Newsletter (National Association of Fleet Managers, 120 Wood Ave. South, Iselin, NJ 08830; phone: 908/494–8100) monthly, $48/nonmember annual subscription to both *Newsletter* and *The NAFA Fleet Executive* (which does not contain job ads), both included in membership package. Jobs listed under "Jobs Available." About five job ads in the typical issue. Many more "Positions Wanted" ads are run.

IFMA News (International Facility Management Association, 1 E. Greenway Place, 11th Floor, Houston, TX 77046–0194; phone: 713/623–4362) monthly, available only to members. Two or three positions in facilities management appear under "FM Jobs."

NAFA Fleet Focus (National Association of Fleet Administrators, 120 Wood Ave., South, Suite 615, Iselin, NJ 08830–2709; phone: 908–494–8100) monthly, $48/annual nonmember subscription (U.S.), $72/Canada, free/members. Two positions in fleet management rest in "Job Talk."

Fleet Owner (FM Business Publications, 342 Madison Ave., New York, NY 10173; phone: 212/889–3174) monthly, free to qualified professionals. Not every issue has job ads, but those that appear are for maintenance directors, supervisors, and fleet management.

Also see **Community Transportation Reporter** *listed below under "Transit management."*

Directories

IFMA Membership Directory (International Facility Management Association, 1 E. Greenway Place, 11th Floor, Houston, TX 77046–0194; phone: 713/623–4362) available only to members, free/members, published each August.

Logistics and physical distribution

Job openings

U.S. Distribution Journal (BMT Publications, 7 Penn Plaza, New York, NY 10001; phone: 800/223-9638) $44/annual subscription (U.S.), $55/Canada, $75/elsewhere. "Classified" has three ads for sales, marketing, warehouse staff, and distributing positions in the candy, tobacco, and grocery businesses listed under "Help Wanted." There are also two or three "Business Opportunities" listed and "Position Wanted" ads.

Job service

Employment Clearinghouse Service (Council of Logistics Management, 2803 Butterfield Rd., Oak Brook, IL 60523; phone: 708/574-0985) free/members only, $175/annual dues. Submit two copies of your resume (no more than two-pages long) which will be duplicated and sent to employers when employers request resumes of job candidates. Every month you must specifically request that your resume be kept on file.

Directories

T&D Warehousing & Distribution Buyers Guide, July issue of *Transportation & Distribution* (Penton Publishing, 1100 Superior Ave., Cleveland, OH 44114; phone: 216/696-7000) free to qualified professionals, call or write for application form; otherwise: $9/issue. This issue includes a directory of products and manufacturers of items used in the physical distribution industry.

Self-Service Storage Membership Directory (Self-Service Storage Association, 4147 Crossgate Dr., Cincinnati, OH 45236; phone: 513/984-6468) $250/nonmembers, free/members, $225/annual dues, published annually. Lists member self-service storage companies.

Salary survey

Materials Management and Distribution Magazine Logistics Salary Survey (Maclean Hunter, 777 Bay St., Toronto, Ontario, M5W 1A7 Canada; phone: 416/596–5709) $25/issue. This is the October issue of the magazine. It covers Canadian salaries and benefits in logistics–related activities.

Traffic engineering and parking

Also see the postings listed below under "Transit management."

Job openings

ITE Journal (Institute of Transportation Engineers, Suite 410, 525 School St., SW, Washington, DC 20024–2729; phone: 202/554–8050) monthly; $50/annual subscription (U.S., Canada, and Mexico), $65/elsewhere. Jobs listed under "Positions." Usually 10 to 30 ads appear each issue.

Traffic World (International Thomson Transport Press, 529 14th St., NW, Washington, DC 20045; phone: 202/626–4500) weekly; $108/annual subscription; $72/six–month subscription, write for student rates. Jobs listed under "Classified."

Roads & Bridges (Scranton Gillette Communications, Inc., 380 Northwest Highway, Des Plaines, IL 60016; phone: 708/298–6622) monthly, $15/annual subscription, $22.50/foreign. Jobs listed under "Classified." Seven to ten job ads in typical issue.

Construction Digest (P.O. Box 603, Indianapolis, IN 46278; phone: 317/297–5500) semimonthly, $40/annual subscription, available in east or west edition. Under "Billboard" you'll find a few ads for project, territory, or service managers in heavy construction and highway construction.

Pavement Maintenance (Cahners Publishing, 1350 E. Touhy, Des Plaines, IL 708/635–8800) monthly, The "Classified" section just started carrying job ads in 1991. The number of job ads is growing. Job openings are for sweepers, patchers, pavers, stripers, sealers, and other positions in road maintenance and building.

Directories

ARTBA Membership Directory & Buyers' Guide (American Road and Transportation Builders Association, 501 School St., SW, Washington, DC 20024; phone: 202/488–2722) contact for price, annual, 196 pages. This really is "the who's who, what, where in transportation construction" guide. It includes an extensive listing of products and services for the transportation construction industry as well as a state–by–state listing of ARTBA member companies.

Association of Transportation Practitioners Membership Directory (ATP, 1725 K St., NW, Suite 301, Washington, DC 20006; phone: 202/466–2080) free/members only, issued in June of odd–numbered years.

International Bridge, Tunnel, and Turnpike Association Membership Directory (IBTTA, 2120 K St., NW, Suite 305, Washington, DC 20037; phone: 202/659–4620) free/members only, annual.

Transit management

Job openings

Passenger Transport (American Public Transport Association, 1201 New York Ave., NW, Washington, DC 20005; phone: 202/898–4119) weekly, $65/annual subscription (U.S. and Canada), $77/elsewhere.

"Help Wanted" features six to 15 vacancies for transit and transportation managers and planners, transportation engineers, marketing directors, and administrators.

Mass Transit (P.O. Box 1478, Riverton, NJ 08077; phone: 516/845-2700) 9 issues/year, $30/annual subscription (U.S. and Canada), $55/elsewhere. Jobs listed under "Classified." Four to ten job ads per issue.

Community Transportation Reporter (Community Transportation Association of America, Suite 900, 725 15th St., NW, Washington, DC 20005; phones: 800/527-8279, 202/628-1480) ten issues/year, $35/annual subscription (U.S), $47/foreign, free to members. Jobs listed under "Employment—Help Wanted." About four ads for transit managers and operators per issue.

METRO Magazine (Bobit Publishing Co., 2512 Artesia Blvd., Redondo Beach, CA 90278; phone: 213/376-8788) seven issues/year, $12/annual subscription (U.S.), $18/Canada, $50/elsewhere. Jobs listed under "Classified Ads." Few job ads.

Bus Ride (Friendship Publications, P.O. Box 1472, Spokane, WA 99210; phone: 509/328-9181) eight issues/year, $25/annual subscription. Three ads for positions in the bus industry are in the typical issue.

Railway Age (Simmons-Boardman Publishing, 345 W. Hudson St., New York, NY 10014; phones: 800/228-9670, 212/620-7200) monthly, $45/annual subscription. Three to five job ads for all aspects of railroad management and operations appear under "Classified."

RT&S: Railway Truck and Structures (345 Hudson St., New York, NY 10014; phone: 212/620-7200) monthly, $35/annual subscription. Two to five positions in the railway industry are under "Classified."

Directories

APTA Membership Directory (American Public Transport Association, 1201 New York Ave., NW, Washington, DC 20005; phone: 202/898-4119) available only to members, published each January.

Community Transportation Resource Guide (Community Transportation Association of America, Suite 900, 725 15th St., NW, Washington, DC 20005; phones: 800/527-8279, 202/628-1480) $10. Includes transportation/transit industry, published every January.

Bus Ride Bus Industry Directory (Friendship Publications, P.O. Box 1472, Spokane, WA 99210; phone: 509/328-9181) $62, released each July. Includes bus companies and transit systems.

Membership Directory of the American Bus Association (ABA, 1015 15th St., NW, Suite 250, Washington, DC 20005; phone: 202/842-1045) free/members only, annual.

Trucking industry

Job openings

Transport Topics (American Trucking Association, 2200 Mill Rd., Alexandria, VA 22314; phone: 703/838-1773) weekly, $59/annual subscription. "Employment/Agents Wanted" runs ads for 50 to 75 vacancies for safety directors, terminal managers, engineers, maintenance, repair, accountants, sales representatives, and upper management as well as positions in insurance sales for the trucking industry.

Owner-Operator: The Business Magazine of Independent Trucking (Chilton Company, Chilton Way, Radnor, PA 19089; phones: 800/345-1214, 215/964-4265) nine issues/year, $16/annual subscription (U.S.), $24/Canada, $30/elsewhere. Four to eight ads for long-haul truck drivers are in "Driver Recruitment."

Directories

National Private Truck Council Membership Directory (NPTC, 1320 Braddock Pl., Suite 720, Alexandria, VA 22314; phone: 703/683-1300) $135/nonmembers, free/members, published each January. Lists over 1,400 private fleet members and 300 suppliers to private fleets.

Transport Topics Directory: Government and Industry (American Trucking Association, 2200 Mill Rd., Alexandria, VA 22314; phone: 703/838–1773) weekly, $59/annual subscription. This directory is in the mid–January issue of *Transport Topics* each year.

Transport Topics Directory: Management Outlook (American Trucking Association, 2200 Mill Rd., Alexandria, VA 22314; phone: 703/838–1773) weekly, $59/annual subscription. This directory is in the late–January issue of *Transport Topics* each year.

Truck Trailer Manufacturers Association Member Directory (TTMA, 1020 Princess St., Alexandria, VA 22314; phone: 703/549–3010) $30/prepaid nonmembers, free/members, published each July. Includes key personnel and types of trucks used at trucking, trailer, tank, and container manufacturing firms as well as suppliers to the industry.

National Tank Truck Carrier Directory (NTTC, 2200 Mill Rd., Alexandria, VA 22314; phone: 703/838–1960) $36/nonmembers, $27/members, issued each January.

Industrial Truck Association Membership Directory (ITA, 1750 K St., NW, Suite 210, Washington, DC 20006; phone: 202/296–9880) free, annual.

The Vehicle (Truck Renting and Leasing Association, 2011 I St., NW, Suite 500, Washington, DC 20006; phone: 202/775–4859) free/members only, annual.

Water transportation

Job openings

Boating Industry (Communication Channels, 6255 Barfield Rd., Atlanta, GA 30328; phone: 404/256–9800) monthly, contact for subscription rates. "Marketplace" contains three or four ads under "Personnel & Positions," largely for salespeople, and almost 20 "Business Opportunities" with marinas and marine businesses for sale.

Cruising World Magazine (5320 Park Ave., Trumbull, CT 06611; phones: 800/727–8473, 401/847–1588) monthly, $23.94/annual subscription (U.S.), $30.97/Canada, $34/elsewhere. "Positions Wanted" carries ads for around 16 sailing crew personnel vacancies.

Sail (Cahners Publishing, 275 Washington St., Newton, MA 02158; phone: 617/964–3030) monthly, $19.95/annual subscription (U.S.), $24.95/Canada, $29.95/elsewhere. Six ads for sailing crew positions are in "Sail—Classifieds—Positions."

NMRA Newsletter (National Marine Representative Association, P.O. Box 957075, Hoffman Estates, IL 60195; phone: 708/213–0606) monthly, free/members only. Up to six jobs for sales representatives for pleasure boats, parts to build a boat from scratch, and aftermarket products are in "Lines Available."

Job services

Captains and Crews (Route 5, No. 11–Long Bay, St. Thomas, Virgin Islands 00802; phone: 809/776–2395) $15 registration fee plus 20 percent of first month's pay if hired or plus $25 if hired to go cruising or deliver a yacht. You complete this service's resume form and are matched to available positions ranging from crew (deck hands, stewards and stewardesses, cooks, etc.) to captain for cruise boats and charter yachts. Resume forms for captains are kept on file indefinitely; forms for crew stay active for a year.

Directories

Commercial Boating Directory (WorkBoat, P.O. Box 908, Rockland, ME 04841) $45, published in even-numbered years. Lists shipyards, fleet owners, and workboat suppliers.

National Marine Representative Association Directory (NMRA, P.O. Box 957075, Hoffman Estates, IL 60195; phone: 708/213-0606) $30/nonmembers, free/members, issued each January.

National Association of Marine Services Membership Directory (1900 Arch St., Philadelphia, PA 19103; phone: 215/564-3484) free, released every September.

If you're having trouble finding job sources for your specialty, you probably should refresh your memory on how to use this book most effectively. Please read Chapter 1 which explains how to get the most out of the *Professional's Job Finder*.

Chapter 38

State–by–state job sources

Obviously most job sources—namely your local classifieds—are not national in scope. In addition to the local classifieds, there are many sources of job openings that are local, regional, or statewide in coverage. This chapter explains what those job sources are and introduces you to the free job recruitment service that every state operates, but of which few habitually–employed workers avail themselves.

State–by–state job sources

State–operated Job Service offices. Perhaps the most underutilized "free lunch" ever offered to job seekers is the Job Service every state government operates. Although the quality of their services varies, each Job Service office provides employment services that include career counseling and a job–matching service of some type.

Popularly known as the "unemployment office," a state Job Service office can put you in contact with job vacancies in the private sector that range from low-paid and entry-level jobs to top-level positions with major corporations. Some companies hire for some vacancies exclusively through the local state Job Service office. For example, in some states, the United Parcel Service does virtually all its recruiting through the state's Job Service offices.

Each Job Service office maintains a frequently updated list of available private sector positions from throughout the state. You are able to read these on a microfiche machine, and in some states, on a computer. You can usually obtain a full job description from the Job Service office for those positions that interest you.

The entries in this chapter note if a state's Job Service offices also operate a job-matching service.

You should be able to find the address and phone number for a nearby Job Service office in your local telephone directory. In case you can't, this chapter offers information that enables you to locate each state's employment services, including Job Service Offices. You should write directly for more information from the state(s) of your choice. Please note that while most states call these "Job Services," some assign a different moniker like "Employment Security Department." So before you go to your local phone directory to find the Job Service office nearest you, be sure to see the entry in this chapter for your state to learn what your state calls its Job Service offices.

In addition, practically all state–operated Job Service offices or centers participate in the Interstate Job Bank Service developed by the U.S. Department of Labor's Employment and Training Administration. Jobs in other states are on microfiche which can be read at your local Job Service office, and in 20 percent of the Job Service offices, are accessible on computers, including computer terminals you can use yourself. Over 7 million non–agricultural job openings are listed during a typical year. About 6,000 vacancies are listed at any one time. These vacancies are typically two weeks old before they get on the list. Many are what are called "constant hires" which means that there are almost always job vacancies for that position. Also keep in mind that many employers take more than two weeks to fill positions, particularly higher–level ones.

If you want additional information on any of the jobs listed, every Job Service Office can call the Interstate Job Bank on its toll–free number to get this additional information on out–of–state positions.

Thirty percent of those who search for a job at a Job Service office find a job there. But note that research shows that more than half of those people who find a job through a Job Service

SYLVIA   by Nicole Hollander

office stay on the job less than a month. Any number of factors may explain this finding. It is very likely that this job loss rate occurs because so few habitually–employed people use the ''unemployment office.'' A disproportionately large percentage of people who use the service may be people who always have difficulty holding a job. But at least they have the good sense to use this free service which is more successful at placing people in appropriate jobs than most private employment agencies (as distinguished from recruiting or executive search firms which usually are more successful at placing job candidates).

The job matching services furnished by Job Service offices really amount to a free employment service for professionals, technical, labor, trades, and office support workers. However, habitually–employed individuals rarely take advantage of these services. Perhaps they are turned off by the generic moniker for these offices: the ''unemployment office.'' Don't let misconceptions steer you away from a state's Job Service offices no matter how high in the private sector hierarchy you wish to work. They are usually an effective source of private sector job openings.

Regional jobs periodicals. In a few instances, a regional jobs periodical covering several states will be an excellent source of local jobs. Several of these that are very specialized were described in earlier chapters of this book. This chapter identifies a few that are broader in scope.

Chapter newsletters of speciality or trade associations. The newsletters produced by the state or local chapters of many professional and trade associations frequently carry job advertisements. Usually, these newsletters are available only to chapter members. Some chapters, however, allow nonmembers to subscribe or join only the chapter. Because officers of state chapters change so frequently, you should contact the national headquarters of the appropriate professional or trade organization to obtain the address of any chapter president you wish to contact. We are not so foolhardy as to try to list these in one book. Many of these local association chapters are listed in the *JobBank* books and *How to Get a Job in "X"* city books described in this chapter.

Job services operated by chapters of specialty or trade associations. Similarly, state or metropolitan chapters of some professional and trade associations operate job–matching services or job hotlines. These services are usually available only to chapter members. Some chapters, however, allow nonmembers to register for a job service or join only the chapter. Because officers of state chapters change so frequently, you should contact the national headquarters of the appropriate professional or trade organization to obtain the address of any chapter president you wish to contact. Many of these local association chapters are listed in the *JobBank* books and *How to Get a Job in X* city books described in this chapter.

Local newspapers. As mentioned earlier, the classified section of local newspapers is usually a pretty good source for local private sector job ads. The sources in this book get you to the job vacancies that generally are not advertised in the local classifieds. If you are seeking a new job in your local area, you would be prudent to use both the local classifieds and the job sources described in this book to find job vacancies. If you are considering jobs outside your local area, the local classifieds usually won't be much of a help. However, the sources described in the preceding chapters, and the sources enumerated in this chapter, will be most helpful.

Job sources: State-by-state

Alabama

To locate **Job Service Offices**, contact the Employment Services Division (Department of Industrial Relations, 649 Monroe St., Montgomery, AL 36131; director's phone: 205/242-8003).

Alaska

To locate **Job Service Offices**, contact the Alaska Employment Security Division (Department of Labor, P.O. Box 3-7000, Juneau, AK 998802; phone: 907/465-2712).

Arizona

Rocky Mountain Employment Newsletter (Intermountain Publishing, 703 S. Broadway, Suite 100-B0, Denver, CO 80209; phone: 303/988-6707) 18 issues/year, $19/three-month subscription to one edition, $30/any two editions, $39/three editions. Two and one-month subscriptions also available. Published in three editions: Colorado-Wyoming, Arizona-New Mexico, and Idaho-Montana. Combined, the three editions include over 300 private sector job openings. The positions tend to orient toward the outdoors, with quite a few in natural resources, environment, and wildlife.

The Phoenix JobBank (Bob Adams Publications, 260 Center St., Holbrook, MA 02343; phones: 800/872-5627) $12.95, annual. Over 250 pages list 1,500 of the major employers in the metropolitan area including whom to contact at each about job vacancies. Also included is a list of professional employment services (always be cautious about these; there are some charlatans out there who have sullied this profession's reputation), the addresses of the local chapter of many professional and trade associations, and profiles of many private sector occupations.

To locate **Job Service Offices**, contact the Employment and Rehabilitation Services Division (Department of Economic Security, P.O. Box 6123-010A, Phoenix, AZ 85007; director's phone: 602/542-4016).

Arkansas

Arkansas Employment Security Division Job–Matching Service (Employment Security Division, Capitol Mall, Little Rock, AR 72201; administrator's phone: 501/682–2121; available at any of the 34 local Employment Security Division offices) free. A job seeker completes the service's resume form and is then matched with jobs. The service contacts matched applicants to arrange job interviews with employers. Applications are kept active for 60 days.

For information on the location of the 34 **Job Service Offices** (known in Arkansas as local Employment Security Department offices), contact the Employment Security Department, (Room 506, ESD Building, P.O. Box 2981, Little Rock, AR 72203; phone: 501/682–2121).

California

Public Interest Employment Report (Public Interest Clearing-house, 200 McAllister St., San Francisco, CA 94102–4978; phone: 415/565–4695) semimonthly, three–month subscription for individuals: $30/employed nonmembers, $15/unemployed nonmembers, $15/members; annual subscription: $125/schools and institutions, $60/non–profit organizations. About 90 professional and support positions described per issue are in legal services.

Directory of Bay Area Public Interest Organizations (Public Interest Clearinghouse) $25. Features 600 organizations working for social change in the nine–county San Francisco Bay Area. Indexed by subject and county. Most recent edition published in 1991.

Public Interest, Private Practice: A Directory of Public Interest Law Firms in Northern California (Public Interest Clearinghouse) $10. Lists over 200 for–profit law firms that devote a substantial portion of their legal work to the public interest.

Public Interest Employment Service Resource Center Clipboards (Public Interest Clearinghouse) free. Members and subscribers to the Public Interest Clearinghouse's publications can drop in between 9 a.m. and 5 p.m. Monday through Friday (open to 7 p.m. on Wednesdays) to examine the five *Job Clipboards* (attorneys, paralegals, more non-attorneys, law students, and other public interest jobs) which are updated daily with new job openings. These vacancies later appear in the next issue of the *Public Interest Employment Report* described above under "California." Also available for examination are other job newsletters and resource files on potential employers.

How to Get a Job in Southern California (Surrey Books, 230 E. Ohio, Suite 120, Chicago, IL 60611; phones: 800/326–4430, 312/751–7330) $15.95 plus $2/shipping, annual, 451 pages. This easy-to-use book tells you whom to contact for job vacancies at over 1,500 top private sector employers in the southern half of the state. It also lists local chapters of professional and trade associations (which may publish a periodical with jobs ads or operate a local job service), local trade magazines, useful local professional publications, directories, and lists of executive search firms and of employment services. Always be careful with employment services. Too many employment services engage in practices that embarrass the legitimate members of the industry.

The Los Angeles JobBank (Bob Adams Publications, 260 Center St., Holbrook, MA 02343; phones: 800/872-5627) $12.95, annual, 392 pages. Includes a list 1,500 of the major employers in the metropolitan area including whom to contact at each about job vacancies. Also included is a list of professional employment services (always be cautious about these; there are some charlatans out there who have sullied this profession's reputation), the addresses of the local chapter of many professional and trade associations, and profiles of many private sector occupations.

The San Francisco Bay Area JobBank (Bob Adams Publications, 260 Center St., Holbrook, MA 02343; phones: 800/872-5627) $12.95, annual, 346 pages. Includes a list 1,500 of the major employers in the Bay Area including whom to contact at each about job vacancies. Also included is a list of professional employment services (always be cautious about these; there are some charlatans out there who have sullied this profession's reputation), the addresses of the local chapter of many professional and trade associations, and profiles of many private sector occupations.

How to Get a Job in the San Francisco Bay Area (Surrey Books, 230 E. Ohio, Suite 120, Chicago, IL 60611; phones: 800/326–4430, 312/751–7330) $15.95 plus $2/shipping, annual, 496 pages. This easy-to-use book tells you whom to contact for job vacancies at over 1,800 top private sector employers in the Bay Area. It also lists local chapters of professional and trade associations (which may publish a periodical with jobs ads or operate a local job service), local trade magazines, useful local professional publications, directories, and lists of executive search firms and of employment services. Always be careful with employment services. Too many employment services engage in practices that embarrass the legitimate members of the industry.

To locate **Job Service Offices**, contact the Employment Development Department (P.O. Box 944216, Sacramento, CA 94244–2160; phone: 916/445–8008).

Colorado

Rocky Mountain Employment Newsletter (Intermountain Publishing, 703 S. Broadway, Suite 100–B0, Denver, CO 80209; phone: 303/988–6707) 18 issues/year, $19/three–month subscription to one edition, $30/any two editions, $39/three editions. Two and one-month subscriptions also available. Published in three editions: Colorado–Wyoming, Arizona–New Mexico, and Idaho–Montana. Combined, the three editions include over 300 private sector job vacancies. The positions tend to orient toward the outdoors, with quite a few in natural resources, environment, and wildlife.

The Denver JobBank (Bob Adams Publications, 260 Center St., Holbrook, MA 02343; phones: 800/872–5627) $12.95, annual, over 250 pages. Lists 1,000 + of the major employers in the metropolitan area including whom to contact at each about job vacancies. Also included is a list of professional employment services (always be cautious about these; there are some charlatans out there who have sullied this profession's reputation), the addresses of the local chapter of many professional and trade associations, and profiles of many private sector occupations.

To locate **Job Service Offices,** contact the Department of Labor and Employment (600 Grant St., Denver, CO 8020-3528; phone: 303/837–3801).

Connecticut

To locate the state **Job Service Offices** in Ansonia, Bridgeport, Bristol, Danbury, Danielson, Enfield, Hamden, Hartford, Manchester, Meriden, Middleton, New Britain, New London, Norwalk, Norwich, Stamford, Torrington, Waterbury, and Willimantic, see the state government section (the blue pages) of the local white pages telephone directory or contact the Connecticut Department of Labor (200 Foly Brook Blvd., Wethersfield, CT 06109; phone: 203/566-8818) for a list of Job Service Offices.

Delaware

To locate **Job Service Offices**, contact the Division of Employment and Training (Delaware Department of Labor, P.O. Box 9499, Newark, DE 19714-9499; phone: 302/368-6825).

District of Columbia

How to Get a Job in Washington DC (Surrey Books, 230 E. Ohio, Suite 120, Chicago, IL 60611; phones: 800/326-4430, 312/751-7330) $15.95 plus $2/shipping, annual, over 300 pages. This easy-to-use book tells you whom to contact for job vacancies at over 1,400 top private sector employers in the metropolitan area. It also lists local chapters of professional and trade associations (which may publish a periodical with jobs ads or operate a local job service), local trade magazines, useful local professional publications, directories, and lists of executive search firms and of employment services. Always be careful with employment services. Too many employment services engage in practices that embarrass the legitimate members of the industry.

The Metropolitan Washington DC JobBank (Bob Adams Publications, 260 Center St., Holbrook, MA 02343; phones: 800/872-5627) $12.95, annual, 336 pages. Lists 1,600+ of the major private sector employers in the metropolitan area including whom to contact at each about job vacancies. Also included is a list of professional employment services (always be cautious about these; there are some charlatans out there who have sullied this profession's reputation), the addresses of the local chapter of many professional and trade associations, and profiles of many private sector occupations.

1992 Internships (Petersons Guides, PO Box 2123, Princeton, NJ 08543-2123; phone: 800/338-3282) $27.95. Updated annually, this 300+ page this book describes more than 200 internship opportunities in and around the District of Columbia, mostly with the federal government, but also a good many in the private sector.

Internships + Job Opportunities in New York City and Washington, DC (Graduate Group, 86 Norwood Rd., West Hartford, CT 06117; phones: 203/232-3100, 203/236-5570) $27.50, published annually.

Washington 91 (Columbia Books, 1212 New York Ave., NW, Suite 300, Washington, DC 20005; phone: 202/898-0662) $60, published annually. Nearly 600 pages of addresses, phone numbers, and information on companies and businesses in the D.C. area. Includes chapters on the media, business, national associations, labor unions, law firms, medicine and health, foundations and philanthropy, science and policy research, education, religion, cultural institutions, clubs, and community affairs.

The Capitol Source: The Who's Who, What, Where in Washington (National Journal, Inc., 1730 M St., NW, Washington, DC 20036; phones: 800/424-2921, 202/862-0644) $30. Published every April and November, this directory includes names, addresses, and phone numbers for corporations, interest groups, think tanks, labor unions, real estate, financial institutions, trade and professional organizations, law firms, political consultants, advertising and public relations firms, private clubs, and the media. All entries are also available on computer diskette. Call 202/857-1469 for information.

For information on **Job Service Offices**, contact the District's Department of Employment Services (500 C St., NW, Washington, DC 20001; phone: 202/639-1000).

Florida

The Florida JobBank (Bob Adams Publications, 260 Center St., Holbrook, MA 02343; phones: 800/872–5627) $12.95, annual, 318 pages. Lists 1,500+ of the major private sector employers in the state including whom to contact at each about job vacancies. Also included is a list of professional employment services (always be cautious about these; there are some charlatans out there who have sullied this profession's reputation), the addresses of the local chapter of many professional and trade associations, and profiles of many private sector occupations.

To locate **Job Service Offices**, contact the Department of Labor and Employment Security (2012 Capital Cr., SE, Tallahassee, FL 32399–2154; phone: 904/488–4398).

Georgia

How to Get a Job in Atlanta (Surrey Books, 230 E. Ohio, Suite 120, Chicago, IL 60611; phones: 800/326–4430, 312/751–7330) $15.95 plus $2/shipping, annual, 490 pages. This easy–to–use book tells you whom to contact for job vacancies at over 1,500 top private sector employers in the metropolitan area. It also lists local chapters of professional and trade associations (which may publish a periodical with jobs ads or operate a local job service), local trade magazines, useful local professional publications, directories, and lists of executive search firms and of employment services. Always be careful with employment services. Too many employment services engage in practices that embarrass the legitimate members of the industry.

The Atlanta JobBank (Bob Adams Publications, 260 Center St., Holbrook, MA 02343; phones: 800/872–5627) $12.95, annual, 323 pages. Lists 1,500+ of the major private sector employers in the metropolitan area including whom to contact at each about job vacancies. Also included is a list of professional employment services (always be cautious about these; there are some charlatans out there who have sullied this profession's reputation), the addresses of the local chapter of many professional and trade associations, and profiles of many private sector occupations.

Job Information Service (Georgia Department of Labor, 148 International Blvd., NE, Atlanta, GA 30303). Descriptions of private sector vacancies throughout the state, and nation, are available on a computerized statewide database. Job opening information can be viewed at any of the department's 35 field offices throughout the state. The largest office is in Atlanta (2811 Lakewood Ave., SW, Atlanta, GA 30315; phone: 404/669-3300). Contact the department for a list of all field offices of this **Job Service** or check the local phone book.

Hawaii

The Honolulu Advertiser/Star-Bulletin (605 Kapiolani Blvd., Honolulu, HI 96813; phone: 808/935-3916) published weekly on Sunday. Write for subscription prices. This is a good source for private sector positions throughout the state.

For information on **Job Service Offices**, contact the Department of Labor and Industrial Relations, 830 Punchbowl St., Honolulu, HI 96813; phone: 808/548-3150).

Idaho

Rocky Mountain Employment Newsletter (Intermountain Publishing, 703 S. Broadway, Suite 100-B0, Denver, CO 80209; phone: 303/988-6707) 18 issues/year, $19/three-month subscription to one edition, $30/any two editions, $39/three editions. Two and one-month subscriptions also available. Published in three editions: Colorado-Wyoming, Arizona-New Mexico, and Idaho-Montana. Combined, the three editions include over 300 private sector job vacancies. The positions tend to orient toward the outdoors, with quite a few in natural resources, environment, and wildlife.

For the addresses and phones of **Job Service Offices**, contact the Department of Employment, 317 Main St., Boise, ID 83735; phone: 208/334-6110).

Illinois

How to Get a Job in Chicago (Surrey Books, 230 E. Ohio, Suite 120, Chicago, IL 60611; phones: 800/326–4430, 312/751–7330) $15.95 plus $2/shipping, annual, 477 pages. This easy–to–use book tells you whom to contact for job vacancies at over 1,500 top private sector employers in the metropolitan area. It also lists local chapters of professional and trade associations (which may publish a periodical with jobs ads or operate a local job service), local trade magazines, useful local professional publications, directories, and lists of executive search firms and of employment services. Always be careful with employment services. Too many employment services engage in practices that embarrass the legitimate members of the industry.

The Greater Chicago JobBank (Bob Adams Publications, 260 Center St., Holbrook, MA 02343; phones: 800/872–5627) $12.95, annual, 370 pages. Lists 1,500 + of the major private sector employers in the metropolitan area including whom to contact at each about job vacancies. Also included is a list of professional employment services (always be cautious about these; there are some charlatans out there who have sullied this profession's reputation), the addresses of the local chapter of many professional and trade associations, and profiles of many private sector occupations.

Illinois Department of Employment Security Offices (Office Manager, Employment Security Consolidated Office South, 1300 S. 9th St., Springfield, IL 62705; phone: 217/524–7838 and 401 S. State St., Chicago, IL 60605; 312/793–8138). Sixty–three of these **Job Service Offices** across the state offer computer–based job searches. For a list of Job Service Offices, contact one of these offices or see the state government section of your local white pages telephone directory.

Indiana

Indiana Department of Employment and Training Service (IDETS) (Room 331, 10 N. Senate Ave., Indianapolis, IN 46204; phone: 317/232-3270) has personnel who specialize in matching applicants with government jobs through the statewide automated **Job Service** Matching System. This service is available only by an in-person visit to a IDETS office. Write for a list of offices or consult the state government section in local telephone directories. All these services are free.

Iowa

To locate **Job Service Offices**, contact the Department of Employment Services (Capitol Complex, Des Moines, IA 50319; phone: 515/281-5387).

Kansas

To find **Job Service Offices**, contact the Department of Human Resources (401 SW Topeka Blvd., Topeka, KS 66603; phone: 913/296-7474) for a copy of the "DHR Office Directory" which lists the 36 offices the Department of Human Resources operates.

Kentucky

To locate **Job Service Offices**, contact Examination and Recruitment (Department for Employment Services, 275 E. Main St., Frankfort, KY 40621; phone: 502/564-5331).

Louisiana

For information on the location of **Job Service Offices**, contact the Department of Employment and Training (P.O. Box 94094, Baton Rouge, LA 70804-9094; phone: 504/342-3111).

Maine

Maine Sunday Telegram and *Portland Press Herald* (390 Congress, Portland, ME 04101; phone: 207/780-9000) are the best sources of job openings for private sector positions throughout the state.

To locate **Job Service Offices**, contact the Bureau of Employment Security (Department of Labor, State House Station #54, Augusta, ME 04333; director's phone: 207/289-3431).

Maryland

Washington 91 (Columbia Books, 1212 New York Ave., NW, Suite 300, Washington, DC 20005; phone: 202/898-0662) $60, published annually. Here are nearly 600 pages of addresses, phone numbers, and information on private sector businesses and companies including suburban Maryland. Included are chapters on the media, business, national associations, labor unions, law firms, medicine and health, foundations and philanthropy, science and policy research, education, religion, cultural institutions, clubs, and community affairs.

Job–Matching Service (Job Training and Placement Administration, Department of Economic and Employment Development, 1100 N. Eutaw St., Baltimore, MD 21201; director's phone: 301/333-7574) free. Matches your skills to job vacancies in the private sector. Available at Job Service offices throughout the state.

To pinpoint **Job Service Offices**, contact the Job Training and Placement Administration (Department of Economic and Employee Development, Room 700, 1100 N. Eutaw St., Baltimore, MD 21201; director's phone: 301/333-5070).

Massachusetts

The Boston JobBank (Bob Adams Publications, 260 Center St., Holbrook, MA 02343; phones: 800/872-5627) $12.95, annual, 355 pages. Lists 1,500+ of the major private sector employers in the metropolitan area including whom to contact at each about job vacancies. Also included is a list of professional employment services (always be cautious about these; there are some charlatans out there who have sullied this profession's reputation), the addresses of the local chapter of many professional and trade associations, and profiles of many private sector occupations.

To locate **Job Service Offices,** contact the Department of Employment and Training (19 Stainford St., Boston, MA 02108; phone: 617/727–6529).

Michigan

The Detroit JobBank (Bob Adams Publications, 260 Center St., Holbrook, MA 02343; phones: 800/872–5627) $12.95, annual, over 250 pages. Lists 1,000 + of the major private sector employers in the metropolitan area including whom to contact at each about job vacancies. Also included is a list of professional employment services (always be cautious with these services; there are some charlatans out there who have sullied this profession's reputation), the addresses of the local chapter of many professional and trade associations, and profiles of many private sector occupations.

Michigan Occupational Information System (4–Sights Network, 16625 Grand River, Detroit, MI 48227; phone: 313/272–3900) free. Updated annually, this computer database includes a description of every job title in the state in both the private and public sectors. Each listing defines the nature of the job, working conditions, methods of entry, earnings, employment outlook, and more. For details on how to connect your computer into this database via modem, contact the 4–Sights Network. This directory is available *only* through computer modem.

To find **Job Service Offices,** contact the Employment Security Commission (7310 Woodward Ave., Detroit, MI 48202; phone: 313/876–5022).

Minnesota

The Minneapolis–St. Paul JobBank (Bob Adams Publications, 260 Center St., Holbrook, MA 02343; phones: 800/872–5627) $12.95, annual, 312 pages. Lists 1,500 + of the major private sector employers in the metropolitan area including whom to contact at each about job vacancies. Also included is a list of professional

"I think it's time I retired. His orders are starting to make sense to me."

employment services (always be cautious about these; there are some charlatans out there who have sullied this profession's reputation), the addresses of the local chapter of many professional and trade associations, and profiles of many private sector occupations.

For information on the location of **Job Service Offices**, contact Jobs, Opportunity, and Insurance (Department of Jobs and Training, 390 N. Robert St., St. Paul, MN 55101; director's phone: 612/296–3625).

Mississippi

For a list of **Job Service Offices**, contact the Mississippi State Employment Service (1520 W. Capitol St., Jackson, MS 39215-1699) for a copy of the "Directory of Employment Service Offices."

Missouri

The St. Louis JobBank (Bob Adams Publications, 260 Center St., Holbrook, MA 02343; phones: 800/872-5627) $12.95, annual, 317 pages. Lists 1,000+ of the major private sector employers in the metropolitan area including whom to contact at each about job vacancies. Also included is a list of professional employment services (always be cautious about these; there are some charlatans out there who have sullied this profession's reputation), the addresses of the local chapter of many professional and trade associations, and profiles of many private sector occupations.

To locate **Job Service Offices**, contact the Division of Employment Security (Labor and Industrial Relations Department, 421 E. Dunklin, Box 59, Jefferson City, MO 65104; director's phone: 314/751-3215).

Montana

Rocky Mountain Employment Newsletter (Intermountain Publishing, 703 S. Broadway, Suite 100-B0, Denver, CO 80209; phone: 303/988-6707) 18 issues/year, $19/three-month subscription to one edition, $30/any two editions, $39/three editions. Two and one-month subscriptions also available. Published in three editions: Colorado-Wyoming, Arizona-New Mexico, and Idaho-Montana. Combined, the three editions include over 300 private sector positions. The positions tend to orient toward the outdoors, with quite a few in natural resources, environment, and wildlife.

Directory of Job Service Offices (Job Service Division, Department of Labor and Industry, P.O. Box 1728, Helena, MT 59624; phone: 406/444-4100) free. Lists detailed information on the state's 24 **Job Service Offices.**

Nebraska

To locate **Job Service Offices**, contact the Job Service Division (Department of Labor, 550 S. 16th St., Lincoln, NE 68509; phone: 402/471-9828).

Nevada

To obtain a list of **Job Service Centers**, contact the Employment Security Department (500 E. Third St., Carson City, NV 89710; phone: 702/687–4630).

New Hampshire

Private sector jobs for the whole state are advertised in local newspapers and the *New Hampshire Sunday News* (35 Amherst St,. Manchester, NH 03101; phone: 603/668–4321), *Maine Sunday Telegram* (390 Congress, Portland, ME 04101; phone: 207/775–5811), and *Boston Globe* (135 Morrissey Blvd., Boston, MA 02107; phone: 617/929–2000).

To locate **Job Service Offices**, contact the Bureau of Employment Services (Department of Employment Security, 32 S. Main St., Concord, NH 03301; phone: 603/224–3311).

New Jersey

Job Service Offices (Division of Employment Services, Department of Labor, John Fitch Plaza, Trenton, NJ 08625; phone: 609/292–2400). Request this list of the 23 full-service **Job Service Offices** and 16 satellite offices. Job vacancies are available on computer.

New Mexico

Rocky Mountain Employment Newsletter (Intermountain Publishing, 703 S. Broadway, Suite 100-B0, Denver, CO 80209; phone: 303/988–6707) 18 issues/year, $19/three-month subscription to one edition, $30/any two editions, $39/three editions. Two and one-month subscriptions also available. Published in three editions: Colorado–Wyoming, Arizona–New Mexico, and Idaho–Montana. Combined, the three editions include over 400 positions, about 75 to 80 percent of them in private sector. The positions tend to orient toward the outdoors, with quite a few in natural resources, environment, and wildlife.

Albuquerque Journal (7777 Jefferson, NE, Albuquerque, NM 87109; phone: 505/823–4400) The Sunday edition is the best source of ads for jobs in three-fourths of the state. For the southern and southeast portions of the state, see the Sunday *El Paso Times* (401 Mills St., El Paso, TX 79901; phone: 915/546–6260). For jobs in the extreme southern section, beginning with Clovis and going south, the Sunday editions of the local newspapers from nearby Texas are the best sources.

To locate **Job Service Offices**, contact the Department of Labor (P.O. Box 1928, Albuquerque, NM 87103; phone: 505/841–8609).

New York

How to Get a Job in New York (Surrey Books, 230 E. Ohio, Suite 120, Chicago, IL 60611; phones: 800/326–4430, 312/751–7330) $15.95 plus $2/shipping, annual, 420 pages. This easy-to-use book tells you whom to contact for job vacancies at over 1,800 top private sector employers in the metropolitan area. It also lists local chapters of professional and trade associations (which may publish a periodical with jobs ads or operate a local job service), local trade magazines, useful local professional publications, directories, and lists of executive search firms and of employ-ment services. Always be careful with em-ployment services. Too many employment services engage in practices that embarrass the legitimate members of the industry.

The Metropolitan New York JobBank (Bob Adams Publications, 260 Center St., Holbrook, MA 02343; phones: 800/872-5627) $12.95, annual, 498 pages. Lists 1,500 + of the major private sector employers in the met-ropolitan area including whom to contact at each about job vacancies. Also included is a list of professional employment services (always be cautious with these services; there are some charlatans out there who have sullied this profession's reputation), the addresses of the local chapter of many professional and trade associations, and profiles of many private sector occupations.

Internships + Job Opportunities in New York City and Washington, DC (Graduate Group, 86 Norwood Rd., West Hartford, CT 06117; phones: 203/232-3100, 203/236-5570) $27.50, published annually.

To find **Job Service Offices**, tagged "Community Service Centers" in New York, contact the Department of Labor (Room 590, State Campus Building #12, Albany, NY 12240; phone: 518/457-7030).

North Carolina

To locate *Job Service Offices*, contact the Employment Security Commission (P.O. Box 25903, Raleigh, NC 27611; phone: 919/733-7546).

North Dakota

Job Service North Dakota (1000 E. Divide Ave., P.O. Box 1537, Bismarck, ND 58502; phone: 701/224-2825). Announcements for private sector jobs can be viewed at any local Job Service Office. Write for a list of local offices.

Ohio

The Ohio JobBank (Bob Adams Publications, 260 Center St., Holbrook, MA 02343; phones: 800/872-5627) $12.95, annual, 348 pages. Lists 1,500+ of the major private sector employers throughout the state including whom to contact at each about job vacancies. Also included is a list of professional employment services (always be cautious with these services; there are some charlatans out there who have sullied this profession's reputation), the addresses of the local chapter of many professional and trade associations, and profiles of many private sector occupations.

To obtain a list of the state's 76 **Job Service Offices**, contact the Public Information Office (Bureau of Employment Services, 145 S. Front St., P.O. Box 1618, Columbus, OH 43216; phone: 614/466-3859).

Oklahoma

To pinpoint **Job Service Offices**, contact the Employment Security Commission (320 Will Rogers Memorial Dr., Oklahoma City, OK 73105; phone: 405/557-7105).

Oregon

Local Office Directory (Employment Division, Department of Human Resources, 875 Union St., NE, Salem, OR 97301; phones: 503/378-3211, 800/237-3710 within Oregon only). Contact these folks for this list of 33 local **Job Service Offices** at which listings of local and state government jobs are available.

Pennsylvania

The Gerater Philadelphia JobBank (Bob Adams Publications, 260 Center St., Holbrook, MA 02343; phones: 800/872-5627) $12.95, annual, 351 pages. Lists 1,400+ of the major private sector employers in the metropolitan area including whom to contact at each about job vacancies. Also included is a list of professional employment services (always be cautious with these services; there are some charlatans out there who have sullied this profession's reputation), the addresses of the local chapter of many professional and trade associations, and profiles of many private sector occupations.

Obtain locations of **Job Service Offices** from the Office of Employment Security (Department of Labor and Industry, Room 1115, Seventh and Forster Streets, Harrisburg, PA 17121; phone: 717/787-3354).

Rhode Island

Find the ten **Job Service Offices**, by contacting the Department of Employment and Training (101 Friendship St., Providence, RI 02903; phone: 401/277-3722) or see your telephone directory. Job Service staff will match job seekers with positions and refer them to potential employers.

South Carolina

To locate **Job Service Offices**, contact the Employment Security Commission (1550 Gadsden St., Columbia, SC 29202; phone: 803/737–2400).

South Dakota

South Dakota Job Order Index (Labor Market Information Center, P.O. Box 4730, Aberdeen, SD 57402–4730; phone: 605/622–2314, 800/592–1881, from within South Dakota only) weekly; free. This periodical lists private sector jobs by geographic area. Each issue includes a list of local **Job Service Offices**.

Tennessee

To obtain a list of **Job Service Offices**, contact the Department of Employment Security (500 James Robertson Parkway, 12th Floor, Nashville, TN 37245–0900; phone: 615/741–7973).

Texas

The Dallas–Ft.Worth JobBank (Bob Adams Publications, 260 Center St., Holbrook, MA 02343; phones: 800/872–5627) $12.95, annual, 298 pages. Lists 1,000+ of the major private sector employers in the metropolitan area including whom to contact at each about job vacancies. Also included is a list of professional employment services (always be cautious with these services; there are some charlatans out there who have sullied this profession's reputation), the addresses of the local chapter of many professional and trade associations, and profiles of many private sector occupations.

How to Get a Job in Dallas/Fort Worth (Surrey Books, 230 E. Ohio, Suite 120, Chicago, IL 60611; phones: 800/326–4430, 312/751–7330) $15.95 plus $2/shipping, annual, over 300 pages. This easy–to–use book tells you whom to contact for job vacancies at over 1,250 top private sector employers in the metropolitan area. It also lists local chapters of professional and trade associations (which may publish a periodical with jobs ads or operate a local job service), local trade magazines, useful local professional publications, directories, and lists of executive search firms and of employment services. Always be careful with employment services. Too many employment services engage in practices that embarrass the legitimate members of the industry.

How to Get a Job in Houston (Surrey Books, 230 E. Ohio, Suite 120, Chicago, IL 60611; phones: 800/326-4430, 312/751-7330) $15.95 plus $2/shipping, annual, over 300 pages. This easy-to-use book tells you whom to contact for job vacancies at over 1,200 top private sector employers in the metropolitan area. It also lists local chapters of professional and trade associations (which may publish a periodical with jobs ads or operate a local job service), local trade magazines, useful local professional publications, directories, and lists of executive search firms and of employment services. Always be careful with employment services. Too many employment services engage in practices that embarrass the legitimate members of the industry.

The Houston JobBank (Bob Adams Publications, 260 Center St., Holbrook, MA 02343; phones: 800/872-5627) $12.95, annual, over 250 pages. Lists 1,000+ of the major private sector employers in the metropolitan area including whom to contact at each about job vacancies. Also included is a list of professional employment services (always be cautious with these services; there are some charlatans out there who have sullied this profession's reputation), the addresses of the local chapter of many professional and trade associations, and profiles of many private sector occupations.

The Texas Employment Commission operates a statewide, computer-assisted job matching system at its 100 offices. Request a list of these **Job Service Offices** from the TEC State Office (101 E. 15th St., Austin, TX 78778-0001; phone: 512/463-2222) or see the state government section of the local telephone directory.

Utah

Jobs listings are available by in-person application at the Utah **Job Service**, 720 South 200 East, Salt Lake City, UT 84111 (phone: 801/536-7000 or 5735 S. Readwood Rd., Salt Lake City, UT 84107; phone: 801/269-4700).

"Certainly I know how to make coffee,
and I do—every morning before I come here!"

To locate other **Job Service Offices**, contact the Utah Department of Employment Security (174 Social Hall Ave., Salt Lake City, UT 84147; phone: 801/533–2202).

Vermont

Vermont Job Service (Vermont Department of Employment and Training, P.O. Box 648, Barre, VT 05641; phone: 802/229–1757) free. Provides job matching services for private sector jobs. Resumes are kept on file up to three years.

To locate **Job Service Offices**, contact the Department of Employment and Training (P.O. Box 488, Montpelier, VT 05602; phone: 802/229–0311).

Virginia

Washington 91 (Columbia Books, 1212 New York Ave., NW, Suite 300, Washington, DC 20005; phone: 202/898–0662) $60, published annually. You'll find nearly 600 pages of addresses, phone numbers, and information on businesses and companies in the D.C.

area including its Virginia suburbs. Included are chapters on the media, business, national associations, labor unions, law firms, medicine and health, foundations and philanthropy, science and policy research, education, religion, cultural institutions, clubs, and community affairs.

Locate a local State Employment Service Office (Job Service) through a local telephone directory's state government section or obtain a list of the 42 local **Job Service Offices** from the Virginia Employment Commission (703 E. Main St., Richmond, VA 23219; phone: 804/786-3001).

Virginia is one of the first states to use ALEX, the *Automated Labor EX*change computer service that enables job seekers to look up job vacancies in Virginia, and nationwide, themselves. If a job is listed with a state Job Service office anywhere in the country, it will be accessible through ALEX. ALEX terminals are being constructed at Job Service Offices and in shopping malls, libraries, and schools.

Washington

How to Get a Job in Seattle/Portland (Surrey Books, 230 E. Ohio, Suite 120, Chicago, IL 60611; phones: 800/326-4430, 312/751-7330) $15.95 plus $2/shipping, annual, over 300 pages. This easy-to-use book tells you whom to contact for job vacancies at over 1,500 top private sector employers in the metropolitan area. It also lists local chapters of professional and trade associations (which may publish a periodical with jobs ads or operate a local job service), local trade magazines, useful local professional publications, directories, and lists of executive search firms and of employment services. Always be careful with employment services. Too many employment services engage in practices that embarrass the legitimate members of the industry.

The Seattle JobBank (Bob Adams Publications, 260 Center St., Holbrook, MA 02343; phones: 800/872-5627) $12.95, annual, 260 pages. Lists 1,000+ of the major private sector employers in the metropolitan area including whom to contact at each about job vacancies. Also included is a list of professional employment services (always be cautious with these services; there are some charlatans out there who have sullied this profession's reputation), the addresses of the local chapter of many professional and trade associations, and profiles of many private sector occupations.

To locate **Job Service Offices**, contact the Division of Employment Services (Employment Security Department, 212 Maple Park, Olympia, WA 98504; phone: 206/438-4804).

West Virginia

To locate **Job Service Offices**, contact the Bureau of Employment Programs (112 California Ave., Charleston, WV 25305; phone: 304/348-2660).

Wisconsin

To locate **Job Service Offices**, contact the Job Service Division (Department of Industry, Labor, and Human Relations, P.O. Box 7903, Madison, WI 53707; director's phone: 608/266-8561).

Wyoming

Rocky Mountain Employment Newsletter (Intermountain Publishing, 703 S. Broadway, Suite 100-B0, Denver, CO 80209; phone: 303/988-6707) 18 issues/year, $19/three-month subscription to one edition, $30/any two editions, $39/three editions. Two and one-month subscriptions also available. Published in three editions: Colorado-Wyoming, Arizona-New Mexico, and Idaho-Montana. Combined, the three editions include over 300 private sector job vacancies. The positions tend to orient toward the outdoors, with quite a few in natural resources, environment, and wildlife.

To get the addresses of the 16 local **Job Service Centers** in Wyoming, contact the Job Service of Wyoming (Department of Employment, P.O. Box 2760, Casper, WY 82602; phone: 307/235-3200).

Chapter 39

Cover letters and resumes

Even if you know how and where to find the job openings, you still have to write an effective cover letter and resume to get the job—unless you are applying for a private sector job that requires submission of only a specified form. There are a lot of fine resume and cover letter books on the market that will help you prepare good cover letters and resumes—and some not so fine books. I've scoured more of them than I care to remember and have refined their best advice for you in this chapter. I've tried to be as concise as possible so you don't have to spend a lot of time reading this chapter.

To take the next step in the job search process, you need to persuade your potential employer that you are worth interviewing. That's where your cover letter and resume make the difference. Once you get the interview, it's up to you to make a good enough impression to be offered the job at the salary you want.

This chapter suggests ways to write an effective application letter to accompany your resume. Then it explains how to prepare an attractive and effective resume. For the student right of out school, these guidelines remove some of the mystery from applying for jobs. For the seasoned worker, they offer a sound refresher course and debunk many of the myths built up over the years, particularly concerning the content of a resume.

Finally, the next chapter reviews ways to adequately prepare for your job interview and recommends productive interview behaviors that can benefit even the most seasoned worker.

Cover or target letters

Cover letters and resumes go hand–in–hand. A target, or cover letter explains why you are particularly well–suited to the specific job for which you are applying. The resume outlines your professional experience, education, and other relevant accomplishments in some detail and can be used for most any job for which you apply.

The purpose of the resume is to market you to a potential employer well enough to get him to invite you to a personal interview. Because the person who does the hiring usually scours scores of applications (sometimes hundreds in today's job market), your cover letter should, in a persuasive, professional, polite, and personable manner, point out your specific qualifications for the job so well that the employer will carefully examine the resume your cover letter accompanies. As Dr. Krannich and William Banis put it in *High Impact Resumes and Letters*, "your letter should be the sizzle accompanying the sell." While the resume can, and should, be mass produced, the cover letter for each job application should be individually typed and targeted to the specific job.

Cover letter guidelines

Use your own personal stationery or blank paper and the appropriate business letter format for your cover letter. It is very bad form to use the letterhead of your current employer when applying for a job elsewhere. Use high quality white or light–colored bond paper.

If at all possible, the letter itself should be addressed to a specific person. If the advertisement or job announcement failed to name the person to whom you apply, it's usually worth a phone call to learn her name. Just ask the receptionist or secretary in the department that is doing the hiring. Sometimes you'll run into a brick wall where nobody will tell you to whom to write. One option is to consult the directories described in this book to identify the proper person. Then call the company to confirm that the individual still works there (personnel do change after directories are published). If you cannot identify a name to which to write, simply address your letter to the "Director of Human Resources" or to the "Director of X," the division or department in which you wish to work.

You'll also want to use these directories if you are writing a "blind" letter seeking employment when there is no job advertised as illustrated in one of the sample resumes at the end of this chapter.

Cover letter content

An effective cover letter is written with a professional tone and style and should include the following items:

∞ *Clearly identify the job* you seek in the first paragraph or sentence.

∞ *Indicate why you are applying* for this particular position (if you wish to state your career objective, this is the place to do it). Try to link your interests to the employer's needs.

∞ *Describe your qualifications.* Explain why you are particularly well-suited for this specific position. Carefully review the job description or job announcement or ad to determine what skills are sought and how you meet them. In your cover letter, show how you meet these requirements. Highlight your enclosed resume and emphasize your qualifications vis-a-vis the employer's needs. In a sense, you should re-write the employer's ad around the qualifications described in it. This approach is low-keyed, but assertive while not appearing to be boastful, hyped-up, or aggressive.

∞ *Refer the reader to the enclosed resume* for details of your experience and education.

∞ *Request the next step* in the hiring process: the interview, an answer to this letter, civil service exam, or a request for references (be assertive, but friendly). Make the employer an open-ended offer she can't refuse, as is done in the sample assistant village manager cover letter at the end of this chapter. This approach softens the request for an interview without putting the employer on the spot to say "yes" or "no" right away. The follow-up phone call lets you know whether or not you have any chance at all for the job. If you don't have a chance, you can move on to more promising job opportunities without waiting any longer. Conversely, the employer may find you sufficiently interesting to invite you to an in-person job interview. Either way, you get results quickly. Alternatively, you can end the letter with the conventional, "Thanks for your time and consideration. I hope to hear from you in the near future." Just be prepared to wait since many employers contact only job candidates they wish to interview and never even acknowledge receiving the application of someone they don't intend to interview.

☞ *Provide any specific information* the employer asked for in his job announcement or ad. If a job ad requests references, you should give their names, addresses, and phone numbers near the end of your cover letter or on a separate sheet. As the discussion on resumes urges, do not include references in your resume. If an employer requests your salary history, include that on a separate sheet, not in the cover letter.

☞ *Thank the reader* for her time and consideration.

If you are writing a so-called "blind" cover letter to learn of a job opening, you will want to adjust your letter accordingly. This sort of approach letter is designed for you to gain access to an individual who will either provide you with contacts, leads, and information on job opportunities within her agency or elsewhere. Be sure to learn the correct name of the person to whom you write. The various directories described throughout the *Professional's Job Finder* will get you her name as will a phone call to her company.

Cover letter style

Your cover letter tells the employer a lot about your competency. No matter what kind of a job you seek, typographical errors suggest that you would be a careless employee. A poorly written cover letter suggests that you do not communicate effectively.

Instead, cover letters should be direct, powerful, and free of errors. Make like a good newspaper copy editor: eliminate unnecessary words; check grammar, spelling, and punctuation. Avoid using the passive voice ("should have been," "it was done by me"). It's suggestions like this one that make so many of us regret paying so little attention in high school English class. Avoid pomposity and overly long sentences. Don't try to be cute or too aggressive like the preceding parenthetical expression did.

Keep the letter short and to the point. There's no reason to overwhelm the reader with a lengthy cover letter that repeats a lot of your resume.

Keep your letter positive. Highlight your past accomplishments and skills as well as your future value to the employer.

References

As mentioned earlier, the ad for the job for which you are applying may have requested references. You should identify your references near the end of your letter or on another sheet of paper. *It is not desirable to list references in a resume since you might want to use different references for different jobs.* In addition, it is prudent to let your references know to which positions you have submitted an application. If you know a potential employer is likely to contact your references, you would be sagacious to send your references a copy of your cover letter and the ad for the job so they can customize their responses to better fit the job.

For each reference, be sure to give the person's correct name and title, and complete address and phone number including area code, so the reference can be contacted easily. If a reference's first name could belong to either sex (Chris, Leslie, Shelley), avoid embarrassment and use "Mr." or "Ms." before the reference's name. A fundamental principle of applying for a job is to make it as easy as possible for the potential employer to follow–up your application because some employers simply toss out an application if they are unable to reach references or obtain other relevant information about the job candidate. It's a buyer's market, and as the applicant, you are the seller.

Be certain to have permission to use these names as references. Use only references you are certain will comment favorably on your performance and ability to work with others. Be prepared to offer additional references if asked.

The resume

Since the individual doing the hiring has to examine so many resumes, you are best off if you keep yours relatively short and sweet. Remember: your resume is both a sales pitch and a summary of your qualifications. Like it or not, those 60–second spots for political candidates nearly always have more impact than a five–minute or half–hour commercial. The same reasoning applies to resumes.

The recent college graduate isn't likely to have any problems keeping his resume down to one–page while the experienced professional may have a tough time limiting her resume to no more than four pages. The keys to making your resume stand out from the crowd—in addition to its substance—are to organize it well and produce an attractive, professional–looking document.

Resume content

By following several general guidelines you can make the content of your resume more effective.

- ☐ *Include only pertinent information.* Do not include material unless it gives potential employers a reason to hire you.

  Include only information from which you can confidently expect a favorable reaction. When in doubt, leave that information out; don't gamble on adverse reactions. A resume simply is not the place to put anything negative about yourself. Remember, you are marketing yourself to the prospective employer as the best person for the job. Would the folks at Dow Chemical, so anxious to build a clean image today, advertise they manufactured the napalm used to burn and kill civilians in Viet Nam or would cigarette advertising voluntarily include warnings on the cause–and–effect relationship of smoking and cancer and other diseases?

- ☐ *Be scrupulously honest.* For example, in 1976, one Illinois municipality offered its village manager job to a man who appeared to have built a successful career in city government in California. Unfortunately for him, the local newspaper learned of his phony credentials when interviewing one of his past employers and exposed the rascal. It seems he failed to earn the degree from Purdue University that he claimed to possess and was ten years older than the 55 years he listed on his resume. He withdrew his name from consideration for the job before the city fathers and mothers could withdraw it for him. During the past few years, many high-level government *and private sector* employees around the country have lost their jobs, and in most cases their careers, for misrepresenting themselves on their resumes or job applications.

Most resume fraud, however, does not become public knowledge. If a discrepancy is found during a job interview, the job simply is not offered. Fraud discovered after someone has been hired, usually results in the employer quietly asking the employee to resign with the not–so–subtle threat of dismissal hanging over his head. An executive of a credential verification service estimates that 30 percent of all resumes contain some fraudulent educational information. And with an increasing number of employers verifying this information, especially in the public sector, honesty and accuracy are essential for any resume or job application. Think about it, how could you ever trust somebody on the job if he lied to get the job?

There are a number of items of information that belong in any resume. An effective resume includes the following information in a clear, concise, and well–written style:

- *Applicant identification.* Your name should go at the top of the first page. If your resume is typewritten, underline your name. If produced on a word processor, place your name in a typeface and style that makes it stand out. See the sample resumes at the end of this chapter. Be sure to include your home address, home telephone number (including area code), and work phone. This is where you can indicate any preference for where you want to be contacted simply by writing: "Contact at [phone number]." You can also provide your birth date and social security number.

- *Education.* Identify your college degree and any advanced degrees earned. Give the names of the school that awarded your degree(s) and the years in which they were received. Include the city and state in which the school is located if that is not apparent from its name. Recent graduates may wish to list major scholarships or honors received. Also note relevant post–graduate education. Recent graduates may want to also list major extracurricular activities and organizational offices they held.

As a professional acquires more work experience, educational information becomes less important to potential employers while practical experience becomes more significant. For the recent graduate, the education section should precede the section on professional experience. The more seasoned professional will want to place the experience section of the education section. Job candidates who lack a college degree should indicate the highest level of education they have had, whether it was a high school degree, or some college or junior college education without receiving a degree.

☞ *Professional experience*. Jobs in your professional field should be described under a heading such as "Professional Experience" or "Work Experience." Jobs should be listed in reverse chronological order with the most recent first. For each position, furnish the following information:

Job title. Place your job title first. Use some emphasis to make it stand out: bold face, italics, borders, or boxing it if your resume is typeset or prepared on computer, underlined if prepared on a typewriter.

Employer's name, address, and phone number. If there is even one former employer you do not want a potential employer to call, leave out the phone numbers of all past employers. Do not give the name of your supervisor here; just give the name of the company or government agency.

Period of employment. If you've frequently changed jobs, like every two or three years, you don't want to advertise it. Employers like to hire people they think will stay with the agency for a long time. It costs them time and money to train a new employee. So, if you've changed jobs frequently, place the dates of employment within the heading for each job as is shown in the first sample resume at the end of this chapter. On the other hand, if you've generally held your jobs for four or more years, place the dates of employment in the left–hand margin as shown in the second sample resume at the end of this chapter.

Responsibilities, duties, skills, and accomplishments. This may be the most important text in your resume. It is your opportunity to tell potential employers what you did in your former positions and what skills you utilized and developed. Using short phrases rather than full sentences presents this information concisely without appearing to be conceit or braggadocio. Unless jobs outside the profession in which you are seeking work reflect on your ability to perform your professional tasks, this list of jobs should concentrate on the professional positions you have held.

Doonesbury

BY GARRY TRUDEAU

∽ *Organization memberships and honors.* Identify the professional organizations to which you belong and offices you have held in them, professional certifications or licenses you have earned, and professional honors you have been awarded. Do not use abbreviations nor acronyms. A potential employer feels pretty dumb when he doesn't recognize the acronym or abbreviation.

Do not include political organizations—that's not any employer's damned business. You can include germane civic and community organization memberships, particularly if you are, or have been, an officer or chaired an important committee.

☞ *Publications.* Clearly identify major relevant publications such as books, plans, reports, budgets, and magazine or newspaper articles so the reader can find them if she wishes. Experienced workers should not include papers or projects from college or graduate school unless they were published. List publications in chronological order with the most recent last or in reverse chronological order with the most recent first.

☞ *Additional professional activities.* List other professional activities such as participation on professional conference programs, guest lectures, commission memberships, courses taught, etc.

☞ *References.* As explained earlier, never identify references in your resume. At the end of your resume, insert a line like "References available upon request." If the job announcement requests references, include their names, addresses, and phone numbers in your cover letter.

Bolstering recent graduates' resumes

For the student or recent graduate with no professional experience, it is appropriate to list nonprofessional jobs and part-time, summer, or volunteer work if you label the section something like "Work Experience." In addition, persons with little or no professional experience can list major school projects that resulted in a written product and projects they may have conducted with a citizen group or a planning commission. See the first sample resume at the end of this chapter for an example of a resume for an entry-level job candidate just graduating from school.

If you have no publications to list, you could label the publications section "Papers" and list selected papers you've written that you feel are pertinent and will generate a positive reaction from a potential employer.

Obviously, if you have no organization memberships, honors, or additional professional activities, leave these sections out of your resume.

Correcting fallacies about resumes

Several common misconceptions about resumes continue to survive despite all the advice job counselors have given. Some items simply do not belong in a resume.

✘ *Salary*. The salaries you earned in former jobs do not belong in a resume. The purpose of your resume is to get you an interview. Don't undermine it. Past earnings could scare a prospective employer into thinking you are too high-priced even if you are willing to work for less or the same as in your current position. Even worse, listing salaries might unwittingly lead the potential employer to reduce the salary she was prepared to offer. Salary should come up only at the end of the job interview after you've had a chance to demonstrate your value to an employer as well as learn about the worth of the position. You cannot realistically discuss or negotiate salary if you prematurely mention it in your resume. However, if the ad for a job requests your salary history, submit it on a separate sheet, but not in your resume. For sound advice on negotiating salary, see *Salary Success: Know What You're Worth and Get It!* (for your convenience, this book is available from Planning/Communications; see the catalog at the end of this book).

✘ *Career Objectives*. If you have the insatiable urge to state your career objectives in writing, describe them in your cover letter. This approach permits an applicant to express his career objectives in terms applicable to a specific job. Do not place career objectives in your resume.

✘ *Hobbies*. Many employers do not care about an applicant's hobbies or outside interests. Frankly, a list of hobbies and outside interests only clutters your resume with irrelevant information. There is also the danger that your hobbies may scare off a potential employer. For example, one Texas planning consultant says she is reluctant to hire anyone who lists skiing or other cold-weather sports on a resume because she thinks such people would vacation a lot on weekends and be unavailable for necessary weekend work. Other employers are reluctant to hire persons with a lot of outside interests because they think it will be hard to get them to do extra work at home or work late hours. Conversely, some employers like their employees to have outside interests.

There's an old story still circulating of the job candidate who won his position over equally-qualified applicants because the agency director wanted a fourth for bridge at lunch—admittedly not a sound hiring criterion. But nobody in good conscience can state that every agency director follows sound hiring procedures. So, list hobbies and outside interests only at your own risk. If your qualifications are any good, you'll make it to an interview where the interviewer can ask about these activities if they are really important to him.

Resume appearance and design

Although most employers are interested in the content of the resume rather than its appearance, design expectations have risen thanks to the accessibility of word processing and laser printers that have made well-designed, typeset-quality resumes today's standard. It used to cost a small fortune to produce a typeset resume. Today, typeset-quality can be produced by anyone with a word processing program and laser printer. Do not use a dot-matrix printers. The results look amateurish even in letter quality mode. Resist the urge to use them.

Today nearly everybody can have access to high-quality resume design at a reasonable cost. Many resume preparation services will convert a one- or two-page typewritten resume into a classy-looking document for fee ranging from $30 to $200. Any resume preparation service that charges $100 or more for a two-page resume should include a major editing or rewrite and redesign of your resume for that price. Resume preparation services appear in the yellow pages under "Resume Service."

There are alternatives that, although more time consuming, cost much less. If you can prepare your resume on a micro-computer, but don't have a laser printer, take a floppy disk with your resume file and word processing program on it to one of the many photocopying shops, like Kinko's, that rent time on desktop computers and laser printers. The one catch is that most of these shops use Apple micro-computers while the dominant personal computer system in the business world is the IBM-compatible,

MS–DOS micro–computer, which, as of this writing, is incompatible with Apple's computers. If you choose this approach, ask the shop what kind of personal computers it has hooked up to its laser printer. Also find out exactly what kind of laser printer it is so you can use the proper printer drivers when preparing your resume file.

On the other hand, you could just rent time on the photocopying shop's computer and prepare your resume there with the shop's word processing and desktop publishing programs. The only difficulty comes about if you are unfamiliar with the shop's programs and computer system. But given enough time, anybody can figure out how to use nearly any word processing program.

Given the relatively high price copy shops charge for each printed page produced on a laser printer (usually around $1/page), plan to print out just one or two copies on the laser printer, and photocopy the additional copies of your resume on a photocopying machine (usually for about 6¢/page).

To assure an attractive, readable resume, type or print it neatly on 8.5 inch x 11 inch paper that is at least 20 pounds in "weight." Unless you've got some very good reason to use bright colored paper, avoid it. Your best bet for a professional–looking resume is a conservative paper color like white, off–white, ivory, light tan, or light gray. Use a dark ink or toner such as black, navy, or dark brown. The exact format or design is up to you. Whatever you choose, keep it clean and professional looking. Two possible designs are suggested by the sample resumes that follow.

Sample cover letters and resumes

Two resumes and cover letters that illustrate these guidelines follow. The first shows a recent graduate who is seeking an entry–level position in architectural graphics with a firm that did not advertise an opening. The cover letter is an example of a "blind" cover letter. The resume is included here because it is so beautifully designed. This is the sort of design that immediately illustrates the applicant's graphic skills.

The second sample resume and cover letter show an experienced worker applying for a higher-level position in response to a job listing on a job hotline. This resume is designed to show how to present your experience when you've risen through the ranks with an employer so it does not look, at first glance, like you simply changed jobs every 18 months.

"Blind" cover letter for entry–level position

1720 North Harlem Avenue
Elmwood Park, Illinois 60635
September 22, 1992

Deanna Troi, Director of Graphic Support
Kahn–Wrath Architects
1312–4 Excelsior Road
Enterprise Park, Illinois 61701

Dear Ms. Troi:

Everywhere I turn, I see new buildings with Kahn–Wrath's innovative architecture springing up throughout the Chicago area. Your firm has helped set a standard for architectural excellence that other architectural firms are only beginning to try to achieve.

I'm very interested in learning more about Kahn–Wrath's work as well as the possiblities of joining your firm. As the enclosed resume indicates, prior to receiving my bachelor's degree in architecture last year I served as an architect's and engineer's assistant.

Perhaps your schedule would permit us to meet briefly to discuss our mutual interests. I will call you office next week to see if such a meeting can be arranged.

Thank you for your time and consideration. I look forward to meeting you.

Sincerely,

Charles Mortel

Enclosure

Charles Mortel
1720 N. Harlem Ave.
Elmwood Park, Illinois 60635
(708)453-0009 fax (708)453-0269

Education

Illinois Institute of Technology,
Bachelor of Architecture, July 1991
- Completed the Architectural Curriculum as well as investigated the realms of Digital Photography and B&W Photograms with their uses in the Architectural field.

Whitney M. Young Magnet High School, 1986
- Two years of mechanical drawing and two years of architectural drawing.

Experience

Kinko's Copies
- Customer Sales Representative: Shift supervisor, layout consultant, production supervisor, key-operator, typesetting consultant.
- Responsible for seeing jobs through from crude originals to presentation quality material.

Air Systems Design
- Engineering Assistant: Updated HVAC drawings, conducted field surveys and produced working drawings from gathered data, light accounting, and layout of HVAC charts.

Lohan and Associates
- Architect's Assistant: Updated roof working drawings for a proposed high-rise building in the down-town area, assisted with construction of presentation models, assisted with study models of DePaul University Physical Education building.

References

Portfolio and slide presentation available upon request.

Response to ad for advanced–level position

2000 Spock Lane
Romulus, California 93560
December 6, 1991

David Marcus, Vice President
Genesis Corporation
4523–3 Q Way
Regula, Wisconsin 52985

Dear Mr. Marcus:

Your announcement on the PRESORT job hotline for a Director of Corporate Planning immediately grabbed my attention as a potentially challenging and very professionally rewarding opportunity. As my enclosed resume indicates, I have been working for over 20 years in planning as a corporate strategic planner, consultant, and municipal planner.

I joined the Harve Bennett Corporation after three years as an economic development planner for the City of El Paso, Texas, and three years as a real estate planner for N. Nichols Consulting Services. In the 15 years I've been with the Bennett Corporation, I've risen from serving as a corporate planner under J. L. Picard, to succeeding him and Tasha Yar as Director of Strategic Planning in 1985. By following the strategic directions my staff and I have recommended, the corporation has expanded its development projects and product sales far beyond what founder Geordi LaForge ever dreamed.

I would like to learn more about this position as well as have an opportunity to meet with you to discuss our mutual interests. I will call you next Friday about any questions we may both have and to arrange an interview if, at that time, we both feel it is appropriate.

Thank you for you time and consideration. I look forward to meeting you.

Sincerely,

Jean Roddenberry

Enclosures

Jean Roddenberry

2000 Spock Lane
Romulus, California 93560
Phone: 310/182–1701

Born: August 19, 1946
Social Security Number:
430–819–5298

Professional Experience

1976+   Harve Bennett Corporation (3141–9 Saavik Row, Ferengi, WI
             56934; 414/176–3025)
             Director of Strategic Planning. 1985+
             Supervise the corporation's 16–person strategic planning di-
             vision. In addition to basic management and administration,
             responsible for preparation of the firm's semiannual strategic
             plan for corporate development and market penetration.
             Responsible for property acquisition.
             Chief strategic planner. 1983—1985
             Headed the section within the Strategic Planning Division
             responsible for corporation projections and short–term corpo-
             rate planning for the Vulcan region. Responsible for supervis-
             ing eight–person research team.
             Senior strategic planner. 1980—1983
             Conducted on–going market analyses and demand projec-
             tions for the Tholian, Beta III, and Scalosian sectors.
             Corporate planner. 1976—1979
             Prepared early projections for market penetration into Betazoid
             regions on the east coast. Responsible for analysis of potential
             properties for expansion of the corporation's Borg units.

1973–
1976   **Senior Planner,** N. Nichols Consulting Services (3451–6
             Uhura Way, Marjel, WA 98652; 509/145–5678)
             Prepared planning studies for real estate developers; made
             presentations to zoning and planning boards. Developed
             computerized real estate valuation programs.

1969–
1972   **Assistant Planner,** Department of Economic Development, El
             Paso, TX 79901; 915/156–5430)
             Conducted planning studies on real estate values, develop-
             ment potential, and tax increment financing proposals.

Education

Master of Urban Planning, University of Illinois–Urbana, June 1969
Teaching Assistant, Sept. 1967–June 1969
B.A. (liberal arts), UCLA, June 1967
Dean's List, 1965–1967
Chairperson, Harry Mudd Dilithium Arts Festival, 1967

Organization Memberships and Honors

American Association of Corporate Planners, 1976+
   Wisconsin Chapter Vice–President, 1984–87
American Planning Association, 1967–84
Metropolitan Development Commission, 1981–1989
Regional Finalist, White House Fellowship, 1980

Publications

"The Undiscovered Country: Where No One has Gone Before," in *Corporate Planning Times*, December 6, 1991, pp. 9–22.
Live Long and Prosper: The Journey Home, published by Planning/Communications Press, 1984, 240 pages.
"City on the Edge of Forever: Is Ferengi's Future Past?" in *Planning* magazine, December 8, 1981, pp. 19–67.
"Amanda as Sarek: The Enemy Within," in *Sunday New York Times*, Feb. 29, 1981, pp. 1,205–1,210.
"Turnabout Intruder: A Daughter for Data," in *Syndication Heaven*, June 3, 1969, pp. 13–20.

Additional Professional Activities

Speaker at American Association of Corporate Planners National
   Conference:
   "Klingons in the Menagerie: Does Strategic Planning Really Pay?" Nov.
   17, 1966
   The Koenig–Nimoy Controversy: Was the Trouble Ever Really with Tribbles?" Dec. 29, 1967
Guest lecturer, St. Elsewhere Series, Boston: "Riker as Number One: The
   Trek Comes to Its First End," June 3, 1969

References available upon request

Chapter 40

Performing your best at your job interview

In the increasingly competitive job market, a job ad often draws well over 100 responses from qualified individuals. An invitation to appear for a personal interview indicates that your cover letter and resume interested a potential employer enough to make you a serious candidate. Now it's up to you to do your best at the job interview to clinch the job. Many well–educated, intelligent, well–qualified candidates lose jobs because they are uncomfortable in interview situations or fail to prepare adequately. Others just have a natural aptitude for personal interviews. Any well–qualified job candidate can improve his performance in job interviews by following the guidelines suggested here and in books on job interviewing such as the Krannichs' *Interview for Success* (available from Planning/Communications; see the catalog at the end of this book).

Few professional, technical, labor, trade, or office support positions require a written examination. Instead there is an oral quasi–examination, more accurately called an interview. Some employers put you before a panel of two to four people who evaluate you. Others simply have the personnel director (or her assistant) or division head interview you. When asked to come in for an interview, try to find out who will conduct the interview and who else will be present for it so you can be adequately prepared.

Preparing for the interview

A personal interview not only gives your potential employer an opportunity to evaluate you in depth and you a chance to sell yourself, but it also gives you the opportunity to learn much more about the employer and the company for which he works. You want to be able to carry on a fairly intelligent conversation with your interviewer, even if he can't. By knowing what is expected of you and by undertaking a few simple preparations, you can make a more favorable impression and minimize any nervousness you may feel.

Interviewers will size you up in terms of the following qualities:

Initial impression	Fitness for the job
Past job performance	Maturity
Analytic ability	Judgment and prudence
Appearance and manner	Leadership
Motivation	Potential to grow in the job
Ability to communicate	Overall personality
Initiative	Mental alertness
Self-confidence	Compatibility with other staff

Some agencies maintain a standard rating form and use a point system to rate candidates. Prior to your interview, try to obtain a copy of the rating form from the Personnel Department so you can tell exactly on what qualities you will be evaluated.

This checklist of fundamental provisions you should take before you meet your interviewer will enhance your performance at the interview:

❑ *Be certain of the exact time and place of the interview.* If you are uncertain how to get there, just ask. Write this information down and don't lose it. If you are really unsure of where the interview location is, check it out on a local street map or take a test drive there.

❑ *Arrive at the interview on time or a little early.* There is no excuse for tardiness for a job interview. Innumerable jobs have been lost because the candidate was late for the interview. If it becomes obvious you are going to be more than five minutes late, call and let the interviewer's secretary know. Try to arrive about 15 minutes early.

❑ *Know how to pronounce the interviewer's name correctly.* If in doubt, call in advance and ask her secretary how to pronounce it.

SYLVIA   by Nicole Hollander

❑ *Learn all you can about your potential employer and the position for which you are applying.* When applying for work with a company, you'll score points with the interviewer if you are reasonably familiar with the company's products or services. You should have enough of an idea of what to company does so you can explain how you can contribute to its success. And if you can't learn all you would like to know about the company, be prepared to ask pertinent questions at the interview. The questions you ask at the interview are often more important than the answers you give to the interviewer's questions.

At least try to learn enough so your potential employer won't feel you are too much of an outsider to learn the vagaries of the company for which you would be working. And by all means try to learn all you can about the person or persons who will interview you and make the hiring decision so you can present the side of you which will appeal the most to their sensibilities. It is possible that other people you know in your field may be able to tell you something about your interviewer and the company for which he works.

❑ *Make a list of points you want to be sure to make in the interview* at appropriate moments. You may have forgotten to make these points or facts about yourself at your last interview. Placing them firmly in mind before this interview should assure you don't forget them again. Even though you should never pull out such a list at the interview, the mere act of writing the list will help you remember the points.

Many interviewers will query you about your career goals. Whether or not you were once a Boy Scout, be prepared! Think this one out carefully because nearly every interviewer will sock you with this some question about your career goals.

❑ *Plan to bring several items to the interview.* Believe it or not, some interviewers lose a candidate's resume and cover letter just before the interview. So be sure to bring a clean copy of each with you. If requested, bring letters of reference and work samples. Students may substitute high-quality term papers or projects. Bring these materials in a folder or brief case and offer them only if asked or if they graphically illustrate a point. The interviewer's desk is probably cluttered enough as is.

Questions interviewers ask

Be prepared to answer the questions that inevitably surface in any job interview. According to the authors of *Interview for Success*, most of the following questions about your education, work experience, career goals, and yourself tend to surface in virtually every job interview.

* Tell me about your educational background.
* Why did you choose to attend that particular college?
* What was your major, and why?
* Did you do the best you could in school? If not, why not?
* What subject did you enjoy most? ...the least? Why?

- If you started all over, what would you change about your schooling?

- Recent graduates are likely to also be asked:

- What was your grade point average? (The more work experience you have, the less likely this inquiry will be made.)

- Why were your grades so high?... so low?

- What leadership positions did you hold?

- How did you finance your education?

- What were your major accomplishments in each of your former jobs?

- Why did you leave your last position? If asked why you left any of former your jobs, give reasons that do not suggest you are a job shopper or jumper. Acceptable reasons include a return to school, better pay, new challenges, more responsibility, and a desire for a different type of work.

- What job activities do you enjoy the most? ...the least?

- What did you like about your boss? ...dislike?

- Which of your jobs did you enjoy the most? Why? ... the least? Why?

- Have you ever been fired? Why?

- Why do you want to work for us?

- Why do you think you are qualified for this position?

- Why are you looking to change jobs?

- Why do you want to make a career change?

- Why should we want to hire you?

- How can you help us?

- What would you ideally like to do?

- What is the lowest pay you would take? (Try, if possible, to deflect this question. See the discussion on salaries later in this chapter.)

- How much do you think you are worth in this job?

SYLVIA   **by Nicole Hollander**

- What do you want to be doing five years from now? (Working here with a promotion or two, obviously.)

- How much do you want to be making five years from now?

- What are your short-range and long-term career goals?

- If you could choose any job and company, where would you work?

- What other types of jobs are you considering? ... other agencies?

- When would you be able to start?

- How do you feel about relocating, travel, and spending weekends or evenings in the office?

- What attracted you to our firm?

- Tell me about yourself.

- What are you major strengths?

- What are your major weaknesses? Never say you don't have any. Turn a negative into a positive with a response like, ''I tend to get too wrapped up in my work and don't pay enough attention to my family. My spouse has suggested, a couple of times, that I join Workaholics Anonymous.''

- What causes you to lose your temper?

- What do you do in your spare time? What are your hobbies?

- What types of books and magazines do you read?

- What role does your family play in your career?
- How well do you work under pressure? ... in meeting deadlines?
- Tell me about your management philosophy?
- How much initiative do you take?
- What types of people do you prefer working for and with?
- How _____ (creative, tactful, analytical, etc.) are you?
- If you could change your life, what would you do differently?
- Who are your references? (Bring a printed list of references' names, addresses, and phone numbers to submit to give the interviewer if requested.)

Stupid interviewer tricks: illegal questions

Unfortunately, despite great strides over the past decade, illegal questions continue to arise in job interviews, especially in the private sector. Sexism, in particular, is alive and well in the hearts and souls of many job interviewers. While equal employment legislation makes it illegal to ask certain questions during an interview, some interviewers ask them anyway. If you are prepared, you can fend them off effectively and still score points with the interviewer. If the questions don't get asked, you've got no problem.

Illegal or inappropriate questions include:

- What's your marital status?
- How old are you?
- Do you go to church regularly?
- What is your religion?
- Do you have many debts?
- Do you own or rent your home?
- What social and political organizations do you belong to? Be wary if the interviewer steers the conversation to politics. Do not be evasive, but temper your remarks to camouflage radical or extremist views. Keep in mind that in some communities a traditionally "liberal" viewpoint is considered "radical."

Your political views are really nobody's business but your own. But don't say that in an interview unless you have found an inoffensive way to express that view. Try to say no more than is necessary to answer the interviewer's broad line of questioning about politics.

- What does you spouse think about your career?
- Are you living with anyone?
- Are you practicing birth control?
- Were you ever arrested?
- How much insurance do you carry?
- How much do you weigh?
- How tall are you?

If an interviewer babbles one of these illegal questions, don't go crazy and shout "That question is illegal and I ain't gonna answer it!" You may be right, but this sort of reaction does not display any tact on your part, which may be what the interviewer is testing, albeit tactlessly. The authors of *Interview for Success* suggest that one type of response is humor. For example, if asked whether you are on the pill, you could respond, "Sure, I take three pills every day, vitamins A, B, and C, and thanks to them I haven't missed a day of work in three years."

Asked if you are divorced, you might respond, "I'd be happy to answer that question if you could perhaps first explain what bearing being divorced, or not being divorced, could have on someone's ability to perform this job?"

As you might have guessed by now, women are the main targets of these unjustifiable questions. But if you're prepared, you can neutralize them. For example, some interviewers will ask women with small children, "What if the kids get sick?" A sound response to this question goes along the lines of, "I have arranged for contingency plans. I have a sitter on standby, or my husband can take a vacation day." This sort of answer indicates to your potential employer that you are a professional (not that you should have to prove your professionalism because you're a woman) and that you've anticipated the problem.

Married women with a family are often asked, "How can you travel?" An interviewer could be trying to find out if the employer will have to pay for the woman's other responsibilities. An employer may be wondering if she is going to put her family before her job. A good answer would be, "Of course I can travel if it's important to my job. I'd be happy to do it. All I have to do is make the proper arrangements."

If an interviewer learns that your spouse works for a company that likes to move its employees around every three or four years, she may ask, "What are your plans if your spouse receives orders to relocate?" That's actually a reasonable question to ask of *either* partner in a two–income household, but for some mysterious reason it is rarely asked of the husband. A good answer is to say, "My husband and I have discussed this issue and we've decided that my work is important for my professional growth and we will work out a plan when and if that time comes." Once a woman has been working for an employer for a while and has proven her worth, she'll have a better bargaining position if spousal relocation threatens her job.

Try to decide how you will handle illegal or inappropriate questions before you go to an interview. With a little preparation, you can turn a negative into a positive when such questions are posed. Your answers to such questions could turn out to be your strongest and most effective of the whole interview.

Questions you should ask

Prepare questions before you go to the interview so you won't be speechless when the interviewer asks you if you have any questions. You may want to ask about the nature of the job and agency, opportunities to exercise initiative and innovation, chances for advancement, and status of the agency. Save questions about fringe benefits (health insurance, leave time, conference attendance) and salary for the end of the interview. As explained later in this chapter, you are best off if the interviewer raises these issues.

The authors of *Interview for Success* and *Careering and Re–Careering for the 1990's* and other job counselors suggest that you be prepared to ask the following questions if the interviewer has not already answered them:

- What duties and responsibilities does this position involve?

- Where does this position fit into the organization?

- Is this a new position?

- What would be the ideal person for this position? Skills required? Background? Personality? Working style?

- With whom would I work in this job?

- Can you tell me something about these people? Their strengths, weaknesses, performance expectations?

- What am I expected to accomplish during the first year?

- How will I be evaluated?

- On what performance criteria are promotions and raises based? How does this system operate?

- Is this a smoke-free office? (Ask this question only if it makes a difference to you. If you ask it, the interviewer will probably want to know if you are a smoker or if you don't want any smoking near you.)

- What is the normal salary range for such a position (assuming it was not given in the advertisement for the job).

- Based on your experience, what types of problems would someone new in this position be likely to encounter?

- How long have you been with this agency? What are your plans for the future? (These two questions are appropriate if the interviewer would be your supervisor or superior.)

- What is particularly unique about working for this company/division/department?

- What does this firms's future look like?

Personal appearance

Face facts: clothes and grooming certainly do not reflect on how decent or qualified a person is for a job, or how well someone will perform on the job. Just look at Albert Einstein, or, at the other extreme, most of the immaculately-groomed men who brought us the savings and loan scandals of the late 1980s and early 1990s.

But since the interviewer does not know you personally, your appearance can greatly influence his first impression of you—and first impressions count a lot at job interviews. You will make a much better first impression if you are well-dressed and well-groomed.

As with your resume, don't take chances with appearance even if it means showing up better dressed than your interviewer. Research shows that women elicit a more favorable reaction from interviewers of either sex when they wear a dress or suit, the classic pump, nylons, and a bra. Jeans, shorts, culottes, mini-skirts, sandals, dirty or unkempt hair, an exposed middle, and flamboyant clothing evoke unfavorable responses. Carry a purse or attache case, but not both. It's hard not to look clumsy trying to handle both. If you opt for the attache case, keep a slim purse with your essentials inside the brief case.

Men should wear a suit and tie. Men make a less favorable impression with a sport coat, and a downright unfavorable one dressed in a sweater or boots. Shorts, T-shirts, jeans, or sandals turn off any interviewer. Some researchers insist that a maroon tie inspires confidence. Others have found that the shorter, more neatly trimmed the hair and beard, if any, the better the impression.

Whatever your everyday mode of dress and grooming may be, you've got to play the game when job hunting. Sometimes you will be better groomed and clothed than your interviewer, but remember that it is *your* appearance that counts. After you've landed the job, you can resume your normal work appearance if it varies from that suggested here and does not violate office standards.

For more information on how to dress for an interview, see any of the dozens of books on interviewing. They'll essentially tell you what you've just read—but they'll take ten to 20 pages to do it.

Conduct at the interview

Common sense, above all else, should govern your conduct at a job interview. For example, be punctual and, if possible, arrive a few minutes early in case there are forms to complete. It only hurts your chances to keep an interviewer waiting.

Similarly, common sense dictates that you do your best to make a good first impression since, fair or not, first impressions are quite strong and seldom change later in the interview. A friendly, warm smile helps establish a good first impression that carries throughout the entire interview. A natural smile in the right places throughout an interview can mean the difference between a favorable and unfavorable response.

Greet your interviewer(s) with a solid handshake—something a bit softer than the Hulkster might use—no matter what your sex is. Most interviewers do not like a "wet fish" handshake.

Throughout the interview try to maintain good poise and posture; sit straight and avoid leaning on your elbow or talking with your hands over your mouth. Look alert and interested throughout the interview. Demonstrate that you can be a wide awake, intelligent listener as well as a talker. If nervous, hide it. Keep your hands still in your lap; do not tap your pencil or twist your purse strap. Don't fiddle with objects on the interviewer's desk, or with your fingernails. Chewing gum, or smoking without being invited to do so, usually makes a bad impression since both are generally regarded as signs of nervousness.

Naturally, you will want to establish and maintain good eye contact. Nearly every interviewer is conscious of eye contact; it is the surest way to convince him you know what you are talking about.

Above all else, be yourself and be honest. Since most interviews follow a simple question and answer format, your ability to respond quickly and intelligently is vital. Confused and contradictory answers can cost you the job. The best preventative against contradictory answers, logically enough, is the truth. An honest answer that seems a little unflattering to you is far better than a white lie that may tangle you up in a later question. If you don't know the answer to a specific question, the best thing you can say is, "I don't know." The odds are good that the interviewer knows the "right" answer to the question and a bad guess can only put you in a poor light.

Following several additional pointers at the interview will enhance your chances of winning the job:

☞ Follow the interviewer's lead. Most interviewers like to think they are in control. Some like to do most of the talking and judge you by your reactions. Because others believe it is your job to sell yourself, they hardly speak at all. When selling yourself, be modest about your accomplishments while getting your points across. Nobody likes, or hires, a braggart. If you seem to self-involved, the interviewer will sense, perhaps rightly so, that you will always place your interests ahead of those of the company—and nobody wants to hire somebody like that! Don't exaggerate your skills or accomplishments since most interviewers pick up on truth stretching very quickly and it hurts your chances for the job. Try to offer concrete examples of your better points.

☞ Do not take notes during the interview. A job candidate taking notes annoys and distracts some interviewers. If you must write something down, make a remark like, "That's very interesting. Do you mind if I jot it down?" Your best bet is to write notes of anything you need to remember after the interview.

☞ Job interviewers like candidates who are enthusiastic and responsive. Let the interviewer know you are genuinely interested in the job. If you are passive or withdrawn during the interview, the assumption can easily be made that you will behave that way on the job. Some employers want passive employees, though. So you will have to use your judgment to determine if your interviewer wants a passive or active employee.

☞ Even if you need the job desperately, do not let the interviewer know. Candidates who call attention to their dire straits are less likely to be hired. Hiring decisions are not based on your need, but on your ability, experience, and attitude.

☛ Be as complete and concise as possible in your answers since many interviewers can give only 30 minutes to an interview. Devote more time to answering important questions that require in–depth responses than to less significant questions. Some hiring executives recommend never spending more than one minute to answer a question. If the interviewer wants you to elaborate, she'll ask you to do so.

SYLVIA   by Nicole Hollander

Sylvia's Interviewing Tips: Don't bad-mouth your previous employer. Some things Are fun to do, but not really worth it, like talking About your divorce.

During an interview, never suggest that your previous employer has the personality of a mass murderer or may actually be one.

☛ Never denigrate a former employer. If you had difficulties, suggest that some of the blame must have rested on you.

☛ Since the last few minutes of an interview can sometimes change things, do not be discouraged if you have the impression that the interview has been going poorly and you have already been rejected in the interviewer's mind. Some interviewers who are interested in hiring you will try to discourage you just to test your reactions. Remaining confident, professional, and determined will help make a good impression.

☛ **Salary** is a sticky question. It is a subject best broached toward the end of an interview, preferably by the interviewer. Some experts believe an applicant should ask for as much money as possible to establish a bargaining position, and that employers offer as little as possible for the same reason. However, ads for most jobs identify a salary range.

Others job notices simply say, "Salary open." The interviewer may choose not to tell you the amount he has to offer and may ask how much you want. Indicate that you are more interested in a job where you can prove yourself than in a specific salary. If interested, the interviewer will usually suggest a figure. Try to find out in advance the standard or average salary for the type of position for which you are applying. The *Professional's Job Finder* describes dozens of salary surveys which can help you determine a reasonable salary to seek. You should also know the salary level beneath which your needs will not permit you to go. For detailed advice, see *Salary Success: Know What You're Worth and Get It!* (for your convenience, this book is available from Planning/Communications; see the catalog at the end of this book).

☛ When given the opportunity, be prepared to offer a closing statement. This will be your last chance to mention any beneficial points you hadn't had a chance to bring up during the interview and to summarize the positive contribution you can make to the company.

☛ Usually no definite offer is made at the interview. The interviewer may want to discuss your application with other staff and may have other candidates to interview. Occasionally a job is offered on the spot. If absolutely certain you want it, you can accept it. However, it is best to ask for 48 hours to decide. But do not give the impression you are playing off one potential employer against another. You can easily lose both job offers that way.

☛ Since most interviews last a half hour or less, an inconspicuous glance at your watch will suggest when your time is almost up. Be alert for signs from the interviewer that the session is almost over, such as when she looks at her watch. Do not keep talking when the session appears to be ending. Summarize your thoughts and stop. Be sure to thank the interviewer for his time and consideration. Tell him to be sure to get in touch with you if he should have any further questions.

☛ Should you send a thank you note right after the interview? Many career counselors say that research shows that a thank you note enhances your chances. But some interviewers regard them as a bother. You certainly should note, for yourself, any further contact your interviewer may have suggested. Follow her instructions exactly, and don't muddy the waters by immediately sending unsolicited correspondence. If the interviewer indicated you will hear from her by a certain date and you don't, write a brief note to remind her about a week after you were supposed to hear from her. Express appreciation for the time and consideration she gave you, and briefly note your continuing interest in the position. You have little to lose at this point by refreshing her memory, and you might get a favorable response.

After the interview

If you don't get a flat rejection or the polite "no" that comes in the type of letter that says, "We will keep your letter and resume in our files and let you know if anything ...." keep in touch if there is still some suggestion that you should. Unless you make a nuisance of yourself, you will be able to stay in the foreground if another vacancy opens.

SYLVIA   by Nicole Hollander

As explained earlier, it's a close call as to whether you should listen to the many job counselors who encourage writing a follow-up letter right after the interview. You will have to use your impressions of the interviewer to determine whether a follow-up letter will help or hurt you.

Following these suggestions should, at least in theory, reduce the hiring decision to one based on qualifications. Not all employers make their hiring decisions the same way. So during your interview be sensitive to hints of what criteria the interviewer will use to make his hiring decision and temper your remarks to comply with them. In general, though, following the suggestions made in this chapter will place you in good stead with a potential employer.

When accepting a job offer, you should send the employer an acceptance letter in which you clarify your assumptions about the job (salary, training, fringe benefits, responsibilities) and indicate your expected date of employment. Once an employer has decided to hire you, you can usually get the starting date changed to one more acceptable to you as long as you are reasonable. Make certain that all conditions of employment are clear and that you have a job offer in writing before you give notice to your current employer that you are leaving. Try to give one month notice if possible, but certainly no less than two weeks.

When rejecting a job offer, you should send a letter as soon as possible that declines the offer and expresses your appreciation for the employer's interest and confidence in you.

When you get rejected, but would still like to work for that employer at some future time, it doesn't hurt to send a pleasant letter thanking the interviewer for her time and expressing your disappointment at not being selected. Emphasize your interest in her department and ask to be kept in mind for future consideration. Suggest that you believe that you would work well together and that you will continue to follow the progress of her agency. Such a letter shows your continuing interest, your recognition that you were not the only qualified applicant, and your genuine desire to work for that agency. Such a thoughtfully–written, brief two– or three–paragraph letter can leave a very favorable impression and enhance your chances should you ever apply there again or encounter the interviewer in another work–related situation.

The *Professional's Job Finder* helps you find the type of job you want in the location you desire, and gives you a leg up on other job seekers who are unaware of the job sources described herein. Armed with the information in this book, you can identify private sector job openings that most job seekers will never know existed because they limit their job search to positions discovered by word of mouth, personal contacts, and the local classifieds.

If you are interested in working for local, state, or the federal government, or in working in the non-profit world, Planning/Communications offers two companion books to this volume, the *Government Job Finder* and *Non–Profits' Job Finder*. Both are available in book stores or through the catalog at the end of this book. These books provide the same service for job seekers in government and non–profit sectors that this book delivers for job hunters seeking positions in the private sector. For some specialties, a few of the sources contained the *Professional's Job Finder* also appear in one or both of these other two books because these sources offer jobs in two or more of these employment sectors. However, each book contains many other job sources that focus on that particular employment sector more than on the other sectors.

Even if you didn't possess these job–quest tools before, you are now prepped to prepare a convincing cover letter and a thorough, yet readable resume with which to interest an employer. Finally, you know how to prepare for that strange phenomenon called the personal interview so you can convey the best impression possible. Effective job hunting is hard work, but by using your common sense and the job–finding techniques explained in the *Professional's Job Finder,* your chances of finding satisfactory employment will soar even in the confusing and sometimes difficult economic times that may face us all in the last decade of the twentieth century.

Reader feedback form

We'd like to make the next edition of the *Professional's Job Finder* even more helpful. You, our readers, are a source of valuable information and suggestions. And you can tell use what we're going right and what we're doing wrong. So, please use this form to:

✍️ Tell us how we can make the next edition of the *Professional's Job Finder* more helpful;

✍️ Tell us about any changes we should make in the entries; and

✍️ Let us know of any useful job sources that somehow escaped our attention or appeared after this book was written.

If you run out of space, just attach another sheet. Please send your comments to me at Planning/Communications, 7215 Oak Avenue, River Forest, IL 60305-1935.

Thanks for your help and support.

Daniel Lauber

Daniel Lauber

Comments and suggestions:

_____
_____
_____
_____
_____
_____
_____
_____
_____
_____
_____
_____

Purely optional: Clearly print your name, address, and evening phone number in case we need to reach you for more information.

About the author

Author Daniel Lauber has written the *Professional's Job Finder, Government Job Finder, Non-Profit's Job Finder, The Compleat Guide to Finding Jobs in Government, The Compleat Guide to Jobs in Planning and Public Administration,* and *The Compleat Guide to Jobs in Planning.*

Prior to entering private legal practice and publishing, he worked for local and state government in Illinois as an award-winning city planner from 1972 through 1980. Since then he has served developers and local and state government as a planning consultant and, since 1985, as a zoning attorney.

At age 35 he was elected the youngest president of the 26,000-member American Planning Association, while attending the Northwestern University School of Law full-time.

He received his Masters of Urban and Regional Planning in 1972 from the University of Illinois-Urbana, and B.A. in sociology from the University of Chicago in 1970.

He has written dozens of articles on planning and law issues in professional publications and the popular press. He created the "Condo Watch" column for the *Chicago Sun-Times* in 1979. When not immersing himself in the preparation of this book, he spends most of his time as an attorney on zoning cases and on behalf of people with disabilities who wish to live in group homes. He is also computer consultant to a number of professional offices and an editor and designer of numerous monographs and newsletters.

Unfortunately, he can't follow his own advice. He resume runs a lot longer than the four pages recommended in this book. No wonder he's a consultant.

Index

As explained in Chapter 1 (remember, that's the chapter that explained how to get the most out of this book—which, of course, nobody wants to read—this Index is intended to supplement the Table of Contents. Use it to locate sources of private sector jobs that you can't find by using the Table of Contents. This Index will get you to job sources for specialties that are not where you would intuitively expect them to be in this book. When you locate a job source by using this Index, be sure to examine the other entries in the section or chapter where the Index leads you. Within that section or chapter, you will often find additional job sources for the specialty which you located by using this Index.

E

T

U

PLANNING/COMMUNICATIONS

For your convenience, Planning/Communications carries these books to help you in your job quest. Several of them are noted in the text of the *Professional's Job Finder*. While most are available in book stores across the country, we've made them available to you by phone and mail order in case you can't find them in your local bookstore or it's simply easier or faster for you to order directly from us.

Ordering information appears on the last two pages of this catalog.

Government Job Finder

$14.95, ISBN 0-9622019-1-X, 1992, 336 pages

It's like a *Professional's Job Finder* for local, state, and federal government vacancies in the U.S. and abroad. "We were **enthralled** with the first edition of this book...and **this is even better**. Like the rear section of **What Color is Your Parachute?**...it is packed with citations (1,400 in all) of resource books, newsletters, job services, etc....Good summary of government jobs at all levels."—*Career Opportunity News*

Non-Profits' Job Finder

$13.95, ISBN 0-9622019-4-4, 1992, 212 pages

Applying the techniques of the *Professional's Job Finder* to the non-profit world, author Daniel Lauber, details over 1,001 job sources for the non-profit sector: education, social services, legal aid, the arts, advocacy, environment, religion, research, fundraising, philanthropy, foundations, housing, community development, public interest groups, child care, adult care, disabilities, museums, and dozens of other non-profit specialties.

Catalog of job-quest books

Photocopying of this catalog is welcome

Careering and Re–Careering for the 1990's

$13.95 ISBN 0–942710–51–7, 1990, 383 pages

Trying to select a new career? This is the book that will help you choose the career that fits you best.

"A **truly impressive** book...**filled with advice** on how to spot jobs of tomorrow, how to best determine your capabilities, how to communicate qualifications, and...an unusual section on how to evaluate the kinds of communities in which you might most like to live."—*Career Opportunity News.*

Discover the Right Job for You!

$11.95, ISBN 0–942710–33–9, 1991, 167 pages

One of the best books for finding the right job, this book helps you assess skills, identify interests, and formulate a powerful job objective *before* writing resumes and letters, responding to job vacancy announcements, or interviewing for jobs. Includes tests and self–assessment exercises.

Graduating to the 9 to 5 World

$11.95, ISBN 0–942710–50–9, 1991, 195 pages

It's a tough world out there on the job, especially for the first time. This book is every student's passport to the realities of the working week. Be prepared for "9 to 5 shock" by learning what it's like to work in a structured world where office politics, productivity, and performance take center stage. Learn how to use your first 90 days on the job to greatly enhance your career.

High Impact Resumes and Letters: How to Communicate Your Qualifications to Employers

$12.95, ISBN 0–942710–30–4, 1990, 257 pages

Twice excerpted in the *National Business Employment Weekly* of the **Wall Street Journal**, this highly praised best–seller is an easy–to–follow guide through the steps necessary to write resumes and cover letters that really stand out from the crowd.

Dynamite Resumes: 101 Great Examples

$9.95, ISBN 0–942710–52–5, 1991, 137 pages

From the authors of *High Impact Resumes and Cover Letters* comes a unique guide for transforming ordinary resumes into outstanding ones that grab the attention of potential employers. Numerous examples illustrate the key principles for revising a resume. Included are two unique chapters that critically review resume guides and computer software used specifically for resume writing.

Order form is at the end of this catalog

Dynamite Cover Letters: 101 Great Examples
$9.95, ISBN 0–942710–53–3, 1991, 135 pages

Dynamite Answers to Interview Questions
$9.95, ISBN 0–942710–60–6, 1992, 163 pages

The perfect companion volume to *Interview for Success*, this book includes sample answers to hundreds of questions interviewers are likely to ask. Learn how to turn negative responses into positive answers that can mean the difference between being hired and being rejected.

Interview for Success: A Practical Guide to Increasing Job Interviews, Offers, and Salaries
$11.95, ISBN 0–942710–31–2, 1990, 218 pages

Packed with solid advice on getting interviews and then using them to your advantage to win the job at the salary you want. Tells how to handle interview stress.

Salary Success: Know What You're Worth and Get It!
$11.95, ISBN 0–942710–35–5, 1990, 151 pages

Praised by the **National Business Employment Weekly,** this book dispells myths and explains how to determine your true value, negotiate salary and employment terms, and finalize your job offer. Shows how to respond to ads requesting a salary history and much more.

Great Connections: Small Talk and Networking for Businesspeople
$11.95, ISBN 0–942710–31–2, 1991, 179 pages

Few people realize that small talk is *the* basic networking tool. The authors explain practical small talk techniques anyone can learn and quickly apply to make great connections that are vital in today's work world.

Network Your Way to Job and Career Success
$11.95, ISBN 0–942710–11–8, 1989, 156 pages

Pinpointing a practice often presented as merely a vague concept, this book shows you how to make the connections that get you to the jobs that aren't widely advertised. Learn to identify, link, and transform networks to gather information and obtain advice and references that lead to job interviews and offers.

Catalog of job-quest books

The Complete Guide to International Jobs & Careers

$13.95, ISBN 0–942710–24–X, 1991, 320 pages

Learn how to enter the international job market: international organizations, contractors, consultants, nonprofit organizations and volunteer opportunities, associations, foundations, research and educational organizations, business, travel industry, and starting your own international business.

The Almanac of International Jobs & Careers

$14.95, ISBN 0–942710–40–1, 1991, 330 pages

Provides the names, addresses, and phone numbers for over 1,000 key employers in the international arena. Plus: work permits, sources of job listings, and relocation resources as well as key in–country contacts for foreign embassies in the U.S., American embassies and U.S. consulates, and American chambers of commerce abroad.

The Complete Guide to Public Employment

$15.95, ISBN 0–942710–23–1, 1990, 528 pages

The perfect companion to the *Government Job Finder*, this book helps people entering government work decide what sort of government jobs to seek, and those who wish to leave government how to shift their government skills into the related worlds of trade and professional associations, contracting and consulting, foundations and research organizations, political support groups, and international institutions.

How to order

Complete the order form on the next two pages, or call us toll–free at 800/829–5220 Mondays through Fridays, 9 a.m. to 6 p.m. Central Time. Be sure to include shipping according to the formula given at the end of the order form and enclose your payment (check, money order, VISA, or MasterCard—individuals must prepay, *purchase orders are accepted only from libraries, universities, bookstores, or government offices*). Call or write for special quantity prices or resale prices. *Please note that prices are subject to change without notice.*

Call or send order to: Planning/Communications
7215 Oak Ave., River Forest, IL 60305

Book Title   Price   x   #   = Total

Book Title	Price	x #	= Total
Professional's Job Finder	$15.95 x	____	= $_____
Government Job Finder	$14.95 x	____	= $_____
Non—Profits' Job Finder	$13.95 x	____	= $_____
Careering and Re—Careering for the 1990's	$13.95 x	____	= $_____
Discover the Right Job for You!	$11.95 x	____	= $_____
Graduating to the 9 to 5 World	$11.95 x	____	= $_____
High Impact Resumes and Letters	$12.95 x	____	= $_____
Dynamite Resumes	$ 9.95 x	____	= $_____
Dynamite Cover Letters	$ 9.95 x	____	= $_____
Dynamite Answers to Interview Questions	$ 9.95 x	____	= $_____
Interview for Success	$11.95 x	____	= $_____
Salary Success: Know What Your're Worth and Get It!	$11.95 x	____	= $_____
Great Connections	$11.95 x	____	= $_____
Network Your Way to Job and Career Success	$11.95 x	____	= $_____
The Complete Guide to International Jobs & Careers	$13.95 x	____	= $_____
The Almanac of International Jobs & Careers	$14.95 x	____	= $_____
The Complete Guide to Public Employment	$15.95 x	____	= $_____

Additional job—quest books available from Planning/Communications:

	Price	x #	= Total
The Almanac of American Government Jobs and Careers	$14.95 x	____	= $_____
How to Get a Federal Job	$14.95 x	____	= $_____
Find a Federal Job Fast!	$ 9.95 x	____	= $_____
The SF—171 Reference Book	$18.95 x	____	= $_____
The Book of U.S. Postal Exams	$13.95 x	____	= $_____
The Book of $16,000–$60,000 Post Office Jobs	$14.95 x	____	= $_____
Great Careers: The Fourth of July Guide to Careers, Internships, and Volunteer Opportunities in the Non—Profit Sector	$34.95 x	____	= $_____

Subtotal: $_____

☞ **Illinois residents: add 7% sales tax**   + $_____

☞ **Shipping: ($3.50 for the first book plus**   + $3.50
    $1 for each additional book)

☞ **Additional books:** ____ **x $1/each**   = $_____

☞ **Overseas orders: add an additional $8 per
book for air mail**   + $_____

☞   **Total enclosed: $_____**

☞ **Please continue on the other side.**

Photocopying of this catalog is welcome

Ship to:

Name _____

Address _____ Apt. _____

For UPS delivery, give full street address and unit number. No post office boxes!

City–State–Zip _____PROJF92–1

☐   Enclosed is my check or money order for $ _____ made payable to Planning/Communications.

☐   Please charge $_____ to my (check one):

☐   VISA
☐   MasterCard

Card number: _____

Expiration date: _____

Signature:

_____

Please sign your name exactly as it appears on your charge card.

Your home phone number is needed only on charge card orders.

Home phone number: _____/_____

Send your order and payment (in U.S. funds only) to:

PLANNING/COMMUNICATIONS

7215 Oak Avenue
River Forest, IL 60305–1935

or call

Toll–Free: 800/829–5220 or 708/366–5200
Monday—Friday, 9 a.m.—6 p.m. Central Time